TARGUM NEOPHYTI 1
A TEXTUAL STUDY

Leviticus, Numbers, Deuteronomy
Volume 2

Studies in Judaism

TARGUM NEOPHYTI 1
A TEXTUAL STUDY

Leviticus, Numbers, Deuteronomy
Volume 2

B. Barry Levy

UNIVERSITY
PRESS OF
AMERICA

Lanham • New York • London

University Press of America,® Inc.

4720 Boston Way
Lanham, MD 20706

3 Henrietta Street
London WC2E 8LU England

Printed in the United States of America

British Cataloging in Publication Information Available

Library of Congress Cataloging-in-Publication Data
(Revised for vol. 2)

Levy, B. Barry.
Targum Neophyti 1.

(Studies in Judaism)
Bibliography: v. 1, p. 80-83.
Includes index.
Contents: v. 1. Introduction, Genesis, Exodus—v. 2. Leviticus, numbers, deuteronomy.
1. Bible. O.T. Pentateuch. Aramaic. Targum Yerushalmi—Criticism, Textual. 2. Codex Neofiti 1. I. Title. II. Series.
BS1224.A77.L48 1986a 222'.1042 86-11117
ISBN 0-8191-6313-9 (v. 2 : alk. paper)
ISBN 0-8191-6314-7 (pbk. : v. 2 : alk. paper)

All University Press of America books are produced on acid-free paper which exceeds the minimum standards set by the National Historical Publication and Records Commission.

In Memory of My Father

David J. Levy

CONTENTS

VOLUME II

PREFACE

This volume concludes my textual study of The Neophyti 1 Targum. Once again I am pleased to thank McGill University and The Social Sciences and Humanities Research Council for their support and M. Joel Linsider for his assistance. The procedures followed in this volume are the same as those used in Volume I. The indices cover both volumes and were prepared by Miss Franceen R. Handelsman.

B. B. L.

Montreal

Erev Sukkot, 5743

ABBREVIATIONS

A	Cairo Geniza targum fragment A published in MdW
ADRN I and II	*Avot deRabbi Nathan*, cited according to the edition of S. Schechter (reprint New York, 1967)
Akk.	Akkadian
Aram.	Aramaic
Aruch	cited according to the edition of *Aruch Completum* edited by A. Kohut (reprint New York, 1955)
A.Z.	*Avodah Zarah*
B	Cairo Geniza targum fragment B published in MdW
B.B.	*Baba Bathra*
BDB	*A Hebrew and English Lexicon of the Old Testament*, edited by F. Brown, S.R. Driver and C.A. Briggs (Oxford, 1962)
Bekh.	*Bekhorot*
Ber.	*Berachot*
BH	Biblical Hebrew
B.M.	*Baba Meṣiᶜa*
BR	*Bereishit Rabbah*, cited according to the edition of J. Theodor and C. Albeck (reprint Jerusalem, 1965)
BT	*Babylonian Talmud*, cited according to the Romm edition (Vilna, 1880-1886) unless noted otherwise
BTA	Babylonian Talmudic Aramaic
C	Cairo Geniza targum fragment C published in MdW
Chron.	Chronicles
D	Deuteronomy, when followed by chapter and verse designations, e.g. D 4:6; when used alone, refers to Cairo Geniza targum fragment D
Dan.	Daniel
Deut.	Deuteronomy
Diqduqei Soferim	R. Rabbinovicz, *Variae Lectionis in Mischnam et in Talmud Babylonicum* (1868-1888 reprint New York, 1960)

DM	Diez-Macho; references are to coments by the editor of _Neophyti 1_ Vol. 1-6 (Madrid, 1968-1979)
E	Exodus, when followed by chapter and verse designations, e.g. E 15:9; when used alone, refers to Cairo Geniza fragment E published in MdW
Esth.	Esther
Ex.	Exodus
Ex. Rab.	_Exodus Rabbah_, cited according to the Romm edition (Vilna, reprint New York, 1952)
Ezek.	Ezekiel
f.	feminine
F	Cairo Geniza targum fragment F published in MdW
Frag.	Fragmentary Targum, cited according to the edition of M. Ginsburger (Berlin, 1899) unless indicated otherwise
G	Genesis, when followed by chapter and verse designations, e.g. G 4:6; when used alone, refers to Cairo Geniza fragment G published in MdW
Gen.	Genesis
Ginzberg	L. Ginzberg, _Legends of the Jews_ (1909-1938, reprint Philadelphia, 1964)
Git.	_Gittin_
Goldin	J. Goldin, _The Song at the Sea_ (New Haven, 1971)
Heb.	Hebrew
HUCA	_Hebrew Union College Annual_
Hul.	_Ḥullin_
I	Interliner notes in the Neophyti 1 manuscript
Ibn Ezra	cited according to the edition of J. L. Krinsky, _Meḥoqeqei Yehudah_ (reprint Benei Barak, 1961)
Is.	Isaiah
JANES	_The Journal of the Ancient Near Eastern Society of Columbia University_
Jastrow	M. Jastrow, _A Dictionary of the Targumim..._, (1903, reprint New York, 1967)
Jer.	Jeremiah

Abbreviations

Jonathan	Targum Jonathan, cited according to the edition of A. Sperber, *The Bible in Aramaic* Vol. II (Leiden, 1959), *Vol. III* (Leiden, 1962).
Josephus	*The Jewish War* and *Jewish Antiquities*, cited according to the edition of S. J. Thackeray and L. Feldman (Cambridge, Mass., 1957-1965)
Josh.	Joshua
JPS	Jewish Publication Society translation of *The Torah* (Philadelphia, 1962)
Ker.	*Keritot*
Ket.	*Ketubot*
L	Leviticus, when followed by chapter and verse designations; e.g. L 19:3
Lam.	Lamentations
Lam. Rab.	*Lamentations Rabbah*, cited according to the edition of S. Buber (Vilna, 1899)
LCL	Loeb Classical Library
Lev.	Leviticus
LR	*Leviticus Rabbah* cited according to the edition of M. Margoliot (Jerusalem, 1953-1960)
LXX	Septuagint, cited according to *Septuaginta*, ed. A. Rahlfs (Stuttgart, 1935)
m	masculine
M	Marginal notes in the Neophyti 1 manuscript, occasionally designated M1, M2, etc.; also Mishnah, but always followed by the name of a tractate. Citations follow the Romm edition (Vilna, reprint New York, 1952) unless indicated otherwise.
Mak.	*Makkot*
Ma^{c}as.	*Ma^{c}aserot*
MdW	P. Kahle, *Masoreten des Westens* II (Stuttgart, 1930)
Meg.	*Megillah*
Mekh. I	*Mekhilta of Rabbi Ishmael* unspecified references to *Mekhilta* are to this text, cited according to the edition of H. S. Horovitz and I. A. Rabin (Jerusalem 1960)

Mekh. S.	_Mekhilta of Rabbi Shimon bar Yochai_, cited according to the edition of J. N. Epstein and E. Z. Melamed (Jerusalem, 1956)
Men.	_Menaḥot_
Meturgeman	E. Levita, _Lexicon Chaldaicum_ (Isna, 1541)
MH	Mishnaic Hebrew; the rabbinic dialects of Hebrew found in the Mishnah, Tosefta, Talmudim and Midrashim
Mid. Hag.	_Midrash HaGaddol_ cited according to the edition of M. Margulies, (Jerusalem, 1967)
Mid. Leqaḥ Ṭov	Mid. Leqaḥ Ṭov cited according to the edition of S. Buber (reprint Israel, n.d.)
Midreshei Geulah	edited by J. Even Shemuel, 2nd edition (Jerusalem, 1968)
Mid. Tan.	_Midrash Tannaim_, cited according to the edition of D. Hoffman (Berlin, 1898)
Mid. Tanḥ.	_Midrash Tanḥuma_, cited according to the editions of H. Zundel (Jerusalem, 1964) and S. Buber (Vilna, n.d.)
Mid. Ps.	_Midrash Psalms_ (_Shocher Ṭov_), cited according to the edition of S. Buber (Vilna, 1891)
Mid. Vayosha	cited according to the edition of J.D. Eisenstein, _Ozar Midrashim_ (reprint Israel, n.d)
Moore	G. F. Moore, _Judaism in the the First Centuries of the Christian Era_ (Cambridge, Mass., 1966)
M.Q.	_Moᶜed Qaṭṭan_
MS	Manuscript
M.S.	_Maᶜaser Sheni_
MSS	Manuscripts
MT	Massoretic Text
N	the base text of the Neophyti 1 manuscript; Numbers, when followed by chapter and verse designations, e.g. N 30:14.
Naz.	_Nazir_
Ned.	_Nedarim_
Neh.	Nehemiah
Num.	Numbers

Abbreviations

Onk.	Onkelos, cited according to the edition of A. Sperber, *The Bible in Aramaic* Vol. 1 (Leiden, 1959)
Onomasticon	*The Onomasticon of Eusebius*, edited and translated by E. Z. Melamed (Jersualem, 1966)
Passover Haggadah	cited according to the edition of D. Goldschmidt *Haggadah Shel Pesach VeToldoteha* (Jerusalem, 1969)
PDRK (PRK)	*Pesikta de Rav Kahana*, cited according to the edition of B. Mandelbaum (New York, 1962)
Pes.	*Pesachim*
Peshitta	cited according to *The Old Testament in Syriac* I, 1 Genesis-Exodus (Leiden, 1977)
Philo	*Moses* (*De Vita Moses*) translated by F. H. Colson (Cambridge, Mass., 1935)
PJ	The Pseudo-Jonathan Targum cited according to the edition of D. Rieder, (Jerusalem, 1974)
pl.	plural
PRE	*Pirqei Rabbi Eliezer* cited according to the edition with commentary of David Luria (Warsaw, 1852)
Prov.	Proverbs
Ps.	Psalms
PT	*Palestinian Talmud*, cited according to the Romm edition (Vilna, 1922)
Q	*Qere*
Qed.	*Qedoshim*
Qid.	*Qiddushin*
R.	Rabbi
Rashi	cited from *Rashi al HaTorah*, edited by A. Berliner (Frankfort, 1905) and from Rashi's commentary on the Talmud printed in BT.
RH	*Rosh HaShannah*
Rosenfeld	A. Rosenfeld, *The Authorized Selichot for the Whole Year* (London, 1962)
s	*Sevirin*
s.	Singular

Sam.	Samaritan Torah, cited according to the edition of A. Sadaqah (Tel Aviv, 1962); when followed by chapter and verse designations, Samuel
San.	*Sanhedrin*
Seder Eliyahu Rabbah	cited according to the edition of M. Friedman (Vienna, 1904)
Seder Olam Rabbah	cited according to the edition of B. Ratner and K. Mirsky (New York, 1966)
Sifra	*Sifra*, cited according to the edition of I.H. Weiss (Vienna, 1862)
Sifrei Deut.	*Sifrei Deuteronomy*, cited according to the edition of L. Finkelstein (Berlin, 1939)
Sifrei Num.	*Sifrei Numbers*, cited according to the edition of H.S Horovitz, *Siphre D'Be Rav* (Liepzig, 1917)
Skinner	J. Skinner, *A Critical and Exegetical commentary on Genesis*, second edition (Edinburgh, 1930)
Soferim	*Massekhet Soferim*, cited according to the edition of M. Higger (New York, 1937)
Sot.	*Soṭah*
Speiser	E. A. Speiser, *The Anchor Bible: Genesis* (Garden City, 1964)
S.T.	Samaritan Targum cited according to the edition of A. Brüll *Das Samaritanische Targum* (Frankfort, 1875) and, for Genesis, M. Heidenheim *Die Samaritanische Pentateuch-Version die Genesis* (Leipzig, 1884)
Suk.	*Sukkah*
T	Tosefta cited from the edition of S. Lieberman, *The Tosefta* (New York, 1955-73) from Berachot to Qiddushin with commentary *Tosefta Ki-Fshutah*, and from the edition of M. S. Zuckermandel (reprint Jerusalem, 1963)
Taᶜan.	*Taᶜanit* cited from BT according to the edition of H. Malter, *The Treatise Taᶜanit of The Babylonian Talmud* (New York, 1930)
Targ. Esth.	cited according to the edition of A. Sperber, *The Bible in Aramaic* Vol. IVA (Leiden, 1968)

Abbreviations

Targ. Job	Targum of Job, cited according to the edition of P. Lagarde, *Hagiographa Chaldaice* (Leipzig, 1873)
Targ. Psalms	Targum of Psalms, cited according to the edition of P. Lagarde, *Hagiographa Chaldaice* (Leipzig, 1873)
Targ. Ruth	Targum of Ruth cited according to the editions of A. Sperber, *The Bible in Aramaic* Vol. IVA (Leiden, 1968) and E. Levine, *The Aramaic Version of Ruth* (Rome, 1973)
Targ. Song of Songs	Targum of Song of Songs, cited according to the edition of R. H. Melamed, *The Targum to Canticles* (Philadelphia, 1921)
TBT	Tiberian Bible Text
T-S NS	Taylor-Schecter, New Series
TS	M. Kasher, *Torah Sheleimah*, (New York and Jerusalem, 1949 ff.)
v.	Verse
vv.	Verses
Werner	Eric Werner, *The Sacred Bridge* (New York, 1959)
Yeb.	*Yebamot*
Y.S.	*Yalqut Shimoni* cited according to the edition of A. Heyman, I.N. Lehrer and I. Shiloni (Jerusalem, 1973ff) unless indicated otherwise
Zech.	Zechariah
11QPs	*The Psalm Scroll of Qumran Cave 11*, ed. J.A. Sanders (Oxford, 1965)

A NOTE ON CITATIONS

All abbreviations are listed above, but the following examples are provided for purposes of clarity:

... N in N 14:22 ...	... Neophyti 1 base text in Numbers 14:22 ...
... M, E 6:19, but fragment D, D 6:4 ...	... Marginalia to Exodus 6:19, but Cairo Geniza Targum text D (published by Kahle in *Masoreten des Westens*) Deuteronomy 6:4 ...
... M G 1:6 is not based on M San. 4:3 ...	... Marginal note to Genesis 1:6 is not based on Mishnah Sanhedrin 4:3 ...

When not accompanied by chapter and verse citations, capital letters A-I, M and N refer to texts. When texts sometimes abbreviated by single capital letters (e.g. E - Exodus) are cited without chapter and verse citations, fuller abbreviations are used (e.g. Gen., Ex., Num.).

Citations frequently appear incomplete, e.g., v. 16, 14:12. In such cases an undesignated verse is found in the chapter being discussed, while an undesignated chapter (with or without a verse) is in the book being discussed. Thus 14:12 in Exodus refers to E 14:12, while in Leviticus to L 14:12.

The manuscript contains a number of forms of the Tetragrammaton, and I have followed Diez-Macho's pattern of printing *yyy*. For convenience and consistency, Hebrew passages containing the Tetragrammaton are also recorded in this way.

LEVITICUS

Chapter 1

1:1 N

a. *whwh kd 'šlm mšh lmqmh yt mšknh*

b. *wrby ytyh*

c. *wqdš ytyh wyt mdbḥh wyt kl mnwy*

d. *ḥšb mšh blybyh w'mr*

e. *ṭwr' dsyny dhwh qdwšy qdwš šᶜh ḥdh*

f. *wrbwyh rbwy šᶜh ḥdh*

g. *l' slqyt lyh*

g. *ᶜd zmn dy 'tmll ᶜmy mn qdm yyy*

i. *mškn zmn' dqdwšyh qdwš ᶜlm*

j. *wrbwyh rbwy ᶜlm*

k. *bdyn' hw' dl' nyᶜwl lgwyh*

l. *ᶜd zmn dy 'tmll ᶜmy mn qdm yyy*

m. *bkn qr' dbyrh lmšh*

n. *wmlyl yyy ᶜmyh mn mškn zmn' lmymr*

Heb.

1. *wyqr' 'l mšh*

2. *wydbr yyy 'lyw m'hl mwᶜd l'mr*

The translation of the Hebrew is found in lines m-n. The rest of the passage is an introduction that first summarizes the preceding events (a-c) and then applies the logic of inference from minor to major to explain Moses' failure to enter the tabernacle, immediately upon completion (d-l). This, of course, serves to introduce God's call to him (m-n).

Lines a-c have been borrowed from N 7:1, which is translated in a manner almost identical to this text:

a whwh bywm' d'šlm mšh lmqmh [cf. DM] yt mšknh

b. wrby ytyh

c. wqdyš ytyh wyt kl mnwy [wyt mdbḥh wyt kl mnwy] ... The words in brackets have been omitted by the scribe and restored by DM. Line c of 1:1 has omitted several words also, and they should probably be restored as well. The term bdyn' has been used in line k as well. The use of this term parallels the Mekh. I, indeed, it is a sign of the school of Rabbi Ishmael (cf. J. N. Epstein, Introduction to Tannaitic Literature, Jerusalem, 1957, pp. 568-9).

1:3 lšmh dyyy (+): now similar to v. 14. Both lyyy and lpny yyy are regularly translated qdm yyy in the first chapter of Lev., but lšmh dyyy is also used thereafter.

1:9 dmtqbl (+): idiomatic; cf. v. 13, 2:2, etc.

1:14 gwzlyh (+): idiomatic; cf. 5:7 etc.

1:16 špykwt qṭm': for Heb. lmqwm hdšn, but in 4:12 for 'l špk hdšn. The Aramaic term combines the Heb. ones. On the use of 'tr byt, cf. E 35:3, L 3:17.

Chapter 2

2:2 wmn ṭwbh: for Heb. wmšmnh.

2:6 mqṣy- tqṣy yth qṣwn: for Heb. ptwt 'th ptym.

2:7 pylh (+): idiomatic usage; cf. e.g. v. 4.

Chapter 3

3:6 Delete mh.

3:9 Note the two ways qrb is translated, here and v. 14.

3:12 gdy br ᶜyzyn: for Heb. ᶜz; cf. 1:14, etc.

Chapter 4

4:2 dy l' kšryn mtᶜbdh: for Heb. 'šr l' tᶜśynh. One might assume that mtᶜbdh is a f. s. participle modifying an understood pronoun "one [of the commandments]," and that kšryn, in the plural, is a late addition; but the full form lmtᶜbdh and the use of kšryn in vv. 13, 22 and 27 belie this claim. Note also that l-mtᶜbdh is actually found here in the MS, divided between the lines, but only mtᶜbdh has been printed.

4:19 khn' (+): cf. vv. 11, 31, etc.

4:20 wyštry wyštbq: for Heb. wyslḥ; in v. 26 only wyšbyq is used. The hendiadys also occurs in v. 31, but wyštbyq alone is found in v. 35. Cf. also TS XXV, p. 240 for additional references. It seems that the double form is most common in N.

4:22 khn' dmtrby: for Heb. nśy'; Onk. PJ: rbh/'.

4:28 'yn (+): expansive.

Chapter 5

5:1 šbwᶜh dḥrwp: for Heb. 'lh.

yqbl ḥwbwy: routine for Heb. wnś' ᶜwnw, deleting the Waw.

5:5 ᶜl (+): idiomatic.

5:19 The Hebrew 'šm 'šm lyyy emphasizes the guilt. N has interpreted this to mean "he should bring the guilt offering": 'šmh yyty qdm yyy. The remaining words that do not translate the Hebrew, i.e. ᶜl ḥwbtyh dy 'tḥyyb, are similar to those found in v. 10.

5:21 'nš: for Heb. npš; npš is used in 4:27, 5:17, etc.

5:23 wyhwy yḥṭ' wytḥyyb: for Heb. whyh ky yḥṭ' w'šm.

yt ḥbr' (+): added from v. 21, but changed from ḥbrh to ḥbr'.

Chapter 6

6:3 ydyh: the equivalent of ytyh.

6:6 The word hmzbḥ is not in N. The word ᶜlwy probably does not include a pronominal ending, so mdbḥh should be added as in M.

6:13 dyrby ythwn: for the passive Heb. hmšḥ 'tw.

ᶜśryn mklth: for Heb. ᶜśyrt h'ph.

thwwn mqrbyn (2x): expansive, based on dy yqrbwn earlier in the verse.

Chapter 7

7:2 *dtkswn* (2x): for Heb. *yšḥṭw*; M: *dy ykswn*, I: *dyt-*.

7:12 *nkst qdšyh*: for Heb. *htwdh*; in v. 12 *twdh* is also called *'wdyh*, as it is in M.

7:18 *l' yqbl brᶜwh*: idiomatic for Heb. *l' yrṣh*.

7:20 *dmprš* (+): expansive.

7:21 *mn qdm yyy*: a routine expression, for the rarer Heb. *'šr lyyy*.

7:31 *qdm yyy*: for Heb. *hmzbḥh*; if an error, it should be corrected to *ᶜl gby mdbḥh* as in v. 5.

Chapter 8

8:10 *wyt kl mnwy* (+): added from v. 11 or N 7:1; cf. L 1:1 also.

8:15 *wrby*: for Heb. *wyḥṭ'*.

8:32 *ytyh* (+): expansive; cf. *tśrpnw*, L 13:55, 57, where N reads *twqdwn ytyh*. In E 12:10 *b'š tśrpw* is translated *twqdwn*.

8:35 *pqdyt*: for passive Heb. *ṣwyty*.

Chapter 9

9:1 *lswp šbᶜty ywmy 'šlmwth* (+): explaining the sudden appearance of "the eighth day."

9:7 ᶜl ydk wᶜl ydyhwn dᶜm' ...: for Heb. bᶜdk wbᶜd hᶜm.... It might seem that bᶜd was read as b'd, comparable to Aram. b'yd = byd, but the phenomenon may be too widespread for such a conclusion. The same expression occurs in N 21:7, where wytpll bᶜd hᶜm is translated wṣly mšh ᶜl ydyhwn dᶜm', and in L 16:6, 11, 17, 24 with the verb kpr + person. However, it appears, in neither D 9:20, E 32:30, 8:24, or G 20:7, which also refer to similar situations of prayer or atonement, nor other contexts where the word bᶜd appears. The word is otherwise translated ᶜl.

9:8 dmn dydyh: for Heb. 'šr lw.

9:22 bṣlw (+): routine expansion when raising the hands is understood to refer to prayer.

Chapter 10

10:3 bmn dmqrb lwwty 'tqdš: for the troublesome Heb. bqrby 'qdš.

wqbl ᶜlwy mklt dynh (+): explanation of Aaron's silence, noted in the previous phrase; cf. MH mdt hdyn.

10:4 ḥbybh: for Heb. dd. The Heb. dd may mean "uncle" or "dear one." The person in question is mentioned in several places, his name spelled both 'lṣpn and 'lyṣpn. According to E 6:14 ff., Amram (the father of Aaron) and Uziel (the father of Mishael and Elsafan) were brothers. Uziel was, therefore, Aaron's uncle. Cf. 18:14, where ḥbybtk means "your aunt."

w'pqw ythwn (+): expansive, as in v. 5.

10:6 tkswn: for Heb. tprᶜw; note that in E 32:25, prᶜ was taken as baring the head. Here the mourning rite of covering the head has been introduced.

10:9 *ḥmr ḥdt wḥmr ʿtyq*: for Heb. *yyn wškr*.

10:16 *mtbʿ tbʿ*: for Heb. *drš drš*. When *drš* means "to inquire of God," *tbʿ wlpn* is used.

10:19 Heb.		N
wydbr 'hrn 'l mšh	a.	*wmlyl 'hrn ʿm mšh*
hn hywm	b.	*h' ywm' hdn*
hqrybw 't ḥṭ'tm w't ʿltm	c.	*qrbw yt ḥṭ'thwn wyt ʿlthwn*
lpny yyy	d.	*qdm yyy*
wtqr'nh 'ty	e.	*w't mlp ytn*
k'lh	f.	*dḥṭ'th ḥmr' mn mʿśrh tnynh*
	g.	*wlyt 'pšr mykl mynyh*
	h.	*w'n' d'rʿ yty yt 'wnsh rbh*
	i.	*ywm' hdyn*
	j.	*wmytw tryn* [*bnyy*] *ndb w'byhw*
	k.	*w'nh 'bl ʿlyhwn*
w'klty ḥṭ't	l.	*h' 'ylw 'klyt mn ḥṭ'th*
hywm	m.	*ywm' hdyn*
hyyṭb bʿyny yyy	n.	*h' špr hwwh qdm yyy*

The Hebrew is difficult in certain places, but understandable, and lines a-e and l-n present a close translation. The one word *k'lh* is not translated, however, but expanded into six lines of text. Building on the translation of *qr'* as *mlp* (line e), the text goes on to explain what Moses actually taught Aaron, i.e. lines f-g; the requirements of the *ḥṭ't* are stricter than those of the second tithe; hence the former may not be eaten.

Formulated in good rabbinic style, line f gives what is claimed to be an halachic teaching in accepted halachic form. Like line l, line g seems to be a presentation of w'klty ḥṭ't. Similarly, line i doubles for line m; in Frag., i is reduced to hdyn and this seems preferable here, too. Lines h and j are similarly somewhat redundant. These duplications may point to two different sources for these materials. Frag. is almost identical to N. PJ contains equivalents of almost all of the lines of N, but in a somewhat different order. The arrangement of N allows us to postulate a time when a-d and l-n may have constituted part of a more literal text, including part, but not all, of e-k, but the presentation of e-k now prevents its being recovered.

10:20 't mylwy d'hrn (+): expansive; dmšh (+): expansive. Both of these expansions help to eliminate any possible confusion about the end of v. 19.

Chapter 11

11:13 'rwm (+): expansive; cf. passim for parallels.

11:19 wyt dyyrh ḥwwrth w'kwmth: for Heb. w't hḥsydh h'nph; dyyrh is for the Heb. hḥsydh h'nph, thus both white and black varieties are included in N.

11:25 ysyṭ: M: dyṭᶜwn; cf. v. 28.

11:30 wpyylt ḥwwyh: for Heb. wh'nqh.

11:37 zrᶜ zryᶜ zrᶜwnyn dy yzdrᶜyn [DM: yzdrᶜwn]: for Heb. zrᶜ zrwᶜ 'šr yzrᶜ, M: [zrᶜ] dmzdrᶜ dy yzdrᶜ. Probably zrᶜwnyn is a double translation of zryᶜ; cf. zrᶜ zrᶜwnyn ... dy yzdrᶜ in PJ and zrʿ zyrwʿ dyzdrʿ in Onk.

11:38 kl (+): expansive; cf. Introduction, chapt. 3.

11:43 ʿl 'rʿ' (+): expansive; probably influenced by v. 42.
wl' tst'bwn bhwn wl' thwwn ms'byn kwwthwn: for the apparently redundant Heb. wl' tṭm'w bhm wnṭmtm bm.

11:45 lmhwy lmhwwy: a double text, the same word spelled in two different ways.

11:46 šrṣh dšrṣ: for Heb. npš hšrṣt.

Chapter 12

12:2 rḥwq ndth: for Heb. ndt dwth; cf. v. 5, 15:19, etc. The word rḥwq is used with ndh; dwth is not translated in N. Onk. uses ryḥwq as the equivalent of ndh, raising the possibility that N contains a conflate term.

12:3 tgzrwn: for Heb. ymwl, M: yg-. This difference between Heb. and N could have been introduced together with ʿmy bny yśr'l, but no such phrase is found here in N or PJ. Other legal subtleties could be intended, but the frequent shift from singular to plural in the translation of the laws belies such a claim.

12:4 ttb tṭr ʿl 'dm ddky: a double translation of Heb. tšb bdmy ṭhrh. The phrase tšb ʿl dmy ṭhrh also occurs in v. 5 and is translated ttb tṭr ʿl 'dm dky. Onk. uses ttyb in both cases. MH frequently uses šmr in similar contexts.

12:8 lmyytyyh (+): expansive.

lḥṭ'th ... lᶜlth: reversed order from the Heb. This order is found in 15:30, but it is unlikely that this alone influenced 12:8.

Chapter 13

13:2 yhwwy, bśryh: lacking in N but added in the margin; cf. the second half of the verse where they are present.

13:5 bḥzwyh: for Heb. bᶜynyw; usually for mr'h, cf. v. 4, etc.

13:16 wytḥzy: for Heb. wb'. Both wb' and whwb' are translated wyyty. This should probably be the reading here as well. Note also v. 19, where wytḥwwy is the translation of wnr'h.

13:33 wyspr ḥzwr ḥzwr lnytq': for Heb. whtglḥ; expanded on the basis of the next phrase. Cf. Onk. wyglḥ sḥrny ntq'....

13:34 lp: read l'.

13:40 śᶜr (+) expansive; cf. v. 41.

13:45 hyk dmbzᶜyn ᶜl 'bylh (+): In the Bible, tearing the garments was a sign of grief, but in rabbinic practice it became of more limited significance, primarily a mourning rite, hence the addition.

The Heb. of the verse ends wṭm' ṭm' yqr'. N perceived this as a warning to passersby, "the unclean will shout 'unclean,' hence whw' mṣrᶜh yhyh [DM: yhwh] ṣwwḥ w'mr rḥwqw mn ms'bh dl' tst'bwn.

13:59 ls'bwtyh: for Heb. lṭm'w, but likely for lṭm'tw when compared to ldkyh ytyh, the translation of lṭhrw.

Chapter 14

14:5 lbr mn dḥsp: for Heb. 'l kly ḥrś; Onk. and PJ have lmn dḥsp, and N reads lgw mn dḥsp in v. 50. DM suggests lgw for lbr, and the presence of this corrected reading in v. 50. supports the idea. Perhaps the use of lbr may be related to the rabbinic prohibition against slaughtering an animal into a vessel? Cf. M Hul. 2:9: 'yn šwḥṭyn ... wl' ltwk klym ....

14:7 wydky: for Heb. whzh; read wydy; wydky occurs elsewhere in the verse.

14:8 lbr mn mšryt': for Heb. mḥwṣ l'hlw. The Aramaic is a common translation for Heb. mḥwṣ lmḥnh, but here the text requires lbr mn mšknh. This same root is used in similar contexts elsewhere, e.g. lbr mn mšryth mšrwyh, 13:46; cf. DM here also. The only correction needed is from mšryt- to mšk-; both are abbreviated mš-; cf. E 33:11.

14:29 ydwy: kp ydwy in the preceding verses.

14:32 lmyytyh qrbn bywm dkwtyh: for Heb. bṭhrtw. The phrase bywm ṭhrtw occurs in 14:2 and N 6:9, where it is translated bywm' ddkwtyh and bywm dkywtyh.

14:35 mryh dbyyth: paraphrase of Heb. zh 'šr lw hbyt, equivalent to b^{c}l hbyt, used in E 22:7 but common in MH.

14:44 wyyty wy^{c}wl: double translation of wb'; y^{c}wl is probably preferable; cf. v. 36.

14:54 *'wryt'*: usually *gzyrt 'wryt'* as suggested in I; cf. v. 57, etc.

14:57 *byn* ... *wbyn*: for Heb. *bywm* ... *wbywm*. Cf. PJ, which contains both elements: *l'lp' khn' l^{c}m' byn ywm'* ... *lbyn ywm'* ... *wbyn br nš' ms'bh lbyn br nš' dky'*. The phrase *byn ḥṭm' wbyn ḥṭhr* (or close equivalents) occurs in 10:10, 11:47 and 20:25. It is easy to see how it replaced the rarer construction in this verse.

Chapter 15

15:12 *ytmrq wyšṭṭp*: for Heb. *yšṭp*.

15:16 *tšmyš dzr^c*: routine for Heb. *škbt zr^c*.

15:19 *bryḥwq ndth*: for Heb. *bndth*; cf. 12:2, where this expression is discussed.

15:31 *dl' ys'bwn yt byt mqdšy d'yqr škyntyh šryh bnyhwn*: for Heb. *bṭm'm 't mškny 'šr btwkm*.

15:33 *'th ms'bh* (+) for Heb. *ṭm'h*, M: *ms'-*.

Chapter 16

16:1 *khn' rbh* (+): Aaron's customary rabbinic title.

qrbn ytyr dl' bzmnh, dy l' 'tpqdw (+): a reference to the events of chapter 10. The phrase *dy l' 'tpqdw* is very close to 10:1 *dl' pqd ythwn*, but the improper act was bringing a strange fire with which to burn incense, not an extra sacrifice, as would appear to be the intention of N.

16:2 *yhwwy*: for Heb. *yb'*. Read either *yyʿwl* as in vv. 26, 29 or *yhwwy ʿll* as in v. 3.

bʿnny 'yqr škynty: for Heb. *bʿnn*; cf. 23:43.

16:3 *lšmšh* (+): also in I but inappropriate with the following *lgw*.

16:21 Heb. *šty* is lacking in N; I: *trtyn*.

Chapter 17

17:3 Read: *twr 'w 'mr*; Heb. *'w* has been omitted; cf. 22:27.

17:4 *'dm ytḥšb* ... *kylw 'dm zkyy špk*: for the different Heb. *dm yḥšb* ... *dm špk*.

17:10 Restore with DM.

17:11 *'dmh hw' ʿl ḥwby npšh ykpr*: for Heb. *hdm hw' bnpš ykpr*.

Chapter 18

18:3 *dyyry* (2x, +): routine; the land does not act, its people do.

18:4 *qyymy d'wryyty*: for Heb. *ḥqty*.

18:5 *kdn 'mr yyy*: for Heb. *'ny yyy*. Used in v. 6 and elsewhere, but not in v. 4, etc. Note, however, 18:30, which is similar to v. 4, and which is translated in this way also.

18:7 d'bwk hw' at the end of the verse is an error copied from v. 8; it should be deleted.

18:9 The Hebrew speaks of mwldt byt and mwldt ḥwṣ, probably meaning born inside or outside the house. This has been taken by N to mean "born to another woman" (sired by the father) or "born to the mother" (sired by another man): mh d'wld 'bwk mn 'th ḥwry 'w mh dylydt 'mk mn gbr 'wḥrn. For these interpretations to apply, mwldt must mean "sired." Otherwise mwldt byt should mean born in the house, i.e. to the mother by an outsider, and mwldt ḥwṣ should mean born outside, i.e. to another woman by the father. Indeed, causative forms of the root wld regularly refer to siring in BH.

18:12 qrybt bśrh: for Heb. š'r, as in v. 13; for š'rh in v. 17.

18:17 ʿrythwn: for Heb. ʿrwth.

znw: for Heb. zmh; cf. 19:29, and 20:14.

18:21 lmtʿbrh bnwr' qdm plḥnh nkryyh: for Heb. lhʿbyr lmlk, generalizing this Molekh worship to include all foreign cults, and applying the standard rabbinic interpretation of this phrase as explained in BT San. 64b, etc. M adds kdn before 'mr yyy, as in 18:5, 19:2, 3, 4, 21:23; this may not be necessary.

Chapter 19

19:3 gbr b'yqryh d'bwy wd'ymyh thwwn zhyryn: for Heb. 'yš 'byw w'mw tyr'w. Quite different from the more literal but inverted rendering of Onk., ... mn 'mh wmn 'bwhy thwn dḥlyn, N reflects the many rabbinic teachings that derive the obligation to care for one's parent's honor from this verse.

šbt qdšyy: for Heb. šbtty.

19:4 The censor's erasure of the translation of h'lylm is virtually complete. There is room for about 6 letters. PJ reads l' tsṭwn lpwlḥn ṭʿwwn wdḥln dmtkn .... Since in N the two words ṭʿwwn dmtkh correspond to PJ's wdḥln dmtkn, some other word must belong. Equally impossible is ṭʿwn wdḥln dmtk' as in Onk. The initial Waw of wṭʿwwn seems certain, so a construction like pwlḥn (d)ṭʿwwn is impossible. In L 26:1 N translates 'lylm, psl, mṣbh and 'bn mśkyt as ṭʿwwn, ..., qyymh and 'bn dmtkh. Since ṭʿwwn dmtkh already exists in our text, this parallel helps very little. In E 34:17, 'lhy mskh is translated dḥln ṭʿwwn dmtkh. D 27:15 presumably contains the terms [ṣlm, ṣwrh] and dmw. Other verses use similar words as well, and frequently these have been obliterated by the censors. Given all of the above, I suggest the following possibilities for 19:4: a) ṣlmyyh; b) ṣlm wṣwrh (a little tight and usually used for psl). These both assume the use of ṣlm, one of the words most consistently erased by the censor. Though the more common translation of 'lyl is ṭʿwwn, forms of ṣlm are attested for Is. 10:10 and Ezek. 30:13, and ṣlm often appears in contexts where ṭʿwwn has already been used. Here, ṭʿwwn is used in the phrase wṭʿwwn dmtkh; ṭʿwwyh wṭʿwwn ... would be clumsy, and there would be no reason to erase ṭʿwwn once but not twice (unless the censor was working from an already censored copy of a slightly different targum). Thus the erased word is, most likely, some form or compound of ṣlm.

19:6 For the first tlytyyh read dbtrh, for Heb. wmmḥrt.

19:8 wmh [DM: wmn?] dy'kl: pl. changed to sing. for consistency. For this use of mh, cf. v. 14. Heb. hhy' has not been translated.

19:9 'wmnh 'ḥryh dḥqlkwn: for Heb. p't śdk.

19:11 For this style of translation cf. E 20:13 ff.

19:14 mh dl' šmʿ: for Heb. ḥrš; wqdm mn dl' ḥmy l' ttn tqlh: for wlpny ʿwr l' ttn mkšl. The second phrase in N may reflect the rabbinic teaching that broadened it to include many other forms of misleading the unknowing person; but this is not necessarily so, particularly give the similarly expansive translation in the first part of the verse, where no such change is intended.

19:15 šqr: for Heb. ʿwl.

bqwšṭ': for Heb. bṣdq; cf. D 16:20 qwšṭ' qwšṭ- thwwn rdpyn, for Heb. ṣdq ṣdq trdp, etc.

19: 16-18	Heb.		N
16-	l' tlk rkyl bʿmyk	a.	l' tyzwl btr lyšnh tlytyh lmrʿyh
		b.	wyt bʿly dynh l' tštwq
	l' tʿmd ʿl dm rʿk	c.	l' tyqwm ʿl 'dm qṭwlwy dḥbrk
		d.	bzmnh d't ydʿ lyh zkw bdyn'
	'ny yyy	e.	'mr yyy
17-	l' tśn' 't 'ḥyk blbbk	f.	l' tśn' yt 'ḥwk blbk
	hwkḥ twkyḥ 't ʿmytk	g.	mwkḥh twkḥ yt ḥbrk

	wl' tś' ᶜlyw ḥṭ'	h.	wl' tqbl ᶜlwy ḥwbyn
	(l' tlk rkyl)	i.	l' thwwn 'zlyn btr lyšn' tlytyyh
		j.	dhw' qš- kḥrb'
		k.	mḥy mn tryn sṭrwy
	(bᶜmyk	l.	dmn tryn ḥwrpwy lmᶜqh bh yt ḥbrk
	(wl' tᶜmd ᶜl dm rᶜk)	m.	wl' tmnᶜ zkwth dḥbr-
		n.	kd tdᶜ bh d'yt lh zkw bdynh
	(wl' tᶜmd ᶜl dm rᶜk)	o.	wl' ttḥšd bḥwbt 'dmh dḥbrk
18-	l' tqm	p.	wl' thwwn nwqmnyn
	wl' tṭr 't bny ᶜmk	q.	wl' nwṭrnyn yt ḥwbrkwn
	w'hbt lrᶜk kmwk	r.	wtrḥmwn lḥbrkwn kwwtkwn
	'ny yyy	s.	kdn 'mr yyy

The translations of vv. 16-18 may be divided into 19 lines that contain many duplications. Lines a-e and i-o translate v. 16; lines f-h translate v. 17; lines p-s translate v. 18.

The Heb. of line a is translated in a and again in i-l. Line a is not literal. Heb. l' tlk rkyl appears to be a prohibition against doing active harm to the injured party, while the Aram. forbids a less active role; l' tyzwl btr, "don't follow." This may be related to the origin of the explanation of lyšnh tlytyh as damaging to three people -- the speaker, the spoken of and the listener (cf. Moore, Vol. II, cited by DM). The word lmrᶜyh may be a Hebraized form comparable to lmb'š' in E 23:2; indeed, there is much similarity between these lines and N in E 23:2, which also contains a double translation: l' thwwn 'zlyn btr swgy' lmb'š' and l' tyzl btr sgy' lmb'š'. N and M in E 23:2 also begin ᶜmy bny yśr'l, as does M here.

The parallel in lines i-l offers an analogy between this

slanderous talk and a sword, and the emphasis on its double edged blade (lines j-1) may hint at the same homiletical notion generally associated with *lyšnh tlytyh*. Lines k and l appear redundant, but line l lacks a finite verb. The differences between these translations are not significant enough to warrant any conclusions about originality. The analogy to the sword in line j is similar to the statement in G 3:24, which is also part of a midrashic addition. Line b does not correspond to any other part of the complex of vv. 16-18. But if line a applies to the judges (as is assumed in many Talmudic interpretations, e.g. BT Ket. 46a) and not to the common man or litigant in a case, line b fits as a second type of advice to the judge about the litigants (*bʿly dynh* are "litigants" not "judges," as translated in the *editio princeps*). The two lines together advise neither following slanderous talk nor silencing the litigants in a case.

Heb. line c is translated in Aram. c, m, and perhaps o as well. Lines c-d take the second part of v. 16 as a command not to withhold evidence of someone's innocence in a capital case. Lines m-n offer a similar expression of the same idea but word it differently. While line c is a literal translation of the Heb., except for the added *qṭwlwy*, m-n are much less closely related to the Heb. text. Line o offers the additional advice of not allowing oneself to be suspected of involvement in another's guilt. This line was obviously inspired by the Heb. of line c, which it translates, with one exception, literally. There is no obvious connection between *tʿmd* and *ttḥšd*, but the verb *ʿmd* clearly can refer to a court appearance in MH if not in BH, and the verse could be understood to mean "Don't stand in court (i.e. allow yourself to be accused = *ttḥšd*) for the guilt of your fellow's blood." In this manner we may see line o as a third alternative to the translation of *l' tʿmd ʿl dm rʿk.*

Returning to E 23:2, we find *wl' ytmnʿ ḥd mnkwn lmlph*

zkwn lḥbryh bdyn' and l' tmnᶜ mn lmymr mh dblbk ᶜl ḥbrk bdyn'. Lines m-n are very close to this other verse, which translates the Heb, wl' tᶜnh ᶜl rb.

The phrase 'ny yyy (e) is frequently translated by kdn 'mr yyy (e.g. line s). Since 'ny cannot be translated by 'mr, it seems best to add kdn here also, but note also 19:25.

Verse 17 is translated quite closely; v. 18 somewhat more expansively. The only unusual usage is ḥwbrkwn for bny ᶜmk.

Onk. translates vv. 16-18 with equivalents of lines 16: a (different), c, e; 17: f, g, h; 18: p, q, r, s. PJ contains equivalents of 16: i, j, l, m, n, e; 17: f (quite different), g, h; 18: p, q, r (+additions), s. Frag. contains ᶜmy bny yśr'l, a or i, a mixture of b-c, d, e ('mr yyy!), but verses 17-18 are not found. N, it would seem, combines Frag. with a shortened, reordered text of PJ (vv. 17, 16, 18); (ᶜmy bny yśr'l would be appropriate before line p). The duplication would therefore be a-e, not i-l, and the preferred material is lines f-s, reordered to follow the Hebrew verses. Of course we may also assume that Frag. was equivalent to vv. 17-18 in N and that the material in i-l is secondary. This would preserve the order of 16-18, and isolate i-l as the intrusion. The duplications of lines k and p are also eliminated in PJ, and the missing equivalent of line e has been retained between lines n and p. The absence of this equivalent to line e leaves i-l as a fragment, further supporting the claim that it is secondary.

19:19	Heb.		N
	't ḥqty tšmrw	a.	yt qymh 'wryyty tṭrwn
	bhmtk l' trbyᶜ kl'ym	b.	bᶜrkwn l' trbᶜwn kl'ym
	śdk l' tzrᶜ kl'ym	c.	ḥqlkwn l' tzrᶜwn kl'ym
	wbgd kl'ym	d.	wlbwš dklym
		e.	ᶜl'r [DM: ᶜmr] wktn

šᶜṭnz — f. šᶜṭnz

l' yᶜlh ᶜlyk — g. l' yswq ᶜlykwn

Line a is similar to 26:3, where bḥqty has been translated bqymh d'wryty. The only significant deviation from the Hebrew is the addition of line e, which reflects the text of D 22:11, l' tlbš šᶜṭnz ṣmr wpštym yḥdw, translated in N as l' tlbšwn šᶜṭnz ᶜmr wkdn (!) mᶜrbyn kḥdh.

19:20 ktb (+): following the rabbinic interpretation as presented in Onk.: 'w ḥrwt' l' 'tyhybt lh bšṭr. For parallels see BT Git. 41b, PT Sot. 2:2, etc.

mrdw 'nwn ḥyybyn: for Heb. bqrt thyh, following the rabbinic teaching that punishment for such behavior is beating; cf. BT Ker. 11a.

19:23 wtprqwn ᶜrltyh: for wᶜrltm ᶜrltw. The translation of wᶜrltm as wtprqwn is problematic. PJ and M have wtgzrwn; Onk. reads wtrḥqwn rḥq'. Given the use of ryḥwq for ᶜrlym later in the verse, a reading of wtrḥqwn for wtprqwn -- a minor change -- is possible. Alternatively the verse may have been influenced by D 14:25, which speaks of redeeming tithes (wtprqwn mᶜśrh in N) and by the redemption of the fourth year of produce; cf. v. 24, Perhaps the same notion was introduced here, intentionally or unintentionally.

19:24 prqn: for Heb. hlwlym.

19:25 kdn is lacking before 'mr as noted above; cf. 18:5, 19:30, 20:7, 8, 21:15.

19:26	Heb.		N
		a.	*ʿmy bny yśr'l*
	l' t'klw ʿl hdm	b.	*l' tyklwn ʿl dm qṭyly snhdryn*
	l' tnḥšw	c.	*wl' thwwn nṭwry nḥšyn*
	wl' tʿwnnw	d.	*wl' ḥrwdy ʿyynyn*

The context of v. 26 is a series of laws that deal primarily with agricultural matters or that are, at least in part, directed at abolishing pagan practices. The prohibition of eating blood (v. 26) can easily be seen as part of this broader purpose. Similar legislation in D 12:16, 23 also prohibits consumption of an animal's blood, however, and the presence of that other, more explicit reference, freed L 19:26 to serve as the basis for some other teaching. Accordingly, in Deut., N follows the Heb. text literally, but here several words that drastically alter the message of the text have been added. The change of Heb. *ʿl hdm* (presumably of an animal) to *ʿl dm qṭyly snhdryn* (b) reflects the teaching recorded in BT San. 63a: Rabbi Akiva says, "Whence do we know that the Sanhedrin that agreed to execute someone should taste nothing during the entire day? It is written, 'Do not eat over the blood.'"

Lines c-d of the Hebrew prohibit two types of sorcery: *l' tnḥšw wl' tʿwnnw*. N has changed the focus of the first phrase by stressing the practitioner, not the action, and paraphrased the text as *wl' thwwn nṭwry nḥšyn*; cf. Onk.: *l' tnḥšwn*, but PJ: *l' thwwn nṭry nḥšyn*. In this form the verse approximates the prohibition in E 22:17, *mkšph l' tḥyh*, but even more so that in D 18:10, where *mnḥš* is translated *nṭwry nḥšyn*. The second phrase, *ḥrwdy* [DM: *ḥrwry*] *ʿyynyn*, also emphasizes the person instead of the act, but the precise meaning of the term is less certain. Outside the Pentateuch, the targumim consistently use m^cnyn as the Aram. term. This is true of Onk. in D 18:10, 14 also; but in L 19:26 the verb t^cnwn is used. PJ has 'ḥwry snhdryn ^cyynyn here, but the middle word is a gloss or error from the equivalent of line b. In Deut., PJ has ḥdwdy ^cynyn (variants: ḥrwry) and ḥdwdy ^cyn (variants: ḥrwr). N has ḥdwdy ^cynyn twice in Deut.; DM has listed many other texts that preserve the reading ḥrwry. The N reading here, ḥrwdy, is very difficult, but in no case does M or I contain alternate suggestions. The similarity between ḥdd and ḥrr (and the abundance of sources that reflect this latter reading) has convinced DM to accept ḥrr throughout. The potential similarity between the PJ 'ḥwry ^cyynyn and the MH term 'ḥyzt ^cyynym (e.g. Sifrei, Deut., p. 219, BT San. 65b) has led Reeder to prefer 'ḥwdy in his edition of PJ to Lev. 19:26; he makes no comment on the Deut. passages. Both of these suggestions are reasonable, but certain problems remain. The Hebrew term for this activity is ^cynwn in PT San. 7:5 and PT Shab. 7:2; I must admit that I have been unable to locate an early text containing the term 'ḥd ^cynyn. Under the circumstances, Reeder's suggestion requires that we assume that PJ to Lev. 19;26 containts a borrowed phrase that is lacking everywhere else, including in PJ of Deut.

Perhaps 'ḥyzt ^cynym and ḥdwdy ^cynym refer to the impact of such magicians on the eyes of the person watching them. The word ḥrr may mean "to penetrate," and also might refer to a hypnotic type of control. If so all of these readings may be acceptable, but the matter needs further evaluation.

19:28 ^cl npš dmyt: taking Heb. lnpš to mean "over a life"; cf. BT Mak. 20b, Onk.: wḥybwl ^cl myt ....

19:29	Heb.		N
	'l tḥll 't btk lhznwth	a.	l' tšhw- yt bntkwn
		b.	mn lmsbh ythwn
	wl' tznh h'rṣ	c.	dl' tzny 'rᶜ'
	wml'h h'rṣ	d.	wttmly 'rᶜ'
	zmh	e.	bnyn dznw

Lines c-d are translated literally, but this is the less important part of the verse. Lines a-b are a paraphrase of the Heb. and comport with the Talmud's encouragement of early marriages to prevent the spread of immorality; cf. BT San. 76a. Leaving one's children unmarried could, in the minds of the rabbis, lead only to improper sexual conduct. For the translation of zmh as bnyn dznw, cf. 18:17 and 20:14.

19:30 wbbyt mqdšy thwwn mṣlyn bdḥl-: for Heb. wmqdšy tyr'w. Reverence for the sanctuary was intended by the Heb., but the frequent omission of Heb. prepositions allowed Heb. wmqdšy to be understood as wbmqdšy, allowing the focus to shift to prayer, the post-Temple form of worship. Cf. 26:2, where the matter is discussed more extensively, and where the text reads wbyt, not wbbyt.

19:31 šw'ly (+): There is a clear distinction between practitioners of these occult acts and those who merely consult them (BT San. 65a), but in all likelihood the term is simply borrowed from D 18:11, š'l 'wb, translated in N š'ly 'wbh.

wmsqy dkwrn: for Heb. hydᶜnym. In D 18:11 the phrase wmsqy zkwrwn is used. (Cf. M and I in both places for variants on dkr / zkr). Note also 20:6, 27.

19:32 ḥkymyn rbrbyn mnkwn b'wryyth: for Heb. śybh. Comparison with the parallel statement that follows led the rabbis to interpret this verse as a reference to honour of sages, not elders; cf. BT Qid. 32b. This being the case, it seems somewhat odd that zqn is translated rbh. Cf. Onk. mn qdm dsbr b'wryt' tqwm wthdr 'py sb' and also PJ mn qdm sbyn dsbryn b'wryyt' tqwmwn wtyqr 'py ḥkym' .... The problem may be resolved by referral to the many places where zqnym, zqny yśr'l, etc. have been rendered ḥkymy. Perhaps rbh was introduced in N to eliminate the repetition of ḥkym and ḥkymyn rbrbyn. If so, this may point to an earlier stage when the original translation of zqn was ḥkym and that of śybh was sb' or the like. (In D 32:25 'yš śybh is translated gbryn sbyn, plural).

19:35 bmtqlh bmklth: for Heb. bmdh bmšql; the order should be reversed, as suggested by M.

19:36 dqšt: for Heb. ṣdq (4x): cf. 19:15, etc.

Chapter 20

20:2 lmʿbrh qdm plḥnh nkryyh: for Heb. lmlk. Cf. 18:21, translated wbnyk l' ttn lmtʿbrh bnwr' qdm plḥnh nkryyh, and D 18:10 mʿbr bryh wbrtyh bnwr'. Cf. also vv. 3, 4, 5. The use of lhʿbyr originates in the Heb. of 18:21.

20:6 Cf. notes on 19:31.

20:9 yzlzl 'yqryh d'bwy wd'mh: for Heb. yqll 't 'byw w't 'mw; a similar usage is found in G 16:4.

20:10 Heb. yn'p is translated yšmš and ygyyr. Cf. gywryn (4x) and *gywr'* in E 20:14 and D 5:18.

20:12 *'tth dbrh*: "his son's wife" for the ambiguous Heb. *kltw*. Heb. *šnyhm* has not been translated, probably unintentionally, since the verbs are in the plural.

20:14 *znw*: for Heb. *zmh*. The regular translation of *bnyn dznw* is impossible here, as it was in the translation of *zmh* as *mrḥqh*, a few words earlier. The phrase *znw bnykwn* means "immorality among you," Heb. *btwkkm*, but the defective spelling of *bynykwn* looks like a reference to "son."

20:17 *dʿbdt ʿm qdmyy lmbny ʿlm' brm mn kdwn kl dy ʿbd kdn* (+): This midrashic addition is a response to two problems -- the use of *ḥsd* in the Heb. of this verse, and the manner in which God provided wives for the men who lived after Adam. Heb. *ḥsd* is normally a positive word meaning "kindness, mercy," but in this verse the Heb. means "abomination." Both meanings are available in Aram. also, but the former is much more frequently attested in N. According to the Sifra, Qed. 11:11 (p. 95a), the world was populated by *ḥsd*, a notion based on a midrashic interpretation of Ps. 89:3, *ʿwlm ḥsd ybnh*. This verse is offered by the Sifra to explain Cain's marrying his sister; this was a special *ḥsd*. The word play is carried throughout the passage, though, and it is unclear whether the point is that Cain did what he did because God wanted it that way, even though the act was an abomination, or that Cain's act was a true *ḥsd*, not at all abominable. The addition in N also allows for either of these interpretations; the second interpretation is paralleled by other midrashim, which had Jacob's twelve sons marrying their sisters.

20:18 *mbwʿ dmh*: for Heb. *mqrh*; the term has been borrowed from the Heb. *mqr dmyh* later in the verse, 12:7, etc.

20:20 *ḥbybth*: for Heb. *ddtw*; *dḥbybth* for *ddw* should probably be corrected to *dḥbybh*.

20:21 *mrḥqh*: for Heb. *ndh*. The translation fits the context, and also note the customary translation of *ndh* as *rḥwq ndth*, e.g. 12:2. But the usage is actually the equivalent of Heb. *twᶜbh hy'* as in v. 13.

20:23 *mrḥqth* (+): expansive. The phrase *'lyyn mrḥqth* was borrowed from 18:26, 27, 29, etc.

Chapter 21

21:1 *dmyt* (+): expansive, influenced by v. 11.

khn' rbh (+): verse 11 contains the rules prohibiting the high priest from coming into contact with a corpse. It is somewhat unexpected for this to be introduced here in the context of the laws for common priest.

21:3 *'tnsbh lgbr*: for Heb. *hyth l'yš*.

lᶜlyh: for Heb. *lh*. This appears to be composed of *ᶜlyh* (cf. *ᶜl npš*, v. 1) and *lh* (*lqryb*, *l'myh*, etc. v. 2); Onk., PJ, M: *lh*.

21:4 *dl' yps yt khnt'*: for Heb. *lhḥlw*; cf. 20:3, 21:6, etc.

21:9 *ṭᶜwh wmpsh*: for Heb. *tḥl lznwt*, but borrowed from v. 7 where it is the equivalent of *znh wḥllh*. Note the same term in v. 14 for Heb. *wḥllh znh*.

21:13 *'th bshdwdth* [DM: *bshdwwth*]: for Heb. *'šh bbtwlyh*. Cf. D 22:17 and my discussion of G 16:5.

21:14 The word *btwlh* has not been translated. In G 24:16, *btwlh* is used in N and it is probably correct here, also; cf. Onk. *btwlt'*, PJ *btwlt' mykšr'*.

21:17 *gbr gbr mn bnyk*: for Heb. *'yš mzrʿk*. Since *gbr gbr* occurs at the end of the line in the MS, the second might be a dittography, but usually the lines are filled with letters from the subsequent word, not the previous one. Note, however, that many laws begin *'yš 'yš* (L 15:2, 17:10, 13, 18:6, 20:2, etc.), and a number of them relate to priests.

21:18 *lmqrbh* (+): expansive, based on v. 17.

21:19 The translation is lacking in the MS; DM has restored the text from PJ. The phrases *šbr rgl* and *šbr yd* occur only here and no other suggestion seems better, but Onk. offers *tbr rgl'* and *tbr yd'*. In 24:20 N translates *šbr* as *tbr* and this seems preferable, as does *dyhwwy* for *dylhy*.

21:20	Heb.		N
	'w gbn	a.	*'w dy gbnwy*
		b.	*ḥpyyn ʿl ʿyynwy*
		c.	*'w dlyt lyh śʿr bgybynwy*
		d.	*'w gbyʿ*
	'w dq	e.	*'w nns*
	'w tbll bʿynw	f.	*'w dḥlzwnh bʿynwy*
	'w grb	g.	*'w dmly ḥzzyyn*
	'w ylpt	h.	*'w dḥzwwy ḥšyk*
	'w mrwḥ 'šk	i.	*'w dmrḥš 'šktyh*

The primary rabbinic discussion of this passage is found in Sifra (p. 95b) and BT Bekh. 45a. The material has been analyzed in detail in J. Preuss, Biblical and Talmudic Medicine (translated by Fred Rosner, New York, 1978) pp. 260 ff; on the possibility that most of the defects are ailments of the eyes, cf. Krinsky, Mehoqeqei Yehudah. a.l. and the sources cited by him. According to the Sifra, the Biblical gbn means a) lacking either one or both eyebrows, or b) having drooping eyebrows (R. Dosa), or c) having a doubled spinal column (Hanina ben Antigonus). These three opinions have been recorded in N as lines c, a-b, and d. According to the Sifra, dq refers to an eye problem -- ḥlzwn nḥš ᶜynyw -- but N translates it nns, "midget." This notion is also found in Frag. (in the text found in some Rabbinic Bibles and in Ginsburger's edition, p. 113, cited from Levita, s.v. nss, where it is not found in the printed text of Meturgeman) and is also attributed to PJ by Preuss; but it appears that PJ, consistent with the Sifra, has translated dq as ḥlzwn bᶜyynwy. N, however, reserves ḥlzwnh bᶜynwy for tbll bᶜynw. According to Kohut (Arukh Completum, Vol. III, p. 398), ḥlzwn means having the black and white of the eye mixed, "cujus albus color nigro commixtus est" -- the precise definition of tbll found in the Sifra, PJ etc., -- cf. bll "to confuse, mix, etc." (Preuss, p. 261). Preuss explains ḥlzwn as the equivalent of nḥš (cf. BT Bekh. 38b), a disease of the eyelids, not eyeballs (p. 262).

The Heb. grb and ylpt are found elsewhere as well. D 28:27 reads ykkh yyy bšḥyn mṣrym wbᶜplym (Qere: wbtḥwrym) wbgrb wbḥrs 'šr l' twkl lhrp'; N translates the diseases as šḥnh dmṣryy wbtḥwryh wbḥrbnh wbḥrsnh. Thus ḥrs is rendered ḥrsnh, leaving grb as ḥrbnh (note the alliteration). The Sifra apparently associated the two verses by having grb (Lev.) = ḥrs (Deut.) and ylpt (Lev.) = šḥyn mṣrym (Deut.); perhaps grb wḥrs was seen as an hendiadys. N has opted for a more general translation mly ḥzzyyn. For ylpt, N reads dḥzwwy ḥšyk, "his appearance is dark," which sounds like the statement of R. Hanina ben Antigonus in Sifra šmr'yw ḥšwkym, but this is the last line of the text and appears to be an alternative to the explanation of mrwḥ 'šk. (Perhaps this gloss in the Sifra is out of place.) The close association of grb and ylpt is seen in PJ also, which translates them as mly ḥrsyn ybšyn and mly ḥzzyt' mṣryt', but this is very close to the Sifra.

The reading dmrḥš for mrwḥ has been questioned by DM, who offers dmḥsr, but this seems to be an unsubstantiated suggestion. Note that Sifra offers šnmrḥw 'škyw and šrwḥ b'škyw. The interpretation of mrwḥ 'šk as kl šmr'yw ḥšwkym would appear to result from redividing the Hebrew as mrw ḥ'šk = mr'w ḥšk.

21:21 lḥm 'lhyh: for Heb. 'šy yyy. This has been introduced from the latter part of the verse; read qrbnwy dyyy, with M.

21:23 lgw mn: for Heb. 'l.

Chapter 22

22:2 Heb. 'ny has been omitted from N; perhaps add 'mr as in vv. 8,9.

22:4 yqrb: for Heb. whngʿ.

br nš (+): expansive, because the laws of purity are different for contact with human or animal dead. That npš might refer to either may be seen from 24:18.

22:7 kdn (+): expansive.

22:10 khn has not been translated, probably it was omitted in favor of the phrase twtb br ᶜmmyn.

22:20 The translation of l' tqrybw ky was omitted through homoioteleuton.

22:22	Heb.		N
	ᶜwrt	a.	dsmy
	'w šbwr	b.	'w dtbyr
	'w ḥrwṣ	c.	'w dgbyyh
	'w yblt	d.	'w nsys
	'w grb	e.	'w dmly ḥzzyyn
	'w ylpt	f.	
	l' tqrybw ...	g.	l' tqrbwn ...

Two of the Heb. terms in this verse, grb and ylpt, correspond to terms in 21:20. In both verses grb is translated dmly ḥzzyyn, but ylpt has apparently not been translated in 22:22. If both h and i in 21:20 are the equivalents of mrwḥ 'šk -- as is suggested in the Sifra -- then ylpt is not translated there either. Several of the Aram. terms are also similar. Eye afflictions are basic to 21:20, and dsmy (22:22) is another. Perhaps dgbyyh is related to the terms in 21:20 also. The term nns for Heb. dq occurs in 21:20, but not here. I suggests nns instead of nnys as the translation of yblt, but the change is not necessarily warranted.

22:27 N

A 1. ᶜydn dtdkr ln qrbynn (!)

2. mh dhwwyyn mqrybyn wmtkpr ᶜl ḥwbynn

3. wkdwn dlyt ln lmqrbyh mn ᶜdry ᶜnynn

4. ytkpr ᶜl ḥṭ'ynn

B 5. twrh 'tbḥr qdmy
6. bgyn lmdkrh qdmyy zkwtyh dgbrh mdnḥyyh
7. dbsybwtyh 'tbrk bkwlh
8. wrhṭ lbqrwtyh
9. w'yyty bt [DM: br] twryn šmyn wṭb
10. wyhb lrbyh
11. w'wḥy lmᶜbd ytyh
12. wpṭyryn 'ph w'yykl lml'kyn
13 wmn yd 'tbśr lśrh
14. dh' śrh yldh lyṣḥq

C 15. wmn btr kdn
16. 'tbḥr 'ymr'
17. bgyn lmdkr' zkwt' dgbr' yḥydh
18. d'tᶜqd ᶜl ḥd mn ṭwry'
19. hyk 'mr lᶜlh ᶜl gby mdbḥh
20. wpdh ytyh
21. wbrḥmwy ṭbyyh
22. wzmn bnwy lmhwy mṣlyyn w'mryn dydhwn (!)
23. bšᶜt 'nnqy ddhwn
24. ᶜny ytn bhdh šᶜth
25. wšmᶜ bql ṣlwtn
26. w'dkr ln ᶜqydtyh dyṣḥq 'bwnn

D 27. wmn btr kdyn
28. 'tbḥr gdyyh br ᶜzyyh
29. bgyn lmdkrh zkwty- dgbr' tmym'
30. dlbš bgw ydwy mškyn dgdyyn bny ᶜzyn
31. wtbšylyn ᶜbd
32. w'yykwl l'bwy
33. w[z]kh lmqblh yt sdr brkth

E 34. 'lyn tlty qrbny qrbny
35. tlty 'bht ᶜlm' 'ynwn
36. 'brhm yṣḥq wyᶜqb

37. bgyn kdn ktyb wmprš bspr 'wryyt- dyyy

38. twr ['w] 'mr 'w gdy 'rwm ytyld

39. yhwy mtrby šbʿh ywmyn btr 'myh

40. wmn ywm' tmynyyh wlhl-

41. yhy kšr lmqrbh ytyh qdm yyy

Heb.

a. šwr 'w kśb 'w ʿz ky ywld

b. whyh šbʿt ymym tḥt 'mw

c. wmywm hšmyny whl'h

d. yrṣh lqrbn 'šh lyyy

This passage can be divided into 5 sections. Section A (lines 1-4) introduces the subject. Sections B (5-14), C (15-26) and D (27-33) explain the symbolism in the choice of the ox, sheep and goat as sacrificial animals. Section E concludes the passage, identifies the animals as the patriarchs (34-36) and translates the verse (37-41).

Section A seems truncated. The idea is apparently that "now," i.e. after the destruction of the Temple in 70, sacrifices, once available as a means of atonement (1-2), can no longer serve this purpose (3-4). Though only line 3 is really clear, lines 1-2 are acceptable; but something is certainly lacking between lines 3 and 4, for line 4 has no point of reference. Perhaps one should insert mh or mh nqrbh (cf. Frag. and M) or hyk.

Section B describes why the ox come first. Presumably, lines 6-14 describe Abraham, identified in line 36. Line 6 notes that he was from the East: mdnḥyyh. This is obviously a possible description of Abraham, who migrated from Mesopotamia to the west, but it appears to be rabbinic rather than Biblical.

Midrashic attempts to associate him with 'ytn h'zrḥy (Ps. 89:1, cf. BT B.B. 15a) are also based on this usage. Line 7 refers to G 24:1, according to which God blessed Abraham with everything. N reads wmmryh dyyy brk yt 'brhm bkl'; Line 7 here is not based on the translation in Gen.

Lines 8-14 refer to the events of G 18:3 ff. Lines 8-11 are similar to 18:7 wlbqrwth rhṭ 'brhm wnsb br twryn rkyk wṭb wyhb lrbyh w'wḥy lmᶜbd ytyh. With one major difference and several minor ones, N is identical in both G 18:7 and here. The major one is in lines 12-13. Here N has mn yd (line 13), but the announcement of Isaac's birth came in G 18:10. Line 12, which interrupts the sequence, poses a problem insofar as it appears to suggest Abraham fed the angels unleavened bread. According to the Bible, Abraham fed the angels various dairy products and beef before Isaac's birth was announced. Though in G 18:6 Abraham requested the preparation of bread, it is not stated that the angels were actually served any. Some midrashic texts assumed that Sarah began to menstruate and thus rendered the dough unclean. Other commentators (e.g. the Rashbam) assume that the bread was served, but was not mentioned because it was not special. In either case, the reference to serving pṭyryn is not found in Gen. 18 but does occur in 19:3, where Lot fed his guests: wmṣwt 'ph wy'klw, translated as wpṭyryn 'ph w'klw. Since pṭyryn is usually the equivalent of mṣwt, its use here, in connection with Abraham, is surprising. The reason for the change may have been a) Isaac's birth was announced on Passover; b) Sarah's sudden menses required the preparation of unleavened bread, which took less time; c) pṭyryh may simply be the equivalent of Heb. ᶜwgwt, since the word ᶜwgwt is used mostly with mṣh. But, directly or indirectly, 19:3 may have influenced this material, for it remains the only Biblical passage that actually mentions feeding these angels unleavened bread. Indeed, some midrashim went to great length to contrast the poor quality of Lot's fare with that offered by Abraham.

The minor differences are in the use of synonyms. They demonstrate the independence of the midrash here from the translation in Gen. 18: *w'yyty* - *wnsb*; *šmyn* - *rkyk*.

Section C explains the inclusion of the sheep among the sacrificial animals. The term *gbr' yḥydh* (17) reflects the use of Heb. *yḥydk* in G 22:2. Line 18 is also based on G 22:2: *whᶜlhw šm lᶜwlh ᶜl 'ḥd hhrym*, translated *wqrb yth tmn lᶜlh ᶜl ḥd ṭwryh d'mr lk*. Deletion of the initial *Waw* of line 21 would make lines 20-21 one complete thought. Parts of lines 22-24 are very reminiscent of G 38:25 (lines 6-7, 13); cf. my notes there. Apparently lines 25-26 are also part of a prayer that requests salvation because of the sacrifice of Isaac, a common liturgical motif for Rosh HaShannah.

Section D contains the rationale for the goat's inclusion. The adjective *tmym'* (line 29) refers to the description of Jacob in G 25:27, which N translated quite differently: *gbr šlm bᶜbd' ṭb'*. Lines 30-32 refer to the events of G 27:16-17, 25, 30. Only line 30 is close enough to the text of Gen. to warrant comparison. In G 27:16, N reads *wyt mšk' dgdyy' bny ᶜyzyy' 'lbšt ᶜl ydwy* ....

Section E contains two parts and mentions the names of the patriarchs for the first time, though the many references in B-D are more than adequate for proper identification. Part one (34-36) is brief and ties together all that has preceded; one *qrbny* should be deleted from line 34. Part two is the translation of the verse; aside from its omission of the first *'w* (identical to the omission from 17:3) and several small paraphrases, it is quite close to the Hebrew. The changes are *mtrby* (+): expansive; and *yhy kšr lmqrbh* for Heb. *yrṣh*. Heb. *yrṣh* is usually translated lrᶜwh, but kšr lmqrbh is appropriate in this context.

Sections B - D are obviously of one cloth, as they present parallel data and contain all sorts of structural similarities. The connections between A, B-D, and E are less certain. Lines 34-36 (E) are very similar to parts of G 40:12 (and 40:18), where three other items are also identified as tlty 'bht ᶜlm' 'nwn, but the differences between these two contexts are striking. In Gen. this characterization precedes the explanation, but here it follows it, and in this position it is really superfluous. Moreover, Section A speaks of the role of sacrifice in atonement and laments the absence of the sacrifices, but it is connected neither with the reasons for choosing particular animals (B-D) nor with the identification of these animals with the patriarchs. Though the texts are not identical in wording, similar sections are found in the lengthy texts of M, F, PJ, and Frag. In general, the version of A found in these other texts is superior to that in N, but the lack of a close relationship between the sections is still a serious problem. In fact we must separate section A from the rest of the text. It is highly liturgical (resembling the beginning of G 35:9 in this respect) and is simlar to other prayers that express anguish over the destruction of the Temple. It is not related to B-E except in the most peripheral way.

B-D form the bulk of this text. Its substance is found in a number of midrashic passages (e.g. LR p. 642; PRK 9,9, p. 157), but in each case the passage is very short, consisting of a reference to each animal followed by a proof text showing some connection between it and the patriarch's merits. This simple form appears to be the original one; N and the other targumic parallels here expanded and embellished it. Since these midrashim contain no component parallel to section A (they usually begin šwr bzkwt 'brhm ...), the translator of N, who needed to flesh out the statement, was forced to provide one. In its present form it is A, but for several reasons a different type of passage should have been used. A comparison of B, C and D and an analysis of other midrashic passages in N point to several features that should have been present in this introduction. Lines 5, 15-16 and 27-28 speak of a conscious selection of these three animals and stress the order of selection as well. All the passages stress merits -- each animal was chosen to serve as a reminder of the meritorious acts of a patriarch -- and each concludes by mentioning God's positive response to the people involved. A proper introduction should have contained these elements. It might have begun with a quotation from the verse listing these animals and might have been organized around the number three. It should have then explained that God searched for appropriate animals to be offered in the Temple and chose these three because of their ability to recall the meritorious acts of the patriarchs, which could aid in the prayers of the people.

Such an arrangement would have obviated E, and it is conceivable that lines 34-36, now part of E, may once have been part of such an introduction. The key phrase here is 'lyn tlty qrbny, which specifically mentions three sacrifices, but neither corresponds to the presentation in B-D (for only C actually mentions a sacrifice) nor refers back to section A in its present form. Perhaps its referent is L 1:2; indeed some, though not most, of the midrashim record this midrash at the beginning of Lev. and L 1:2, which introduces the whole matter of sacrifices, is a more fitting location. But the earlier midrashim, which locate this passage in chapter 22, are almost all part of the cycle of homilies correlated to special Sabbath readings -- that do not comment on the first part of Lev. -- and, for lack of a better choice, associate the matter with chapter 22, rather than the seriatim reading of the Torah. The equivalent of lines 34-36 is lacking in all of the parallel translations, and it is conceivable that it originated elsewhere.

Whether originally tied to 22:27 or 1:2, lines 34-36 must have followed some reference to the animals, which could then be associated with the patriarchs, i.e. the phrases from 1:2 (or 22:27). But since these lines lack some of the components of a proper introduction to B-D (described above), the text most likely to have followed 36 is the shorter version of the midrash presented in LR, Mid. Tanh., etc. As already suggested above, this short midrash was later expanded into B-D. Apparently, N now contains one part of this older text (34-36) together with the expanded version of another part (B-D). When first brought together, N had 34-36 plus the short midrash side by side with the long midrash, B-D. Since B-D was more developed than the short version, the short version was dropped, leaving B-D + 34-36. The absence of a fitting introduction may then have prompted the addition of Section A, conceivably to replace a different introductory piece now lost. And the translation itself (38-41) is another independent piece that has been used as the anchor for these midrashim. In its present form and setting it bears no relationship to the contents of lines 1-36 at all.

22:28 Restore with DM.

22:29 Restore with DM.

22:31 mṣwwth d'wryyty: for Heb. mṣwty.

'nh hw' yyy: for Heb. 'ny yyy. Since hw' is unnecessary, this may be another form of circumlocution to avoid 'nh yyy. Cf. also v. 32.

dyhb 'gr ṭb lnṭry mṣwwth d'wryyty (+): based, perhaps on wᶜśh ḥsd l'lpym l'hby wlšmry mṣwty, translated nṭr ḥsd ... wlnṭry- pyqwdy' (M: mṣwwty- d'wryyt-) in E 20:6 and wlnṭry mṣwwth d'wryyty in D 5:10.

22:32 ᶜmy yśr'l: for Heb. bny yśr'l.

22:33 dprqt l'bhtkwn wᶜtyd lmprq ytkwn (+): This correlation between the past redemption from suffering in Egypt and the future redemption from ongoing suffering is too vague to be of help in dating the targum.

Chapter 23

23:2 ywmyn ṭbyn w'yrᶜwn qdyš: routinely for Heb. mqr'y qdš.

zmn sdry mwᶜdwy: for Heb. mwᶜdy. This is probably a conflate phrase. The word sdr is often added in N, but zmn is the MH equivalent of BH mwᶜd; cf. v. 4 where bzmnyhwn is the translation of bmwᶜdm, and the parallel in 23:44.

23:3 tᶜbd: for Heb. tᶜśh. The Heb. is vocalized as a passive form 3 m. s.; it is very likely that tᶜbd was intended to be active, 2 m. s.; cf. E 20:9, 23:12, D 5:13.

23:5 nkyst (+): expansive; Heb. psḥ is taken as the sacrifice, not the holiday.

23:6 Heb. hzh has not been translated. In N 28:17 the identical phrase contains hdn.

23:11 mn btr ywm' ṭb' qdmyy' dpysḥ': for Heb. mmḥrt hšbt. This follows the standard rabbinic interpretation on an issue of great calendrical importance in antiquity; cf. also vv. 15, 16.

23:12 *wtᶜbdwn wtqrbwn*: a double translation of Heb. *wᶜśytm*; cf. v. 19, where only *wtqrbwn* is used.

The order of the words *br šṭyh šlm mn mwm* does not follow the Heb.; cf. M. In the listing of sacrifices in Num. 28-29, *tmymym* usually follows rather than precedes the description of the sacrifice. The change here may reflect these other verses; cf. also v. 18.

23:13 The words *lryḥ drᶜwh lšmh dyyy* also follow the more frequent Heb. order, rather than that of this verse.

23:14 *wlḥm ḥdt*: for Heb. *wlḥm*.

wqmḥ qly: for Heb. *wqly*.

The words *ᶜd ᶜṣm hywm hzh* have been omitted from N but added in I.

23:15 Heb. *lkm* has not been translated.

23:16 *mn dtmnwn lhwd mn btr ywmʼ ṭbh qdmyh dpysḥʼ* (+): added here for the third time in 10 verses. The present form of N presents these words as a gloss to the first phrase in the verse. Since it is a gloss here, it may have replaced the literal translations of *hšbt* in vv. 11 and 15 also. The constant repetition reflects the significance of the issue.

23:17 *ḥlyn* (+): expansive.

23:20 *mtnh lkhnʼ ytyhbwn*: for Heb. *lkhn*.

23:21 *ḥyyn wqyymyn* (+): expansive with *wtᶜrᶜwn*.

23:22 Add ḥṣdh, with I.

'wmnh 'ḥryh d'yt bḥqlykwn: for Heb. p't śdk; cf. 19:9 for a similar usage.

23:24 šbt šbth: for Heb. šbtwn; cf. E 31:15, 35:2, L 25:5, etc.

dkrn ṭb tqyᶜh wybbw: for Heb. zkrwn trwᶜh; ṭb was added as part of the Aramaic idiom. For the use of tqyᶜh and ybbw, cf. BT RH 29b-32a.

23:27 ṣwmh dkypwryh: for Heb. ywm hkpwrym; cf. v. 28.

wtṣwmwn bh yt npštkwn: for Heb. wᶜnytm 't npštykm; cf. L 16:29 and N 29:7, where the same construction is found, also F: wtṣymwn bh yt npštkwn.

23:29 The text in the MS is 'rwm kl npš gb- dy t'kl ..., not as printed.

Heb.		N
ky kl hnpš	a.	'rwm kl npš gb- (!)
'šr l' tᶜnh	b.	dy t'kl lmṣwm wl' ṣyymh
bᶜṣm hywm hzh	c.	kzmn ywm ṣwmh dkypwryyh
wnkrth mᶜmyh	d.	wtštyṣ' mn gw ᶜm'

The routine translation of npš is npš. The addition of gb[r'] may exclude those groups understood by the rabbis not to be included in the prohibition, e.g. children. It is also possible that gb[r'] is a double reading of nps. In either case we must understand gbr as "person," not "man"; cf. the usage in L 24:17.

The Heb. 'šr l' tᶜnh (b), vocalized teᶜuneh, is taken by Onk. as an active rather than a passive form: ... dy l' mtᶜny.... N follows this understanding of the verse but adds the rabbinic moderation t'kl lmṣwm "is able to fast." The spelling t'kl is suited to the root 'kl and obviously could make a difference in the context but apparently does not, though it is possible that texts reading dy t'kl and dy tykl lmṣwm wl' ṣyymh for line b were joined. Elsewhere in N the verb ʿnh is translated by form of ṣwm, e.g. 16:31, 23:32. M and F suggest dy kmst lmṣwm. (On the form tʿnh cf. also BT Yoma' 80a).

The Heb. bʿṣm hywm hzh is frequently rendered hkzmn ywm' hdn (e.g. vv. 28: 30). The phrase ywm ṣwmh dkypwryyh occurs in v. 28 and replaced this expression. There is no clear grammatical justification for the omission of the initial Heh on kzmn. Perhaps the Heh of ṣyymh led a copiest astray. This would not be the scribe of N, however, who omitted ṣyymh completely; it was added in the margin later.

23:30 w'yšyṣy: for Heb. wh'bdty, usually for krt not 'bd; cf. Sifra a.l.

23:32 wtṣymwn: cf. v. 27.

The following four lines correspond to Heb. tšbtw šbtkm:

a. ... thwn ṣymyn qwmykwn

b. wšbtyn šbykwn

c. wʿbdyn zmny mwʿdykwn

d. bḥdwh

Line b corresponds to the Heb. phrase. Line a may have been necessitated by the emphasis on fasting in vv. 27 ff; c-d reflect the inclusion of the unit about Yom Kippur in the section of Lev. that deals with all holidays. Together they recognize the conflicting emotional and ritual aspects of the day. Line c contains the expression zmny mwʿdykwn, similar to 23:2, which I have perceived to be conflate. For a text similar to c-d, cf. N

10:10.

23: 35-36 The verses should be restored: (35) bywm' qdmyh [ywm ṭb w'yrwᶜ qdyš kl ᶜbydh dplḥn l' tᶜbdwn (36) šbᶜh ywmyn tqrbwn qrbnyn lyyy bywm' tmynyh] ywm ṭb w'rwᶜ qdyš .... DM added 'yrwᶜ qdyš, lacking in the MS, but usually the translation of mqr' qdš is ywm ṭb w'yrwᶜ qdyš (e.g. vv. 37, 39), and this should probably be the case here as well. Interestingly, F reads ywm w'rwᶜ qdyš in v. 36, while v. 35 lacks all four words. Kahle has restored them as dḥgh 'rwᶜ qdyš, but the reading ywm ṭb ... is preferable there also.

23:36 knyst ḥdwwh: for Heb. ᶜṣrt; cf. also v. 32.

23:38 br mn qrbnyh dyyy dy 'twn mqrbyn bšwby qdšwy dyyy: for Heb. mlbd šbtt yyy. Usually šbt refers to the "Sabbath day," as seems to be the case here as well, but the series of sacrifices in the verse suggests the notion of "Sabbath sacrifices" (cf. psḥ in 23:5). N has actually accomodated both positions in the translation. The use of dyyy twice may point to a double text, i.e. original readings of br mn qrbnyh dyyy and br mn šwby dyyy. The latter is supported by br mšby' dyyy (Onk.), br šwby qwdšwy dyyy (F). br mn ywmy šby' dyyy (PJ).

23:39 ḥgh qdm yyy: for Heb. ḥg yyy.

23:40

Heb.		N
... pry ᶜṣ hdr	a.	... pyry 'yln mšbḥ
	b.	trwgyn
kpt tmrym	c.	wlwlbyn
wᶜnp ᶜṣ ᶜbt	d.	whds
wᶜrby nḥl ...	e.	wᶜrbh dnḥlh ...

Lines c-e are translated in keeping with the regular rabbinic understanding of the verse (cf. Sifra, etc.), and b provides the rabbinic understanding of Heb. line a as referring to the *'etrog*. The Heb. of line a, however, has also been translated word for word in Aram. line a, with *hdr* rendered as *mšbḥ*. This same arrangement appears in F and PJ. Note also Onk. *pyry 'yln' 'trwgyn*.

23:43 *bʿnny 'yqr škynty bdmwt mṭlyn*: for Heb. *bskwt*; cf. F: *bʿnnyn hyk mṭlyn*; and Onk., PJ: *bmṭlt ʿnny*. This follows the opinion of Rabbi Eliezer (BT Suk. 11b) that the verse refers to *ʿnny kbwd* and reflects the absence in the exodus narrative of any mention of God's having provided booths to house the people. Cf. Ibn Ezra a.l.

23:44 *w'lp ythwn* (+): expansive; cf. Onk., F, PJ, which are almost identical.

Chapter 24

24:2 *wyysbwn wyytwn*: for Heb. *wyqḥw*.

24:4 The words *lpny yyy* have not been translated; I: *qdm yyy*.

24:5 *bkl ḥlh ḥdth*: for *hḥlh h'ḥt*. This may betray two attempts to translate the phrase -- *bkl ḥlh* and *ḥlh ḥdth* (the latter is found in M and is closer to PJ also) -- or a Heb. text *bḥlh h'ḥt*, but it is most likely an example of *Bet pretii*.

24:6 *šth sdwryn ḥlyn bkl sdwr*: for Heb. *šš hmʿrkt*. DM suggests deleting sdwryn, but cf. Onk.: wtšwy ythwn tryn sdryn šyt sydr' ᶜl ptwr' ....

24:7 Heb. 'šh has not been translated; cf. M.

24:11 The verse is translated literally except for Heb. wyqb, which has been rendered wprš ... bgdpyn, and the extra qdyšh. Note that yt šmh qdyšh is lacking in N and added in I, but this seems to have been an accidental omission; cf. v. 12 line 11, and vv. 15-16 for the same phrase.

24:12 N

1. dn ḥd mn 'rbᶜh dynyn dqmw qdm mšh
2. wskm ythwn [not ytkwn] bdᶜtyh dlᶜyl
3. btryn mnhwn hwh mšh zryz
4. wbtryn mnhwn hwh mšh mtyn
5. b'lyyn wb'ylyn 'mr l' šmᶜyt
6. bms'byn dl' yklw lmᶜbd pysḥh
7. wbdyn bnth dṣlpḥd
8. hwh mšh zryz
9. mn bgll dhwwh dynyhwn dyny mmwn
10. bmqwššh dḥll šwbth bzydnw
11. wbmḥrph dprš šmyh qdyšh bgdpyn
12 hwh mšh mtyn
13. mn bgll dhwwn dynyhwn dyny npšn
14. wbgyn lmlph ldyynyh dqyymyn btr mšh
15. dyhwwn zryzyn bdyny mmwnh
16. wmmtynyn bdyny npšth
17. dl' yhwwn qṭylyn bpryᶜ
18. yt mn dḥmy lyh lmtqṭlh bdynh
19. dylmh dyštkḥ lh zkw mn zwy ḥwry bdynh
20. dl' yhwwn bhtyn lmymr l' šmᶜnn

21. dmšh rbhwn 'mr l' šmᶜyt
22. w'ṣnᶜw yth bmṭrth
23. ᶜd zmn dytprš lhwn mn qdm yyy
24. bhydyn dyn' mqṭlyn ytyh

The long midrashic insertion that precedes the translation tells how Moses consulted with God about four cases, from which lessons for the rabbinic judges are derived. Lines 1-5 introduce this material; lines 6-21 present the four cases and derived lessons; lines 22-24 translate the verse. The introductory materials in lines 1-5 are well organized and presage the structure and substance of lines 6-21. Lines 6-9 expand on line 3 and lines 10-13 expand on line 4. Lines 14-21 build on the reasons for Moses' actions as explained in lines 6-13. The only possible problem is in lines 14-21, to which I shall return.

Lines 6 and 7 identify the two cases, alluded to in line 3, where Moses acted quickly. Line 6 refers to people who were unable to offer the Passover sacrifice in its proper time; cf. gbryn dhwwn ms'byn ... wl' yklw lmᶜbd pysḥh, N 9:6. Line 7 recalls the claim of Zelophehad's daughters to inherit a portion of the promised land (N 27:1-11). In neither case did Moses know how to proceed, and in both cases he consulted God without delay (line 8). Line 9 suggests that this haste was prompted by the fact that both cases were civil rather than capital.

The parallel unit beginning in line 10 (and anticipated in line 4) is similar. Line 10 refers to the events of N 15:32-36, while line 11 refers to L 24:12. In both cases the the criminals were incarcerated pending the outcome of consultation with God. The Bible stresses neither Moses' lack of knowledge nor his concern over the lives of the accused, but the midrash adds this nuance, attributing Moses' deliberateness to the capital nature of the cases. This explanation is set forth in lines 12-13, which parallel 8-9.

Lines 15-16 (part of an 8-line unit beginning with line 14) are similar to 8-9 and 12-13 in that all lines emphasize the difference between the treatment of civil and capital cases; cf. Avot 1:1, which seems to counsel caution in all cases, but which may have influenced the presentation here. Lines 17-19, which are not balanced by any other lines in this passage, appear to explain 15-16. Elaborating on the caution mentioned in line 16, they present what was probably the major concern of the passage; but their position renders them relatively unimportant and makes them look like a later gloss. Lines 20-21 follow synactically after lines 15-16 (dyhwwn zryzyn ... wmmtynyn ... dl' [read wdl'] yhwwn bhtyn); this places 17-19 in series with 20-21 and possibly with 15-16 also. These lines also tie up the loose ends from lines 5, referring back to the matter of Moses having said l' šmᶜyt. There is no reference in any of the Biblical passages to Moses' saying anything like that, but the assumption is understandable, since in each case he consulted God for an answer.

The translation of the Heb. in lines 22-24 is close to the original. Line 22 corresponds to wynyḥhw bmšmr. Line 23 includes a routine circumlocution for God's addressing men, though it hardly seems necessary in this case because the Heb. assumes that Moses explained the law, not God. Line 24 provides the complement of dytprš, somewhat more necessary in Aram. than in BH. This addition assumes (as does the entire midrash) that Moses knew that the death sentence was applicable, but he did not know which mode of execution was appropriate.

Other than the reference to v. 12 in line 11 and the common assumption that the verse refers to a capital crime, there is no obvious connection between the translation in lines 22-24 and the midrashic passage in lines 1-21. In fact, the entire passage has been incorporated, with slight changes, in N 9:8, 15:34 and

27:5 as well; in each case the verse's translation follows. Surely lines 1-21 (including 17-18 which are found in all three texts, but perhaps excluding lines 2 and 18 which are found only here) formed an independent literary unit that was introduced to supplement the translation. Given the presence of lines 17-18 in each passage, we must assume that these were present in the text before it was placed in all four contexts and, therefore, that the original context of the midrash was one of the verses dealing with capital crimes, i.e. either Lev. 24 or Num. 15. Internal evidence provides no clue by which we may designate one or the other location as primary. PJ contains this material in each case, also; M seems to suggest all but the last occurence. Integration of the midrash into the text is best demonstrated in N 9:8, offering a third choice. Additional differences among the texts are noted in N 9:8 and 15:34.

24:14 *yt*: for Heb. *kl*.

24:15-21 Verses 15, 17 and 19 use a form of *'yš*, while 16, 18 and 21 use a participle to describe the perpetration of a crime. N routinely translates *'yš* as *gbr*, while the participle is rendered *mn d-* or *mn dy-*.

Chapter 25

25:5 *šbt šbth*: for Heb. *šnt šbtwn*. Given the similarity between *šnt* and *šbt*, it is understandable that the more common expression has been introduced.

25:8

Heb.	N
... *šbʿ šbtt šnym*	a. ... *šbʿ šmyṭyn*
šbʿ šnym	b. *šwbʿh zmnyn*

šbᶜ pᶜmym c. *mn šwbᶜh šnyn* ...

The relationships between the phrases are clear; cf. Onk., PJ: *šbᶜ šmyṭn dšnyn šbᶜ šnyn šbᶜ zmnyn*. Apparently N switched the order of b and c.

25:9 *ṣwm'* (+) cf. 23:29, etc.

25:10 *l'rᶜ'*: for Heb. *b'rṣ*.

25:16 *ksp* (+): expansive (2x).

25:38 The second *dmṣrym* is an error; read *dknᶜn*, with DM.

25:42 *ytkwn*: for Heb. *'tm*, an important change in emphasis for the listener. Note the statement in the Passover Haggadah "Every person is obligated to see himself as a refugee from Egypt." DM's change to *ythwn* is unwarranted.

knymwsy ᶜbdyh: for Heb. *mmkrt ᶜbd*. The expression is also used in E 21:7.

25:49 *'ḥwy d'bwy*: for Heb. *ddw*, elsewhere *ḥbybh* is used.

25:51 The word *ksp* has not been translated.

25:55 *lšmy*: circumlocution for heb. *ly*.

Chapter 26

26:2 *qwdšwy* (+): idiomatic.

wbyt mqdšy thwwn mṣlyyn bdḥlh: for Heb. *wmqdšy tyr'w*. The Heb. demands revering God's sanctuary, while the Aram.

instructs the listener to pray in awe in the sanctuary. Since *byt mqdšh* is the routine translation of *mqdš* and frequently is taken to refer to the Temple, this translation poses a certain inconsistency. If the Temple were available for prayer, it surely could be revered, (unless *tyr'w* was considered an inappropriate word for the *mqdš*), therefore eliminating any need for a change from the literal meaning of the Hebrew. If this is not a reference to the Temple, *knyštyhwn* or *mdršyhwn* could have been used instead of *byt mqdšh* (cf. G 34:31 where these terms do occur). Conceivably the verse refers to praying in a non-functioning Temple, a situation reminiscent of the period after 135 when Jews went to Jerusalem to pray and to mourn the destruction of the Temple. The same thought is expressed in 19:30, where the use of *wbbyt* relieves the feeling that the translation was originally literal and that *thwwn* ... *bdḥlh* replaced the original verb. Note PJ: *wlbyt mwqdšy thwn 'zlyn bdḥlt'*, M: *thbwn ᶜlyn bdḥl'* and Onk. *wlbyt mqdšy thwn dḥlyn*. One text of Onk. cited by Sperber (Biblia Hebraica, Ixar, 1490) reads *wbyt*).

26:4 *mṭr 'rᶜkwn bzmnh*: for Heb. *gšmykm b'tm*. Apparently the familiar *mṭr 'rṣkm* was borrowed from D 11:14, which deals with the same subject. The change, however, might emphasize the foreign perspective of the listener: the rain is in "your land," i.e. Israel.

26:5 *wtśbᶜwn*: for Heb. *lśbᶜ*. Perhaps the presence of *w'kltm* recalled D 11:15 *w'klt wśbᶜt*, translated in N as *wtyklwn wtśbᶜwn*.

26:6 *ytkwn* (+): expansive.

ršwthwn dmlkwwth dmtyln bḥywwt br': for Heb. *ḥyh rᶜh*; possibly a reference to the Romans; cf. Dan. 8:1-12 and N to G 15:11-12.

dśny (x): "of the enemy," parallel to the above.

26:7 *qṭyly* (+): expansive, as in v. 8.

26:9 *w'pny mymry myyṭbh*: for Heb. *wpnyty*.

26:12 All of the additions are routine idiomatic translations with the exception of *qdyšyn*, which may have been added on the basis of E 19:6.

26:13 *mšʿbdyn* (+): expansive; cf. E 21:6.

wtbryt nyr šʿbwdyhwn dmṣryy mʿylwwykwn dhwh qšy ʿlykwn hyk nyr przlh: for Heb. *w'šbr mṭt ʿlkm*. The phrase *ʿl brzl* occurs in D 28:48 and Jer. 28:14, but neither verse refers to the Egyptian period.

26:14 *l'wlpn 'wryyty*: for Heb. *ly*. The way to follow God is to follow his Torah; cf. vv. 18, 21, etc.

26:16 Heb. *'p* has been omitted, probably because the first words of the Heb. and Aramaic are both *'p*.

23:17 *'py tqwp rwgzy*: possibly a double translation of Heb. *pny*.

26:18 *mrdwwth* (+): expansive; as in v. 23.

26:19

Heb.		N
wšbrty 't	a.	*w'ḥrb yt byt mqdšy*
g'wn ʿzkm	b.	*dhw' tqwp ḥyylkwn*
wntty 't šmykm	c.	*w'šwy yt šmyyh dy ʿlwykwn*
kbrzl	d.	*bryryn hyk przlh*

	e.	mn lmḥth lkwn ṭlyn wmṭryn
w't 'rṣkm	f.	wyt 'rᶜ' dy tḥtkwn
knḥšh	g.	ḥsymh hyk nḥsh
	f.	mlmrbyh lkwn ṣmḥyn

Lines c and f end with routine expansions, while lines d and g begin with added clarifications. Lines e and h spell out the punishment in detail, not unlike the manner of E 11:17. The most important change is the insertion of byt mqdšy in line a. The phrase g'wn ᶜzkm occurs in Ezek. 24:21 and, with other pronominal suffixes, in Ezek. 7:24, 30:6, 30:18 and 33:28. The phrase in Ezek. 24:21 is hnny mḥll 't mqdšy g'wn ᶜzkm, sufficient evidence to warrant the interpretation in Lev.

26:25 šlpy (+): expansive; sword bearers, not swords, will be sent, as in v. 33.

lmtprᶜh mnkwn ᶜl dy prᶜtwn yt qyymy: for Heb. nqmt nqm bryt.

26:26 š' or ś' lḥm: for Heb. mṭh lḥm. DM has suggested that the first word may be śᶜd' (cf. M: śᶜdy, PJ: sᶜdy) or šbṭ'. Also possible is s'h, though it usually is followed by slt, qmḥ, etc., not by lḥm. The phrase sᶜyd lḥm' occurs in the Targum to Ps. 105:16; sᶜyd mykl' is used in Jonathan to Ezek. 4:16, 5:16, etc.

26:29

Heb.		N
	a.	'y mh qšyyn 'ynwn ḥwbyyh
	b.	wtqypyn ḥṭ'yh
	c.	dgrmw l'bhtn byrwšlm
w'kltm bśr bnykm	d.	lmykl bśr bnyhm
wbśr bntykm t'klw	e.	wbśr bnthwn 'klw

Despite the parallel in D 28:53 and specific references to such cannibalism in Jer. 19:9, II Kings 6:29, Lam. 2:20 ff, Zech. 11:9, Josephus, Wars, VI, 201-213, BT Taᶜan. 5a, etc., it is impossible to assign lines a-c to any specific event.

It seems that neither the composer of the targum nor his audience was in Jerusalem, though their forefathers had been; and the length of the intervening period is unknown. Structurally the verse resembles the exclamations in G 49:11,12, etc., but there is no connection other than the unnecessary shift from translation to exclamation. Apparently the translator of L 26:29 wanted to emphasize that this, perhaps the most horrible of the predictions, had actually come true.

The redundant use of lmykl (d) and 'klw (e) points to a close correlation with the Hebrew, where the parallel lines both contain the verb 'kl. Apparently the translator joined the intitial text to an existing translation; probably the seam is between lmykl and bśr. Interesting, by comparison, is PJ, which places the equivalent of lines a-c between translations of most of the verse:

1.	wtyklwn bśr bnykwn	= Heb. d
2.	wbśr bntykwn	similar to Heb. e
3.	'mr mšh nby'	
4.	kmh qšyyn hynwn ḥwby'	= N a
5.	dy grmw l'bht'	= N c
6.	lmykwl bśr bnyhwn	= N d
7.	wbntyhwn	similar to N e
8.	ᶜl dl' nṭrw mṣwwt' d'wryyt'.	

PJ 6-7 and N demonstrate that this part of the targum is not really a translation of the Hebrew, for PJ also contains one. The pronominal shift reapplies the curse to others and, in fact, claims that it has already been fulfilled. This is similar to the many other circumlocutions whose purpose was to avoid insulting or cursing the listeners.

26:31 'qbl brᶜwwh: for Heb. 'ryh. Note the inconsistency between brᶜwwh and bryḥ, possibly pointing to a time when 'ryḥ was translated literally.

26:32 'wp (+): added here but lacking in v. 16.

26:34 kl ywmyn dhy' ṣdy (!) mnkwn: for Heb. kl ymy hšmh, as in v. 35.

glyn (+): expansive.

26:36

Heb.		N
whnš'rym bkm	a.	wmh dmštyyr bkwn
whb'ty mrk blbbm	b.	w'ᶜl tbrh blbbykwn
b'rṣt 'ybyhm	c.	b'rᶜ bᶜly dbbykwn
wrdp 'tm qwl	d.	wyrdwp ql
ᶜlh ndp	e.	ᶜlyh dšp ᶜm ḥbr wnṭr
wnsw	f.	wyᶜrqwn
mnwst ḥrb	g.	kmqdm šlpy ḥrbh
wnplw	h.	wyplwn
w'yn rdp	i.	wlyt dr[d]p

The translation is quite close to the Hebrew except in lines d-e and g. Line d has omitted Heb. 'tm, and line c has expanded the two Hebrew words. The word šp means "rub"; while šqp is attested elsewhere (Onk.), the text makes sense as it stands. For šlpy ḥrb instead of Heb. ḥrb, cf. vv. 25, 33, 37, etc.

26:39 *b'rʿ bʿly dbbyhwn*: a common phrase, used here in spite of the Heb. pl. *b'rṣt*.

26:41 *lbhwn zydnh*: for the figurative Heb. *lbbm hʿrl*.

26: 42-44 These verses are lacking in N, and DM has printed the text of MS Paris 110. Certain inconsistencies between this text and the style of N prelude the assumption that this text actually contains the correct wording of the missing lines.

26:45 *qyymh dy qyymt ʿm qdmy*: for Heb. *bryt r'šnym*.

Chapter 27

27:1 *ʿlwyh*: for *ʿrkk*; cf. passim.

27:10 The words *wl' ymyr 'tw* are lacking in N but found in M; cf. v. 33 *wl' yprg ytyh*.

27:21 *'pršw*: for Heb. *ḥrm*, as in v. 28.

27:27 *ḥmšyn dmwy*: an error in the text substituted for N; cf. vv. 15, 31, etc.

27:32 *kl mh dy yʿbr šrbyṭh*: for Heb. *kl 'šr yʿbr tḥt hšbt*.

TABLE OF CROSS REFERENCES

The following cross references facilitate finding discussions of N that are not found in the expected place in the commentary. All Pentateuchal Hebrew and Targumic references are included.

Leviticus

1:1	Intro., ch. 1, 3, 4; L 8:10; N 7:1.
1:2	Intro., ch. 3; L 22:27.
1:3	Intro., ch. 3.
1:5	Intro., ch. 3.
1:13	L 1:9.
1:14	L 1:3; 3:12.
2:2	L 1:9.
2:4	L 2:7.
3:14	L 3:9.
3:17	E 35:3; L 1:16.
4:11	L 4:19.
4:12	L 1:16.
4:13	L 4:2.
4:20	Intro., ch. 3.
4:22	L 4:2.
4:26	L 4:20.
4:27	L 4:2; 5:21.
4:31	L 4:19, 20.
4:35	L 4:20.
5:7	L 1:14.
5:10	L 5:19.
5:15	N 5:6; D 32:51.
5:17	L 5:21.

5:21	L 5:23.
6:2	E 12:43.
6:7	E 12:43.
6:18	E 12:43.
7:5	L 7:31
7:26	E 35:3.
8:9	D 35:10.
8:11	L 8:10.
9:22	G 49:3.
10:1	L 16:1; N 26:61.
10:2	N 3:4.
10:5	L 10:4
10:10	L 14:57; D 12:15.
10:11	Intro., ch. 3.
10:19	Intro., ch. 4.; L 10:20; D 26:14.
11:19	D 14:18.
11:28	L 11:25.
11:37	Intro., ch. 4.
11:42	L 11:43.
11:47	L 14:57; D 12:15
12:2	L 15:19; 20:21.
12:3	D 7:26.
12:5	L 12:2; 12:4.
12:7	L 20:18.
13:4	L 13:5.
13:6	G 35:2.
13:19	L 13:16.
13:41	L 13:40.
13:46	L 14:8.
13:55	L 8:32.
13:57	L 8:32.
14:2	L 14:32.

14:5	G 26:19; N 19:17.
14:36	L 14:44.
14:50	G 26:19; L 14:5; N 19:17.
14:57	L 14:54.
15:2	L 21:17.
15:8	G 35:2.
15:11	G 35:2.
15:19	L 12:2.
15:30	L 12:8.
16:3	L 16:2.
16:6	L 9:7.
16:10	N 33:8.
16:11	L 9:17.
16:17	E 28:30; L 9:7; N 7:16.
16:21	N 33:8.
16:23	E 28:30.
16:24	L 9:7.
16:26	L 16:2.
16:29	L 16:2; 23:27.
16:31	L 23:29.
17:3	L 22:27.
17:10	L 21:17.
17:13	L 21:17.
18:4	L 18:5.
18:5	Intro., ch. 3.; G 26:24; E 6:2; L 18:21; 19:25.
18:6	L 18:5; 21:17.
18:7	Intro., ch. 3; L 22:27; D 23:1.
18:8	L 18:7; D 27:20.
18:13	L 18:12.
18:14	L 10:4.
18:17	L 18:12; 19:29.
18:21	G 26:24; L 20:2.

18:26 L 20:23.

18:27 L 20:23.

18:29 L 20:23.

18:30 Intro., ch. 3.; L 18:5.

19:2 L 18:21.

19:3 L 18:21.

19:4 L 18:21.

19:9 L 23:22.

19:12 E 23:1.

19:14 L 19:18.

19:15 L 19:36.

19:16 Intro., ch. 4; E 6:2; 23:2.

19:17 Intro., ch. 4.; G 4:8; 6:2; 23:2.

19:18 Intro., ch. 3.; ch. 4.; E 6:2; 23:2.

19:19 Intro., ch. 2.; ch. 4.; L 23:22; D 22:10.

19:20 Intro., ch. 3.

19:24 L 19:23.

19:25 E 6:2; L 19:16-18.

19:26 N 23:23; D 18:10.

19:29 L 18:17.

19:30 L 19:25, 26:2.

19:31 L 20:6.

19:32 Intro., ch. 4.

19:36 N 21:6.

20:2 L 21:17.

20:3 L 20:2; 21:4.

20:4 L 20:2.

20:5 L 20:2.

20:6 L 19:31.

20:7 Intro., ch. 3.; L 19:25.

20:8 Intro., ch. 3.; L 19:25.

20:13 L 20:21.

20:14 L 18:17; 19:29.

20:19 D 28:23.

20:25 L 14:57.

20:27 L 19:31.

21:1 L 21:3.

21:2 L 21:3.

21:6 L 21:4.

21:7 G 34:31; L 21:9.

21:8 N 28:2.

21:9 Intro., ch. 3.

21:10 N 3:3.

21:11 L 21:1.

21:12 Intro., ch. 3.

21:14 G 34:31; L 21:9.

21:15 L 19:25.

21:17 L 21:18.

21:20 Intro., ch.2.; L 22:22.

21:23 Intro., ch. 3.; L 18:21.

22:4 N 3:13; 5:2.

22:8 L 22:2.

22:9 L 22:2.

22:10 E 12:45; D 32:16.

22:12 D 32:16.

22:13 D 32:16.

22:27 Intro., ch. 4.; L 17:3.

22:28 Intro., ch. 3.

22:31 Intro., ch. 4.

22:32 L 22:31.

23:2 Intro., ch. 3.; L 23:32; N 15:3; 28:26.

23:3 Intro., ch. 3.; E 12:16.

23:4 L 23:2.

23:5 L 23:38; N 28:16.

23:7	E 12:16.
23:11	L 23:16.
23:13	N 28:7.
23:15	L 23:11; 23:16; N 33:3.
23:16	L 23:11; N 33:3.
23:18	L 23:12.
23:19	L 23:12.
23:21	E 12:16.
23:24	Intro., ch. 3.
23:27	E 12:16; L 23:32; N 29:7.
23:28	L 23:27; 23:29; N 15:40.
23:29	L 25:9.
23:30	L 23:29.
23:32	L 23:29; 23:36; N 29:7.
23:36	E 12:16; N 29:35.
23:37	L 23:35-36.
23:39	L 23: 35-36.
23:40	N 15:40.
23:41	Intro., ch. 3.
23:43	L 16:2; N 24:6.
23:44	L 23:2.
24:2	N 19:2.
24:11	N 9:6.
24:12	Intro., ch. 4.; L 24:11; N 9:8; 15:34; 27:5; D 32:2.
24:14	Intro., ch. 3.
24:15	L 24:11.
24:16	L 24:11.
24:17	L 23:29.
24:18	L 22:4.
24:20	L 21:19
25:5	L 23:24
25:29	E 35:3.

25:33	Intro., ch. 3.
25:34	Intro., ch. 3.
25:42	Intro., ch. 3.
25:55	Intro., ch. 3.; N 21:6.
26:1	L 19:4; D 4:16.
26:2	L 19:30.
26:3	L 19:19.
26:4	Intro., ch. 2.
26:6	E 12:15.
26:8	L 26:7; D 32:30.
26:14	Intro., ch. 4.
26:16	L 26:32.
26:18	L 26:14.
26:19	D 28:23.
26:21	L 26:14.
26:23	L 26:18.
26:25	L 26:36.
26:30	L 19:19.
26:33	L 26:25; 26:36.
26:35	L 26:34.
26:37	L 26:36.
26:38	G 49:5.
26:39	G 49:5.
26:40	G 49:5; D 32:51.
26:41	G 49:5.
26:42	G 49:5; D 1:1.
26:43	G 49:5.
26:44	G 49:5.
27:1	G 34:31.
27:3	Intro., ch. 3.
27:6	Intro., ch. 3.
27:14	G 34:31.

27:15 G 27:27.

27:25 L 27:10.

27:28 L 27:21.

27:31 L 27:27.

27:33 L 27:10.

NUMBERS

Chapter 1

1:2 *qbylw yt ryš skwmyhwn*: for Heb. *nś' 't r'š*; cf. e.g. v. 49.

1:3 *kl npqy ḥyl qrb'*: for Heb. *kl yṣ' ṣb'*. The use of *kl npqy qrb'* in vv. 22, 24, 26, etc. suggests that the phrase here is a double translation; cf. Onk. *kl npyq ḥyl' byśr'l*. Note, however, 4:3, 4:23, etc. where the phrase is translated *kl dy yᶜwl lḥyl qrbh*.

1:4 *mkl šbṭ*: for Heb. *lmṭh*.

1:5 *mn šbṭh dbnwy d-* + Name: for Heb. *l-* + Name; *bnwy* is routinely added, perhaps to prevent reading these as referring to Jacob's sons.

ṣwry šdy: 2 words, also in 2:12.

1:8 *bn*: for Heb. *bn*, but in the other verses *br*; also *br* in 7:23.

1:10 *pdh ṣwr*: 2 words, also in 2:20.

1:12 *ᶜmy šdy*: 2 words, also in 2:25.

1:20 *yḥwsyhwn*: for Heb. *twldtm*, as in vv. 22, 24, etc. In G 2:4, etc. the phrase *yḥws twldt* is used.

1:22 *skwmy*: DM suggests *skwmwy*, but the word is lacking in the parallel passages throughout the chapter and is probably an error.

1:32 *hw' šbṭh dbyt 'prym*: for Heb. *lbny 'prym*.

1:45 The word *šnh* has been omitted; read *mbr ʿśryn šnyn*.

1:51 *lmšmšh* (+): expansive, as in 3:10, 3:38 and 18:7. The contexts of 3:10 and 18:7 clearly allow for use of *lmšmšh*. It is less appropriate here and in 18:7, but not impossible.

Chapter 2

2:3 *wrb šbṭh dbnwy dyhwdh*: for Heb. *wnśy' lbny yhwdh*. In v. 5, the phrase is again treated in this manner, but v. 7 lacks the phrase *wrb šbṭh* because of a scribal error. In the subsequent verses, the phrase is translated *wrbh dhwh mmny ʿl šbṭh dbnwy d-*, e.g. vv. 10, 12, etc. M notes this difference in vv. 3 and 5 and translates the phrase *wrbh hwh mmny ʿl ḥyylwt šbṭh db-*.

2:7 Restore as in the bottom margin of the MS, printed by DM.

Chapter 3

3:3 *dy 'šlmw qrbn ydyhwn lmšmšh bkhnth rbth*: for Heb. *'šr ml' ydm lkhn*. This is the idiomatic translation of these phrases; cf. E 28:41, L 21:10, etc.

3:4 The first *lpny yyy* has been omitted from N; both are in L 10:2 in N.

bḥywy d-: for Heb. *ʿl pny*, as in G 11:28.

3:8 *mšknh*: for Heb. *'hl mwʿd*, perhaps influenced by the end of the verse, though the tent is frequently referred to simply as *h'hl*.

3:10 *tṭks*: for Heb. *tpqd*; DM suggests *tskm*.

3:13 *'mr yyy*: for Heb. *'ny yyy*; cf. L 22:4, N 10:10.

Chapter 4

4:4 *bbyt qwdšy'*: for Heb. *qdš hqdšym*.

4:7 *ptwrh dlḥm 'pyh*: for Heb. *šlḥn hpnym*; the expansion results from the common term *lḥm hpnym*.

4:15 *bmškn* (+): deleted in M.

4:20 The Heb. *kblʿ* is problematic, but one possible explanation is offered by the expansion *kd mšqʿ khnh rbh yt kl mny byt qwdšh*.

Chapter 5

5:2 *dms'b btm' npš dbr nš*: for Heb. *ṭm' npš*; cf. L 22:4 where *npš* has been expanded in this manner.

5:6 *lmšqry šqr bšmh dyyy*: for Heb. *lmʿl mʿl byyy*, as in L 5:15; closer to the use of *mʿl* in Prov. 16:10 than the standard rabbinic usage of the word.

5:13 *dlyt*: for Heb. *'yn*; I: *lyt*.

5:15 Add ʿlwy before DM's restoration.

5:17 lgw: for Heb. b-; M: bgw is only a little less expected.

5:19 br mn ršwth dbʿlyk: for Heb. tḥt 'yšk; cf. v. 20. The use of ršwt allows the verse to refer to straying from either the husband's house or his social domain.

5:22 'mn dl' 'st'bt 'mn dl' 'st'b (+): cf. Sifrei, p. 20, BT Sot. 18 a-b, etc. Rabbi Meir is credited with this explanation of the repetition of 'mn in the Sifrei, but the sages offered other possibilities.

5:24 lmmrh lh: for Heb. lmrym.

5:27 krsh: for Heb. bṭnh, but in v. 21 mʿyk is used in N.

5:28 wtʿbr wtld br dkr: for Heb. wnqth wnzrʿh zrʿ. Although the Heb. zrʿ does not specify the sex of the offspring, it is taken to be male. This is consistent with the use of zrʿ dbnyn for zrʿ in G 19:32 M, 21:12, etc. Here, however, the phrase br dkr, more frequently used for Heb. bn, is used to promise the exonerated woman a son. Assuming that wtʿbr wtld corresponds to wnzrʿh, the word wnqth has not been translated.

5:29 tsṭh: add the relative pronoun with I.

br mn bʿlh: for Heb. tḥt 'yšh. In vv. 19-20 the phrase is br mn ršwth dbʿlyk. In 19, M suggests tḥwt ršwth lbʿlyk [read dbʿlyk], and tḥwt is added in v. 20 to indicate a similar construction. In v. 29, M has ḥwlp bʿ-. Onk. uses br mbʿl-

throughout, as found in N of v. 29. PJ uses br mn rswt' dbᶜl- throughout.

5:30 qyymyh d'wryth h'lyn: for plural of Heb. htwrh hz't.

Chapter 6

6:3 ḥmr ḥdt wᶜtyq: for Heb. yyn wškr; routine.

ḥl dḥmr ḥdt wḥl dḥmr ᶜtyq (following DM): for Heb. ḥmṣ yyn wḥmṣ škr.

6:4 ndr (+): cf. vv 2, 5 ndr dnzyrw, etc. The more common term has been used.

6:9 dsmyk lyh btkyp dl' ydᶜ: for Heb. ᶜlyw bptᶜ pt'm. The phrase dsmyk lyh corresponds to Heb. ᶜlyw. For bptᶜ pt'm, Onk. and PJ have btkyp šlw and btkwp šlw. In 35:22 bptᶜ is rendered btkwp, while in 12:4 it is the translation of pt'm. The use of both terms here thus must have appeared redundant, so pt'm was translated as it is explained in the Sifrei, p. 34, pt'wm lhby' 't hšwgg, i.e. dl' ydᶜ.

6:10 gwzlyn (+): idiomatic.

6:13 dšlmwn yt: for Heb. ml't.

6:23 'zl mšh mn šmy [DM: šmy']: an unexpected addition. The most recent location of God's speaking to Moses is the Wilderness of Sinai (3:14). Various Biblical passages and midrashim speak of Moses' going up to God or heaven, but N usually translates descent by nḥt, not 'zl. Taken together, these facts offer little support for DM's suggestion that v. 23 speaks of Moses' return from the heavens. But there is another possibility. In vv. 22-23, Moses is told to speak to Aaron and the priests. The Torah does not report that Moses spoke to them, and vv. 24-26 appear to be God's words. But, according to N, these three verses are Moses' words. N has understood 'mr lhm as a 3 m.s. perfect verb, rather than an imperative, and has translated it 'zl mšh w'mr lhwn in order to stress this interpretation of 'mr and to present vv. 24-26 as Moses' words, not God's. If the above is correct, we may assume that mn šmy is an intrusion. Perhaps it should be associated with v. 27, where it may have served as part of a translation of the phrase wśmw 't šmy. N already contains two translations of the phrase 't šmy, yt šmy and yt mmry. Perhaps a third one existed in the margin and was inserted in v. 23 by mistake. (Cf. further my notes to v. 27). Onk. and PJ offer yt brkt šmy; Frag. contains yt šmy qdyš', as does M, but neither provides a sure source or parallel for mn šmy.

6:24-26 Following M Meg. 4:10, these verses are not translated.

6:27 yt šmy yt mmry: a double translation of Heb. 't šmy. M adds qdyš', probably attesting to the šmy reading. Note the use of mymry later in the verse.

Chapter 7

7:1 bmšḥ rbwth (+): The phrase šmn hmšḥh, translated mšḥ' drbwt', appears in E 31:11, 35:15, etc.

The missing piece, correctly restored by Diez-Macho, can be found in L 1:1, which begins by translating most of N 7:1. The word lmqmh is found there also.

7:2 dhww mmnyn: for Heb. hm h^{c}mdym.

7:3 ^{c}gln mzwwgn: for Heb. ^{c}glt ṣb.

7:7 mšh (+): expansive; cf. also v. 9.

7:8 Heb. hkhn is translated khnh rbh whenever possible. The missing adjective has been supplied by M.

7:9 l' mn ^{c}glth wl' mn twryh (+): providing an object for the verb ntn; the subject mšh has also been added as in vv. 7-8.

yt 'rwnh (+): providing the assumed object of the verb yś'w.

7:11 rb šbṭ: for nśy', passim.

rbwth (+): supplementary to ḥnwkt, as in v. 84.

Verses 7:12-7:83 comprise 12 essentially similar units of 6 verses each. Recurring matters are discussed with respect to vv. 12-17 only.

7:13 dy qrb (+): expansive, as in vv. 14, 16, 17.

sl^{c}yn bsl^{c}y byt qwdš' (+): the equivalent of bšql hqdš. The phrase occurs once in the Heb. after šb^{c}ym šql; it has been added after m'h wtltyn sl^{c}yn, in imitation of the later phrase.

tql (+): added in imitation of mtqlh in the previous phrase.

mnyh (+): expansive.

qrb ythwn (+): expansive.

pyylyt' wmzrqh (+): seemingly out of place, but present

in the second verse of every unit.

7:14 Heb.		N
kp 'ḥt	a.	bzk ḥdh
ʿśrh	b.	mtqlyh ʿśr slʿyn dksp
	c.	hwwt ʿbydh
zhb	d.	why' hwwt ddhb
ml'h	e.	qrb ytyh mlyyh
	f.	r'šy qṭrt bwsmnyn
	g.	bṭbyn mqṭmyn wdkyyn
qṭrt	h.	lqṭrth

The term ʿśrh zhb was explained by conversion to a silver standard (b-d). Lines f-g explain the items with which the utensil was filled. The added qrb ytyh is similar to the two usages in vv. 13, etc. In line g, read ṭbyn, as in v. 20, etc.

7:15 The Heb. specifies the age of the lamb (kbś) as one year, but refers to no corresponding requirement for the other animals. N has added br tlt šnyn for the bull (pr) and br trtyn for the ram ('yl).

7:16 lḥṭ'th lšbqwt ḥwbyn wlšlwwn, lmkprh b'dmh dṣpyrh ʿl ḥwbwy wʿl ḥwby šlwt šbṭh: for the Heb. lḥṭ'th, which is translated in the first Aramaic word. The last part of the addition appears to borrow elements from L 16:17, which reads wkpr bʿdw wbʿd bytw wbʿd kl qhl yśr'l, though N a.l. translates that verse without using most of the key phrases here. Even closer is the following line from the Musaf prayer for the New Moon: ... ḥdš ʿlynw 't hḥdš hzh ... lmḥylt ḥṭ' wlslyḥt ʿwn wlkprt pšʿ ....

7:17 dy 'tndb wqrb mnksy grmy rb šbṭh dbnwy dyhwdh (+): This emphasizes that the leader did not use community funds for the donation.

In general, the additions found in vv. 13-17 are not significant alterations, but the resulting verbosity is surprising in light of their lack of substance and the more literal style evidenced in the preceding six chapters and elsewhere in Numbers. Particularly noteworthy is the addition of the verb qrb in every verse and twice in vv. 13 and 17. The addition of these explanatory glosses -- and, especially, the verb qrb in v. 13 -- may perhaps be explained by a liturgical need. According to M Meg. 3:6, the portion of the "princes" (i.e. Num. 7) is read from the Torah on Hannukah. Assuming that each daily reading corresponded to one day's offering, the six verses of the MT (e.g. 12-17) would be divided into three portions, but according to M Meg. 4:4, a portion may be no less than three verses. The inclusion of extra verbs in the targum of this passage may reflect an attempt to divide our vv. 12-17 into nine verses. Thus, verses 13, 14 and 17 could each be split into two verses, making, together with 12, 15, and 16, a total of nine. (The required overall minimum of 10 verses may not be followed, though a verse may be formed without a verb, e.g. E 1:2-4). While this suggestion correlates to the Aramaic better than the Hebrew, it would, if correct, obviate reading two days' princely offerings on each day of Hannukah, as is done in synagogues today. Further evidence to this surmise is the absence of these flourishes in the summation, vv. 84 ff., where they are not needed for liturgical purposes but should have been included had they been regarded as expansive idiomatic translations of the Heb., required in order to translate the terms.

7:18 dḥnwkt rbwth dmdbḥh (+) not in v. 12 but in vv. 1, 18, 24, etc.

7:85 This verse lacks the repetition of bslᶜy byt qwdšh of v. 13 and parallels.

7:86 This verse lacks the embellishment r'šy qṭrt bwsmnyn ṭbyn mpṭmyn of v. 14 and parallels.

7:87 Note the absence of the ages of the bulls and rams.

7:89 ql dbyrh: for Heb. hqwl.
mn tmn hwh dbyrh mmll ᶜmyh: for Heb. wydbr 'lyw.

Chapter 8

8:4 bṣl'l (+): The subject is added following E 31:1. Moses did not actually carry out the construction or art work.

8:13 Delete lmkprh ᶜl lywyy -- copied from the end of v. 12--with DM.

8:16 mtnh: for Heb. ntnym ntnym; cf. v. 19, etc.

8:20 kl: for Heb. kkl.

8:21 Restore with DM.

8:24 lmplḥ: for Heb. bᶜbdt.

8:25 mn ḥyl qrbh: for Heb. mṣb' hᶜbdh

Chapter 9

9:1 *bzmn 'pqwthwn*: for Heb. *lṣ'tm*.

dbny yśr'l (+): expansive, as in 1:1.

9:5 *kl*: for Heb. *kkl*.

9:6 *bṭm' npš dbr nš*: for Heb. *lnpš 'dm*; cf. vv. 7, 10, etc.

DM's reconstruction of the missing second half of the verse is based on PJ but is probably inaccurate in its use of *lqdm*. The same notion is expressed by *qdm* in N 27:2 (4x) and by *lwwt* in N 15:33 (3x) and L 24:11 (1x). These are both preferable to *lqdm* (2x).

9:8 The midrash has been discussed at length in my comments to L 24:12. Only additional differences from the text there are noted here.

The phrase *b'lyyn wb'ylyyn 'mr l' šmʿyt* (=L 24:12, line 5) is lacking in N 9:8, but present in N 15:34 and 27:5.

The phrase *dyhwwn zryzyn* appears in four forms: 1) *dyhwwn* (L 24:12); 2) *dy hwwyn* (N 9:8); 3) *dy hwyn* (N 15:34); and 4) *dy hwwn* (N 27:5). In the fourth case, the words may be joined to produce the preferable reading, found in the first. The others may be corrected to follow suit.

mtqṭlh (N 9:8) differs from *lmtqṭlh* of the other texts, but no emendation is required.

l' šmʿth: in other passages *l' šmʿnn* (L 24:12), *l' šmʿyt* (N 27:5), *l' šmʿt* (N 15:34); *l' šmʿth* is probably not an error but a verb with accusative pronominal suffix, cf. I *-tyh*.

wbtryn bnth dṣlpḥd: read *wbdyn* as in the other texts; N 27:1 mentions that there were five daughters. N 15:34 lacks the word dynyhwn (line 13). Moses is described as rbhwn in line 21 of L 24:12 and N 27:5 and as rbn in the other two texts. This has been extended to line 1 of N 15:34 also. Apparently rbhwn has been shortened to rbn.

Only in N 9:8 is the originally independent midrash integrated into the verse, as is N's practice with respect to other midrashim. The passage begins w'mr lhwn, for Heb. wy'mr 'lhm and concludes with a full translation of the verse w'mr lhwn mšh .... This may mean that the midrash was first added here; cf. further L 24:12.

9:12 yʿbdwn yʿbdn: alternate spellings for the same word; DM has printed the former. Add yth following yʿbdwn; a part of it may be indicated at the end of the line in the MS.

9:16 'klh 'š' (+): The phrase, added also in the midrash in G 38:25, etc. appears earliest in rabbinic literature. It is found in BT Yoma 21b and also in the liturgical poetry for Rosh HaShannah. Its use here obviously glorifies the clouds even more than the Biblical description; cf. E 24:17.

9:18 dy šry: for Heb. yškn. Perhaps read dyšry; cf. M: dy yšry.

9:20 Add dyyy after the first mymryh.

9:21 dy hwwy: Perhaps read dyhwwy; cf. v. 20, etc.

9:22 sgyn (+): expansive.

Chapter 10

10:9 ʿl bʿly dbbykwn ʿl śn'h dmʿyq lkwn: a double translation of Heb. ʿl hṣr hṣrr 'tkm. Since ʿl śn'h dmʿyq lkwn is a complete translation of the Hebrew and ʿl bʿly dbbykwn is not, the latter phrase is probably the intruder; cf. Onk., PJ: ʿl mʿyqyy dmʿyqyn lkwn, I: sn'h dmʿtyq lkwn. The words ṣr and 'wyb frequently appear together (though not here), a factor that may have influenced this double translation. In the similar context of E 23:22, Heb. w'ybty 't 'ybyk wṣrty 't ṣrryk is translated w'śny lmn dśny ytkwn wʿyq lmn dʿyq ytkwn; cf. also N 10:35.

10:11 The words bḥdš hšny have not been translated; add byrḥh tnynh.

10:14 wrbh dhwh mmny ʿl ḥyylwwt šbṭh dbnwy dyhwdh: for Hebrew. wʿl ṣb'w as in vv. 18, 22, 25.

10:29 'mr lmytyh ṭbh wnḥmn: for Heb. dbr ṭb.

10:30 The addition of 'zl may be unnecessary.

10:31 nsy' dʿbd yyy ʿmn bkl 'tr dḥzynn [DM: dhwynn] šryn wnṭlyn bmdbrh: for Heb. ḥntnw bmdbr. Jethro's knowledge of God's actions is mentioned in E 18:1 ff.

lshdwth: for Heb. ʿynym. Apparently Moses asked Jethro to be their guide, literally "eyes." N has changed this to the request that Jethro remain an impartial, non-Jewish witness to God's saving the Jews.

10:33 mṭwr byt mqdšh: for mhr yyy. Identifying this mountain as the Temple Mount is problematic; cf. M: mn ṭwrh dyyy; Onk.:

mṭwr d'tgly ᶜlwhy yqr' dyyy; PJ: mṭwr' d'tgly ᶜlwy 'yqr šknt' dyyy. Similar problems have been circumvented in E 3:1, 4:27, 18:5, etc.

10:35 The Heb. wy'mr mšh is translated twice, by w'mr and by whwh mšh mṣly w'mr. Introduction of ṣly is common in N and fits the following line of text, both in Heb. and Aram., but the presence of w'mr may show that the more literal translation, w'mr mšh, is older.

The word bbᶜw is frequently used in N to introduce prayers, but here it follows qwm. It would appear that qwm bbᶜw is the translation of qwmh, but qwm kᶜn is more appropriate in N; cf. M: qwm kᶜn and ḥzwr kᶜn in v. 36. In 11:11 Moses' speech to God is broken by the insertion of kᶜn after the first word. Even if one assumes a Heb. text qwmh n', kᶜn is still preferable. Perhaps bbᶜw should precede qwm.

10:36	Heb.		N
	wbnḥh	a.	wkd hwh šry
	y'mr	b.	hwh mšh mṣly w'mr
	šwbh yyy	c.	ḥzwr kᶜn yyy mn tqwp rwgdk [DM: rwgzk]
		d.	wtwb ᶜlynn brḥmyk ṭbyyh
		e.	w'šry 'yqr škyntk bgw 'lpyh wrbwwth
	rbbwt	f.	ysqwn rbwwth
	'lpy yśr'l	g.	wbrk 'lpy dbny yśr'l

The terse, obscure Hebrew has been expanded. Line a is a routine substitution for the BH construction. Line b is parallel to v. 35, etc. Line c translates part of E 32:12, šwb mḥrwn 'pk, though yyy has been inserted to accommodate the Heb. of this verse. Line d is parallel to e.

Chapter 11

11:1 *hgyn* (+): expansive.

wšmʿ qdm yyy: for Heb. *wyšmʿ yyy*. The word *qdm* was probably added later.

11:3 *byt yqydth*: translation of Heb. toponym *tbʿrh*.

11:4 *'lwwyy* (+): expansive, with *my*, as in v. 18.

11:6 *ln* (+): expansive.

[*mnth hdh*] *dʿyynynn tlyyn bh*: for Heb. *'l hmn ʿynynw*. The words in brackets are lacking but restored by DM from M. The form *mnth* is not found in N, however. In E 16:15, 31, 33, 35, N 11:7, 9, and D 8:3, 16, N uses *mnh* or *mn'* for both the absolute and determined forms. Accordingly, *mnth* should be *mnh* or *mn'*, and *hdh* is unnecessary.

11:8 Heb. *brḥym* has not been translated; in E 11:5 and D 24:6 *rḥym* is translated *rḥy'* and *ryḥyyh*; cf. I *brḥyh*.

ššyyn bdbš: in E 16:31 the manna is described *wṭʿmyh kšyšyn bdbš*, for Heb. *kṣpyḥt bdbš*, and the sweet taste was inserted here in place of Heb. *lšd hšmn*.

11:10 *qlhwn* (+): expansive.

11:11 *kʿn* (+): idiomatic with *lmh* (2x).

Insert *ḥn wḥsd* for *ḥsd*, following M; cf. v. 15.

11:14 *ṭwrḥthwn* (+): expansive, perhaps influenced by D 1:9 and 1:12.

11:15 The addition of *kʿn* in *'yn kʿn 'škḥt ḥyn wḥsd b'pyk* makes this phrase identical to G 18:3, 30:27, E 33:13, etc.

wl' 'ḥmy bbšthwn dʿmk: for Heb. *w'l 'r'h brʿty*. This is one of the Tiqqunei Soferim. According to the Massorah, this verse should have said *w'l 'r'h brʿtm*; N follows this suggestion in the translation.

11:17 *w'tgly bmmry*: to eliminate the objectionable *wyrdty*; cf. v. 25, etc.

11:18 *bmšmʿh dyyy*: routine for Heb. *b'zny yyy*.

11:19 *wl' ʿśrh ywmym* has not been translated; add *wl' ʿśrh ywmyn* after *ḥmšh ywmyn*.

11:20 *srbtwn ʿl pm gzrt mmrh dyyy*: problematic for Heb. *ky m'stm 't yyy*; cf. M also.

11:21 *rglyyn gbryn*: possibly a double translation of Heb. *rgly*, but note *kštyn rbbwwn dgbryn rglyyn* in E 12:37.

11:23 *h' 'yt qdm yyy mḥswr*: to eliminate the objectionable *hyd yyy tqṣr*.

11:24 *gbry*: delete; it is probably an error for *ḥkymy*, influenced by the preceding *gbryn*.

11:25 *qwdšh* (+): idiomatic with *rwḥ* (2x), as in v. 26.

11:26 N

1. w'štyyrw tryn gbryn bmšryth
2. šmh dḥd 'ldd wšmh dtnyynh mydd
3. wšrt ʿlyhwn rwḥ qwdšh
4. 'ldd hwh mtnb' w'mr
5. h' slwy slq mn ym'
6. wyhwy lyśr'l ltqlh
7. wmydd hwh mtnb' w'mr
8. h' mšh nby' mstlq mn gw mšryth
9. wyhwšʿ br nwn mšmš nśywtyh btryh
10. wtrwyhwn mtnbyyn kḥd' w'mryn
11. bswp ʿqb ywmy'
12. gwg wmgwg slqyn lyrwšlm
13. wbydwy dmlk' mšyḥ' 'ynwn nplyn
14. wšbʿ šnyn ydlqwn bny yśr'l mn mny zyynyhwn
15. wḥrš l' ypqwn
16 w'ynwn hwwn mn šbʿty ḥkymyh dmtpršyn
17. wl' npqw šbʿty ḥkymyh mn mšryth
18. ʿd 'ldd wmdd mtnb'yn bmšryth

Heb.

a. wyš'rw šny 'nšym bmḥnh
b. šm h'ḥd 'ldd wšm hšny mydd
c. wtnḥ ʿlhm hrwḥ
d. whmh bktbym
e. wl' yṣ'w h'hlh
f. wytnb'w bmḥnh

Lines 1-3 translate lines a-c of the Hebrew and tell of two men left in the camp who were possessed of the holy spirit. The Hebrew does not report the contents of their prophecies, but lines 4-15 provide several midrashic suggestions. Lines 4-6 contain the prophecy of Eldad, while lines 7-9 contain that of Medad. A joint prophecy is found in lines 10-15. Eldad's prophecy refers to the quails that were to be blown in by God (vv. 31 ff.) and notes that they will become an ensnarement (tqlh) for the people. Medad's prophecy notes that Joshua will replace Moses as the leader of the people (N 27:18-23). Their joint prophecy concerns the defeat of Gog and Magog in Jerusalem. Lines 16-18 conclude with the translation of the remaining Heb., lines d-f. My consideration of the Midrashic insertion follows a brief discussion of the translation.

With the exception of the idiomatic qwdšh in line 3 (cf. v. 25, etc.), lines 1-3 offer a literal translation of the Heb. of a-c. The last part of the actual translation (16-18) is less literal than the first part (1-3), but it corresponds to the Hebrew of lines d-f. Line d is virtually unintelligible because of the word bktbym; it was frequently explained by the rabbis as referring to the initial inclusion of Eldad and Medad's names in the list of seventy-two elders (six per tribe) and their subsequent deletion from that list to reduce it to the requisite seventy names. (cf. Rashi a.l., based on Sifrei, pp. 95-96). According to N, they were two of the seventy (line 16) who were designated (read dmtpršyn bšmhwn with M). Lines 17-18 have the 70 remaining in the camp, while the two continued their prophecy.

Perhaps the most significant aspect of the midrashic material in this verse is that the prophecies it recounts (i.e. lines 5-6, 8-9, and part of 11-15), like Biblical prophecies, may be poetry. (Cf. Introduction, chapter 4.). Only lines 14-15 appear to be non-poetic, and even they, if redivided as

14a wšbᶜ šnyn ydlqwn bny yśr'l
14b mn mny zyynyhwn
15 wḥrš l' ypqwn,

have a measure of poetic rhythm and balance and even a near rhyme between zyynyhwn (15a) and ypqwn (15b). Their parallelism, however, is not as strong as that of the earlier lines, and, as will become clear below, the first two lines are one unit and should not be redivided in this way. (Recognizing that lines 14-15 thus pose a problem, we can proceed to consider common aspects of the three prophecies).

In addition to the similarity of setting and sources, the passages are structurally similar. Lines 5, 8 and 12 begin with common or proper nouns (5 and 8 have h' first) followed by participal forms of slq followed by a preposition (once l- but twice mn, in vv. 5 and 8) followed by a place. Allowing for the added line dating Gog and Magog in the distant future (11), these similarities all revolve around the first line in each passage. They demonstrate the unified nature of the three prophecies, but offer no suggestion as to how one might evaluate the difficult 14b-15 other than to declare it secondary, because no parallel for it exists in the first two passages. This step, however, is definitely unwarranted.

Comparison with Frag. offers additional support for the authenticity of lines 14-15.

(11) bswp ʿqb ywmy'

(12) ʿtyd gwg wmgwg wḥylwwtyh slqyn lyrwšlm

(13) wbydwy dmlk' mšyḥ' 'ynwn nplyn

(14) wšbʿ šnyn [d]ywmyn dlqyn bny yśr'l mn m'ny zyynyhwn

(15) lḥwrš l' ypqwn

(15a) w'yln l' yqṣṣwn

Frag. contains equivalents of all lines in N (sometimes with minor changes), but adds an important extra piece (15a) that parallels 15 and helps restore some of the poetic balance. (PJ is extremely expansive and offers no close parallel; M omits the equivalent of lines 10-15 altogether). The authenticity of this extra stich can be supported from the Biblical texts on which it was based. Ezek. 39 speaks of the defeat of Gog and Magog. Ezek. 39:9-10 read:

9a. *wyṣ'w yšby ᶜry yśr'l*
b. *wbᶜrw whśyqw bnšq wmgn wṣnh*
c. *bqšt wbḥṣym wbmql yd wbrmḥ*
d. *wbᶜrw bhm 'š šbᶜ šnym*
10a. *wl' yś'w ᶜṣym mn hśdh*
b. *wl' yḥṭbw mn hyᶜrym*
c. *ky bnšq ybᶜrw 'š*
d. *wšllw 't šllyhm*
e. *wbzzw 't bzzyhm*
f. *n'm 'dny yyy*

Verse 9 is frequently cited in eschatological midrashim (e.g. *Sefer Eliyahu*, lines 76-77 and *Pereq Eliyahu*, lines 98-99, in *Midreshei Ge'ulah*). The texts usually jump from v. 9 to v. 12, which describes the burial of the attackers, but N has opted to continue with v. 10. Line 14 of N contains the translation of 9d, expanded to fit the context, and line 15 clearly refers to Ezek. 39:10a. Under the circumstances, 15a of Frag. should be seen as the equivalent of 10b of Ezek, 39. Whether this line was ever present in N is impossible to determine, but it is clear that lines 14-15 in N are paraphrased, non-poetic translations of of parts of successive verses in Ezek. They were thus not created by the midrashist and do not follow the same style.
Cf. Jonathan on the passage in Ezek.:

9d. *wydlqwn bhwn nwr' šbᶜ šnyn*

10a wl' ysbwn 'ᶜyn mn ḥql'

b. wl' yqṣwn mn ḥwršy'

The use of ḥwršy' in 10b of Jonathan (for Heb. hyᶜrym) comports with the use of wḥrš and lḥwrš in line 15 of N and Frag., but does not add to our knowledge of N. N's use of ypqwn may have been influenced by the frequent appearance of yṣ' and npq in this verse.

Even assuming that N is defective in the omission of Frag.'s 15a, it seems to contain an earlier form of these prophecies than does either PJ or Frag. Minor additions that break the rhythm and parallelism and rearrangements that destroy the rhyme all point to a period of transmission during which the poetic qualities were either unnoticed or disregarded. Unless we are prepared to assume that some transmittor of N converted the prose accounts found in these other texts into poetic form, we must conclude that N, as the most poetic text, preserves the earliest version of these lines. Whether the minor changes needed to produce perfect rhyming should be maintained is far from clear (see further 21:6); and other aspects of the material, such as the attribution of the identification of these prophecies with three different rabbis in BT San. 17a must still be investigated. Also of note is the location of this material in the middle of v. 26, a point on which N, M, PJ and Frag. all agree. One would expect, however, that this material would follow v. 26 or v. 27. In both places the Torah actually notes that these men prophesied (wytnb'w, mtnb'ym), and these are the most logical places for the catch words that introduce the material: 'ldd hwh mtnb'... (4), wmydd hwh mtnb' ... (7), wtrwyhwn mtnbyyn ... (10). Apparently the translation of Hebrew originally existed intact, and the midrashic material (lines 4-15) was inserted in the middle, a phenomenon noted in many other verses as well.

11:28 *mnᶜ mnhwn rwḥ qwdšh*: for Heb. *kl'm*, changing the harsh BH to a more restrained phrase, on the assumption that Joshua believed that Moses had the power to deny prophecy to someone.

11:30 Read *dyśr'l* for *wyśr'l*.

11:31 *rwm* (+) expansive.

11:33 *ᶜd kᶜn*: for Heb. *ᶜwdnw.*

11:34 *qbry š'lth:* for Heb. toponym *qbrwt ht'wh*. In v. 35 the name is given as *qbry tḥmwdth*, which is more offensive but closer to the Hebrew. M corrects v. 34 to *tḥmdnh*; cf. also *twḥmdnyyh* and DM a.l. This change points to two problems: 1) the root *š'l* compared with the root *ḥmd*, and 2) the choice between the abstract noun *tḥmwdth* and the *nomen agentis tḥmdnh*. Onk. translates *qbry dmš'ly* (2x) and PJ has *qybry dmšyyly byśr'* (2x). In both cases these translations of the toponym correspond to the translation of Heb. *hᶜm hmt'wym* (34 end): *ᶜm' dš'ylw* (Onk.), *ᶜm' dšyylw byśr'* (PJ). Since N translates this phrase as *ᶜm' dhwwn mtḥmdyn*, it would seem that the usage in v. 34 is an intrusion and the root *ḥmd* is preferable, but the name appears in N 33:16-17 and D 9:22 also, and the data there do not support this conclusion. N 33:16 has *qbry š'ly š'lth* (M: *dmšyly byśr'*), while N 33:17 has *qbry twḥmdth*. D 9:22 reads *wbqbry š'lth* (M: *wbqbry š'lt tḥmdth*, designated conflate by DM). Apparently both translations were acceptable. In the light of N's use of *ḥmd* to describe the people's desire (= Heb. *t'wh*), the reading *qbry tḥmwdth* must be the closest to the Hebrew. The form *qbry š'lth* is morphologically similar but lexically different, while qbry twḥmdnyyh, etc. is lexically the same but morphologically different. Both tḥmdnh and tḥmdnyyh may be plural forms, but it seems more likely that the former is singular and may even be equivalent to twḥmdth. The appearance of both names together in two different contexts hardly seems accidental, but aside from possible interference from another translation (e.g. Onk), no solution is obvious.

11:35 bḥṣrwt ... bḥṣyrwt: The first should probably be ḥṣrwt, without the preposition, which may have been added in imitation of the second. Note, however, that in Num. 33, where the wilderness journey is charted in detail and the places are repeated, the first occurrence is always b- (wšrwn b-) while the second is m- (wnṭlw m-). M reacts to the problem here by suggesting mn hṣy- for the first bḥṣrwt, but this makes no sense. The gloss must refer to the second usage (bḥṣyrwt) and not the first one (bḥṣrwt).

Chapter 12

12:1

Heb.		N
wtdbr mrym w'hrn bmšh	a.	wmllt mrym w'hrn bmšh
ʿl 'dwt h'šh hkšyt 'šr lqḥ	b.	ʿl ʿsq 'tth kwšyth dy nsb
ky 'šh kšyt lqḥ	c.	
	d.	whlw 'th kwšyh hwt ṣypwrh 'tth dmšh
	e.	'l' hyk mh dkwšyh
	f.	šny bgwph
	g.	mn kl bryyth
	h.	kdyn hwt ṣypwrh 'tth dmšh
	i.	y'yh brywh wšpyrh bḥyzwh

j. *wšnyyh* *bᶜwbdy-* *ṭbyh*

k. *mn* *kl* *nšyyh* *ddrh* *hhw'*

Lines a-b are translated literally, but c was omitted when the translation was joined to the midrashic addition in d-j.

The problem of Moses' foreign wife vexed many Jews, from Miriam and Aaron through the rabbis of later millenia. Lines d-j were one attempt to explain away the problem -- *kwšyt* did not mean "Kushite" or "Ethiopian," but "different." The reasoning was simple: Zipporah was a Midianite not a Kushite (cf. E 2:21 and Sifrei here, the basis of d); but she was called Kushite, because just as the Kushite differs from all other people in appearance, so did Zipporah differ from the other women of her generation (h, k) with respect to her appearance (i) or actions (j).

Some midrashic texts stress the uniqueness of Zipporah's beauty (e.g. Sifrei, pp. 98-99); others the uniqueness of her behavior (e.g. BT M.Q. 16b); some refer to both (e.g. Sifrei, p. 99). The text of N is almost identical to that of Frag. and confirms the presence of both her beauty and fine behavior in the text. Line i, of course, is a common description of women (e.g. G 29:17), but is not applied to Zipporah by the Bible itself. The emphasis on her beauty appears in Onk. as well: *ᶜl* *ᶜsq* *'ytt'* *špyrt'*. The rabbinic logic aside, note the Arabic *kuwayisun*, which means "beautiful" and may play a role in the formation of this midrash because of its similarity to Heb. *kwšyt* or Aram. *kwšyth*. Also, note the similarity between *ṣypwrh* and Aram. *špyrh* "beautiful."

12:6 *'yn* *yhwwy* *bynykwn* *nbyyh*: for Heb. *'m* *yhyh* *nby'km*.

12:7 *l'* *kwwt* *kl* *nby'h*: for Heb. *l'* *kn*.

bkl ʿwlmy dbryt: for Heb. bkl byty.

12:8 mmll lqbl mmll: to eliminate the anthropomorphism in the Heb. ph 'l ph.

12:12 N

a. l' kʿn tyhwy mrym ms'bh b'hylh kmytyyh
b. wh' mtmy' (!) lwwldh dʿbd bmʿyh d'myh
c. tšʿh yrḥyn bmy' wb'št'
d. wl' mtnzq
e. wkywn dmṭ' qṣh lmpwq lgw ʿlm-
f. 't'kl plgwt bśryh
g. kdyn kd hwyn' mštʿbdyn bmṣrym
h. wḥzryn wmṭrpyn bmdbr-
i. hwwt 'ḥtn ḥmyyh bšʿbwdn
j. wkywn dmṭh qṣh lmḥsnh yt 'rʿ'
k. lmh hy' mtmnʿh mnn
l. ṣly ʿl bśrh myth dbh wyḥy
m. lmh ʿbd yt zkwth

Heb.

1. 'l n' thy kmt
2. 'šr bṣ'tw mrḥm 'mw
3. wy'kl hṣy bśrw

The Hebrew is concise; it voices dismay at the possiblility that Miriam's leprosy will leave her like a half devoured, dead foetus. The translation of these three lines is much longer, and the Hebrew lines are separated and worked into the fabric of the targum.

Line a, an expansion of the first line of the Hebrew, contains the additions mrym ms'bh b'hylh. The addition of the name is routine. The phrase ms'bh b'hylh refers to the rabbinic concept twm't 'hl, impurity caused by a dead body in an enclosed area (cf. N 19:14 and M Kelim 1:1 ff). The impurity of mṣrᶜ "leper" is a much lower form than that of 'hl "enclosure." However, according to some authorities, a leper is considered as if dead (BT Ned. 64b), and the plea here is that she not be allowed to remain in this state and that Moses pray on her behalf (1).

Lines b-k contain the logical inference explaining the ironic tragedy of Miriam's situation. She is like a foetus who survived nine tortuous months in the womb without injury (b-d) but was half devoured when born (e-f). More explicitly, she survived the enslavement in Egypt and travels in the desert (g-i), and now that acquisition of the promised land is at hand, she is withheld (quarantined) (j-k). The remainder of line l continues Aaron's plea that Moses save her; line m marshals yet another argument in favor of it. Lines 2-3 of the Hebrew have been incorporated into the mashal, line 2 in b and line 3 in f, and the absorption of the Hebrew is thorough and complete. There is no indication that the midrash is based on a Biblical text. A dead foetus is also capable of conveying impurity through "enclosure." Aaron wanted to remove Miriam from this category. The thrust of the passage may thus be: Let Miriam no longer convey impurity through enclosure, like the dead. She is comparable to a foetus that was carried alive and born dead, in others words, whe survived the ordeals of the exodus and desert (pregnancy) only to be consumed at the time of acquiring the land (delivery). Cure her.

12:13 bbᶜw brḥmyn mn qdmyk yyy (+): This formulaic introduction to a prayer routinely ends with yyy, so the request itself begins 'lhh (so M, also). The wording 'lhh ḥnnh wrḥmnh 'sy yth is not a literal translation of Heb. 'l n' rp' n' lh. The phrase 'lhh ḥnnh wrḥmnh is borrowed from Moses' prayer in E 34:6, 'l rḥwm wḥnwn, translated in N 'lhh ḥnn' wrḥmn'. Note, by way of comparison, 'lh bbʿw 'sy kʿn yth (Onk.) and bbʿw brḥmyn 'lh' rḥmn' bbʿw 'lh' dšlyṭ bnyšmt kl byśr' 'sy bbʿw lh (PJ). Perhaps the introductory formula in N substitutes for one n', but at least one was left untranslated. The length of these translations contrasts somewhat with the emphasis on the brevity of Moses' prayer found in BT Ber. 34a.

12:14 mn qdmwy (+): expansive.

tt'sy: for Heb. t'sp, M: ttknš. Apparently N has been influenced by the similarity of the Aram. and Heb. roots 'sy and 'sp; cf. 't'syt for Heb. h'sp in vv. 15 and 16;

12:16 N

a. 'p ʿl gb d'tḥyybt mrym nbyyth lmṣṭrʿh
b. 'yt 'wlpn sgy lḥkymy wlnṭry 'wryth
c. dmṣwh zʿyrh d'nš ʿbd hw' mqbl ʿylwy 'gr sgy'
d. lpm dqmt lh mrym ʿl gyp nhr'
e. lmydʿ mh yhwwy bswpyh dmšh
f. hwwn yśr'l 'štyn rbwwn
g. d'nwn skwm [with DM] tmnyyn lygywnyn
h. wʿnny 'yqrh wbyrh l' hwwn zyyʿyn wl' nṭlyn mn 'tryhwn
i. ʿd zmn d'tsy't mrym nby'th mn ṣrʿth
j.1. [wmm btr kn]
2. DM: [wmn btr d'tsyt mrym nby'th mn ṣrʿth btr kn]
k. nṭlw ʿmh mn ḥṣrwt wšrwn bmdbrh dp'rn

The targum of v. 16 may be divided into several sections.

Lines a-c note the rabbinic concept of great reward for even a small meritorious act. Miriam's meritorious act of guarding Moses while he was in a basket in the Nile follows (d-e). Her reward was that the people (f-g), the clouds of God's glory, and the miraculous well (h) remained stationary until her return from quarantine (i). Lines j-k translate the Hebrew.

Lines d-e are based on E 2:4, translated in N w'tᶜtdt 'ḥtyh mrḥwq lmydᶜ 'ḥtyh mh 'tᶜbyd lyh. There is clearly no connection between the translations, but similar phrases are used elsewhere in N. Line f refers to the census tabulation of N 1:45-46, rounded in rabbinic parlance to 600,000. N translates N 1:46 ... štyn rybwwn ..., which is similar to the form elsewhere in N but not here. The gloss in g correlates the figure with contemporary ones, i.e. the Israelites composed 600,000 men or 80 legions of 7500 men.

The clouds mentioned in h are those Moses and the people followed. The well is less certain, but presumably refers to the legendary source of water that travelled with the people in the desert. The association of Miriam and the well is probably based on N 20:1-2, where the lack of water is noted right after the record of Miriam's death.

Line j is lacking in N and has been restored by M, but it is uncertain if the full text is needed. DM has followed M for the most part, but elsewhere N translates w'ḥr as wmn btr kn (cf. PJ wmn btr kdyn), and it is offered as another possibility. Line k, of course, is the literal translation of the Heb. nsᶜw hᶜm mḥṣrwt wyḥnw bmdbr p'rn.

The major point of this passage is found in lines a-i: the time spent by Miriam in waiting for Moses was of great merit. This is followed by her reward, namely that the people waited for her to be restored to health before moving on. Actually, the material in lines a-i fits better in v. 15, after šbᶜt ymym. The similarity of the end of the verse *whᶜm l' nsᶜ ᶜd h'sp mrym* and lines f-i of v. 16 shows that lines a-i, in fact, belong to this earlier verse. Line i is as good a translation of the end of verse 15 as the text of N, while line h offers a midrashic alternative to *whᶜm l' nsᶜ*. The presence in v. 16 of this second translation of part of v. 15 argues against the authenticity of one or the other passage. Given the presence of literal renditions of v. 15 and most of v. 16 (in line k), it would seem that 16 a-i are the secondary addition. The lost line j and k are the original translations of v. 16, and originally followed the literal translation of v. 15.

Chapter 13

13:2 The Heb. reads *'yš 'ḥd* twice, but N has translated the phrase only once.

13:3 *mšh* has been omitted.

mmdbrh: for Heb. *mmdbr p'rn*.

13:17 *mšh* (+): The second occurrence is extra.

13:19 *h' qry kprnyn 'ynwn 'w tlyln*: for Heb. *hbmḥnym 'm bmbṣrym*.

13:21 *'ntwkyh*: for Heb. *ḥmt*.

13:22 *klb* (+): The singular verb *wyb'* (the *Sevirin* *wyb'w* notwithstanding) prompted the observation that only one spy went to Hebron. This was supported by Josh. 14:13-14, which tells how Caleb received this portion as an inheritance.

gybr' (+): expansive; cf. v. 28. Both are probably based on v. 33.

13:23 nḥl sgwlh: for the similar sounding Heb. nḥl 'škl.
wkn (+): expansive (2x).

13:26 Heb. kl has not been translated.

13:27 wh' mn pyrh: for the less precise Heb. wzh pryh.

13:29 wᶜl mgyzth dyrdnh: for Heb. wᶜl yd hyrdn.

13:32 ṭybh: cf. G 37:2.
mry ᶜyynn byšh (+): The accusation of sorcery was real and frequent during late antiquity, but the exact nature of the activity often evades precise definition. National heroes, enemies and leaders of alien groups were endowed with magical powers in ancient literature. This designation is lacking in the other targumim here, but hardly unexpected in the light of contemporary documents. More noteworthy is the fact that mry ᶜyynn byšh and gbryn dmšyḥh are apparently both intended as equivalents of 'nšy mdwt. For materials related to the magical powers of e.g. Moses, Solomon and Jesus see John G. Gager, Moses in Greco-Roman Paganism (New York, 1972), especially chapter 4; James B. Pritchard (ed.), Solomon and Sheba (London, 1974); Morton Smith, Jesus The Magician (New York, 1978).

Chapter 14

14:1 The word kl is not translated in N but is added in M; it has also been omitted from v. 5 twice.

14:4 mlk: for Heb. r'š. Since r'š is translated ryš in this context elsewhere, the use of mlk is potentially significant; cf. mlyk lryš (PJ), ryš' (Onk.), mlk (Frag.).

14:5 knyšth: for Heb. qhl ʿdt; the words kl ʿm have not been translated.

14:9

Heb.		N
'k byyy 'l tmrdw	a.	lḥwd b'yqr škynth dyyy l' tmrdwn
w'tm 'l tyr'w 't ʿm h'rṣ	b.	w'twn l' tdḥlwn mn ʿm' d'rʿ'
ky lḥmnw hm	c.	'rwm hyk mh dlḥm' qlyl ln lmykl
	d.	kdn 'ynwn qlylyn b'pynn lmšyṣy' ythwn
sr ṣlm mʿlyhm	e.	ʿbr tlyhwn mʿylwyhwn
wyyy 'tnw	f.	wmymr dyyy ʿmn
'l tyr'm	g.	l' tdḥlwn mnhwn

The verse is translated literally except for lines c-d, where the reference to the enemies as "food" has been related to the manna -- it will be as easy to destroy them as it is to eat manna. The association is based on 21:5, where some of these same words are used, and eliminates any possible notions of the Israelites' devouring the flesh of their enemies. Line c is similar in some respects to 21:5.

14:11 yrgzwn qdmy: for Heb. yn'ṣny, as in v. 23.

14:12 w'šṣy ythwn: for Heb. w'wryšnw, "I will disown them" (JPS).

w'yt yklh qdmyy lmmnyh ytk: for Heb. w'ʿśh 'tk. The literal translation may have been avoided to prevent the impression that God made a promise he did not fulfull, but this is the routine translation of the phrase. Cf. notes to D 9:14.

14:14 d'yqr škyntk bgw ʿm': for the Heb. ky' 'th yyy bqrb hʿm.

ḥzyw bḥzyw: for Heb. ʿyn bʿyn; cf. mmll lqbl mmll for Heb. ph 'l ph, 12:8.

Heb. ʿmd has not been translated; cf. M: q'ym.

14:18

Heb.		N
yyy 'rk 'pym	a.	yyy 'ryk rwḥ
	b.	wrḥyq rgz
	c.	wqryb rḥmyn
wrb ḥsd	d.	wmsgy lmʿbd ḥsd
nś' ʿwn	e.	šry wšbyq lḥwbyn
wpšʿ	f.	wmʿbr ʿl mrwdyn
	g.	wmkpr ʿl ḥṭ'yn
wnqh l' ynqh	h.	wmzkyyh l' mzky
	i.	bywm dynh rbh
pqd ʿwn 'bwt	j.	mdkr ḥwby 'bhn ršyʿn
ʿl bnym	k.	ʿl bnyn mrwdyn
ʿl šlšym	l.	ʿl dr tlytyy
wʿl rbʿym	m.	wʿl dr rbyʿyy

All of the Hebrew is present in the Aramaic. The same expressions are used, for the most part, in translating the parallel passages E 20:5, D 5:9 and especially E 34:6-7. Parts of E 34:6 are translated exactly like part of lines a-d, and both contain b-c, even though not based on this verse. E 34:6 has wqšwṭ at the end of line d for Heb. w'mt; this is lacking here in the Heb. and in N, but is added by M. Similarly, the translation of E 34:7 is identical, in part, to lines e–m. The equivalent of i has been added in Ex.; and line g has been borrowed from Ex., where it translates *wḥṭ'h*. Even were we to attribute the absence of *wqšwṭ* from line d to an accident, we could not conclude that the translation of v. 18 was simply replaced by the translation of E 34:6-7, because there are other phrases in Ex. 34 that were not borrowed. Perhaps Ex. 34 was better known to the translator because of its use in the liturgy, and where possible it, or its liturgical derivative, influenced the translation of N 14:18.

14:19 *šry kʿn wšbwq*: for Heb. *slḥ n'*. It is interesting that the hendiadys *šry wšbwq* has been split by the insertion of *kʿn*.

14:21 *ḥy wqyym*: for Heb. *ḥy*, as in v. 28, etc.

lʿlm (+): expansive, but necessitated by the application of *ḥy* to God.

14:24 *rwḥ dqdš*: for Heb. *rwḥ 'ḥrt*. The translation specifies the spirit and also eliminates the sometines negative connotation that *'ḥr* carries in rabbinic literature.

14:27 *dqmyy ʿlwyy*: a double translation of Heb. *ʿly*. Hebrew regularly uses *ʿl* with the verb *mlynym*. Where applied to things or people, N uses *ʿl* also, e.g. 14:2, 14:36, 16:6, etc. When applied to God, *qdm* is preferred, e.g. 14:29, 14:35. Both forms appear in this verse, but this is probably just a case of standardization, since the idiom is applied to God only rarely.

14:29 *wkl*: for Heb. *lkl*, changed by M to *lkl*.

14:34 The Heb. phrase 't h'rṣ has been omitted.

ywm ḥd bkl šnh: for Heb. ywm lšnh (2x). This is not a casual error. Rabbinic lore suggests that this day, the Ninth of Av, was established as a permanent day of mourning to commemorate the people's lack of faith.

14:36 Heb. 't has not been translated.

14:41 lmh kʿn: using a common idiom for Heb. lmh zh.

14:45 ʿd šṣyw: for the toponym ʿd hḥrmh. Note the translation of the verb wyḥrm in 21:3, where the toponym remains ḥrmh.

Chapter 15

15:3 bzmny (+): expansive; cf. L 23:2.

15:8 bpyrwš: for Heb. lpl'.

15:11 ʿm 'mrh b'mryh 'w bgdyh 'w bʿzyh: for Heb. lśh bkbśym 'w bʿzym. N appears to contain a double reading. Elsewhere śh is translated 'ymr or 'mr, e.g. E 12:3, 12:5, 21:37; kbś is translated 'mr, E 12:5, 29:40; ʿz is translated ʿz, G 32:15, 37:31; and gdy is translated gdy, e.g. G 38:17, 38:20. The problem in this text may be corrected by comparison with E 12:5, where ʿzym is translated gdyy' bny ʿzy'. Apparently this text should read bgdyh bny ʿzyh also; cf. M: ldgy ʿzyyh.

15:14 mn mh (+): perhaps a double text.

15:15 lkwn (+): cf. v. 29. The same change is found in v. 16 also.

kwwtkwn gywrh: for Heb. kkm kgr. The similar expression kmwk kprʿh in G 44:18 is paraphrased several times in N but is not translated literally.

15:18 Delete 'rwm. Perhaps this has been influenced by the many places that read ky tb'w, some of which are translated 'rwm, e.g. N 10:9, 15:2.

15:20 r'šyt šrwy: for Heb. r'šyt; cf. v. 21 where only šrwy is used.

k'pršwt ʿbwrh mn 'drh wtmrh [DM: wḥmrh] mn mʿṣrth: Though the Heb. contains only ktrwmt grn, the complementary phrase is based on 18:30, which reads ktbw't grn wktbw't yqb and is translated ʿybwr mn 'drh wḥmrh [not wtmrh] mn mʿṣrth.

15:25 Heb. 'šh is not translated.

15:27 br: for Heb. bt.

15:29 lkwl mn mn dʿbd: for Heb. lkm lʿśh. The scribe wrote lkwl and changed it to lkwn for Heb. lkm, but possibly both belong. Only one mn is needed. Read either lkwn lkl mn dʿbd or lkwn lmn dʿbd. Prefixed la- is frequently translated lkl (cf. Introduction, chapt. 3).

15:33 dbny yśr'l (+): idiomatic.

15:34 The midrash has been discussed in L 24:12. Here it is followed by the translation of the Heb., literal except for Heb. ky l' prš (foraš), which N renders ʿd zmn dytprš lhwn qdm yyy. Perhaps the translator assumed God to be the subject of prs; cf. L 24:12 where lprš lhm is also translated in this manner.

15:38 The missing words are found in the margin.

glwth (+): "prayer wrap."

šyᶜ tklth: for Heb. ptyl tklt; M: ṣnpt gylyhwn šzyr dtklh; cf. v. 39.

15:39 lmṣnpn: for Heb. lṣyṣt; cf. ṣnypn in D 22:12.

hrhwry lbkwn, hrhwry ḥzyw: expansive; eliminates the literalist doubt about following the heart and eyes.

15:40 Heb. wᶜśytm has not been translated.

qdm yyy 'lhkwn: for l'lhykm. The phrase lpny yyy 'lhykm occurs in L 23:28, 23:40, etc., while lyyy 'lhykm is found, e.g., in E 8:24, 10:16. Either could be translated in this way.

Heb. 'ny yyy 'lhykm has not been translated, possibly to avoid the translator's saying that he is God; verse 41 is thus read as part of v. 40. Apparently this problem could not be avoided as easily at the end of the verse.

Chapter 16

16:1 wplyg: The problem caused by the lack of an object for the Heb. verb wyqḥ has been eliminated by translating it as an intransitive verb, albeit of a different meaning; cf. Ont.: w'tplyg.

16:8 lkwn: read lqrḥ, with DM.

16:11 ḥšyb (+): expansive.

16:13 hy' (+): expansive.

Restore the end of the verse with DM.

16:15 *l' tqbl brʿwwh yt qrbnhwn*: for Heb. *'l tpn 'l mnḥtm*; cf. G 4:8.

16:16 Heb. *whm* has not been translated.

16:22 *'lhh*: for Heb. *'l 'lhy*.
Heb. *'ḥd* has not been translated.

16:24 *kl* (+): expansive, perhaps influenced by v. 23.

16:26 *mškn*: read *mškny* for Heb. *'hly*.

16:28 *mn qdm yyy 'štlḥt*: for Heb. *yyy šlḥny*, as in v. 29.
mn dʿty: for Heb. *mlby*.

16:29 *dmytn* (+): expansive.

16:30 *ḥdth* (+): expansive; cf v. 29.

16:32 *bryyth*: for Heb. *h'dm*. This is part of a phrase lacking in N but recorded in the margin. Almost invariably N translates *'dm* as *br* or *bny* (*'*)*nš* when it refers to people in general. The other reading in M seems preferable in this respect (*bny 'nš'* ...), but *bryyth* is used in v. 29.

16:33 *š'wl*: for Heb. *š'lh*, M: *lš'wlh*.

Chapter 17

17:3 *dḥyybyh h'lyyn dḥbw bnpšthwn*: for Heb. *hḥṭ'ym h'lh bnpštm*, taking *hḥṭ'ym* as both noun and verb.

17:11 Moses has been omitted as the subject of the verb w'mr.

šry ḥblh mḥbl bᶜm': for Heb. hḥl hngp, perhaps influenced by v. 12, where N translates hḥl hngp bᶜm in the same way.

17:13 The Hebrew describes Moses standing between the dead and the living members of the group. This, apparently, ended or coincided with the end of the plague; thus the addition of bᶜy rḥmym ᶜl, which gave him credit for stopping the plague. Perhaps Moses' praying was derived solely from the verb wyᶜmd, itself a code word for prayer in rabbinic literature, e.g. BT Ber. 26b. In any case, N has avoided the possible misreading of Moses' act as magical.

17:14 mytyh dmytw: for Heb. hmtym (2x), translating the verbal and nominal aspects of the participle by separate words. Usually singular participles are translated mn d- + participle.

dhwwn ᶜl ᶜṣth dqrḥ: for Heb. ᶜl dbr qrḥ. The phrase dmytw dhwwn is redundant, and one word should be deleted.

17:18 Heb. 'ḥd has not been translated.

17:20 'trᶜy byh: for Heb. 'bḥr bw.

17:23 wgmr wᶜbd lwzyn br lylyh: for Heb. wygml šqdym.

17:27 Heb. 'l mšh has not been translated.

mynn mytw bmgpth wmnn blᶜt 'rᶜ' wmmn npqt 'šth (+): The verse's three references to destruction of the people have been correlated with the three events recently narrated.

17:28 yqrb lmqrbh: for Heb. hqrb hqrb.

h' [not hw'] spnn h' 'štyṣynn: for Heb. h'm tmnw lgwʿ, dividing the verbal phrase into two; cf. 21:29.

Chapter 18

18:1 w'nšy bytk; has been substituted for wbyt 'byk; cf. v. 13, etc. where it is used for Heb. bytk.

18:2 lwwtk: for Heb. 'tk; clearly making the Levites subservient, as specified later in the verse.

18:9 byt qdš qdšyh: not as in Heb. qdš hqdšym; cf. also v. 10.

18:11 yhwwy (+): perhaps expansive, but perhaps influenced by D 18:3, where a similar idea is expressed as wzh yhyh mšpṭ hkhnym, translated wdyn yhwwy sdr dynyhwn ....

18:12 ṭwb: for Heb. hlb (2x).

wḥmr: for Heb. wdgn.

šrwy brthwn: for Heb. r'šytm; brthwn is the equivalent of śdwtyhm, but the word is not found in the Heb.

18:15 dydk yhwwy: for Heb. yhyh lk. Frequently the order of the Heb. is lk yhyh.

18:17 tsdr for Heb. tqṭyr; the rest of the verse is the idiomatic translation of the last 4 Heb. words.

18:19 btrk: for Heb. 'tk, emphasizing the importance of this law for future generations; cf. D 4:40, 12:25, etc., where the phrase *wlbnyk* *'ḥryk* is used.

18:27 *wḥmrh* *mn* *mᶜṣrth*: for Heb. *kml'h* *mn* *hyqb*, cf. v. 30.

18:29 *ṭwbh*: for Heb. *mqdšw*; cf. M and vv. 30, 32.

Chapter 19

19:2 *wysbwn* *wyytwn*: for Heb. *wyqḥw*; cf. E 27:20 and L 24:2, where the same idiomatic translation is used.

šᶜbwd (+): expansive.

19:5 *yth* (+): expansive.

19:6 *wyqlq* *wyṭlq*: double translation of Heb. *whšlyk*.

19:7 *wmrḥq* *mn* *qdšyh* (+): expansive.

19:11 *kl* (+): *mn* is expected.

ṭm' (+): cf. v. 13. Even contact with part of a body renders the person unclean. Note, however, v. 16, where *ᶜṣm* is translated *grm*.

19:13 *ᶜd* *kᶜn*: for Heb. *ᶜwd*. This seems like a mechanical translation; the Hebrew may mean "while."

19:15 *mn* *dḥsp*: for Heb. *kly*; cf. M Kelim 10:1, v. 17.

gwph *dšyᶜ*: for Heb. *ṣmyd*.

19:16 *dqṭyl*: for Heb. *bḥll*; read *bqṭyl*.

19:17 myn dmbw^c dkyn: for Heb. mym ḥyym, a double translation. In L 14:5, 50 only myyn (d)mbw^c is used.

19:19 wytdky: for Heb. wḥṭ'w.

19:22 byh (+): idiomatic; cf. vv. 11, 13.

Chapter 20

20:3 ^{c}mh: for Heb. ^{c}m mšh; note also the change in word order.

20:5 k^{c}n (+): idiomatic with lmh.

l' 'tr špr lbyt zr^c: for Heb. l' mqwm zr^c, perhaps a double translation of mqwm as 'tr špr and byt.

wl' mṣb (+): perhaps a supplement to the preceding phrase or a double translation of zr^c rather than an additional item in the subsequent list.

ln (+): expansive; cf. E 15:24, N 21:5.

20:8 qdmyhwn l^{c}yynyhwn: a double translation of l^{c}ynyhm; cf. 21:6, line 1.

20:10 ^{c}mh dmlpyn mlpnyhwn dy ṣrkw lmylp: for Heb. hmrym.

20:11 ḥwṭrh: for Heb. ydw; added to explain how he struck the rock with the staff when he only raised his hand.

tnyn tryn zmnyn: possibly a double translation of Heb. p^{c}mym; cf. G 27:36 and 43:10 tryn zmnyn, but trtyn zmnyn in G 41:32. Onk. uses trtyn zmnyn in all three cases.

20:12 l' hyymntwn ly bšm mymry: a double translation of l'

h'mntm by:

bšbwʿh bgyn kdn: a double translation of lkn; Heb. lkn is frequently translated bsbwʿh in N, cf. G 4:15, etc.

l'tr': for Heb. 'l h'rṣ. The promised land was frequently referred to as hmqwm, but this change probably resulted from interchanging the Aram. 'rʿ for 'tr'.

20:14 Add d'dmyy (or the like), deleted by the censor because taken as a reference to Rome.

20:16 wṣlynn: for Heb. wnṣʿq.

bql ṣlwtn: for Heb. qlnw.

[ml'k] drḥmyn: for Heb. ml'k. The word [ml'k], lacking in N, has been added by DM because it sometimes accompanies drḥmyn.

wšyzb ytn: for Heb. wyṣ'nw.

20:17 tḥwmk nʿbr: for Heb. nʿbr gbwlk.

20:18 mlkyhwn d'dwmyy: for Heb. 'dwm; only the officials negotiated such arrangements. (The verse is lacking in N and was added from the margin.)

20:19 'rḥ mlk: for bmslh, based on drk hmlk in v. 17.

ksp zbwnyhwn: for Heb. mkrm.

lyt ml' byšh: for Heb. 'yn dbr.

20:20 wb'dr mnṭl': for Heb. wbyd ḥzqh; M: wbyd tqyph; Onk.: wbyd tqyp'; PJ: wbyd' tqypt'. Elsewhere, e.g. D 4:34, N uses this phrase for yd ḥzqh also, while 'drʿ mnṭlh is used for zrwʿ nṭwyh; every place zrwʿ nṭwyh occurs in the Torah it applies to God. The phrase wb'drʿ mnṭl' seems quite inappropriate here, even if we assume that it is additional to bydh tqyph, which originally preceded it and was deleted.

20:21 dhwwn mpqdyn mn 'bwhwn dbšmy' dl' lsdrh lqblyhwn sdry qrbh (+): It is obvious from the context that Moses preferred not to fight the Edomites, but it is not obvious that this was at God's command. Cf., however, D 2:5, 19, where God prohibited fighting against the descendants of Esau -- the Edomites -- and the Ammonites.

20:23 d'dwmyy: for Heb. 'rṣ 'dwm.

20:26 w'šlḥ 'hrn yt lbwšwy: for Heb. whpšṭ 't 'hrn 't bgdyw; wtlbš ythwn 'lʿzr, for Heb. whlbštm 't 'lʿzr. Under the circumstances, DM's addition of yt in v. 28 is suspect, but not impossible; cf. w'lbš ythwn yt 'lʿzr, v. 28, and G 37:23, where a similar phrase has been translated yt ... yt.

Chapter 21

21:1	Heb.		N
	wyšmʿ hknʿny mlk ʿrd	a.	wšmʿ knʿn'h mlk' dʿrd
	yšb hngb	b.	dhwh šry bdrwmh
		c.	'rwm 'stlq 'hrn gbr' ḥsydh
		d.	dbzkwtyh hwwn ʿnny 'yqrh mpqyn [read: mqpyn] yt yśr'l
		e.	w'rwm 'stlqt mrym nby'th
		f.	dbzkwth hwwt byrh slqh lhwn
	ky b' yśr'l	g.	'rwm mṭwn yśr'l

drk h'trym	h.	'rḥh dy slyqw bh yllyh
wylḥm byśr'l	i.	wsdrw qrbh ᶜm yśr'l
wyšb mmnw šby	j.	wšbwn mnhwn šbyh

The Hebrew is translated quite closely. Line b adds dhwh, perhaps under the influence of N 33:40, which reads wyšmᶜ hknᶜny mlk ᶜrd whw' yšb bngb .... Lines c-f are an obvious insertion; no conjunction has even been added to reintroduce the translation. Lines c-d and e-f are two balanced units that refer to the associations of Miriam with the well (cf. N 20:1-2) and Aaron with the clouds of glory. Otherwise the translation is literal except for line h. Onk., PJ, and M agree with N in this respect. The precise meaning of the hapax legomenon drk h'trym is unknown; cf. LXX odon atharin (Aramaized).

21:3 bydyhwn (+): needed in the Heb. also.

21:5 btr: for Heb. b-.

'trᶜmw (+): added to describe the reaction to Moses, but a different verb is used for the reaction to God (mlylw, for Heb. wydbr), though 'trᶜmw is used in similar contexts. Perhaps it is a double translation of wmlylw. It is similar to the translation of v. 7, which also has one verb in Heb. but two in Aram.:

N, N 21:5	N, N 21:7
wmlylw ᶜmh btr mmrh dyyy	mllnn btr mmrh dyyy
wᶜl mšh 'trᶜmw	wᶜlyk 'trᶜmnn

lyt ln lḥm lmykl wl' myyn lmyšty: for Heb. 'yn lḥm w'yn mym.

blḥmh hdyn dmyklyh qlyl: for Heb. blḥm hqlql, translated

with a similar sounding word.

21:6 N

a. brt ql' npqt mn gw 'rʿ'

b. w'yštmʿ qlyh brwmh

c. 'twn ḥmwn kl bryyth

d. w'twn 'ṣytw kl bny bśr'

e. lṭyt ḥwyh mn šrwyh

f. w'mryt lyh

g. ʿpr' yhwwy mzwnk

h. 'sqt ʿmy m'rʿ' dmṣrym

i. w'ḥtt lhwn mn' mn šmyy'

j. w'sqt lhwn byr' mn thwm'

k. w'gyzt lhwn slwwy mn ym'

l. wḥzrw ʿmy lmtrʿm' qdmyy

m. ʿl ʿsq mnh dmykly qlyl

n. yyty ḥwyh dl' 'trʿm ʿl mzwnh

o. wyšlṭ bʿm' d'trʿmw ʿl mzwnyhwn

p. bgyn kdn bry [DM: gry] yyy bʿm' yt ḥwyh śrpyth

q. wnktw yt ʿm'

r. wmytw ʿm sgyn mn yśr'l

Heb.

1. wyšlḥ yyy bʿm 't hnḥšym hśrpym

2. wynškw 't hʿm

3. wymt ʿm rb myśr'l

Lines a-b and c-d are rhymed, parallel stichs. Line b echoes Jer. 31:15 qwl brmh nšmʿ, translated by Jonathan as ql' brwm ʿlm' 'štmʿ, and basic to N and PJ as well. Lines a-b, unlike the poetic passages in N 11:26 and here in c-d ff., introduce rather than contain prophetic material. Lines e-g describe the punishment of the Snake in G 3:14, i.e., he will eat the dust; but f may be out of place. Lines h-m describe God's having provided manna, quails, etc. for the Israelites in the desert, who, however, ungraciously complained about them. The result is that the Snake, who acquiesced in his diet of dust, will rule over the Israelites (n-o). Accordingly, God sent poisonous snakes who bit and killed many of the people (p-r).

Lines p-r, contain the translation of the present verse, but many of the other lines are based on other Biblical passages. First, we consider the snake's punishment:

	N, N 21:6		N, G 3:14
f.	w'mryt lyh	(1)	w'mr yyy 'lhym lḥwyh
		(2)	'rwm ^{c}bdyt d'
e.	lṭyt ḥwyh mn šrwyh	(3)	lyṭ thwh ḥwyh
		(4)	mn kl b^{c}yr' wmn kl ḥywt'
		(5)	d^{c}l 'py brh
		(6)	^{c}l m^{c}k thwy šḥp
g.	^{c}pr' yhwwy mzwnk	(7)	w^{c}pr yhwy mzwnk
		(8)	kl ywmy ḥyyk

The connection between lines e-g and G 3:14 is unquestionable, though, the material has been reworded for inclusion here. These changes notwithstanding, the similarity between g and line (7) of G 3:14 is striking, particularly since they are not literal translations of the Hebrew, which reads w^{c}pr t'kl. This is all the more significant because Onk. and PJ translate G 3:14 literally, but PJ has ^{c}pr yhwy mzwnyh in N 21:6. (Frag., which is lacking to G 3:14, has ^{c}pr' yh' mzwnk). There are several possible directions in which we may proceed in evaluating these data. One may argue that the midrash in N 21:6 focuses on food rather than on eating. It is the Snake's food that is compared to the Israelites', and this necessitates the changes in N 21:6, attested in PJ and Frag. as well. Such a line of reasoning would consider the appearance of the same translation in G 3:14 as either coincidence or influenced by the passage in Numbers. The alternative would be to argue that the Genesis passage is primary and influenced the translation in Numbers. This would necessitate assuming that a differentiation between eating and food is unwarranted, and that the translation of PJ in G 3:14 has been altered to a more literal format (perhaps following Onk.). Both of these positions can be accommodated, however, if we assume that a common tradition of translating the phrase underlies the translation of both passages. The Palestinian way of translating wᶜpr t'kl was wᶜpr' yhwwy mzwnk, and this shows up everywhere except in PJ of G 3:14, which has been influenced by Onk. Thus there would be no interdependence of the translations of N 21:6 and G 3:14.

Lines h-m retell God's actions in caring for the Israelites. Line h resembles many verses (E 12:17, 29:46, L 19:36, 25:55, etc.), but is not identical to any of them. The main difference is the change of bny yśr'l or 'tm to ᶜmy. This personal touch further points up God's annoyance (cf. line l). N usually translates hwṣ'ty ... m'rṣ mṣrym as 'pqyt ... pryqyn mn 'rᶜ' dmṣrym; almost invariably the word pryqyn is included (E 29:46 is an exception). While M corrects its omission here and in E 29:46, the translation here belies the claim of a relationship between this midrash and N's translation of these verses.

Lines i-k describe the three types of food God provided: manna, water and quails. The lines, obviously similar in structure and rhythm, also rhyme; and I assume that this is not accidental. Lines i and k are based on Ex. 16 and Num. 11. The well in line j is less certain but, in all liklihood, refers to the events described in E 17:1 ff. These three events are associated in v. 5, in Ex. 16-17, and again in Ps. 78:20 ff. and Ps. 105:40-41. The association is thus not original with N, but the phrasing appears to be, even though it uses the standard words for each event.

Ungrateful for God's help, the people complained about the poor fare. Lines l-m are based on N 21:5, though there are other parallels as well. While lines h-m are based on the material in the previous verse, they are not a translation of it. The persons have been changed and God has mirrored the Israelites' complaints by repeating them as a list of his gifts. This same procedure has been followed in lines n-o, as well, where God states that he will send snakes against the people, mirroring the description of this action in v. 6. The punishment is made to fit the crime, because the Snake did not complaint about eating dust, while the Israelites complained about eating God's special food. The comparison, the explanation of this seemingly inappropriate punishment, and the story are now complete. While the translation of v. 6 is appended in lines p-r, it is unnecessary for the story line. Lines a-o are independent of lines p-r and may very well have existed independently.

The snakes described in v. 6 and in the translation (lines q-r) are not the Snake of the midrash. One might argue that *ḥwyh śrpyth* may be either singular or plural, but the verbs in q-r are definitely plural, while the *ḥwyh* of lines e-g and n-o is definitely singular (cf. *hnḥš*, v. 7). The point of the midrash is that the Snake of Gen. 3 will dominate the people (*wyšlṭ bᶜm'*), The point of the translation (lines p-r) is that God sent snakes against the people. Connecting them (lines n-o) makes the snakes the tools of the Snake, but in reality it is God, not the Snake, who controls them. The entire matter of domination by the Snake and his descendents is the substance of the curse as translated by N in G 3:15, but the emphasis on observance of the Torah in Gen. 3 belies any close relationship between the passages. (For additional discussion of some of this material cf. Bruce Malina, *The Palestinian Manna Tradition* (Leiden, 1968), Chapter II "The Manna Tradition in the Palestinian Targums.")

The linguistic differences between a-o and N are significant and probably point to a different origin for the midrash. Note, for example, *mn* for manna in line i, while N routinely uses *mn'* or *mnh* (cf. notes to 11:6). Verses 5 and 7 use the prhase *mlylw btr mmrh dyyy*, but line 1 has *lmtrᶜm' qdmyy*, which, though not improper, does not fit the established context.

21:7 Cf. v. 5.

ᶜl ydyhwn: routine for Heb. *bᶜd*.

21:8 *ḥywy dnḥš*: For Heb. *śrp*. Note, however, that in 21:6, line p *hnḥšym hśrpym* is translated *ḥwyh śrpyth*. This inconsistency results from borrowing the phrase *ḥwy dnḥš* from v. 9. God's instructions in the Heb. lack any reference to the material from which the snake should be made. This is provided by N.

'l 'tr tly: for Heb. *ᶜl ns*. The preposition *'l* is all but nonexistent in N. The text should probably read *ᶜl* as in Heb., M and I.

21:9 *wyḥy*: for Heb. *wḥy*, elsewhere translated as *'sy*, but this does not invalidate the authenticity of the omitted piece that DM added from the margin.

21:11 *bmgzt ᶜbryh*: for Heb. *bᶜyy hᶜbrym*.

21:14	Heb.		N
	ᶜl kn y'mr	a.	bgyn kdn ktyb wmpr̆š
	bspr	b.	bspr 'wryyth dyyy
	mlḥmt yyy	c.	dmtylh bspr qrbyyh
		d.	nsyyh dᶜbd yyy ᶜm yśr'l
	't whb bswph	e.	kd hwwn qyymyn ᶜl ym' dswp
		f.	wgbwrth dᶜbd ᶜmhwn
	w't hnḥlym 'rnwn	g.	kd hwwn ᶜbryn bnḥly 'rnwnh

The Hebrew is difficult, the targum less so. The JPS translation of the Hebrew suggests: (14) Therefore, the Book of the Wars of the Lord speaks of "... Waheb in Suphah, and the wadis: The Arnon (15) with its tributary wadis, stretched along the settled country of Ar, hugging the territory of Moab ...," reading vv. 14-15 together and seeing the bulk of the material as a fragmentary quotation. The above breakdown of the lines shows the correlation between the Heb. and N. N has focused on three elements in the Heb: the meanings of spr mlḥmt yyy and swph and the events associated with hnḥlym 'rnwn. The Heb. word swph (c) has been taken as an alternative of ym swp, The Sea of Reeds (cf. Onk.), where the Egyptian army was destroyed, and 'rnwn (g) is seen as the location of the victory over the Amorites (cf. vv. 21 ff.). Lines d and f expand the descriptions of these places and provide subjects for the participles ktyb wmpr̆š. The full texts of d-e and f-g, as well as the paraphrase of y'mr as ktyb wmpr̆š, eliminate any hint that lines e and g may be a quotation. They are paraphrases of the Torah, thus confirming and exemplifying the statement of b-c, that the Torah is like a book of wars.

Lines a-c are very similar to lines f-g of N in G 40:23 and must be the direct or indirect source of that passage, because the phrase spr mlḥmt yyy occurs only here. The notion in Gen. 40 that Joseph forgot what the passage from spr 'wryt' dyyy dmtyl' bspr qrby' is, of course, not in any way related to the passage in Numbers, -- indeed the idea he forgot is based on Jeremiah 17:5 -- but the terms come from N 21:14. The association is that God's military feats, recorded in the Bible, should have been known to Joseph, and he should therefore not have relied upon a mere mortal for help.

There is a grammatical inconsistency between the use of the singular ktyb wmpwrš in a and nsyyh (d) and wgbwrth (f). Frag., I, and (to some extent) PJ contain this inconsistency also. While it may point to a seam in the text, this is not certain. Lines d and f cannot be deleted, and converting nsyyh to a singular form is of no value, because there is still a compound subject with gbwrth (cf. 21:15 line k). The phrase ktyb wmprš is idiomatic and in N, at least, seems to occur only in the singular. It preceeds the subject by quite a few words and is an acceptable if imperfect construction.

21:15 The Hebrew v. 15 continues the material begun in v. 14, but this is not evident from the targum, which begins a whole new story.

N

a. kd hwwn yśr'l ᶜbryn bnḥly 'rnwnh

b. 'ṭmrw 'mwryy bgw mᶜryh dnḥly 'rnwnh

c. 'mryn kd yhwwn bny yśr'l ᶜbryn

d. 'nn npqyn lqblyhwn wmqṭlyn ythwn

e. wrmz rbwn kl ᶜlm' yyy

f. dydᶜ mh blbbyh

q. wgly qdmwy mh bkwlyth

h. rmz lṭwryh w'qpw ryšyhwn 'lyn l'lyn

i. wrṣyṣw ryšy gybryhwn

j. wšṭpw nḥlyh mn 'dmyhwn

k. *wl' hwwn ydᶜyn nsyh wgbwrth*

l. *dᶜbd yyy ᶜmhwn bnḥly*

m. *wmn btr kdn 'tpršw w'zlw lhwn l'tryhwn*

n. *lḥwwt qrth dy l' hwwt bᶜṣthwn 'štyzybt*

o. *wh' hy' smykh ltḥwmyhwn dmw'byy*.

Heb.

1. *w'šd hnḥlym*

2. *'šr nṭh lšbt ᶜr*

3. *wnšᶜn*

4. *lgbwl mw'b*

Lines a-d tell of the Amorites' plot to attack the Israelites, while e-l describe how God thwarted their plans. All of this material is apparently elicited by the Heb. *'šd hnḥlym*, translated "bottom of the ravines" (BDB) and "tributary wadis" (JPS), but in Onk. as *špwk lnḥly'*, subject to the interpretation "spilling blood" instead of "spilling water." Lines m and o expand lines 2-3 of the Hebrew; line n is supplementary. This story, prompted as much by the landscape as the Biblical context, helps explain the very difficult Heb. passage, while also relieving some of the tedium of a dry narrative.

The passage poses no serious textual problems. The word *'rnwnh* in b is redundant. Lines f-g are redundant, or, by other standards, parallel; Frag. also contains both. Line k contains the phrase *nsyh wgbwrth*, used to expand v. 14. The publicizing of God's heroic acts (*nsyh wgbwrth*) in v. 14 inherently contradicts the people's ignorance of them in v. 15, though the passages may refer to different events. There is a certain similarity between the styles of 14 d-g and 15 m-o. Allowing for the absence of an equivalent for line 1 of 15:1 (*'šd hnḥlym*), which would have been eliminated when 15 a-l were added, one might assume that the text of vv. 14-15 was once much briefer and consisted of 14 a-g, the equivalent of line 1 of Heb. 15, and 15 m-o, which translates the bulk of v. 15.

21:16 *'thybt lhwn byrh*: for Heb. *b'rh*; cf. Onk. *wmytmn 'tyhybt lhwn byr'*, and the end of v. 18.

21:17 *šyrt twšbḥth*: for Heb. *hšyrh*.

hwwn mzmryn lyh why' slq': for Heb. *ᶜnw lh*.

21:18

Heb.		N
b'r ḥprwh	a.	*byr' dḥprw yt* [read *yth*]
śrym	b.	*rbrbny ᶜlm' mn šrwyh*
	c.	*'brhm yṣḥq wyᶜqb*
krwh	d.	*šklylw yth*
ndyby hᶜm	e.	*skltnyhwn dᶜm'*
	f.	*šwbᶜyty ḥkymy dmpršyn*
bmḥqq bmšᶜntm	g.	*mšḥw yth bḥwṭryhwn*
	h.	*spryhwn dyśr'l*
	i.	*mšh w'hrn*
wmmdbr mtnh	j.	*wmn mdbrh 'tyhbt lhwn mtnh*

The Hebrew is composed of four stichs. Lines a-b and d-e form a synonymous parallelism; line g appears to be an extension of a-b and d-e. Line j is unrelated and could have been joined to v. 19, were it not the regular pattern of Heb. versification to limit verses like 19 to units the size of the present verse. N has treated j differently from the rest of the verse, but not literally. Mattanah is mentioned only in vv. 18-19 and is otherwise transcribed Manthanain (LXX) and Mathanem (*Onomasticon*, p. 61). It appears that *mtnh* in N is intended as a toponym; if not, its use of Heb. *mtnh* instead of Aramaic (Greek) *dwrwn* is noteworthy. Cf. ST mtnh, also the treatment in line a of v. 19.

The treatment of the rest of the verse is more significant. While the Heb. comprises two parallel lines (a-b and d-e) and one line of extension (g), the targum has created a text of three parallel units corresponding to the Heb.: a-b, d-e and g-h. These three units have similar structures (except for the very common mn šrwyh added in b), but each has been supplemented by one additional line a-b + c; d-e + f; g-h + i. In each case the supplementary line identifies the rulers mentioned in the previous line. The text of N flows smoothly and presents three nicely balanced units, belying the inconsistent treatment given to the Hebrew. What has happened here is very similar to the process described in G 27:29, where the Hebrew has been translated and glossed. In this case N presents the final stage of development, and the intermediate stage is found in Frag., where the third unit is explained, not simply translated and glossed:

g. spry' bḥwṭryhwn
h. hn hn spry' dyśr'l
i. mšh w'hrn
j. mn mdbr' 'ytyhybt lhwn mtnh

In this version, line g, Heb. bmḥqq bmšʿntm, has been translated spry' bḥwṭryhwn, not mšḥw yth bḥwṭryhwn (N, line g); and the introduction of hn hn is a clear statement of interpretation, identifying the people understood to be mentioned in g. This presentation would apper to be a little closer to the structure, if not the meaning, of the Heb., and corresponds to the inconsistent developmental stage preserved in N to G 27:29.

Also of note are differences in the contents of lines e-f. M glosses N with snhdryn dyśr'l šw-, while I has swkltny ʿlm' šwbʿyn (Ginsburger also notes the varient ʿm' / ʿlm' in line b). In this case, the use of skltnyhwn dᶜm' (e) in N appears preferable to the other versions, but dmpršyn (f) is difficult; bšmhwn may be needed, but note 11:26, line 16.

21:19-20	Heb.		N
19-	wmmtnh	a.	wmn d'tyhybt lhwn byr' mtnh
	nḥly'l	b.	ḥzrt lmhwwy lhwn lnḥlyn mtgbryn
	wmnḥly'l	c.	wmn dhwwt lnḥlyn mtgbryn
	bmwt	d.	ḥzrt lmhwwy (!) slqh ᶜmhwn lryš ṭwryh
		e.	wnḥth ᶜmhwn lḥlth ᶜmyqth
20-	wmbmwt	f.	wm dhwwt slqh ᶜmhwn lr'šy ṭwryyh rmth [DM: rmyh]
	hgy'	g.	wnḥt ᶜmhwn lḥlth ᶜmyqth
	'šr	h.	ytgnzt mnhwn bḥlth
	bśdh mw'b	i.	dbtḥwmyhwn dmw'byy
	r'š hpsgh	j.	ryš rmth
	wnšqph	k.	wh' hy' mṣṭpyyh
	ᶜl pny hyšymn	l.	kl qbl byt yšymwn

These two overlapping verses continue the description of the well. The general idea is that the well, known from previous Biblical encounters (v. 18), travelled over mountains and valleys, wherever the Israelites went (vv. 19-20). This notion explains the juxtaposition in vv. 17-20 of the account of the well, the song about it, and the seemingly unrelated travel information. To propose this idea, N treated the Hebrew quite expansively, transferring the places into categories of terrain in which the well travelled.

On mtnh, cf. notes to v. 16. Apparently line e is a dittography from v. 20, g. Lines d and f are almost identical except for the word *rmth*. This word is parallel to *ᶜmyqtn* in line g and the expected translation of *bmwt*; it should probably be added to line d (it is found in PJ but lacking in Frag. in both lines d and f). Lines g and h appear to be alternatives to the expansion of Heb. *hgy'*, but this results from the repetition of *lḥlth* / *bḥlth* (cf. the readings in Onk., Frag., and PJ). Our division of the material has retained both lines, thus following the pattern of one word in Hebrew to a line of Aramaic. While the pattern does not clearly govern lines h-i, the word *ytgnzt* may be associated with *'šr*, an idea that is sustained if *'šr* is perceived midrashically as *'šr* or *ᶜšr*.

21:24 *wšyṣy ytyh*: for Heb. *wykhw*.

21:26 *mlkyhwn dmw'byy qdmyyh*: for Heb. *mlk mw'b hr'šwn*. Though translations of singular nouns by plural ones are very frequent in N, this case is exceptional.

21:27 *mtwly mtlyyh*: for Heb. *hmšlym*.

21:28

Heb.		N
ky 'š	a.	*'rwm ᶜm gybryn bᶜryn hyk 'št'*
yṣ'h mḥšbwn	b.	*npqw mn ḥšbwn*
lhbh	c.	*ᶜbdy qrb kšlhbyth*
mqryt syḥn	d.	*npqw mn qrt' dsyḥwn*
'klh	e.	*šyṣwn*
ᶜr mw'b	f.	*lḥwwt mw'byy*
bᶜly	g.	[*qṭylw kwmryh* with DM]
bmwt 'rnwn	h.	*dhwwn mdbḥyn qdm bmth d'rnwnh*

The verse speaks of the Amorites' victory over the

Moabites in metaphoric terms; the translation has changed them to a simile but remains close to the Hebrew. The other significant change is in g-h, where *bʿly bmwt 'rnwn* "the masters of the Hights of Arnon" has been understood as a reference to the cultic high places (*bmwt*) and their priests (*bʿly* = *kwmryh*). This offers a justification for the destruction of Moab and fits well with the rabbinic need for Moab to have been absorbed by Sihon and his people: *ʿmwn wmw'b ṭhrw bsyḥwn*, BT Hul. 60B.

The expansion in line a seems to accomodate the Hebrew *'š* as both "man" (*'yš* = *gbryn*) and "fire" (*'š* = *'št'*). The word *kšlhbyth* (M: *b-*, I: *-hw-*) is a variation of *šlhbtyh*, Song of Songs 8:6, understood by the targum and other rabbinic texts as "the fire of Hell." It is not clear if the change of *-btyh* to *-byth* results from weakening of the *Yod*, scribal reordering of the letters, reading the Heb. as an Aramaic word, or some other influence.

21:29 *spwn 'štyswn*: for Heb. *'bdt*; cf. 17:28.

dhwwn mdbḥyn qdm ṭʿwwth (+): an added attack on Moabite paganism; cf. v. 28.

šlyln bqwlry': for Heb. *plṭym*.

lmlkyhwn: is a singular noun with a plural pronominal suffix "their king"; cf. v. 34, end.

21;30	Heb.		N.
	wnyrm 'bd ḥšbwn	a.	*wpsqt mlkw mn ḥšbwn*
	ʿd dybn	b.	*wšlṭwn mn dybwn*
	wnšym ʿd npḥ	c.	*wṣdyyn 'rḥtyh ʿd krkh dnpḥyh*
	'šr ʿd mydb'	d.	*dsmyk lmytb'* (!)

The translation is expansive, but keeps to the general theme of the text. The poetic qualities of the translation are more noticeable, in some respects, than those of the Hebrew. Addition of *wšlṭwn* in b not only creates the word pair *mlkw* / *wšlṭwn* (a common hendiadys in N), it also improves the meter and rhythm. Lines a-c rhyme with b and d respectively, but the defective rhythm of c-d suggests this may be by coincidence as much as by design.

21:32 *wšyṣwn*: for Heb. *wyyrš* (*Qere*: *wywrš*).

21:34 N

a. *whwh kd ḥm' mšh lᶜwg mlk' dbwtnyn*

b. *dḥl w'rtt mn qdmwy*

c. *w'mr hl' dyn hw' ᶜwg*

d. *dhwh mḥsd l'brhm wśrh*

e. *w'mr lhwn 'brhm wśrh mdmyyn l'lnyn y'yn*

f. *qyymyn ᶜl mbwᶜyn dmyyn*

g. *brm pyryn l' ᶜbdyn*

h. *bgyn kdn qyym yyy ytyh*

i. *ᶜd zmn dḥm' bnyhwn wbny bnyhwn*

j. *w't' wnpl bydyhwn*

k. *wmn btr kdyn*

l. *'mr yyy lmšh*

m. *l' tdḥl mn qdmwy*

n. *'rwm bydk msryt ytyh wyt kl ᶜmyh*

o. *wtᶜbd lyh hyk mn dᶜbdt*

p. *lsyḥwn mlkyhwn d'ymwryy*

q. *dy hwwh šry bḥšbwn*

Heb.

1. wy'mr yyy 'l mšh
2. 'l tyr' 'tw
3. ky bydk ntty 'tw w't kl ᶜmw w't 'rṣw
4. wᶜśyt lw k'šr ᶜśyt
5. lsyḥn mlk h'mry
6. 'šr ywšb bḥšbwn

The Heb. of vv. 33-34 describes how the Israelites, when confronted by the soldiers of Og, were told by God not to be afraid because he would render them victorious. The translation of the Hebrew is found in lines l-q and is literal, except that w't 'rṣw has been omitted from N (but added in I). Line k is a transition to l-q from the introductory midrash in a-j. The midrash itself amplifies the reason for Moses' fear, which is assumed to be the stimulus for God's reassurance in l-q (cf. N, G 1:19) and is articulated in a-b. N goes on to tell how Og mocked Abraham and Sarah (c-d) by comparing them to beautiful but fruitless trees (e-g). God, therefore, kept Og alive (h) until he could be defeated by the multitudes of descendents of Abraham and Sarah (i-j), punishing him for his crime in rabbinic fashion, measure for measure.

Upon close reading there appears to be little connection between a-b and c-j, though a-b relate closely to l-q. To join a-b to c-j, one must explain why Moses was afraid if he, in fact, knew that Og's destiny included being defeated by Abraham's descendents. Possibly, Moses knew of Og's future defeat, but did not know it was imminent, hence the emphasis on "you" in the Hebrew (bydk). Moses' fear may then have been based on a concern for the immediate present and the possibility, suggested by Og's advanced age, that the latter was immortal. Accordingly, God assured him that Og's time had run out. Alternately, one might argue that h-j are not presented as Moses' words, but as the comment of the midrash. Moses would then know about Og's curse, but not about God's promise of punishment. In fact, lines h-j are unnecessary, for m-q provide an equally strong divine reassurance. And the curse in c-g is similarly not needed, though it helps to explain the possible cause of Moses' fear. The only really important addition is a-b, which reacts to the Hebrew verse at hand and explains why the verse recounts God's reassurance to Moses. Lines a-b begin by introducing the statement that Moses was afraid. The units c-d, e-g and h-j in sequence embellish this fear, but each unit or sequential group of units from a-b on may exist independently of those subsequent to it.

The occurence of the passage (with minor differences) in PJ and Frag. and in M to D 3:2, argues for its unity; and indeed it makes sense and flows smoothly as preserved. But a prehistory also seems recoverable and points to a time when the units may not have been joined. The real point of c-j is to explain why Og survived until the time of Moses, while a-b are concerned with why God told Moses not to fear Og, though no such warning was needed for the battle against Sihon. Moses' fear may have been aroused by Og's arrival; but, if so, the midrash has devoted too much space to Og's attack on Abraham and not enough to the real issue. To some extent this results from the use of Ps. 1:3 in e-g (discussed below), but even if this were reduced or omitted, little would change. The text is thus clearly composite.

Lines e-g are based on Ps. 1:3, which describes the ideal righteous man:

(a) whyh kʿṣ štwl ʿl plgy mym

(b) 'šr pryw ytn bʿtw ...

Lines c-f are close to line (a), while line g expresses a notion almost diametrically opposed to line (b). The Targum of Psalms reads wyhy k'yln ḥyy dnṣyb ʿl ṭwrpy mwy dy 'ynbyh mbšl bʿydnyh.

This is obviously not the basis of the midrashic text in N. Lines 4 ff in G 49:22 read *mdmy 'nh lk ywsp bry lgpn štylh ʿl mbwʿyn dmyyn*..., but my analysis there demonstrated that passage to be closer to Jer. 17:8 than to Ps. 1:3. The image is a popular one in N, but the translations are not interdependent.

Chapter 22

22:3 *tqypyn*: taking Heb. *rb* as "strong" rather than "multitudinous," Cf. G 1:22, etc., where *prw wrbw* is translated *tqypw wsgwn*, and v. 5. In v. 6, *tqypyn* is used to translate *ʿṣwm*.

22:4 *kl qyrwy' dy ḥzwr ḥzwr*: an expansive translation of Heb. *'t kl sbybtynw*; cf. Onk.: *yt kl sḥrnn'*, PJ: *yt kl ḥzrnwtn'*.

blšnyh (+): expansive.

22:5 *ḥlmyyh* (+): According to the following story, Bilaam had visions and nocturnal communication from God, but the word "dream" (*ḥlm*) does not appear in the Hebrew. Even if it is an appropriate description of some of his prophecies, the word seems out of place in N. If it means "dreamer" it should precede *ptwrh* and be a singular form. The word *ptr*, however, is the verb for interpreting a dream, and, according to M, Frag. and PJ, the toponym Pethor is to be understood as *ptr ḥlmyh*; hence M: *ptwr*, Frag.: *ptwr ḥwlmy'* and most clearly PJ: *hy' ptwr ʿl šmyh ptyr ḥlmy'*. This reads the Heb. *ptwrh* as Aramaic "the interpreter" and reapplies the subsequent *'šr ʿl hnhr* to Bilaam rather than to the place.

sgyn (+): expansive. This may be based on the Heb. *rb*

in v. 3, but there it was translated *tqypyn*. Note also v. 11.

22:7 *wgryn dqsmyn*: for Heb. *wqsmyn*.

ḥtymyn (+): expansive, making the magical materials (*qsmyn*) inscribed or sealed in their hands.

22:8 *ywm' hdyn* (+): Unless the messengers arrived at nightfall, they would have had to wait part of that day as well. Note, in contrast, v. 19.

22:11 *mh y'ykwl*: read *mh dylm' d'ykwl*.

22:13 *lyt rᶜwh mn qdm yyy*: for Heb. *m'n yyy*.

22:19 *sqwn* (+): not supported by M, Frag., PJ or Onk.

mh ywsyp mn qdm yyy lmtmllh ᶜmy: for Heb. *mh ysp yyy dbr ᶜmy*. Note the mixture of active and passive constructions that betrays an earlier literal translation.

22:30 N

a. *w'mrt 'tnth lblᶜm*
b. *lhn 't 'zl blᶜm ršyᶜ' ḥsyr dᶜth*
c. *mh 'n 'nh*
d. *d'nh bᶜyr ms'b*
e. *wmyth bᶜlm' hdyn*
f. *wl' 'tyyh lᶜlm' d'ty*
g. *lyt 't ykyl lmlwṭ yty*
h. *ᶜl 'ḥt kmh wkmh*
i. *bnwy d'brhm dyṣḥq wyᶜqb*
j. *dbgllhwn 'tbry ᶜlm' mn r'š*
k. *wbzkwwthwn hw' mdkr* [DM: *mdbr*] *qdmyhwn*

l. mh 't ykyl lmylṭ ythwn

m. wdy ṭlmt b'pyhwn dgbryh h'lyyn

n. lyt hd' 'tnth dydy

o. š'lh hy'

p. hl' 'nh 'tnk dy rkbt ᶜlyy

q. mn ṭlywtk ᶜd ywm' hdyn

r. h' mtkwwnh mtkwwnt lmᶜbd lk kdyn

s. w'mr l'

Heb.

1. wt'mr h'twn 'l blᶜm

2. hlw' 'nky 'tnk 'šr rkbt ᶜly

3. mᶜwdk ᶜd hywm hzh

4. hhskn hsknty lᶜśwt lk kh

5. wy'mr l'

The Hebrew contrasts the lively statement of Bilaam's ass with Bilaam's rather meek response, and the translation stresses this disparity even more by expanding the ass's 4 lines of Hebrew to 17 of Aramaic, while retaining Bilaam's one-word answer as it is. The ass's statement -- now a speech -- has been augmented by adding a lengthy passage (b-o), comprised of two unrelated sections, between lines 1 and 2 of the Hebrew. Lines b-l mock Bilaam for his failure to realize his lack of power. If he cannot effectively curse his ass, an impure beast with no share in the world to come, how can he fare better against the Israelites, for whom the world was created? Lines m-o rebuke Bilaam for excusing his inability to handle the animal properly by telling his fellow travellers that she belongs to someone else and are responsible, as will be shown, for the insertion of lines b-l.

The Hebrew of v. 30 seems to play on the emotional

attachment between Bilaam and the ass: they have been through a lot together; the animal has been loyal; how can Bilaam be so cruel as to curse her ? The Aramaic has preferred to see v. 30 as emphasizing the authenticity of the relationship, thus responding to some unstated denial by Bilaam of its veracity. This interpretation of the Heb. is made explicit by the insertion of lines m-o, which refer to Bilaam's claim not to own the ass, but that insertion simultaneously creates a gap in the story line, for Heb. v. 30 is no longer seen as a reaction to the curse in v. 29. Accordingly, lines b-l have been introduced to respond to Bilaam's curse by pointing to its futility and, going further, to Bilaam's *a fortiori* powerless state vis a vis the Israelites.

Lines b-l are a logical deduction, introduced by *mh 'n*, executed by *ʿl 'ḥt kmh wkmh*, and completed by *mh 't ykyl*. Similar formulations are common in rabbinic texts, but it is interesting that the Hebrew form of the expression is used in line h, not the Aramaic *ʿl ḥd kmh wkmh* as in G 44:18. Similarly *mn r'š* (j) is Heb., while N routinely has *mn šrwyh*, Frag. *mn šyrwy'*. Note also *mh 't* for the expected *lyt 't* (l). Lines j-k are somewhat redundant. Frag. and PJ both contain equivalents of j but not k, which may be secondary.

The translation itself, begun in a and completed in p-s, is quite close to the Hebrew. Heb. *mʿdk* (line 3) is translated simply as *mn ṭlywtk* and the root *skn* (line 4) is presented as *kwn* (r).

22:31 *qym mtʿtd*: sometimes used for Heb. *nṣb*; cf. Onk. and PJ: *mʿtd*; but note *h' 'n' qyym mʿtd ʿl ʿny' dmy'*, G 24:13, 43; *h' 'n' qyym mʿtd ʿl ryš rmt'*, E 17:9, It is always used for Heb. *hnh 'nky nṣb*, also in v. 34, where this is not the case, but usually N has *qyym* or *mʿtd*, e.g. *wh' yyy qyym ʿlwy*, G 28:13, *qyymyn ᶜlwy*, G 18:2, or *wh' 'tᶜtd*, N 23:6 (M: *mᶜt-*).

22:32 *lmsṭn lk*: for Heb. *lśṭn*, but cf. *lśṭn lw* in N 22:22, translated *lmsṭn lh*.

22:33 *'ylw*: for Heb. *'wly*.

Heb. *gm* has been omitted from the translation.

22:34 *l'tryh*: for Heb. *ly*.

22:39 *lkrkh dmlkwth hy' mryšh* [DM: *bryšh* or *brwšh*] : for Heb. *qryt ḥṣwt*. PJ in N 32:37 reads *byryš* (for *qrytym*), but here *byrwś'*; most vocalized texts have a *Shin*. Onk. has *qryt mḥwzwhy* here, but *qrytym* in 32:37 (variant: *qryt*); cf. *Onomastikon*: *Kareatha*, and *Bare*, noted by Eusebius to be near Medaba, known also as Baris. The reading in N is unusual, but whether it is a simple error or a phonetic interchange of *b-m* is difficult to say.

22:41 *mn qṣt ᶜm'*: for Heb. *qṣh hᶜm*; cf. 23:13.

Chapter 23

23:1 Delete the first *twryn*.

23:2 *ᶜl kl mdbḥ*: for Heb. *bmzbḥ*, taking it to refer to each of the seven built in v. 1; also in vv. 4, 30, etc.

23:3 *yhwwy yyy*: for *yr'ny*; perhaps *yyy* should be *yty*.

w'zl blᶜm blb yḥydy špy lmylwṭ yt yśr'l: for Heb. *wylk špy*. Heb. *špy* is difficult, but it is clear that N contains a double text *blb yḥydy* and *špy*. Note also the double texts with blbh šlmh (for Heb. yḥdw) in G 22:6, 8. Addition of the subject (here blᶜm) has been documented frequently, and lmylwṭ yt yśr'l is a simple expansion.

23:7 bmtl nbwth: for Heb. mšlw; note that Heb. wy'mr has been omitted from the translation.

zᶜyr ly: for Heb. zᶜmh, M: w'zᶜr; PJ, Frag.: zᶜyr; Onk.: tryk. The word lwṭ is often used for zᶜm in the translation of other parts of the Bible, but it was already used in this verse, and a substitute was required. Here, and in v. 8, the targumim apparently preferred the homophony and lack of repetition to the literal translation. Note the emphasis on the multitude of Israelites in 22:5, 11, etc. In this context zᶜyr is very appropriate, suggesting the curse would reduce their numbers.

23:8

Heb.		N
mh 'qb	a.	mh 'nh lyyṭ [Add: ythwn?]
l' qbh 'l	b.	wmmryh dyyy msgy [DM: mbrk] ythwn
wmh 'zᶜm	c.	mh 'nh mzᶜr ythwn
l' zᶜm yyy	d.	wmmryh dyyy msgy ythwn

Most interpreters understand this verse as two questions that mean "How can I curse those not cursed by God?" Assuming that mbrk should be added (with DM), God's actions are rendered with positive rather than negative terms: mbrk for l' qbh and msgy for l' zᶜm. But it is not clear that N should be read as questions; it may also be seen as containing two statements. Note the use of zᶜr and sgy, the concern of v. 7.

23:9 Heb.		N
ky *'r'nw*	a.	*'rwm* *ḥmy* *'nh*
	b.	*ᶜm'* *h'lynn* *mdbryn* *w'tyyn*
mr'š (note the change	c.	*bzkwt* *'bhth* *ṣdyqyh*
ṣrym in word order)	d.	*dmtylyn* *bṭwwryh*
	e.	*'brhm* *yṣḥq* *wyᶜq-*
wmgbᶜwt *'šwrnw*	f.	*wbzkwt* *'mhth* *ṣdyqth*
	g.	*dmtyln* *bglmth*
	h.	*śrh* *rbqh* *rḥl* *wl'h*
hn *ᶜm* *lbdd* *yškn*	i.	*h'* *ᶜm'* *h'lynn* *šryyn* *lblḥwdyhwn*
wbgwym *l'* *ytḥšb*	j.	*wbnymws* *'wmyh* *l'* *mtᶜrbyn*

The targum has replaced the first two lines of synonymous parallelism with expansive, non-literal translations. Lines a-b of the Aramaic have replaced *'r'nw* and *'šwrnw*, while *r'š* *ṣrym* and *gbᶜwt* have been understood figuratively as the patriarchs (c-e) and matriarchs (f-h). The genders of *ṣwrym* and *gbᶜwt* have facilitated this association, but the association is a very common one in rabbinic literature. Cf. e.g. BT R.H. 11a, PT San. 10:1, *Torah* *Temimah* to G 1:27 and Song of Songs 2:8, etc. The word pair *hrym* - *gbᶜwt* is quite common in the Bible, and it seems to have become almost routine for it to have been interpreted in this manner.

The last two lines have been translated quite literally. One may question if the Aramaic is based on a reading of *wkgwym* or *wbgwym*, but the use of the preposition in *wbnymws* supports the MT.

23:10 Heb.		N
my *mnh*	a.	*mn* *ykyl* *lmymny*
yᶜqb (note the	b.	*ᶜwlymyhwn* *dbyt* *yᶜqb*
changed order)	c.	*d'yt'mr* *ᶜlyhwn*

ᶜpr	d.	dy hwwn mbrkyn kᶜpr' d'rᶜ'
wmspr	e.	'w mn ykyl mskwm
't rbᶜ yśr'l	f.	ḥdh mn 'rbᶜty ṭksy mšryth dbny yśr'l
	g.	d't'mr ᶜlyhwn
	h.	yhwwn msgyn kkwkby šmy'
	i.	'mr blᶜm bmtl nbwth
	j.	'n qṭlyn ytyh yśr'l bḥrbh
	k.	mbśr hw' blᶜm
	l.	dlyt lyh ḥwlq lᶜlm' d'ty
tmwt npšy mwt yšrym	m.	brm 'n myyt blᶜm mwtyn qšyṭyn
	n.	lwwy tyhwy swpyh
wthy 'ḥryty	o.	'lwwy tyhwy 'ḥryth
kmhw	p.	kzᶜyrh dbhwn

The Hebrew consists of four stichs that form two pairs of two lines each. Lines a-h present the first two and j-p the last two; more precisely, the text may be divided a-d, e-h, i, j, k-l, and m-p.

The first half of the verse was perceived as Bilaam's reaction to the fullfilment of God's promise about the number of Israelites (wmspr in e may reflect a vocalization of umesapper not umispar as in MT). The first Hebrew stich uses the metaphor "dust" ᶜpr to describe the numerous descendents of Jacob, parallel to rbᶜ, taken as a reference to the four Israelite camps that travelled together in the wilderness (cf. Num. 2). This interpretation of rbᶜ, found in e-f, is anticipated in b, where ᶜwlymyhwn has been introduced. This change in order is similar to e-h and has been supported rather artfully by line d's having been based on the recurring phrase ᶜpr h'rṣ, which occurs in G

13:10 etc., but also is part of God's promise to Jacob in G 28:14.

Line h, the last in the unit, contains, like line d, a paraphrase from Genesis. G 15:5 expresses God's promise that Abraham's descendents would be as numerous as the stars, a commitment repeated to Abraham in G 22:17 and to Isaac in G 26:4 and also found frequently in Deut. Though this promise was not made directly to Jacob (the closest parallels are G 28:14 and 46:4), it is mentioned with respect to all three patriarchs in E 32:13, where Jacob is called Israel, the name used in this half of the Hebrew verse as well.

While the non-literal translations in a-d and e-h are balanced and relate to passages in Genesis, the expansion, in fact, grows out of the metaphoric use of *ᶜpr* in the Hebrew. It is this word that stimulated the use of *ᶜwlymyhwn* and the accompanying explanation *d't'mr ᶜlyhwn* .... Stylistic considerations, together with the expansive translation of *rbᶜ*, generated the parallel structure of e-h.

If line i is taken as the conclusion of a-h, rather than the introduction of j-p, the contents of a-h are labeled a prophecy, called *mtl* (Heb. *mšl*) in v. 7. Line i thus forms an *inclusio* with the beginning of v. 7 *wnṭl bmtl nbwth* ... *'mr blᶜm bmtl nbwth*. This emphasizes the difference in content between the text presented in vv. 7, 8, 9 and the first half of v. 10 and the two lines at the end of v. 10. These concluding statements, though poetic, were not perceived as part of Bilaam's prophecy about Israel, and the insertion of line i at this point separates them from the other prophetic material. The other poetic units in these chapters are 23:18-24, 24:3-9, 24:15-19, 24:20, 24:21-22, and 24:23-24. In each case the poetry is introduced by the phrase *wyś' mšlw wy'mr*. In 23:23, 24:4, and 24:16 (one verse from each of the lengthy passages), N includes comments relating parts of Bilaam's oracles to his own situation, thus pointing to two different types of material believed to be present in the oracles -- prophecies about Israel and prophecies about Bilaam's own situation. Note, also, that Joseph's interpretations of dreams (at least as now preserved in N) also contain applications to the dreamer and to Joseph (the Israelites). Similarly, Jacob's statements to his sons as presented in N (Gen. 49) fluctuate between predictions of the future and personal matters.

The second half of v. 10 thus deals with Bilaam's personal situation. The Hebrew records Bilaam's wish to die a righteous man and have his future ('ḥryty) be like Israel's. The Hebrew is in the first person and undoubtedly convey's Bilaam's desire to identify with the nation he was brought to curse. The translation in N has altered both aspects of the material. The Aramaic speaks of Bilaam only in the third person (ytyh, lyh, swpyh, etc.) and allows him to identify with Israel only under certain conditions (m) and only as an insignificant (or cursed, cf. zyᶜr in vv. 7-8) member of the group. Anticipating his wish to die the death of the righteous (Heb. m), lines j-l note that if Bilaam were to be killed, he would declare, as did his ass in 22:30, his lack of a share in the world to come. The alternate possibility is expressed in lines m-p, the paraphrase of the rest of the verse. Lines n and o are a double text; o is found in Frag. and M and is closer to the Hebrew, but n is paralleled in Onk. and PJ. Apparently o is preferable.

23:11 mbrkh (+): There is no obvious reason for this addition here, but it is paralleled in PJ and Onk. and may reflect the Heb. brkt brk in 24:10.

23:12 Read mymryh dyyy.

23:14 lḥql skyyh: for Heb. śdh ṣpym.

23:18 wnṭl bmtl nbwth w'mr: for Heb. wyś' mšlw wy'mr; cf. notes to v. 10.

23:19

Heb.		N
l' 'yš 'l wykzb	a.	l' kmymr bny 'nš'
	b.	mymryh dyyy
wbn 'dm wytnḥm	c.	wl' kᶜwbdhwn dbny 'nš'
	d.	ᶜwbdwy dyyy
hhw' 'mr wl' yᶜśh	e.	bny 'nš' 'mryn wl' ᶜbdyn
wdbr wl' yqymnw	f.	gzryn wl' mqyymyn
	g.	wḥzryn wkpryn bmylyhwn
	h.	brm 'lhh 'mr wᶜbd
	i.	gzr wmqyym
	j.	wptgmy nbw'th qyymy lᶜlm

Lines a-b correspond to the Heb. of line a, while c-d correspond to c. N has expanded and paraphrased the Hebrew, avoiding the metaphor in its regular way. Lines e-f correspond to the Heb., to which they are very close (changes of singular to plural are routine), so g appears to be extra. As presented, g provides a third line in the unit e-g, parallel to the third line of h-j; but it is also possible that it is a double translation of the end of either e or f, wl' ᶜbdyn and wl' mqyymyn. Both e and f are closer to the Hebrew, however, and no internal evidence favors replacement of one or the other. Frag. is like N. Note, however, the parallel in Onk.:

1. l' kmly bny 'nš' mymr 'lh'
2. bny 'nš' 'mryn wmkdbyn
3. w'p l' kᶜwbdy bny bśr'

4. d'nwn gzryn lmᶜbd

5. tybyn wmtmlkyn

6. hw' 'mr wᶜbyd

7. wkl mymryh mtqyym

The lack of rhythm in Onk. stems from the intrusion of line 2 between lines 1 and 3. Line 3 should probably conclude with ᶜwbdy 'lh'. Line 2 would be most appropriate after line 3, corresponding to its position in N as line e. This creates a three line unit (2, 4, 5) corresponding to that found in N as e, f, g and explains both the origin of g and its relationship to the rest of this passage. In Onk. lines 4-5 are one thought, but line f of N (=4) has been expanded to parallel e (=2), while g (= 5, but originally the second half of 4) has been left as an incomplete phrase (actually a paraphrase from the Aramaic of Onk. to the Aramaic of N).

The Hebrew of the verse is clear but asymmetrical. The first two lines are parallel, as are the last two, but the latter pair dwells on the failure of man to carry out his promises rather than on the ability of God to carry out his. The desire to correct this imbalance lies behind the addition of h-j, paralleled in Onk. 6-7. As noted, the final text of N contains two antithetical three-line units. e-g and h-i. It is difficult to determine if both were expanded simultaneously, but the unit e-g seems less redundant and perhaps stimulated the other addition. Also of note in this regard are the liturgical parallels to h-j. Both 'mr wᶜbd (h) and gzr wmqyym (i) are found together in the prayer Barukh SheAmar: brwk 'wmr wᶜś́h, brwk gwzr wmqym, based, in all likelihood, on the formula suggested in BT Ber. 57b. Line j is similar to the line found in the High Holiday Amidah, wdbrk 'mt wqym lᶜd, but the similarity is not as close as that noted for lines h and i. The wish for literary balance and the availability of appropriate liturgical prose have helped in the development of the text.

23:20	Heb.		N
	hnh brk lqḥty	a.	*h' lmbrkh 'dbryt*
	wbrk	b.	*mbrk 'nh yt yśr'l*
	wl' 'šybnh	c.	*wbrkh lyt 'nh mnʿ mnhwn*

Line a apparently read Heb. *lqḥty* as passive, not active. Lines b-c are expansive.

23:21	Heb.		N
	l' hbyṭ	a.	*lyt 'nh ḥmy*
	'wn	b.	*ʿbdy šqr*
	byʿqb	c.	*bdbyt yʿqb*
	wl' r'h	d.	*wl'*
	ʿml	e.	*ʿbdy plḥn nkryy*
	byśr'l	f.	*bdbyt yśr'l*
	yyy 'lhyw ʿmw	g.	*mymr yyy 'lhhwn ʿmhwn*
	wtrwʿt mlk	h.	*wybbwt zyw 'yqr mlkyhwn*
	bw	i.	*mgn ʿlyhwn*

The person of *l' hbyṭ* has been changed to *lyt 'nh ḥmy* (as if it said *l' 'byṭ*), but otherwise a-i are simple expansions, where virtually every word in the Hebrew has become a line of Aramaic. Many of the expansions are routine, i.e. *bdbyt yʿqb* for *byʿqb*, *bdbyt yśr'l* for *byśr'l*, addition of *mymr*, etc. Noteworthy is the omission of *r'h* (d); *ḥmy* in line a is used for both *hbyṭ* and *r'h*. Also *wtrwʿt mlk bw* has been modified to eliminate the anthropomorphism. The nouns in b and e have been read as *nomina agentis*; cf. v. 23.

23:22 pryqyn is lacking in N, M and I, but routinely used in such constructions. It is found in PJ and Frag. but not in Onk.

dy twqp' wtwšbḥth wrwmmwth dydh 'ynwn: for the anthropomorphic ktwᶜpt r'm lw. The phrase twqp' wtwšbḥth wrwmmwth is of standard doxological fabric, similar to, though not based on, 1 Chron. 29:11 (which was incorporated into the liturgy and is recited at least four times per week). The line in Chron. was expanded in the targum a.l. also, but there is no connection with the material found here.

23:23 Heb.		N
ky l'	a.	'rwm lyt 'nh ḥmy
nḥš	b.	nṭwry nḥšyn
byᶜqb	c.	bdbyt yᶜqb
wl' qsm	d.	wl' qsmy qsmyn
byśr'l	e.	bdbyt yśr'l
kᶜt	f.	bᶜdn' hdyn
y'mr lyᶜqb	g.	yt'mr lbyt yᶜqb
	h.	ṭbth wnyḥmth dᶜtyd myytyyh ᶜlykwn
wlyśr'l	i.	wddbyt yśr'l
	j.	'mr blᶜm bmtl nbwth
	k.	twbykwn ṣdyqyh
mh pᶜl 'l	l.	mh 'gr ṭb mtqn lkwn mn(!) qdm yyy
	m.	lᶜlm' d'ty

Stylistically v. 23 is like v. 21, but the expansions are sometimes more extensive. The phrase lyt 'nh ḥmy (a) has been borrowed from 21 a (or the untranslated r'h of 21 d). Heb. nḥš is vocalized naḥaš and is assumed by the MT to be the object used for divination, or perhaps the act itself; but N read it as the nomen agentis. The identical procedure has been followed with *qsm* (d) and occurred in 21 lines b and e, as well. The translation *nṭry nḥšyn* occurs in L 19:26 also.

The Hebrew *y'mr lyʿqb wlyśr'l* has a referent, *mh pʿl 'l*. N preferred to split *yʿqb* and *yśr'l*, and added line h for this purpose; line h is associated with the verb *yt'mr* in g, and lines k-m with the verb *'mr* in j; *ṭbth wnyḥmth* in h is a routine hendiadys. Line j resembles 23:10, line i, and introduces Bilaam's concern for the world to come. The phrase *ṭwbykwn ṣdyqyh* is probably a vocative construction, *ṭwbykwn* being "leaders," *agathoi*. Line l is quite expansive, but at least part of this change results from the avoidance of the anthropomorphism. Note, also, the similarity between lines g-m and the second version of 24:5 (lines c-d).

23:24 Heb.		N
hn ʿm klby' yqwm	a.	*h' ʿm' k'ryyh šryyn*
wk'ry ytnś'	b.	*wk'rywwth mtnṭlyn*
	c.	*'rwm hyk mh d'ryh*
l' yškb	d.	*l' nyyḥ wl' dmk*
ʿd y'kl ṭrp	e.	*ʿd zmn d'kyl pšwṭ*
wdm ḥllym yšth	f.	*wšty 'dm* [with DM]
	g.	*kdn ʿm' h'lyyn*
	h.	*l' nyyḥyn wl' škdyn* [DM: *šdykyn*]
	i.	*ʿd dqṭlyn bʿly* [d]*bbykwn*
	j.	*wyšpkwn 'dm qṭwlyhwn kmyy'*

Though it is clear that the people are compared to a lion, the Hebrew is ambiguous about whether the description (d-f) applies literally to the lion, figuratively to the people, or simultaneously to both. (A literal application to the people is ruled out by rabbinic canons of taste, if not Biblical ones). N applies the description to both; but treats it literally for the lion (c-f) and figuratively for the people (g-j). The two descriptions are contained in a standard rabbinic rhetorical frame *hyk mh d- ... kdn ....* This procedure thus avoids the possible implication that the Israelites consumed human flesh and blood and the problem of identifying the subject of the description. In all other respects the translation is quite close to the Hebrew.

23:28 *ṭᶜwwth pᶜwr*: for Heb. *hpᶜwr*.

byt hyšymwn: for Heb. *hyšymn*.

Chapter 24

24:1

Heb.		N
wyr' blᶜm ky ṭwb bᶜyny yyy	a.	*wḥmh blᶜm 'rwm špr hwh mn qdm yyy*
lbrk 't yśr'l	b.	*lmbrkh yt yśr'l*
wl' hlk	c.	*wl' 'zl*
kpᶜm bpᶜm	d.	*hyk mh dhwh 'zl bkl zmn*
lqr't nḥšym	e.	*lmš'lyh bdkryh* [DM: *bdykrh*] *lqdmwt qsmyh*
wyšt 'l hmdbr pnyw	f.	*w'zl wšwy lmdbrh 'pwy*
	g.	*whwh mdkr lhwn ᶜbdh dᶜglh*

Much of the verse has been translated quite closely, but additions have been made in d, e, and f, while g is entirely new. Lines d and e are simple expansions, and *w'zl* in f was introduced because of *wl' 'zl* in c. The extra line g results from Bilaam's desperate situation. Having failed to curse the Israelites through conventional means, he has chosen to recall their sin with the golden calf, in the hope it will serve to break down their defenses by denying them God's favor.

24:2 lṭksyhwn: for Heb. lšbṭyw; cf. 23:10.

23:3 dpᶜwr: for Heb. bᶜwr. This may be a phonetic shift b-p, or a conscious attempt to associate Bilaam with Peor as in 23:28, etc; or both.

dyqyr mn 'bwy mh d'ksy mn kl nbw'h 'tqly ᶜlwy: The phrase dyqr mn 'bwy is added, but the remaining words embellish the Heb. štm hᶜyn.

24:4

Heb.		N
n'm šmᶜ 'mry 'l	a.	'ymr dšmᶜ mymr mn qdm yyy ᶜlyh
'šr mḥzh šdy yḥzh	b.	dy ḥzyw šdy hwh ḥzy
	c.	wkd hwh ḥzy
npl	d.	hwh mšṭṭḥ ᶜl 'pwy
wglwy ᶜynym	e.	wrzy nbw't[h] mtglyn lh
	f.	whwh mtnb' ᶜl npšyh
	g.	dnpyl bḥrb'
	h.	wswp nbw'tyh lmtqyymh

The translation begins in a literal manner (for ᶜlyh, cf. notes to v. 16) but changes after line b. Line c is a double translation of Heb. b that takes 'šr as k'šr "when," rather than as "who," as in b, dy .... It has been added to introduce d, expanded in N by the idiomatic ᶜl 'pwy. Line e is also expanded for clarification. Lines f-h are added to continue the series of Bilaam's prophetic references to his own future. The line 'mr blᶜm bmtl nbwth (e.g. 23:10, i) is lacking. Line g is an alternate interpretation of Heb. npl (d), while h corresponds to wglwy ᶜynym (e). The latter was rendered in e as wzrzy nbw't[h] mtglyn lh. In h, the same word nbw'tyh is applied, but the prophecy is to come true: wswp nbw'tyh lmtqyymh. Though presented for two different purposes, d-e and g-h are, in essence, parallel translations of the same Hebrew words. Line g (and h), of course, is based on N 31:8 w't blᶜm bn bᶜwr hrgw bḥrb.

24:5 N

1 a. mh y'yyn mšknyhwn dbyt yᶜqb

b. bzkwt mšknyh dytyb bhwn yśr'l 'bwkwn

2 c. kmh ṭbn wnḥmn mmryh ᶜtyd myytyyh ᶜlykwn ddbyt yᶜqb

d. bzkwt byt mdršyyh dšmyš bhwn yśr'l 'bwkwn

3 e. mh y'y hw' mškn zymn' dšry bynykwn ddbyt yᶜqb

f. wmšknyhwn dy ḥzwr ḥzwr lh dy dbyt yśr'l

Heb.

1. mh ṭbw 'hlyk yᶜqb
2. mškntyk yśr'l

The two lines of Hebrew have been presented three times in succession, lines a-b, c-d and e-f. Additional translations are found elsewhere:

M: a. mh ṭbn hnwn byt [DM: bty] mdršyyk dbyt yᶜqb

b. wbty knštk dbyt yśr'l

Onk: a. m' ṭb' 'rᶜk yᶜqb

b. byt mšrk yśr'l

Frag: a. mn' ṭbyn 'ynwn mšknyn dṣly bhwn yᶜqb 'bwhwn

b. wmšknyn dᶜbdtwn lšm' dyyy

c. wmšknykwn ḥzwr ḥzwr lkwn byt yśr'l

PJ: a. *km' y'wwn hynwn bty mdryšykwn bmškny' dy šmyš bhwn yᶜqb 'bwkwn*

b. *wmh y'y hw' mškn zymn' dmyyṣᶜ bynykwn wmšknykwn dḥzwr ḥzwr lyh byt yśr'l*

ST: a. *mh ṭbym mšknyk yᶜqb*

b. *wmšrwyk yśr'l*

Aside from the literal Samaritan Targum, Onkelos (who translated the verse in a non-literal manner), and the citation in Rashi that says that *mškntyk* is translated *ḥnywtyk*, all of the other texts focus on one or more meanings of *'hl* and *mškn* in other Biblical contexts in order to explain the occurrence here. "Tent" (*'hl*) may refer to simple tents in which the Israelites lived, as in N, a; to the "tent of meeting (*'hl mᶜd*) as in N, c, e; or, by extension, to the tent used by Jacob in Genesis. These associations usually begin with G 25:27, where Jacob is called *yšb 'hlym*, but allow for all sorts of interpretations that tie in with the standard rabbinic interpretation of *'hl* as academy or synagogue (cf. M, Frag, PJ, etc). The second line of the text uses the word *mškn*, which immediately calls to mind the Tabernacle (Heb. *mškn*), but use of *'hl mᶜd* = *mškn zymn'* in the first line precluded repetition in the second. Since Aramaic *mškn* means "tent," it was quite simple for the second line of the Hebrew to refer to any tent that could be associated with the one mentioned in the first line, e.g. Israelite tents surrounding the Tabernacle (N e-f, Frag., PJ) or synagogues with academies (M). The logic of these associations notwithstanding, other groupings, mixtures, and apparent lacunae have produced the various versions noted above.

Comparison of the three texts in N reveals certain marked similarities and differences. The first and third begin *mh y'yyn* and *mh y'y*, a fairly common expression in N (cf. G 49:11, 12, etc.); the second begins *kmh ṭbn* ... Translations 1 and 2 begin the second line with *bzkwt*, while 3, which refers to the tents surrounding the Tabernacle, does not (an observation true of this text in PJ and Frag. as well). It is impossible to determine which reading is the original one in N, if there ever was only one, but 3 seems to be the most likely. Translation 2 does not conform to the accepted associations and uses the less frequent introduction *kmh* ..., though phrases like *ṭbn wnḥmn* have been used routinely. Translations 1 and 3 appear in slightly different form in PJ, while 3 is also found in Frag.

24:6	Heb.		N
	knḥlym nṭyw	a.	*knḥlyn mtgbryn*
		b.	*kdn yhwwn yśr'l mtgbryn ʿl bʿly dbbykwn* (!)
	kgnt ʿly nhr	c.	*kgynyn štylyn ʿl mbwʿyn dmyyn*
		d.	*kdn yhwwn qwryyhwn mpqn ḥkymyn wbny 'wryyh*
	k'hlym nṭʿ yyy	e.	*kšwmh dmtḥzy* [DM: *kšmyyḥ dmth yyy*] *lbyt škynh lh*
		f.	*kdn yhwwn yśr'l ḥyyn wqyymyn lʿlm*
	k'rzym ʿly mym	g.	*y'n wmšbḥyn k'rzyyh dmyyn*
		h.	*wmšbḥyn wmnṭlyn bbrywth*

Though lines a, c, e and g correspond to the Hebrew, they are not really translations of it. In line a, *nḥlym* is understood as "rivers," whence the use of *mtgbryn*; the gloss in b applies the word to Israel. Line c corresponds to the Hebrew but expands *ʿly nhr* into the customary *štylyn ʿl mbwʿyn dmyyn*. The gloss in d explains the simile, as did b; in this case, the water symbolizes the study of the Torah. Line e continues the comparison, taking *'hlym* as "tents," a symbol for the heavens (accepting the reading suggested by DM). The association of earthly dwellings and the heavens may seem a little far-fetched, but compare the interpretation of *sukkot* in L 23:43 as the clouds of glory. The meaning of *skh* as "covering" was applied to both the booths and to the cloud overhead, and a similar association may be intended here between *'hl* and the heavens.

Lines a-f follow the pattern of paraphrasing a line of Hebrew (a, c, e) and glossing it with an explanation that relates it to Israel (b, d, f). One might anticipate the same treatment of the fourth line of Hebrew, but this has not occurred in N. N's arrangement is evident in PJ to some extent, but there is no evidence of a paraphrastic rendition of the Heb. of g, which might have introduced g-h but has been lost. Lines g-h are repetitive, at least structurally, but the repetition lends a note of finality to the end of the passage and retains the balance of paired lines even though it breaks the established pattern of glossing. Had the Hebrew been translated, it would have read *k'rzyh* *štylyn* *ʿl* *mbwʿyn* *dmyyn*, and the similarity to line c may have prompted the translator to prefer this other format.

24:7	Heb.		N
	yzl mym mdlyw	a.	*yqwm mlkyhwn mn bynyhwn*
		b.	*wprwqhwn mnhwn yhwwy*
		c.	*yknš lhwn glwthwn mn mdynt bʿly dbbyhwn*
	wzrʿw bmym rbym	d.	*wbnwy yšlṭwn b'wmyn sgyn*
		e.	*ytqp mn š'wl*
	wyrm m'gg mlkw	f.	*rḥm ʿl 'gg mlkyhwn dʿmlqyy*
	wtnś' mlktw	g.	*wytrwmm mlkwtyh dmlk' mšyḥ'*

Associative links for lines e, f and g are obvious; that for yzl mym mdlyw is less so. The Hebrew continues to describe the scene in v. 6, but N has given the entire passage a messianic orientation. In the process, the first two lines of Hebrew have been expanded into four lines of Aramaic, while the last two lines of Hebrew have become three lines of Aramaic. This lack of symmetry results from the addition of line e, which introduces Saul in order to clarify the reference to Agag (cf. 1 Sam. 15:4 ff). The line is found in Frag., also, but it is not really essential for the meaning and interrupts the rhythm of the verse.

Line f begins rḥm in N, but Frag. has dy ḥs and DM prefers dḥs. The two words look very much alike, but it is far from clear that such a change is needed. According to 1 Sam. 15:9, Saul had compassion on Agag (Heb. ḥml, Jonathan wḥs š'wl ...). But the word rḥm is no less appropriate, and provides another link between the Hebrew and the Aramaic. Assuming a weakened Heth and/or a connection with Akkadian rêmu, wyrm and rḥm correspond quite closely.

24:8 Heb.		N
'l mwṣy'w mmṣrym	a.	'lh dy 'pq ythwn pryqyn mn mṣrym
ktwᶜpt r'm lw	b.	tqph wtwšbḥth wrwmmwth dydh [with DM] 'ynwn
y'kl	c.	y'klwn bny yśr'l
gwym ṣryw	d.	nksy 'myh bᶜly dbbyhwn
wᶜṣmtyhm ygrm	e.	wgwbrhwn yqṭlwn
wḥṣyw ymḥṣ	f.	wqwryyhwn yṭlwn wyplgwn

The Aramaic follows the Hebrew but varies with respect to literal treatment of it. Line a is close to the Hebrew; note mwṣy'w (sing.) but 'pq ythwn (pl.), corresponding to mwṣy'm in the Heb., based on 23:22. Line b replaces the comparison of God to an animal with a commonly used doxology. Line c has been augmented by the addition of the subject, while *nksy* has been added to d to eliminate any possibility of reading the text as a reference to cannibalism. Lines e and f have been paraphrased, the latter building on a possible word play of *ḥṣ*, "arrow," and *ḥwṣ*, literally "outside" but frequently used as part of a city or the surrounding territory.

24:9	Heb.		N
	krʿ škb k'ry wklby'	a.	*nyḥyn wšryn k'ryh wk'rywwth*
	my yqymnw	b.	*wlyt 'wmh wmlkw dtqwm lqb [lyhwn]*
	mbrkyk brwk	c.	*mn dmbrk ythwn yhwwy mbrk*
	w'rryk 'rwr	d.	*wmn dlyyṭ ythwn yhwwy lyṭ*

The similarities with G 49:9 are obvious in both the division of the Hebrew (after *wklby'*) and the translation of lines a-b.

24:11 Add *ytk* after *'yqr*. Perhaps the word occurs after *yyy* in the phrase *ytk mnk*, but this looks like a double translation of the pronominal suffix on Heb. *mnʿk*. DM, following the scribe, has omitted *ytk* before *mnk*.

24:14 N

a. *wkdwn h' 'nh 'zl lwwt ʿmy*

b. *'t' 'ʿwṣ ytk ʿṣh*

c. *'ḥty ythwn*

d. *w'yn l'*

e. *lyt 't ykyl šlyṭ bhwn*

f. *brm ʿtydyn 'ynwn ʿm' h'lyyn*

g. mšlwṭ bᶜmk

h. swp ᶜqb ywmy'

Heb.

1. wᶜth hnny hwlk lᶜmy

2. lkh 'yᶜṣk

3. 'šr yᶜśh hᶜm hzh lᶜmk

4. b'ḥryt hymym

Lines a, b and h are close to the corresponding Hebrew of lines 1, 2 and 4. Line 3 is not translated, but a specific prediction in f-g has replaced the general one of 3. Line c contains the advice offered but not specified in b (=2), and d-e warn of the consequences of failing to cause the Israelites to sin. Bilaam now advises causing new sins, for merely mentioning past ones is not sufficient.

24:15 Cf. notes to v. 3; with minor orthographic differences, the verses are the same.

24:16 Verses 4 and 16 are identical in Hebrew except for the addition of wydᶜ dᶜt ᶜlywn, which is found in v. 16. N has translated this wydᶜ dyᶜh mn qdm ᶜlyh here, of which ᶜlyh is also found in v. 4. It is probably testimony either to the clause having once been found there also or to a copying error (it is lacking in Frag. to v. 4). For other analysis cf. v. 4.

Given the similarity between the verses and their relative proximity, the orthographic differences between them are remarkable.

N, N 24:4		N, N 24:16
'ymr dšmʿ mymr mn qdm yyy	a.	'mr dšmʿ mymr mn qdm yyy
ʿlyh	b.	wydʿ dyʿh mn qdm ʿlyh
dy ḥzyw šdy hwh ḥzr [or ḥzh]	c.	wḥzyw šdy hwh ḥzy
wkd hwh ḥzy	d.	wkd hwwh bʿy
hwh mšṭṭḥ ʿl 'pwy	e.	hwwh mšṭṭḥ ʿl 'pwy
wrzy nbw't (!) mtglyn lh	f.	wrzy nbw'tyh mtglyyn lyh
whwh mtnb' ʿl npšyh	g.	whwh whwh (!) mtnb' ʿl npšyh
dnpyl bḥrb'	h.	dhwh npl bḥrbh
wswp nbw'tyh lmtqyymh	i.	wswp nbw'tyh lmtqyymh

Following the order of lines there are at least six minor differences in spelling and four in word usage: 'ymr - 'mr; the difference noted above for line b; dy - w-; ḥzr - ḥzy; hwh - hwwh (3x, but not everywhere in v. 16); ḥzy - bʿy (bʿy is probably to be preferred); nbw't - nbw'tyh (both should be nbw'tyh); dnpyl - dhwh npl; bḥrb' - bḥrbh. These passages were copied by the same scribe.

24:17 Heb.		N
'r'nw wl' ʿth	a.	ḥmy 'nh lyh wl' kdwn
'šwrnw wl' qrwb	b.	mstkl 'nh byh wlyt hy' qrybh
drk kwkb myʿqb	c.	ʿtyd mlk lmqwm mn dbyt yʿqb
wqm šbṭ myśr'l	d.	wprwq wšlyṭ mn dbyt yśr'l
wmḥṣ p'ty mw'b	e.	wyqṭl tqypy mw'byy
wqrqr kl bny št	f.	wyšyṣy kl bnwy dšt
	g.	wyrwqn mry nksyyh

The substitutions of *mlk* (c) and *prwq wšlyṭ* (d) for *kwkb* and *šbṭ* are so unobtrusive, that were it not for their messianic content they would be worthy of almost no special mention. The phrase *prwq wšlyṭ* occurs rarely; much more frequently N uses *mlk wšlyṭ*. As seen in v. 8, etc., parts of the body are translated as references to warriors.

Line g is unnecessary, but does provide a parallel line to f. Frag. has *wyrwqn kl bny mdynḥ'* for the Heb. of line f. Onk. generalizes even further with *wyšlwṭ bkl bny 'nš'*. PJ offers a different approach:

(1) *wyrwqn kl bnwy dšt*

(2) *mšyrytyh dgwg dʿtydyn lmsdr' sydry qrb' byśr'l*

(3) *wyplwn pygryhwn kwlhwn qdmwy*

While line (2) is a gloss for (1), line (1) combines the important features of f and g. N and PJ are related; perhaps g is best seen as a double or expansion of f.

24:18 *yṣlḥwn bnksyn sgyn*: for Heb. *ʿśh ḥyl*; cf. D 8:18 for a similar usage.

24:19	Heb.		N
	wyrd myʿqb	a.	*ʿtyd mlk lmqwm mn dbyt yʿqb*
	wh'byd śryd mʿyr	b.	*wyšyṣy mn dmtḥyyb mn krkh ḥyyb'*
		c.	*hy'* ...

See the description of the lacuna and suggested restorations in DM. It seems that the gap existed in the text copied by the scribe of N,

24:20

Heb.		N
wyr' 't ʿmlq	a.	wḥm' yt ʿmlq'h
wyś' mšlw wy'mr	b.	wnṭl bmtl nbwth w'mr
r'šyt gwym ʿmlq	c.	šrwy 'wmyh dsdrw [qrbh] ʿm yśr'l ʿmlqyy
	d.	wbʿqbh bywmwy dgwg wmgwg
	e.	'ynwn ʿtydyn msdrh lqblyhwn sdry qrbh
w'ḥrytw ʿdy 'bd	f.	wswpyhwn l'bdn yhwwy
	g.	w'bdnhwn ʿd lʿlm

The beginning of the verse is translated literally, but the word 'ḥrytw (f), with its apocalyptic associations, stimulated the expansion in lines c-g. The extra words in line c refer to the first Amalaqite attack in E 17:8-16; that expected in the days of Gog and Magog (d-g) will be the last. The contrast between "first" (c) and "last" (f) has been reworked into this historical scheme.

The duplication in f-g is similar to those noted in vv. 6, 17, 24, etc., but is suspect nevertheless. Frag. is very similar to N; M reads only brm swpyhwn l'wbdn ʿlmy', but its text in this verse is nowhere identical to N; PJ concludes brm swpyhwn d'ylyyn wd'ylyyn ʿd ʿlm' yhwy l'wbdn', but it, too, varies throughout.

24:21 šlmyyh: for Heb. hqyny; cf. v. 22, G 15:19, etc.

Heb.		N
... 'ytn mwšbk	a.	... mh tqyp hw' mšrwyk
wśym bslʿ qnk	b.	wšwyt bnyqr' dkyph yt mdwrk

Line a interprets the Hebrew as an exclamation, rather than a prophecy or counsel. Line b takes qnk as "dwelling" (mdwrk) and expands bslʿ into two words. The reference may point to Petra, the Nabatean capital. The expression nqrt hṣwr occurs in E 33:22; but there it refers to where Moses was kept safe from the glory of God's presence and is translated nqrh dṭynr' in N.

24:22 lbyzh: for Heb. lbʿr.

ʿd kʿn: for Heb. ʿd mh, also Frag.; PJ: ʿd kdy, Onk.: ʿd m'.

24:23

Heb.		N
wyś' mšlw wy'mr	a.	wnṭl bmtl nbwth w'mr
'wy my yhyh	b.	'lwwy mn yyhy bywmy' h'ynwn
mśmw 'l	c.	kd yšwwy yyy tqwp rwgzyh
	d.	lmtprʿh mn ršyʿyh
	e.	lmytn 'grhwn dṣdyqyh
	f.	wbzmnh [with DM] dy ygrh mlkwth
	g.	'lyn l'lyn

Line a is formulaic; cf. 23:7, 18; 24:3, 15, 20, 21. The addition of bywmy' h'ynwn (b) helps introduce the future scene described in c-g. The presumably negative 'wy (b) has been rendered in a positive sense as 'lwwy, and mśmw (c) has been translated as yšwwy. The stock phrases in d and e are also used in G 3:24, 4:8, etc. and might have once concluded the passage. Though wbzmnh is balanced with bywmy' h'ynwn in b, lines f-g are extra and may anticipate the following verse.

24:24	Heb.		N
	wṣym	a.	*ypqwn 'wklwsyn sgyn* [*blbrnyyh*
	myd ktym	b.	*ʿzy*] *lšwn mn mdynt* [*'yṭly'* + ?]
		c.	*dhy'* ...
		d.	*wyṣṭrpwn ʿmhwn lgywnyn sgyn mn* [*drwmyy*]
	wʿnw 'šwr	e.	*wyšʿbdwn 'twryyh*
	wʿnw ʿbr	f.	*wyṣʿrwn ʿbr nhr'*
	wgm hw' ʿdy 'bd	g.	*wswpyhwn l'bdn yhwwn*
		h.	*w'bdnhwn ʿd lʿwlm*

The verse 24 continues the description of the eschaton. Scribal omissions or censorship have complicated the analysis, and the words in brackets follow the suggestions of DM. Lines e-f are close translation; and g-h are very similar to the end of v. 20. The major problem is with *wṣym myd ktym* (a-b). If *ṣym* is taken as "ships," it has been translated as *lbrnyyh* (a), but there is no reference to *myd ktym* in a. Most scholars agree that *ktym* in the Dead Sea Scrolls refers to the Romans, and this same usage may be reflected here and in the association *mn mdynt 'yṭly'* in b. There is no indication of the length of the lacuna in line c, so no judgement can be made on the relationship of d to c; but even if *drwmyy* (d) is taken as "Romans," *ktym* is probably best understood as the basis for b, not d.

The literature describing Jewish messianic speculations frequently cites material from this chapter of Numbers as sources and proof texts for the predictions; cf. *Midreshei Geulah*, pp. 102-3, 135, 278-9, etc. In several places, e.g. p. 135, 278, the Hebrew of a-b is associated with the Romans, thus supporting DM's reconstructions. BT San. 106a also contains an interpretation of this passage, but it exists in a wide array of versions, e.g. *lbyn 'spr*, *lybwn 'spyr*, *lyyw'bn spwr*, *lyybw 'spyr*, *lykwn 'spwr*, etc. (cf. Rabinowitz, Diqduqei Soferim, a.l.). Jastrow (p. 96b) notes lgywn also (cf. Y.S., a.l.,). but prefers the identification as Leon the Isaurian. The use of lgywn in d, together with drwmyy, allows us to perceive line d as a possible double for part of b, but the proliferation of warring parties in this literature is so great that no certain conclusion is possible. The ᶜzy lšwn (b) is a variant of ᶜz pnym (Dan. 8:11), a routine element in texts that deal with this material.

24:25 ḥzr l'tryh: for Heb. hlk ldrkw. The Heb. says that Bilaam went home and Balaq "also went his way" The "also" (wgm) may have prompted using the same expression for both men.

w'qym bntyh ᶜl prh rbh (+): This addition details how Balaq carried out Bilaam's advice in v. 14 -- that the only way to overcome Israel is to cause them to sin. According to other midrashic sources, Bilaam suggested tempting the Israelites to promiscuity and they succumbed (cf. Philo, Moses 1:54-55, Josephus, Antiquities 1V 6:6-9, Sifrei, pp. 131, 157, Mid. Tanḥ., Balaq 15, etc.). Balaq used Moabite girls for the plot (hence bntyh); but it is very unlikely that their purpose was for propagation, as suggested by N. The standard MH term for fertility is pryh wrbyh (with a conjunction); N reads prh rbh. The reading rbyh in I notwithstanding, there is no reason why Balaq would have wanted his women impregnated by Israelites, even though this might have cemented the relationship between the two already related nations. The spelling prh is probably a variant of brh "outside," used to translate ḥwṣ in D 23:13-14 (in a different context), G 24:31, etc. The word ḥwṣwt regularly refers to "the open places," "streets," etc. In fact a prostitute is called npqt br, e.g. G 34:31, 38:15, etc. Balaq's women went to prh rbh, "the great outdoors," to seduce the Israelites. Cf. prwyr for Heb. mgrš in 35:3, 4, etc.

Specific places where hwṣ means "street" are usually translated šwq, especially when used for a street where special items were sold (e.g. Jer. 37:21, 9:20). The idea here, however, is not that they met outside or in the streets but in the open, uninhabited areas. The Hebrew term rḥwb, usually translated as rḥwb, is of no use in understanding the passage. The strongest support for the notion comes from PJ, which has a longer version of the story and locates the places bpršt 'wrḥt'.

According to PJ, Balaq located his people from byt hyšymwt to ṭwwr tlg', but their purpose was commerce, a notion which might be derived from the statement that he went ldrkw "on his way" (as a travelling salesman). PJ does not mention prostitution, though in some midrashim the men were initially attracted by low prices and then seduced. The texts of both PJ and N can thus be understood without the prostitution motif, which derives from the first verse of the next chapter. N can be understood in the light of this explanation as well, prh rbh, read as prt rbh "The Great Euphrates," could replace the geographic areas listed in PJ; note that in BH bnwt frequently means "cities."

Chapter 25

25:4	Heb.		N
	wy'mr yyy 'l mšh	a.	w'mr yyy lmšh
	qḥ 't kl r'šy hᶜm	b.	dbr yt kl r'šy ᶜm'
	whwqᶜ 'wtm lyyy	c.	w'qym ythwn bsnhdryn qdm yyy wyhwwn dyynyn
		d.	kl mn dmtḥyyb qṭlh
		e.	yṣlbwn ytyh ṣlybh
	ngd hšmš	f.	wqbryn yt nblthwn ᶜm mṭmᶜy šmš'

wyšb ḥrwn 'p yyy	g.	*bkdn yḥzwr tqwp rwqzh dyyy*
myśr'l	h.	*mn yśr'l*

Lines a-b and f-h are close to the Hebrew. Lines d-e derive from v. 5. The phrase *ngd hšmš* (f) "in broad daylight" has been understood in the very limiting sense of "only in daylight"; hence the admonition to bury the executed before nightfall, based on D 21:23. The seriousness of the punishment described here is emphasized in D 21:23. The phrase *ᶜd mṭmᶜ' šmš'* is used in E 22:25 to translate *ᶜd b' hšmš*.

25:5 *'nšy ᶜmyh*: for Heb. *'nšyw*.

lplḥy (+): expansive.

25:8 *qhl'*: for Heb. *hqbh*; DM suggests *qwlh*.

25:13 *wlzrᶜyt*: read either *wlzrᶜytyh* with I or *wlzrᶜyt bnwy*; cf. 26:5 ff.

25:14 Read *dšbṭh dbnwy dšmᶜwny*, following the pattern established in chapter 1 and followed throughout the book.

Chapter 26

26:2 Add *dbny yśr'l* before *mn br*.

npqy qrbh: for Heb. *yṣ' ṣb'* (sing.). Note also the expression *npqy ḥyl qrbh* used in 1:3 and other terms discussed there.

26:9 *dy plgw qdm yyy*: for Heb. *'šr hṣw*. The word *hṣw* is rare, and *plg* is an appropriate translation, but it may also have been helped by the similarly sounding *ḥṣw*; cf. *hmsw 't lbbynw*, D

1:28, explained in PT Maʿas. 1:2 as plgwn lbbynw.

26:10 bzmnh d-: for Heb. b-; cf. v. 10.

kd tklt: for Heb. b'kl.

lnsywn: for Heb. lns, also in PJ.

26:11 ʿl dy l' hwwn bʿṣth d'bwhwn (+): explanatory gloss; cf. 27:3 where a similar claim is made by the daughters of Zelophehad about their father.

26:12 Note the inconsistency between the use of zrʿyth dbnwy d- in vv. 7, 18, 22, 25 etc. and zrʿyth d- in vv. 12, 14, 15. The longer form seems to be preferred throughout N.

26:54 lšbṭ' dʿm' sgyn: explanation of Heb. lrb, to eliminate other possible meanings of the word.

wlšbṭ' dʿm' zʿyryn: for Heb. wlmʿṭ; cf. v. 56.

26:61 'š' bryh: for Heb. 'š zrh, as in L 10:1.

Chapter 27

27:2 wqdm (+) the fourth time is extra, to follow the established pattern in the verse.

27:3 wbnyn dkryn: for Heb. wbnym. Here and in the following verses the problem centers around the lack of male offspring, so the emphasis on bnyn dkryn is appropriate, though the word bnyn, if not the story line, should have sufficed to eliminate any misunderstanding. In fact, the usage is idiomatic, as bn is often translated bn dkr.

27:5 For a full evaluation, see L 24:12. Some details are also discussed in N 9:8 and 15:34. The verse is translated at the very end of the passage.

27:7 *kdyn*: for Heb. *kn*. The translation is attested elsewhere, but may be incorrect in this context; cf. *y'wt wqwšṭ' mllt* in E 10:29, a double translation of *kn dbrt*, and *y'wt* in N 36:5. Can *kdyn* be *kadin*?

27:9 Read *brth* or *brh nqbh* (not *brh* as in I) for Heb. *bt*: cf. G 30:21, E 1:16, 21:31, N 36:8.

27:14 *bmy dyyny ʿm knyšth*: for Heb. *bmrybt hʿdh*. Cf. *nsyywnyh wdyynwwtyh*, E 17:7; *my' dyynyh*, N 20:13, 24.

27:16 *'lh dšlyṭ bnšmt kl bśr'*: for Heb. *'lhy hrwḥt*, as in 16:22.

mhymn (+): expansive, following 12:7.

27:17 *lsdry qrb', mn sdry qrb' bšlm* (+): explanatory additions that play on the use of *yṣ'* as military activity elsewhere. Note the lack of this translation in v. 21.

27:18 *qdš mn qdm yyy* (+): routine expansion with *rwḥ*.

27:19 *wqdm rbrbnyh* (+): The addition is appropriate and reflects the inclusion of the leaders elsewhere (e.g. v. 2). It is not found in the repetition in v. 22.

27:20 *yt mn*: possibly a double translation of Heb. *m-*; cf. Onk., PJ: *m-*. DM suggests reading *mn* as *m'n* "garment," but the emendation is unnecessary to support this meaning. This use of the garment would make the transfer of authority from Moses to Joshua parallel those from Aaron to Elazar and from Elijah to Elisha. The interpretation that would underlie a translation of yt (rather than mn) was rejected in BT B.B. 75a, where the word mhwdk is glossed by mhwdk wl' kl hwdk, a common rabbinic interpretation of the preposition m-.

27:21 gzyrt (+): expansive; eliminates literalness of the BH (2x).

Read hw' wkl bny yśr'l.

27:23 Read hyk mh with I.

Chapter 28

28:2	Heb.		N
	ṣw 't bny yśr'l w'mrt 'lhm	a.	pqd yt bny yśr'l wtymr lhwn
	't qrbny lḥmy	b.	yt qrbny lḥmy
		c.	lḥm sdwr ptwry
	l'šy	d.	mh dy 'twn mqrbyn qdmyy
		e.	hl' 'št' hy' d'klh ytyh
	ryḥ nyḥḥy	f.	why' mtqbl mnkwn qdmy lryḥ drʿwh
		g.	ʿmy bny yśr'l
	tšmrw lhqryb ly bmwʿdw	h.	hwwn zhyryn lmqrbh ytyh bzmnyh

Lines a-b are literal translations, but c is a gloss to b, if not a double translation (cf. E 25:30). Lines d and e explain l'šy. Normally, the singular 'šh is translated qrbn (e.g. E 29:25, 30:20), and the word sdr is a frequent addition.

The expansion in d-e is, therefore, not only unusual, it also makes this passage seem like an introductory one, explaining a term already used dozens of times in Exodus and Leviticus. Liturgical usages may account for this development. According to M Meg. 3:6, N 28:11-15 was read on the New Moon, but a few paragraphs later in 4:2 (or earlier in those editions where chapters 3 and 4 reversed) the Mishnah notes that four portions (of three verses each) were required on that day. Since it is impossible to divide N 28:11-15 into twelve verses, the reading was expanded to encompass N 28:1-15, making N 28:2 a monthly opportunity for the translator to add to the text in the interest of educating his listeners and possibly demonstrating his skills. Indeed, since 28:1-8 describe the daily sacrifices, the text may have been used every day. (Cf. my comments on 7:17).

The term ryḥ nyḥḥ is usually translated mtqbl lryḥ drᶜwh. This eliminates the anthropomorphic objection, but the more expansive way it is translated in f seems also to be motivated by educational concerns. Whatever its purpose, the explanation in e-f effectively alters the syntax of the verse and splits the Hebrew into two sentences. The first states that the sacrifice is accepted as ryḥ nyḥḥ, reading this term as a predicate complement, instead of an appositive. The second, consisting of the now disassociated clause in h introduced by the insertion in g, sets forth the brief law concerning the sacrifice. It also provides an extra verse if needed to meet the minimum verse count for Torah readings on the New Moon.

Line h appears close to the Hebrew, but Heb. ly has been rendered as if it meant "to him," as it can in Aramaic.

Comparison with PJ discloses the seeming absence from N of several significant lines of text:

(1) yyklwn khny' (after c)

(2) lyt ršw lgbr dyykwl mynyh (after d);

hence the note of DM transmissio hujus v mendosa. Actually, however, the translation is fine, except for line c. If lḥmy is understood as "bread," its identification with the show bread, arrayed on the table (ptwry), makes sense, and DM is correct in looking for the distinction between this and the sacrifices, as in PJ. But lḥmy should, in all likelihood, be understood as "food" or "meat" (cf. Arabic lḥm and the rabbinic references to this meaning in Ex. Rab. 42:4, etc.). Unless N is just a truncated version of the text in PJ, line c is either a gloss or an alternate translation of b. As a gloss it would only confuse the issue, but perhaps sdwr ptwry was intended as a replacement for lḥmy in an attempt to eliminate God's referring to the sacrifices as "my food." The desire to remove offensive anthropomorphisms is well documented throughout N. (Note, however, that the term lḥm 'lhyk, L 21:8, etc. is translated literally.)

28:4 ytyh (+): unnecessary, also in v. 8.

28:7 ḥmr (+): cf. the expression wnskw yyn rbyᶜt hhyn, L 23:13, translated wnswkwy ḥmr rbᶜwt hynh in N and F.

tqrbwn (+): expansive.

bmny byt qwdšh: for Heb. bqdš.

ḥmr bḥyr: for Heb. škr.

28:9 tqrbwn (+): added in imitation of vv. 7, 8, etc., as in v. 10.

'ynwn wnskyhwn: for Heb. wnskh.

28:10 bywm šbth: for Heb. bšbtw.

tqrbwn ytyh (+): adding a verb and forming a sentence.

28:11 The MS reads ... twryn bny šthwn twryn tryn .... It should say twryn bny twryn tryn. The word šthwn has been added in imitation of the many places where bny šthwn is used (e.g. later in the verse). DM has omitted an extra word; cf. v. 19.

28:13 mtqbl seems misplaced, but cf. 29:6.

28:14

Heb.		N
wnskyhm	a.	wnswkyhwn
	b.	mh dy thwwn mqrbyn ᶜmhwn
ḥṣy hhyn yhyh lpr	c.	plgwt hyn' tqrbwn ᶜm twr'
wšlyšt hhyn l'yl	d.	wtltwt hyn' tqrbwn ᶜm dkr'
wrbyᶜt hhyn lkbś yyn	e.	wrbᶜwt hyn' tqrbwn ᶜm 'mr' ḥmr
z't ᶜlt	f.	d' ᶜlth
	g.	dy thwwy mqrbh
ḥdš bḥdšw	h.	bkl ryš yrḥ wyrḥ bhtḥdtwtyh
	i.	khdyn sdr' thwwn mqrbyn ᶜmy
lḥdšy hšnh	j.	bkl r'šy yrḥy št'

The many additions of tqrbwn make the presentation much longer in Aramaic than in Hebrew. Lines f, h and j are very similar to Onk. d' ᶜlt ryš yrḥ b'tḥdtwtyh kyn lkl ryšy yrḥy št'. Lines g and i are the routine insertions, but the use of khdyn sdr' (i), analagous to kyn in Onk., turns i-j into a full sentence and may add another verse, possibly needed for liturgical reasons, to the section.

28:15 Add ḥd (with M) after ᶜzym.

28:16 *nkst psḥ'*: for Heb. *psḥ*, as in E 12:11, 27, etc., where *mks psḥ'* is used, and L 23:5 *nkyst*.

28:21 *mklth* (+): cf. v.5.

khdyn sdr' tqrbwn ʿm šbʿtyh 'mryh: for Heb. *tʿśw*; cf. v. 14, 29, 29:4, 14, etc.

28:22 *wṣpyr lḥṭ'th ḥd*: for Heb. *wśʿyr ḥṭ't 'ḥd*; cf. *passim*.

28:26 *mnḥh mn ḥdt*: for Heb. *mnḥh ḥdšh*.

bzmn bḥgy šbwʿykwn: for Heb. *bšbʿtykm*; perhaps a double reading of *zmn* and *ḥg*; cf. L 23:2.

Chapter 29

29:1 *ywm tqyʿh dšwpr wybbw*: for Heb. *ywm trwʿh*; M: *dybbw*, probably an alternative to *tqyʿh wybbw*. N may contain a double translation. In N 10:5-6 *wtqʿtm trwʿh* is translated *wttqʿwn ybbw* (note in v. 6 the phrase *ybbwn ytqʿwn*, for *trʿwh ytqʿw*); cf. also v. 7 *ttqʿwn wl' ttyybbwn* for *ttqʿw wl' tryʿw*. The *ybbw* reading in M and N seems to be the proper one, and *tqyʿh dšwpr* is the intrusion. The double readings are *ywm tqyʿh dšwpr* and *ywm dybbw*.

29:7 *tṣwmwn byh yt npštkwn*: Cf. L 23:27, 32; also N 30:14 where *ṣʿr npš* is used for Heb. *lʿnt npš*.

29:15 Add *'mryyh* with M.

29:17 *dḥg' dmṭly'* (+): as in vv. 20, 23, etc.

29:18 wḥmr (+): cf. vv. 21, 24, etc., where the word is not added.

mh dythwwn mqrybyn ᶜmhwn (+): as in vv. 21, 24, etc.

29:31 wṣlwḥyt my' dhwwt mtqrbh bywm' štytyh ᶜl gby mdbḥh dkrn ṭb lrbyᶜwt mṭrh wnyswkh wnyswk my' (+): added in keeping with the water libation observed on this occasion. The words wnswkh wnyswk my' are the translations of wnskyh (pl.) and refer to the regular libation as well as the water libation; cf. BT Taᶜanit. 2b (p.5). This makes the preceding passage wṣlwḥyt ... mṭrh a double text. Perhaps when this was added, mnḥth was lost; add it with DM. Cf. PJ ... br mn ᶜlt tdyr' wṣmyd' dḥnṭy' lmnḥth wḥmr nyswkh wṣlwḥyt dmy' hwwn mnskyn bywm' dḥg' dwkrn ṭb lrbyᶜ dmyṭr'.

29:35 wbywm': for Heb. bywm, but following the established pattern of wbywm for vv. 17, 20, etc.

knyšyn thwwn mn mṭlykwn lgw btykwn bhdwh and knyšyn dmṣwwn tyhwwy lkwn are double translations of ᶜṣrt thyh lkm. In D 16:8 the phrase ᶜṣrt lyyy 'lhyk (referring to the seventh day of Passover) is translated knyšt ḥdwh... In L 23:36 the translation is knyšt ḥdwwh. On the meaning of ᶜṣr, cf. Sifrei, p. 196: 'yn ᶜṣyrh 'l' knyšh. The use of lkm in Heb. (cf. ᶜṣrt lyyy 'lhyk in D 16:8) may have prompted the comment that on the eighth day the people should gather in their houses rather than in their sukkot. Whether this supports the practice of dwelling in sukkot on this day or not depends on whether entering the houses was done on the eighth day or in anticipation of it.

29:39 khdn sydr' thwwn mqrbyn: for Heb. 'lh; the marginal reading 'lyn is an alternative; cf. 28:14 lines f and i.

Chapter 30

30:1 kl: for Heb. kkl, as in v. 3.

30:3 lšm' dyyy: in place of Heb. ᶜl npšw, perhaps influenced by the beginning of the verse. Read ᶜl npšh instead; cf. Onk., PJ: ᶜl npšyh.

30:16 bᶜlh (+): adding the subject, probably an imitation of v. 13.

Chapter 31

31:3 'zdyynw: for Heb. hḥlṣw; cf. v. 7 where it is the translation of wyṣb'w, and v. 42 where hṣb'ym is translated d'tḥylw.

31:4 'lp mn kl šbṭ 'lp mn kl šbṭyhwn: a double translation of Heb. 'lp lmṭh. The first expression occurs in vv. 5, 6.

31:5 mzyyny qrbh: for Heb. lṣb' (cf. v. 7), but a few words later lṣb' is translated lsdry qrbh.

31:14 mn ḥyl qrb': for Heb. mṣb' hmlḥmh, the literal equivalent; note also v. 21 where the phrase is used for mlḥmh.

31:16 tqlh (+): according to the story at the end of chapt. 24.

31:21 ᶜm' ᶜbdy qrb': for Heb. 'nšy hṣb'.

31:22 wyt bᶜṣh wyt ksyṭr': a double translation of Heb. w't

hbdyl, the first in Aramaic and the second in Greek.

31:28 'pršw: for Heb. mks, normally used for trwmh (e.g. v. 29) and used here with wtpršwn; cf. also vv. 37, 39, 40, etc.

31:41 tlš (+): cf. v. 30.

31:50 N

a. wqrbnn yt qrbnh dyyy
b. gbr
c. mdhwwynn ʿllyn bbtyhwn dmdyynyy
d. bqyṭwny mlkyhwn
e. whwynn ḥmdyn bnthwn
f. y'th wšpyrth mḥṭyth wmprnqth
g. whwwynn šryn
h. qryh
i. klylyyh ddhbh mn r'šyhwn
j. qdyšyn mn 'dnyhwn
k. šyšlyn mn ṣw'ryhwn
l. qṭlyn mn 'drʿyhwn
m. šyryn mn ydyhwn
n. ʿzqyn mn 'ṣbʿthwn
o. mʿzqyn mn bytryhwn [DM: mn byt tdyhwn]
p. kl kdn
q. l' 't'ḥd ḥd mnn ʿm ḥdh mnhwn bʿlm' hdyn
r. dl' mhwy ʿmh bgyhynm bʿlm' d'ty
s. d' tyqwm ln bywm dynh rbh
t. lmkprh ʿl npštn qdm yyy

Heb.

1. wnqrb 't qrbn yyy
2. 'yš

3. 'šr mṣ'

4. kly zhb

5. 'ṣᶜdh

6. wṣmyd

7. ṭbᶜt

8. ᶜgyl

9. wkwmz

10. lkpr ᶜl npštynw lpny yyy

Lines 1-2 and 10 have been translated in a-b and t, but the six Hebrew words in lines 4-9 have been expanded into 8 lines (i-o), introduced by c-h and followed by p-t. Line 3, properly the continuation of 2, may be reflected in g, but really has been omitted.

The beginning and end of the passage thus comprise the entire translation, and c-t are an independent story based on the verse but nevertheless superimposed. (It is not clear if line t is part of the translation or the story, but it is now integrated into the story). The midrashic addition describes how the Israelite soldiers conquered the Midianites, entered their bed chambers and, without succumbing to sexual temptations, stripped the Midianite women of their costly golden jewelry. The story is, in general terms, the antithesis of Bilaam's suggestion, alluded to in 24:25, that Balaq, the King of Moab, cause Israel to sin by having them seduced. The story also portrays the self-discipline required by the laws concerning the capture of attractive women (D 21:10-14), but does not reflect the legislative contents of that passage.

Though lines c-t are based on the Biblical verse, the story line has been embellished quite erotically. In the midst of reports about military spoils, we are suddenly introduced to soldiers who enter the enemies' bedrooms and find their ornately adorned women there. Four adjectives are used to describe the women's beauty, and we are told that the soldiers lusted after them. (There is no reason to change ḫmdyn in line e to ḫmyyn, even though it is attested in PJ and Frag.). The soldiers began to remove their jewelry, their head dresses, earrings, etc., until they loosened the clasps over their breasts (added over the Hebrew list). But they only wanted the gold; no one dared get involved with the women in this world for fear of being permanently banished with them in the world to come. The religious message with which the passage concludes has been presented very forcefully, but the Hellenistic tendency to introduce erotic passages where there are none in the original has also been accommodated.

While the story has been designed to deal with the immediate context, there are important parallels with other passages as well. The list of jewelry is reminiscent of the lists in G 49:22 (where women tossed their jewels at Joseph to attract his attention) and in E 35:22 (which lists the items contributed to the building of the tabernacle). The balanced phrases bᶜlm' hdyn (q) and bᶜlm' d'ty (r) have been introduced in many other places as well, as have Gehinnom and The Day of The Great Judgment. Of particular interest, however, is the similarity between q-r and G 31:10. The latter contains a midrashic expansion of lškb 'ṣlh lhywt ᶜmh: ... lmšmšh ᶜmh bᶜlm-hdyn dl' lmhwy ᶜmh lᶜlm' d'ty. This expansion may underlie the text here.

Lines q-s are closely paralleled in Judah's midrashic speech in G 38:25. There, too, the context is suspicion of sexual misconduct, and Judah's confession of having impregnated Tamar uses the ᶜlmh hdyn and ᶜlmh d'ty terms twice (lines 28-32). Reference to dyn' rb' (line 24) is included in Tamar's speech, and even the term ᶜzq, which occurs here in line n, is used in G

35:18 as one of the pieces of collateral given to Tamar. This last reference may be coincidental, but the sexual connotations of jewelry in this passage are not. Even today, certain groups of oriental women, especially royalty and brides (who are treated as royalty), are adorned with what western standards would consider highly excessive quantities of golden jewelry. Cf., for example, Y. K. Stillman, "The Costume of the Jewish Women in Morocco," *Studies in Jewish Folkore*, ed. F. Talmage (Cambridge, Mass., 1980) pp. 343-375, especially the photographs. The erotic associations with the jewelry are brought out here and thus help clarify G 49:22 also. Perhaps they also further underscore the sacrifice of the women who contributed them.

The precise identification of the items of jewelry is not my major concern, but lines g-h are somewhat problematic and require further analysis. The MS reads *whwwynn* *šryn* *qryh*, but the *Nun* of *šryn* is medial, and the words are really joined together as *šrynqryh*. It is possible for this to be some feminine ornament, possibly a "choke," (cf. *šnq*). This would require the assumption that *whwwynn* should be *wḥwwynn*, also easily justified. Such a proposal would leave 7 phrases containing the removal of objects from parts of the body (possibly 8 if the phrase is needed here also) without a complete verb that describes the removal (*šryn*), and, under the circumstances, the proposal is weak. The lack of a complementary phrase for *qryyh* then becomes a question, but it is perhaps easier to accommodate it and the use of the medial *Nun* than to add the missing verb. Note also the use of *šyryn* in G 49:22.

31:52 Hebrew *kl* has not been translated.

Chapter 32

32:1 'rᶜ mbkr [DM: mkbr with v. 3]: for Heb. 'rṣ yᶜzr.

špr l- (+): expansive.

32:3 The names ᶜṭrwt and dybwn have been delted.

byt nmryn: for the Heb. toponym nmrh; cf. byt nmrh in the Heb. of v. 36.

w-symt: for the Heb. toponym w-śbm.

32:4 dkbš: for Heb. 'šr hkh, a little less strong, perhaps, but no less accurate.

sgyn (+): added from v. 1 for emphasis.

32:11 Add: l' 'šlmw btr mmry; cf. vv. 12, 15. As presented, vv. 11-12 have been telescoped.

32:12 'lhn: for Heb. blty; note however ky 'm klb ... in 14:30 and 26:65 where 'lhn and 'rwm 'lhn are used, respectively.

32:13 mh dśny wmrḥq: for Heb. hrᶜ.

32:17 nᶜbr mzyynyn: for Heb. nᶜbr ḥšym; cf. the similar translations of ḥlṣym in v. 30 and ḥmšym in E 13:18.

32:18 The verse is lacking, and the reconstruction of DM seems in keeping with the language of N, but lbtm should probably be lbtynn as in E 12:27.

32:19 The Hebrew reads ky b'h nḥltnw 'lynw and could be translated literally, e.g. 'rwm mṭt 'ḥsntn' ln' (PJ) or paraphrastically as "we received our share ...." The use of pronominal elements in qblnn and lwwtn seems redundant, even though it is similar to the construction in Onk.: qbyln' 'ḥsntn' ln'. Perhaps this attests to a combination of two separate readings like 1) qblnn 'ḥsntn and 2) mṭt or 'tt 'ḥsntn lwwtn.

32:34 lḥyyt: for the Heb. toponym ʿrʿr.

32:36 byt rmth: for Heb. toponym byt hrn.

32:37 'lʿlh: for Heb. spelling 'lʿl', but in v. 3 the Hebrew has final Heh and a number of witnesses follow this reading here as well.

32:38 mqpn šwryn rmyn: for Heb. mwsbwt šm, understood as "famed for being encircled" i.e. "encircled by high walls."

32:40 glʿd: for Heb. hglʿd; probably read glʿdh with M.

Chapter 33

33:3 pylwsyn: for Heb. rʿmss, as in E 1:11, etc. The word should also occur in v. 5, but it has been copied as pylwswpyn, an interesting change, to say the least.

33:3 mn btr ywm' ṭb' qdmyh dpysḥ': for Heb. mmḥrt hpsḥ. This verse is important for the chronology of the events told in Exodus and the calendrical ruling on the meaning of mmḥrt hšbt in L 23:15-16, which served as the basis of much sectarian debate over the date of the holiday Shavuoth. See notes a.l.

33:4 dynyn šnyn: for Heb. špṭym, as in E 12:12.

33:7 m-'lym: for Heb. m-'ytm. The error is based on v. 10 and may be in the Heb. not the Aram. The word wnṭlw is also lacking.

33:8 bmdbrh: As printed, bmdbrh seems to be the translation of Heb. hmdbrh, but the lacuna in N is really for the Hebrew words hmdbrh wylkw drk šlšt ymym, not wylkw drk šlšt ymym bmdbr, notwithstanding that M begins w'zlw and ends bmdbrh. The word hmdbrh occurs in E 4:27, L 16:10, 16:21, N 21:23 and D 1:40, where it is translated lmdbr' (I: bmdb-) or lmdbrh, and it probably should appear this way here. In E 4:27 I substitues bmdb-, obviously identical to the gloss here. The only exception seems to be D 2:1, where the situation is reversed, N: bmdbrh and M: lmd-, but this may actually be the intention of the verse.

33:9 kl qbl try ʿśrty šbṭyh dyśr'l, kl qbl šbʿyn [with DM] ḥkymy dbny yśr'l (+): these glosses associate the number of tribes and elders with the number of wells and trees. The style of translation + gloss has been discussed in G 15:12, etc.

33:22 Add wšrwn with DM.

33:35 krk trnwglh: for Heb. ʿṣyn gbr. A translated toponym, as in v. 36 and D 2:8.

33:38 bswp 'rbʿyn šnyn bzmn 'pqwthwn: for Heb. bšnt h'rbʿym lṣ't. The addition of bswp is correct but perhaps misleading. Aaron died towards the end of the forty years, but not at the end of the fortieth year. As noted later in the verse, he died in the fifth month of that year.

33:40 'rwm: for Heb. w-; bzmnh (+): These two changes alter

the Hebrew quite a bit. The Heb. *wyšmᶜ* ... *bb'* means "he heard of the coming." The phrase *bb' bny yśr'l* is the object of *wyšmᶜ*, not an adverbial clause describing when the King of Arad lived in the South of Israel. N has chosen this other possible, but less likely, alternative, thus necessitating the addition of *bzmnh* and the translation of *w-* as *'rwm*.

33:44 *mgzt ᶜbryyh*: for Heb. *ᶜyy hᶜbrym*, as in 21:11; cf. 27:12, 33:47-48, and D 32:49 (*hr hᶜbrym*). Note that in v. 45 only the form *ᶜyyn* is used, based on Heb. *ᶜyym*.

33:53 *dyyry* (+): The land can be acquired but not destroyed, hence the addition of *dyyry*, which is based on vv. 52, 55.

33:54 *lkl*: for Heb. *'l*.

33:55 *yt kl mh dy*: for Heb. *'šr*.

Chapter 34

34:3 The following verses contain the word *gbwl* over a dozen times, but not every boundary is so designated. N has translated *gbl* as *tḥwm* and has introduced it in many additional phrases where it does not appear in Heb.

34:4 *bṭwr przl'*: for Heb. *ṣnh*.

tyrt 'dryyh: for Heb. toponym *ḥṣr 'dr*.

šwq msyy: for Heb. *ᶜṣmnh*; PJ: *lqysm*. This is a phonetic alternative to *šwq mzyy* in the midrashic addition to v. 15. The word *bqsm* in N and M may be a double translation of *ᶜṣmnh*. The name *ᶜṣmwn* occurs here and in v. 5, (where it is translated *lqsm*), and its only other occurrence is in Josh. 15:4, where it is transcribed into Aramaic. Bones (Heb. *ʿṣm*) were often used for magical praxis (*qsm*), but there may be no connection.

34:6 N

a. *wtḥwm ymh rbh*

b. *'wqyynws*

c. *'ynwn my br'šyt*

d. *mswy* [DM: *nyswy*] *mʿwzwy wspynth*

e. *ʿm myy' qdmwyy dy bgwwh*

f. *dyn yhwwy lkwn tḥwm ym'*

Heb.

1. *wgbwl ym*
2. *whyh lkm hym hgdwl wgbwl*
3. *zh yhyh lkm gbwl ym*

Lines a and f begin and end the translation in keeping with the Hebrew (1, 3), but lines c-e are a substitution for line 2, which is itself barely reflected in this passage at all. M suggests a sequence of b, d, e, c, which is probably the best. The order in Frag. is a, b (*whw' 'wqy'nws*), d, e, c, f, also, but this correlates no more closely to the Heb. and only provides additional variants. PJ, by comparison, is longer and clearer:

PJ

1. *wtḥwm mʿrb'*
2. *wyhwy lkwn ym' rb' 'wqynws*
3. *wtḥwmyh hynwn my br'šyt ʿm my' qdm'y dhwwn bgwyh*
4. *'byrwy wprbyrwy krkwy wmdyntyh nyswy wmḥwzwy spyntyh w'lgwwtyh*

5. dyn yhwy lkwn tḥwm mᶜrby'

The order, in terms of N, is a, b, c, e, d, f.

In order to make sense of N, it is necessary to see it in the light of these other texts as well as the translation procedures used throughout the chapter. The phrase wgbwl ym (line 1) can mean the western or seaward border, and should be translated tḥwm ymh, as it is line f. The term tḥwm ymh rbh (a) means "the border of the Great Sea" and makes sense, but is not likely. Line a should read either 1) wtḥwm ymh, like tḥwm ṣpwnh in vv. 7, 9 (deleting rbh), or 2) wtḥwm mᶜrbh, like PJ, assuming that mᶜrbh became corrupted to ymh rbh (it is not inconceivable that some intermediate text had m'rbh for "western"), or 3) wtḥwm mᶜrb' ymh rbh, combining them as in PJ.

The terms my br'šyt (c) and myy' qdmwyy (= qdmyy) (e) are synonymous, unless one has some special significance of which I am unaware; cf. Zech. 14:8. The use of 'ynwn in c requires a plural antecedent. This cannot be wtḥwm in a. In v. 3 the plural form of tḥwm was introduced -- ᶜd tḥwmyhwn d'dwmyy for ᶜl ydy 'dwm. Thus the word tḥwmyh, or the like, might have occured somehwere between tḥwm in a and 'ynwn in c, but this seems forced. Either the terms my br'šyt and myy' qdmwyy must be equated as in Frag. and M or joined as in PJ, in which case the plural myy' in e would serve as the antecedent of 'ynwn in c. N's placement of line d between c and e is intelligible but very strained, and M's suggestion that c follow e is correct.

The Hebrew term hym hgdwl (2) is undoubtedly ymh rbh, frequently identified by the Latin oceanus (b). The word wgbwl at the end of line 2 defies any attempt to fit it into the Aram. sentence as presented, but if wgbwl is taken as an abridged form gbwlwt, and joined to hym hgdwl, it could lead into a list of locations on the Great Sea. This list varies from three items in

N (d), M, and Frag. to eight in PJ (line 4). The list must follow the translation of hym hgdwl, glossed, if necessary, by oceanus. Indeed, the foreign name may have recalled these varied aspects of sea travel and may be an integral element in the addition of this list in d and PJ, line 4.

Accordingly, I suggest that N be restored as follows:

a. wtḥwm [mᶜrb' wyhwy lkwn] ymh rbh [ltḥwm]

b. 'wqyynws

c. mswy [DM: nyswy as in PJ] mᶜwzwy wspynth

e. ᶜm myy' qdmwyy dy bgwh

c. 'ynwn my br'šyt

f. dyn yhwwy lkwn tḥwm ym'

In this way, lines a and f translate the Heb. literally. Lines b, d, and e are a midrashic insertion explaining ymh rbh, while 'ynwn my br'šyt (c) is a later Heb. gloss on myy' qdmwyy. The word ltḥwm (a) may have been deleted when b-e were added; but it is present in PJ. The general tone of this reconstructed text is quite different from PJ, which may extend the Israelite border to the far corners of the unknown sea and all the surrounding land. The shorter list in d of N simply gives the description some local color.

34:7 lhwmyns ṭwwrws: for Heb. hr hhr: cf. ṭwwrws mnws in v. 8 and the usual rendering of the phrase as hr ṭwr'.

mzrḥ (+): perhaps added in imitation of the directions in vv. 3, 5, etc.

34:8 lmᶜlny 'ntwkyyh: for Heb. typonym lb' ḥmt, as in 13:21.

l'wwls dqylqy: for Heb. ṣddh.

34:9 ṭyrt ᶜnbth: for Heb. ḥṣr ᶜynn; cf. ṭyrt ᶜnwwth in v. 10.

34:10 l'pmyh: for Heb. špmh.

34:11 ldpny: for Heb. hrblh.
sypwwy: for Heb. ktp.
ymh dgnysr: for Heb. ym knrt.

34:15 N

a. tyrn šbṭyyh wplgwt šbṭh dmnšh qblw 'ḥsnthwn
b. mn ᶜbr lyrdnh dyryḥw qdmyn mn mdnḥh
c. [mn myšr ymh dmlḥ']
d. npq lhwn tḥwmh lknrt
e. krk mlkyhwn d'mryy
f. [wmn knrt]
g. npq lhwn tḥwmh lkrk' dᶜywn
h. dmn mdnḥ lbyt yrḥ
i. wmmdnḥ ym' dbyt yrḥ
j. npq lhwn tḥwm' lydywqyṭ'
k. wmydywqyṭws trngyl [DM: trngwl] qsrywn dmmdnḥ mᶜrbh [DM: mᶜrh] ddn
l. npq lhwn tḥwmh lṭwr tlg'
m. ltḥwmh lbnwn dmṣpwn ᶜyynwwtyh ddrmśq
n. wmṣpwn ᶜyynwwtyh ddrmśq
o. npq lhwn tḥwm' lnhr' rwb' nhr' prt
p. dᶜlwy sdr nṣḥny qrbwy dyyy mdᶜbdyn (!)
q. wmnhr' rwb' nhr' prt
r. npq lhwn tḥwm' lqrn zwwy dbtryh
s. wkl ṭrkwn byt zymr'
t. byt mlkwt' dsyḥwn mlkwt' d'mwryy

u. wbyt mlkwt' dʿwg mlk' dbwtnyyn

v. mh dy qṭl mšh nby' dyyy

w. npq lrpywn wlšwq mzyy wlmʿrt ʿyn gdy

x. ʿd mṭy spr [read: sypy] ym' dmylḥ'

y. dyn hw' tḥwm' dtryn šbṭyh wplgwt šbṭ'

Heb.

1. šny hmṭwt wḥṣy hmṭh lqḥw nḥltm

2. mʿbr lyrdn yrḥw qdmh mzrḥh

Verse 15 begins with the translation of the Hebrew (a-b; 1-2). The Bible does not specify which 2½ tribes are intended, and it is rather odd for N to name the half-tribe but not the two full ones (cf. PJ, which omits all references). Either delete dmnšh or add dr'wbn wdgd after šbṭyyh.

Lines c-y supposedly describe the borders of the territories belonging to the 2½ tribes. Other lists of boundaries are scattered throughout rabbinic literature and provide some clarification: Sifrei, Eiqev, 51 (pp. 117-118); T Sheviʿit, 4:11 (p. 181) and Lieberman's notes; PT Sheviʿit 6:1; etc. Also useful is S. Klein, "Das Tannaitische Grenzverzeichnis Palaestinas" HUCA V (1928), pp. 197-259. In general, the borders run from the Jordan to the Euphrates and from the Dead Sea area to north of Damascus. The borders contain both Biblical and post-Biblical names, and we are not told which territories belong to which tribe.

The rhythm of the text necessitates the addition of the material in lines c and f. Line c has been taken from M, but the equivalent of f in M contains the repeated identification in e and leads to l, so I have reconstructed f in keeping with the literary patterns of N.

The boundary begins with the Dead Sea Valley (c) and

extends northward to the city Kinnereth (d) on the western bank of the Sea of Galilee. From there it extends to the city of Iyyon (g) east of Bait Yerech (i). Bait Yerech is located on the south western side of the Sea of Galilee, and this further identification eliminates any confusion with the other city called Iyyon, further north. From the Sea of Bait Yerech (i.e. the Sea of Galilee) the border extends to a place known as Iodioqita (j) or Iodioqitos Tarnegol Caesarion (k), though the first word is given as Dioqitos or the like in M, and the spelling dywwqynws occurs in PJ, 34:8. Lieberman has cited a number of variants for the names in lines j-k, and Klein has interpreted dywqynws trngwl' dqysryn as "the image of the rooster of Caesarion," i.e. Caesarea Philippi (p. 232). If this is the correct reading, and the three words in k are all one toponym, the word lydywqyṭ' in j is an abbreviated or faulty equivalent.

From there the border extends to Tur Talga (Mt. Hermon), identified further in m as the border of Lebanon north of the Wells of Damascus. The border then heads in an easterly direction to the Euphrates (o) and from there to qrn zwwy, corrected by DM to refer to the cities of Nave, capital of Bashan i.e. qrywn nwwy. If this identification is correct -- and it does fit with the location of Terachon (s)--it is difficult to explain the subsequent use of dbtryh -- "after it" or "behind it". Presumably that means that Qeren Ziwwi (Nave?) is located on the far side of the Euphrates; alternatively, if we maintain DM's identification on the western side of the Euphrates, the perspective of the text, at least in this midrash, is Mesopotamian. I suggest, instead, the possibility that the scribe copied qrn zwwy, thinking it to be a variation of the common talmudic term qrn zwyt "corner," but that is not the correct reading. A number of the texts cited above list qrwn zkwt' or skwt' equivalent to byt skwt. Klein has accepted this reading and corrected the subsequent word to wgbt' dḥṭmwn'.

Terachon (s) is northeast of Bashan, used in D 3:4 to translate ḥbl 'rgb. The identity of Bait Zimra is not clear, but given its context, it cannot refer to the Phoenician Simirra identified in N, G 10:18, as zymryy' (=Heb. hṣmry), bordering on the mountains of Sana (= Zawie), in spite of the use of qrn zwwy in line r. (For additional data cf. H. J. Katzenstein, The History of Tyre, Jerusalem, 1973, p. 211). Diez-Macho identifies it as Bet Zamaris in Bashan. The location of the capital cities of Sihon and Og are Heshbon and Ashtarot-Edrei, located east of the Jordan. The former is slightly north-east of the Dead Sea, while the latter cities are east and south east of the Sea of Galilee. The border then returns to the Dead Sea (x) via Rafyon (w), suggested by Diez-Macho to be Raphon, east of Ashtarot in Bashan, but rpyḥ is a possible choice also and appears in some of the lists. Shuq Mazai and Ein Geddi follow. Diez-Macho has identified Shuq Mazai as Sycamazon, south of Gaza, but perhaps the place should be located east of the Jordan to prevent having the border run from the Bashan right through the country. N identifies Azmon (ʿṣmn) in v. 4 as šwq msyy, and ʿṣmn is usually located near Qadesh Barnea, also south and west of the Dead Sea. The same argument applies to Raphiach, and Klein has suggested that these western places have been copied from the source containing the other sites, even though they are not properly the boundaries of the 2½ tribes. A number of texts carry the border to the Mediterranean, and N seems to follow this pattern, at least in part. Our text should end with Ein Geddi, located on the western side of the Dead Sea, possibly reached from Raphon.

Several of the identifications are tentative, but the purpose of the text is clear. The greater part of the list focuses on the northern and eastern area, places in and around Syria, from Lebanon to the Euphrates. The emphasis of the text is also national rather than tribal, though this follows the pattern established in the earlier part of the chapter, where the total claim to the land is given rather than the individual areas outlined in Joshua. It is related to D 3:5-13 but is not a translation of these verses. The territory is far more extensive than that alloted to these 2½ tribes in Josh. chapt. 13, and is closer to the description of the Davidic-Solomonic empire whose control extended through Syria, Palmyra and Jordan, up to the Euphrates. In general terms, these borders approximate, but overstate, those outlined in Ezek. 47 and include the territory of the Assyrian conquest in the eighth century and the Seleucid share of the region in the pre-Christian centuries. The borders of the Roman empire extended to the Euphrates and included all of this territory as well.

Frag. and PJ omit this passage, but part of it is cited by Levita, as noted by Ginsburger, *Das Fragmententhargum*, p. 118. The significant differences are *mn ywqynws twrngl' dqysrywn* for (part of?) line k and *lrpyḥ*, for *lrpywn* in line w. The various Rabbinic Bibles also preserve a number of versions, including some already noted variants and corrections. (Cf. Vilna *Miqra'ot Gedolot*, IV, p. 451-453 (N 34:15) and the Venice 1525 Rabbinic Bible, *Targum Yerushalmi* a.l.) M, on the other hand, contains a more extensive fragment:

(1) ... *mʿbr ywrdnh dyryḥw qdm'yn mn mdnḥh*

(2) *mn myšr ymh dmlḥ'*

(3) *npq lhwn tḥwmh lknrt*

(4) *krk dmlkwthwn d'ymwr'y*

(5) *wmn knrt krk mlkwthwn d'ymwr'y*

(6) *npq lhwn tḥwmh lṭwr tlg' wlḥwmth dlbnn*

(7) *wmn ṭwr tlgh wlḥwmth dlbnn*

(8) *npq lhwn tḥwmh lḥwbh*

(9) dy mn ṣpwn ᶜyynwwth ddrmsq

(10) wmn ṣpwn npq lhwn tḥwmh ldywqṭs twrngl' dqysrywn [with DM]

(11) dy mn mdnḥ mᶜrb [DM: mᶜrt] dn

(12) npq lhwn tḥwmh lnhrh rbh dprt

(13) dᶜlwy sd- ...

This text corresponds to lines b, c, d, e, f, l, m-n, k, o, p. A gap of the type I have reconstructed in lines c and f of N is also present in line 10 of M, where wmn ṣpwn should be followed by a place. The major difference between the texts is the order of the places, of value in reconstructing the general borders but not in identifying the places.

The basis of these texts is impossible to determine. They are not grounded on Josh. 13 or Ezek. 47; though references to Sihon and Og do occur in Josh. 13:21. By making boundary markers of places so insignificant or obscure that we cannot now identify them, they evince an extreme concern with the details of these borders. The text also shows various literary influences. Lines t-v, for example, have been reversed, to reflect the routine Biblical sequence Sihon ... Og, instead of mentioning Og first, as one would expect in a list going from north to south. Moses, however, proceded from south to north and is said to have killed Sihon and Og in D 1:4, etc.

Some of the places mentioned in the earlier part of the chapter (e.g. vv. 9-11) are used as border points in this text as well, and Klein has demonstrated the similarities by printing this text parallel to the translation of vv. 15, 11, 8, 11, 9 and 11 from PJ. The text ends with an inclusio (line y) parallel to the end of v. 12.

34:18 mn kl šbṭ: for Heb. mmṭh.

34:29 yt mšh (+): providing a different object for the verb.

Chapter 35

35:12 tbwᶜ 'dm': for Heb. g'l; the full term is used in v. 21, etc.

35:14 Heb. mqlṭ has not been translated.

35:16 Add hw' after qṭyl as in v. 17.

35:17 ml' yd': for Heb. yd; cf. v. 18.

35:18 Heb. kly has not been translated, and perhaps was influenced by 'bn yd in v. 17. The Heb. quotation contains bkly.

35:20 bkmnh: for Heb. bṣdyh; DM suggests bkwwnh; cf. v. 22.

35:23 dl' ḥmh ytyh: for Heb. bl' r'wt.
bšth dnpšyh: for Heb. rᶜtw.

35:24 Correct the printed text ᶜm to ᶜl as in the MS.

35:27 lyt lyh ḥwbt špykwt 'dm zkyy: for Heb. 'yn lw dm, as in E 22:1. The phrase dm nqy is found in D 21:8, 9, etc. It is used with the verb špk in D 19:10. The MH term for this act is špykwt dmym.

35:30 ytqṭl qṭwlh: for Heb. yrṣḥ 't hrṣḥ. The verb ytqṭl may be active in meaning, but the absence of yt argues against this explanation. The syntax of the Hebrew is somewhat awkward, but *mkh npš* is synonymous with *hrṣḥ* of the second clause and is not the subject of the verb *yrṣḥ*; hence the appropriateness of N. (Cf. Onk. and PJ for two other options).

35:32 *rbh* (+): added in keeping with v. 28, etc.

Chapter 36

36:1 *r'šy šybṭyyh*: for Heb. *r'šy h'bwt*. This error occurs in the Hebrew quotation before the Aramaic also, and may result from confusion with 30:2 where the Heb. reads *r'šy hmṭwt*.

36:5 *tbᶜyn*: for Heb. *dbrym*.

y'wt: for Heb. *kn*; gives priority to *y'wt* in the double translation *y'wt wqwšt'* in E 10:29.

36:8 *dyrth*: for Heb. *yršt*, emphasizing that the Heb. *yršt* ... is a subordinate clause and eliminating any doubt that the verse means that all daughters inherit their father's land.

lbr: for Heb. *l'ḥd*.

36:11 *lbnwy d'ḥwy d'bwhwn*: for Heb. *lbny ddyhn*.

36:13 Read *ᶜl ydwy dmšh*. The MS seems to contain a letter after *yyy*, but the artistic layout of the words precluded filling in the words once they had been omitted.

TABLE OF CROSS REFERENCES

The following cross references facilitate finding discussions of N that are not found in the expected place in the commentary. All Pentateuchal Hebrew and targumic references are included.

Numbers

1:1	E 12:31; N 9:1.
1:3	N 26:2.
1:5	Intro., ch. 2.
1:10	Intro., ch. 2.
1:12	Intro., ch. 2.; N 11:14.
1:22	N 1:3; 1:20.
1:24	N 1:3; 1:20.
1:26	N 1:3.
1:45	N 12:16.
1:46	N 12:16.
1:49	N 1:2.
1:50	D 32:10.
1:51	D 32:10.
1:52	D 32:10.
1:53	D 32:10.
2:2	D 32:10.
2:5	N 2:3.
2:7	N 2:3.
2:10	N 2:3.
2:12	N 1:5; 2:3.
2:13	N 14:28.
2:20	N 1:10.

2:25	N 1:12.
3:10	N 1:51.
3:12	E 34:19.
3:14	N 6:23.
3:16	D 32:2.
3:23	D 33:23.
3:38	N 1:51.
3:39	D 32:2.
4:3	N 1:3.
4:23	N 1:3.
5:6	D 32:51.
5:19	N 5:29.
5:20	N 5:19; 5:29.
5:21	N 5:27; D 32:24.
6:2	N 6:4.
6:5	N 6:4.
6:9	L 14:32.
6:22	N 6:23.
6:24	N 6:23.
6:25	N 6:23.
6:26	N 6:23.
6:27	Intro., ch. 4.; N 6:23.
7:1	Intro., ch. 1.; L 1:1; 8:10; N 7:18.
7:7	Intro., ch. 3.; N 7:9.
7:8	N 7:9.
7:9	Intro., ch. 3.; N 7:7.
7:11	Intro., ch. 3.
7:12-83	See paragraph before 7:13
7:12	N 7:17; 7:18.
7:13	N 7:14; 7:17; 7:85.
7:14	N 7:13; 7:17; 7:86

7:15 N 7:17.

7:16 N 7:13; 7:17.

7:17 N 7:13; 28:2.

7:20 N 7:14.

7:23 N 1:8.

7:24 N 7:18.

7:66 Intro., ch. 2.

7:84 N 7:11; 7:17.

7:87 G 32:16.

7:88 G 32:16.

8:12 N 8:13.

8:19 N 8:16.

8:20 D 1:3.

9:1 E 12:31.

9:6 L 24:12.

9:7 N 9:6.

9:8 Intro., ch. 4.; E 14:13-14; L 24:12; N 27:5.

9:10 N 9:6.

9:20 N 9:21.

10:5 N 29:1.

10:6 N 29:1.

10:9 Intro., ch. 4.; N 15:18.

10:10 L 23:32; N 3:13.

10:18 N 10:14.

10:22 N 10:14.

10:25 N 10:14.

10:35 Intro., ch. 3.; ch. 4; N 10:9; 10:36.

10:36 Intro., ch. 4.; N 10:35.

11:1 Intro., ch.3.; G 4:5-6.

11:4 N 11:18; D 1:1.

11:5 N 11:26.

11:6 Intro., ch. 1.; N 21:6.

11:7 N 11:6.

11:8 N 11:26.

11:9 N 11:6; 11:26.

11:10 N 11:26.

11:11 Intro., ch. 3.; N 10:35; 11:26.

11:12 N 11:26.

11:14 Intro., ch.3.

11:15 Intro., ch. 2.; ch. 3.; N 11:11.

11:17 Intro., ch. 3.

11:18 Intro., ch. 3.; N 11:4; D 1:1.

11:25 Intro., ch. 3.; N 11:17; 11:26.

11:26 Intro., ch. 4.; N 11:25; 21:6; 21:18; 24:24; D 32:1.

11:27 N 11:26.

11:31 N 11:26; D 32:10.

11:33 D 1:1.

11:35 N 11:34; D 1:1.

12:4 N 6:9.

12:7 N 27:16; D 33:8.

12:8 Intro., ch. 3.; N 14:14; D 35:10.

12:11 Intro., ch. 4.

12:12 Intro., ch. 2.; ch. 3.; ch. 4.

12:13 Intro., ch. 4.

12:15 N 12:14; 12:16; D 32:1.

12:16 Intro., ch. 1.; ch. 4.; N 12:14; D 1:1.

13:1 D 1:1.

13:2 D 1:1.

13:3 D 1:1.

13:20 Intro., ch. 3.

13:21 N 34:8.

13:26 Intro., ch. 3.

13:28 N 13:22.

13:32 G 37;:2.

13:33 N 13:22.

14:1 Intro., ch. 3.; D 1:1.

14:2 N 14:27.

14:3 Intro., ch.3.

14:5 Intro., ch.3.; N 14:1.

14:12 D 9:14.

14:14 Intro., ch. 3.

14:18 Intro., ch. 4.; D 5:9.

14:21 Intro., ch. 3.

14:22 D 6:16; 33:8.

14:23 N 14:11.

14:24 Intro.; ch. 3.

14:27 Intro., ch. 4.

14:28 N 14:21; D 32:27.

14:29 N 14:27; D 1:1.

14:30 N 32:12.

14:32 D 1:1.

14:33 D 1:1.

14:34 Intro., ch. 3.

14:35 N 14:27.

14:36 G 37:2; N 14:27.

14:37 G 37:2.

14:45 D 1:44.

15:1 N 21:5.

15:2 N 15:18.

15:11 Intro., ch. 4.

15:16 N 15:15.

15:21 N 15:20.

15:29 N 15:15.

15:30	Intro., ch. 4.; G 40:18-19; D 32:27.
15:32	L 24:12.
15:33	L 24:12; N 9:6.
15:34	Intro., ch. 4.; L 24:12; N 9:8; 27:5.
15:35	L 24:12.
15:36	L 24:12.
15:39	Intro., ch. 3.; G 49:22; N 15:38.
16:6	N 14:27.
16:11	G 4:15.
16:22	N 27:16.
16:23	N 16:24.
16:29	N 16:28; 16:30; 16:32.
16:32	E 15:12.
17:12	N 17:11.
17:22	G 49:33.
17:28	G 49:33, N 21:29.
18:7	N 1:51.
18:10	N 18:9.
18:13	N 18:1.
18:15	E 34:19.
18:21	D 26:12.
18:27	D 16:13.
18:30	N 15:20; 18:27; 18:29; D 16:13.
18:32	N 18:29.
19:2	E 12:43; D 21:3.
19:11	N 19:22.
19:13	N 19:11; 19:22.
19:14	N 12:12.
19:16	N 19:11.
19:17	N 19:15.
20:1	N 12:16; 21:1.

20:2 E 17:1; N 12:16; 21:1.

20:5 Intro., ch. 3.

20:9 E 4:28.

20:12 Intro., ch. 4.; G 4:15; D 32:51.

20:13 N 27:14; D 32:51.

20:16 Intro., ch. 3.; ch. 4.

20:17 N 20:19.

20:20 D 32:51.

20:24 N 27:14; D 32:51.

20:26 D 32:1.

20:28 N 20:26.

20:29 G 49:33.

21:1 Intro., ch. 4.; E 15:9.

21:3 Intro., ch 4.; N 14:45; D 1:44.

21:5 Intro., ch. 3.; ch. 4.; N 14:9; 20:5; 21:6; 21:7; D 1:1.

21:6 Intro., ch. 4.; G 3:14; N 11:26; 20:8; 21:8; D 1:1.

21:7 L 9:7; N 21:5; 21:6.

21:8 Intro., ch. 3.

21:9 N 21:8.

21:11 N 33:44.

21:14 G 40:23; N 21:15.

21:15 N 21:14.

21:16 N 21:19-20.

21:17 N 21:19-20.

21:18 G 27:29; N 21:16; 21:19-20.

21:19 N 21:18.

21:21 N 21:14.

21:23 N 33:8.

21:28 N 21:29.

21:29 N 17:28.

21:30 Intro., ch. 3.; ch. 4.

21:33 N 21:34.

21:34 Intro., ch. 3.; ch. 4.; G 49:22; N 21:29; D 2:1; 3:2.

22:3 N 22:5.

22:5 Intro., ch. 3.; N 22:3; 23:7; D 23:5.

22:6 N 22:3.

22:10 Intro., ch. 4.

22:11 N 22:5, 23:7.

22:13 Intro., ch. 3.

22:19 N 22:8.

22:22 Intro., ch. 3.; N 22:32.

22:29 N 22:30.

22:30 Intro., ch. 4.; N 23:10.

22:31 G 44:18; 24:13.

22:34 N 22:31.

23:1 G 32:16; N 23:2.

23:4 N 23:2.

23:6 N 22:31.

23:7 N 23:8; 23:10; 24:23.

23:8 Intro., ch. 3.; N 23:7; 23:10.

23:9 N 23:10; D 32:12; 33:15.

23:10 Intro., ch. 2.; G 44:18; N 23:18; 23:23; 24:2; 24:4; D 32:14.

23:13 N 22:41.

23:18 N 23:10; 24:23.

23:19 Intro., ch. 4.; N 23:10.

23:20 N 23:10.

23:21 N 23:10; 23:23.

23:22 Intro., ch. 4.; N 23:10.

23:23 N 23:10; 23:21; D 32:14.

23:24 Intro., ch. 3., N 23:10.

23:28 N 24:3.

23:29 G 32:16.

23:30 N 23:2.

24:1 Intro., ch. 3.

24:3 N 23:10; 24:15; 24:23.

24:4 Intro., ch. 4.; N 23:10; 24:16.

24:5 Intro., ch. 4.; N 23:10; 23:23; D 28:6.

24:6 N 23:10; 24:7; 24:20.

24:7 Intro., ch. 4.; N 23:10.

24:8 N 23:10; 24:17; D 32:39.

24:9 Intro., ch. 2.; G 49:9; N 23:10.

24:10 N 23:11.

24:14 N 24:25.

24:15 N 23:10; 24:23.

24:16 N 23:10, 24:4.

24:17 N 23:10; 24:20; D 32:39; 33:5.

24:18 N 23:10.

24:19 N 23:10.

24:20 N 23:10; 24:23; 24:24.

24:21 N 23:10; 24:23.

24:22 N 23:10; 24:21.

24:23 N 23:10.

24:24 N 23:10; 24:20; D 28:68.

24:25 N 31:50.

25:1 D 33:9.

25:2 D 33:9.

25:3 D 33:9.

25:4 D 33:9.

25:5 N 25:4; D 4:3; 33:9.

25:6-11 D 33:9.

25:12 G 4:15; D 33:9.

25:13 D 33:9.

25:14 D 33:9.

25:15 D 33:9.

26:5 N 25:13.

26:7 N 26:12.

26:14 N 26:12.

26:15 N 26:12.

26:18 N 26:12.

26:22 N 26:12.

26:25 N 26:12.

26:56 N 26:54.

26:65 N 32:12.

27:1 L 24:12; N 9:8.

27:2 L 24:12; N 9:6; 27:19.

27:3 L 24:12; N 26:11.

27:4 Intro., ch. 3.; L 24:12.

27:5 Intro., ch. 4.; L 24:12; N 9:8.

27:6 L 24:12.

27:7 L 24:12.

27:8-11 L 24:12.

27:12 N 33:44; D 32:51.

27:13 D 32:51.

27:14 D 32:51.

27:15 D 32:51.

27:17 D 32:51.

27:18 N 11:26.

27:19 N 11:26.

27:20 N 11:26.

27:21 N 11:26; 27:17.

27:22 N 11:26; 27:19.

27:23	N 11:26.
28:1	N 28:2.
28:2	Intro., ch. 2.
28:3	Intro., ch. 3.; N 28:2.
28:4	N 28:2.
28:5	N 28:2; 28:21.
28:6	N 28:2.
28:7	N 28:2; 28:9.
28:8	N 28:2; 28:4; 28:9.
28:9	N 28:2.
28:10	N 28:2; 28:9.
28:11	G 32:16; N 28:2.
28:12	N 28:2.
28:13	N 28:2.
28:14	N 28:2; 28:21; 29:39.
28:15	N 28:2.
28:17	L 23:6.
28:18	E 12:16.
28:19	G 32:16; N 28:11.
28:25	E 12:16.
28:26	E 12:16.
28:29	Intro., ch. 3.; N 28:21.
29:4	Intro., ch. 3.; N 28:21.
29:6	N 28:13; 29:1.
29:7	L 23:27; N 29:1.
29:14	N 28:21.
29:17	N 29:35.
29:20	N 29:17; 29:35.
29:21	N 29:18.
29:23	N 29:17.
29:24	N 29:18.

29:31	Intro., ch. 3.
29:39	Intro., ch. 3.
30:2	N 36:1.
30:3	N 30:1
30:13	N 30:16.
30:14	N 29:7.
31:2	Intro., ch. 2.; D 32:1.
31:5	N 31:4.
31:6	N 31:4.
31:7	N 31:3; 31:5.
31:8	N 24:4.
31:10	G 10:2.
31:21	E 12:43; N 31:14.
31:22	Intro., ch. 4.; D 32:42.
31:29	N 31:28.
31:30	N 31:41.
31:37	N 31:28.
31:39	N 31:28.
31:40	N 31:28.
31:42	N 31:3.
31:50	Intro., ch. 4.; D 22:7.
32:1	N 32:4.
32:3	N 32:1; 32:37.
32:12	N 32:11.
32:15	N 32:11.
32:29	G 49:19.
32:30	N 32:17.
32:36	N 32:3.
32:37	N 22:39; 32:3.
33:2	D 32:2.
33:3	Intro., ch. 4; G 40:18-19; D 32:27.

33:5 Intro., ch. 1.; N 33:3.
33:7 E 14:2.
33:8 E 14:2.
33:10 N 33:7.
33:14 E 17:1.
33:15 D 3:8; 3:10.
33:16 N 11:34.
33:17 N 11:34.
33:36 N 33:35.
33:38 D 1:3.
33:40 N 21:1.
33:45 N 33:44.
33:47 N 33:44.
33:48 N 33:44.
33:52 N 33:53.
33:55 N 33:53.
34:3 N 34:6; 34:7.
34:4 N 34:15.
34:5 N 34:4; 34:7.
34:6 G 9:2.
34:7 N 34:6.
34:8 N 34:7; 34:15.
34:9 N 34:6; 34:15.
34:10 N 34:9; 34:15.
34:11 N 34:15.
34:12 N 34:15.
34:15 Intro., ch. 4.; N 34:4; D 3:13; 33:23.
34:29 Intro., ch. 3.
35:3 N 24:25.
35:4 N 24:25.
35:5 D 33:23.

35:11	E 21:13; D 19:2; 19:3.
35:13	E 21:13.
35:16	D 27:5.
35:17	N 35:16; 35:18.
35:18	N 35:17.
35:21	G 3:15; N 35:12.
35:22	G 3:15; N 6:9; 35:20; D 4:42.
35:23	E 4:19; 10:28.
35:25	D 32:13.
35:28	N 35:32.
35:31	Intro., ch. 3.
36:5	N 27:7.
36:8	N 27:9.
36:13	D 1:1.

DEUTERONOMY

Chapter 1

1:1 N

a. 'lyn ptgmyyh dy mll mšh ᶜm kl bny yśr'l

b. w'wkḥ ythwn ᶜd 'ynwn yhybyn bᶜbr yrdnh

c. ᶜny mšh w'mr lhwn

d. hl' bmdbrh wbṭwr' dsyny

e. 'ytyhybt lkwn 'wryth bny yśr'l

f. wbmyšryh dmw'b 'tpršt lkwn

g. kmh nysyn ᶜbd yyy ᶜmkwn bny yśr'l

h. kd hwwytwn qyymyn ᶜl ym' dswp

i. 'tbzᶜ qdmykwn ym'

j. w'tᶜbd trtyn ᶜśry 'ysṭrṭyn 'srṭ lkl šbṭ

k. 'rgyztwn qwdmwy ᶜl ym'

l. wsrbtwn ᶜl ym' dswp

m. wᶜl ᶜsq ylylyh dy šlḥtwn mn mdbrh dpr'n lmyllh yt 'rᶜ' dknᶜn

n. wᶜl ᶜsq mnh dy 'mrtwn

o. npšn mᶜyqh blḥmh hdyn dmyklyh qlyl

p. wbḥṣrwt nplw pygrykwn

q. wᶜl ydy bśr' dy 'tḥmdtwn

r. wᶜl ᶜsq ᶜyglh dy ᶜbdtwn

s. 'mr yyy bmymrh lmyšyṣy ytkwn

t. 'lwly d'dkr lkwn qyymh dy qyym ᶜm 'bhtkwn

u. ᶜm 'brhm ᶜm yṣḥq wᶜm yᶜqb

v. wmškn zymn' dy ᶜbdtwn lšmyh

w. w'rwn qyym' dyyy dy 'ᶜltwn bgwwh

x. whpytwn ytyh bdhb' snynh

y. 'mr bmymryh wkpr ᶜl ḥwbykwn

Heb.

1. 'lh hdbrym 'šr dbr mšh 'l kl yśr'l

2. bᶜbr hyrdn bmdbr bᶜrbh mwl swp

3. byn p'rn wbyn tpl wlbn wḥṣrt wdy zhb

The Hebrew is an introduction to what follows and announces that the subsequent material is a review of what Moses already told the people during their travels. The obvious associations of some of the places, the novelty of others (e.g. dy zhb), and the general tone of the exhortations in the following chapters have contributed to the reinterpretation of some of these place names. Some are sites of God's wonderous acts on behalf of the people; some are taken as places that recall sins of the people; others are taken as objects reminiscent of the sins. The bulk of this midrash has Moses summarize and chastise the Israelites for the many times they angered, rejected or sinned against God during their travels in the desert. It also explains that though the people deserved to be punished for all of these sins, their merits assuaged God's anger.

The overall purpose of the midrash is thus clear and the text in its present form glows smoothly. Nonetheless, the text betrays its history. It begins with a literal translation of line 1 (a), but rapidly changes in line b, to the midrashic expansion. The phrase w'wkḥ lhwn anticipates the contents of the midrash, but the first geographic term, bᶜbr yrdnh, has been taken as the location of Moses' speech, not as referring to another Israelite sin (as, e.g., in the Sifrei). These factors permit seeing lines a-b as remnants of an original translation of the verse that was shortened and grafted to the midrash. (It is also possible to divide a and b after _ythwn_, but that would not alter the meaning at all).

Moses' speech begins in c and introduces the rest of the text as well as the next literary unit, d-f. These three lines focus on the giving of the Torah "in the desert" (_bmdbrh_) and include references to Mt. Sinai and the Plains of Moab, (_bᶜrbh_ f), the latter being the subject of N 36:13, the previous verse. The assumption of these lines is that the entire Torah was given on Mt. Sinai and explained in the Plains of Moab -- a deviation from the statement at the end of Numbers, but more in keeping with D 1:5. The use of _bny yśr'l_ (e), frequent in Deut., is interesting for its similarity to the commonly used _ᶜmy bny yśr'l_; cf. Introduction, chapter 4.

Lines g-j correspond to Heb. _mwl swp_ (line 2) and describe another positive experience, the miracles done at the Red Sea; and again the phrase _ᶜm- bny yśr'l_ is used. Lines g-i follow the account in Exodus chapt. 14, but line j, which speaks of 12 separate paths paved through the sea for the 12 tribes, is mentioned neither in the Heb. nor in N. Lines g-h and i-j may be two independent interpretations of _mwl swp_, but it is also possible that they are one long passage composed of an exclamation (g-h) and a statement (i-j). Either way, the recollection of positive experiences ends with line j. This line also marks the seam between the parts of the midrash, for k-l, though also about the events at the Red Sea, begin a series of negative comments about the Israelites' behaviour (k-s). It is quite different from g-h and i-j and, together with line l, offers a second (or third) interpretation of _mwl swp_.

While structurally line k is part of a series of offences committed by the Israelites, lines k-l contain a truncated version of part of Ps. 106:7 (itself part of a lengthy list of Israelite sins committed in the desert). The Hebrew is _wymrw ᶜl_ ym bym swp, translated a.l. as wsrybw ᶜl mymrk ᶜl ym' bym' dswp. The addition of ᶜl mymrk provides an object for the verb srybw, comparable to qwdmwy in N, but otherwise the translation is quite literal. This verse underlies the text in lines k-l and confirms the reading wsrbtwn, unnecessarily emended by DM to wsbtm. The events following line l and introduced by ᶜl are governed by 'rgyztwn not wsrbtwn. It therefore seems that either the use of Ps. 106:7 was an after thought or k-l have replaced the original verb. As things stand, it is not clear exactly how the Israelites sinned. They seem to have angered God by either failing to believe that He would protect them from the Egyptians or refusing to enter the sea, though other possibilities also exist.

Line m refers to the incident of the spies who were sent from the Wilderness of Paran (N 13:1-3). Lines n-o refer to the incident of the serpent infestation following the complaint about the manna wnpšnw qṣh blḥm hqlql (N 21:5). N translates this line wnpšn 'tyᶜqt blḥmh hdyn dmyklyh qlyl, which is almost identical to the translation here and to that used in Onk.

The relation of n-o to the Hebrew is problematic. The Hebrew reads byn p'rn wbyn tpl wlbn wḥṣrwt. Since Paran has been covered in line m and ḥṣrwt is mentioned in p, either 1) the material in lines n-o must be divided into two parts corresponding to the two places wbyn tpl wlbn; or 2) the phrase was understood to be an hendiadys; or 3) something is missing. The Sifrei a.l. poses the exact same problem; i.e. the catch words for the explanation of the relevant phrase are lacking (and restored by R. Elijah of Vilna. as wbyn tpl wlbn). The reason for his change is the explanation dbry tplwt: štplw ᶜl hmn, obviously a play on tpl. The text of Mid. Tan. is even clearer; for it refers to the fruitless search in the Torah for a place name tpl wlbn and, reading tpl wlbn as tplw lbn, mentions the play on tpl / tplwt together with E 16:31, which describes the manna as kzrᶜ gd lbn. It thus seems that lines n-o are an abridgement of or assume the explanations given in the text of Mid. Tan. and that both tpl and lbn should be seen as included in these lines even though there is no direct or indirect reference to the former.

Lines p-q present a different problem. The Israelites' arrival in Haserot is reported in N 11:35 and their departure in N 12:16. Chapter 12 deals with Miriam's leprosy, which is the only event associated with the place in the entire Bible. The Sifrei, which follows the same general pattern as our text, explains the reference to ḥṣrwt by referring to the story of Miriam, but the Mid. Tan. relates the place to the events of the quail. The prooftext cited there is E 16:3, which describes the Israelite complaint about leaving the flesh pots of Egypt (bšbtnw ᶜl syr hbśr), to which God responded by giving them manna. This took place in mdbr syn 'šr byn 'ylm wbyn syny (E 16:1). Hoffman, the editor of Mid. Tan., suggested replacing this verse with my y'kylnw bśr, which he cites to N 14:1. But N 14:1 describes the complaint in Paran that followed the report of the spies sent by Moses, and the required phrase is found in N 11:4 and 18 (a mixup of 11:4 and 14:1 is possible in both Arabic and Hebrew numerals). It describes the Israelite complaint about the lack of proper food, which preceded the arrival of the quails and the plague. As noted above, this all occurred before the arrival at Haserot, reported in N 11:35. Hoffman's explanation, repeated by Fish in his edition of Midrash HaGaddol, is simply that the complaint was associated with Ḥaṣerot because of the proximity to this name in the text.

Line q undoubtedly refers to the plea for meat; for the words bśr' and 'tḥmdtwn are both used in translating Numbers chapter 11, and, as in the Mid. Tan., the event is here erroneously associated with Haseroth. But line p remains a problem, because the statement nplw pgrykwn in no way reflects that event. N 11:33 records the affliction sent by God and the deaths of many people, but the use of pgrykwn comes from N 14:29, 32 and 33, where the Israelites who rejected the spies' reports were told they would die in the desert. N, like Hoffman's citation, thus relates the desire for meat to Num. 14; but presumably the phrase was borrowed only for its powerful language, and not for the association with the spies' report.

All of these associations aside, there is yet another problem in p-q. Assuming that the verbs 'rgyztwn and wsrbtwn govern the subsequent list of incidents, each event should be introduced by ʿl or wʿl; thus: ʿl ym' dswp (l), wʿl ʿsq ylylyh (m), wʿl ʿsq mnh (n-o), and wʿl ʿsq ʿyglh (r). It is improper for p-q to begin wbḥṣrwt, and, as it stands, wʿl in q must be corrected to ʿl. Under the circumstances it is only logical that p-q be reversed so that the event may begin wʿl, as preserved (though Frag. retains the order and has only ʿl). But if line p is out of place, would it, or at least the phrase nplw pgrykwn, be best situated following line m, which actually describes the episode of the spies, from which the phrase is drawn? If these two words are joined to m and wbḥṣrwt is placed after q instead of before it, the manna and quail incidents of n-o and q become one unit, associated with the phrase tpl wlbn. The place Haserot then stands (after q) without any explanation of the sin. The most obvious suggestion is something to do with Miriam, as in the Sifrei, though the Pesikta Zutreta (Mid. Leqaḥ Ṭov) mentions the rebellion of Korah (as noted by Hoffman).

It may not even be necessary to move nplw pgrykwn. Frag is similar to N in most of this passage, as M also seems to be, but both Frag. and M offer a different ending for m. Instead of lmyllh yt 'rʿ' dknʿn, Frag. (and M) reads ... gzr ʿlykm dl' tʿlwn l'rʿ' dyśr'l, a close alternative to the nplw pgrykwn of p, should that be placed following m. However, following the reference to the complaint about the manna in lines n–o, Frag. (and M) reads wgry bkwn ḥywn, a reference to the serpent attack that followed the complaints about the manna in N 21:6, and punished the people for rejection of lḥm qlql (cf. line o). Though the phrase nplw pgrykwn (p) is borrowed from elsewhere, this evidence in Frag. (and M) confirms that it may really belong after line o, in which case the only suggested changes in the text would be moving wbḥṣrwt from p to follow q and/or completing a line such as wᶜl x bḥṣrwt to fill in the line and make it parallel to the others.

As appealing as all this may be, the association of the complaint for meat with Ḥaṣerot (p) is found in Frag., PJ, N, and the Mid. Tan. If this is a simple error, it was an old and established one, for the same problem exists in Josephus. In *Antiquities* III 295, after describing how Moses broke camp at Sinai, Josephus says: "... he ... came to a place called Esermoth. There the multitude began to revolt once more and to reproach Moses ..."; then follows the story of the quails in Num. 11. Esermoth is not phonetically equivalent to Ḥaṣerot, nor is it found in the LXX, which has Aseroth in N 11:35 and 12:16 (but Aulon "courts" in D 1:1). According to a suggestion of J. Weill, accepted by Thackery (Loeb edition, p. 462), Esermoth is related to the name Asarmoth = Ḥaṣarmaweth, a person listed in G 10:26. While there is no connection between this name and our verse, it seems that the meaning of the name ḥṣr-mwt "Field of Death" was associated with the place ḥṣrwt, and various Biblical events not originally placed there, but in which people died, were associated with it. Note the explanation of Rav Huna (BR 37, p. 350) Ḥaṣarmawet: "This is a place whose name is ḥṣr-mwt where the people eat grass (kryšym) and wear "linen" clothes (kly ppyr) and wait for death every day ...." Apparently Ḥaṣeroth was understood as the equivalent of Ḥaṣarmawet, "Field of Death," sometimes used as the equivalent of "cemetery" e.g. BT Ber. 18b (see also Aruch, s.v. ḥṣr) and the associations of other Biblical events became permanent. (Aramaizing ḥṣrwt as ḥaṣerwat or ḥaṣerwata may have helped the association). Perhaps it was not even seen as a specific place but rather conceptualized as any place where people died (e.g. Israelites, Korah). Note also ḥṣrym in 2:23 and the fact that it is translated, not transcribed, and Eusebius' comment in The Onomastikon (p. 4). If so, p may remain as recorded, though it still lacks the appropriate introduction of wᶜl.

Returning to the analysis of N, we note that line r refers not to a place but to the golden calf (E 32:1-10). The place name in the Hebrew is dy zhb, the association being the gold from which the calf was made, but which is not actually mentioned in the verse.

This part of the midrash ends with line r. Of the places listed in the Heb., one was the site of Moses' speech, two were places where good things happened to the Israelites, and the rest recalled sins against God. As a result, God considered ('mr) destroying them (s, based on E 32:10), but he did not do so because of his promise to the patriarchs (t-u) and the meritorious acts of the Israelites themselves (v-y).

Lines t-u are a paraphrase of L 26:42: wzkrty 't bryty yᶜqwb w'p 't bryty yṣḥq w'p 't bryty 'brhm, reordered chronologically to follow the language of D 1:8. Lines v-x refer to the Tent of Meeting, the Ark of the Covenant placed in it, and the gold with which it was made and because of which God wiped away the sins of the people. The salvation noted in v is dependent, in part, on the gold donated by the Israelites to decorate the Tabernacle (x). Though there is no sure indication, an association with dy zhb is very possible. This assumes a reading dai zhb "enough gold" and could easily derive from E 36:5-6, where Moses requested that the people stop making contributions to the construction of the Tabernacle because mrbym hᶜm lhby' mdy hᶜbdh. (Sources about atoning for the golden calf through giving gold for the tabernacle are listed in Ginzberg, Vol. VI, p. 63, n. 322). In general, the contents of this list of sins and God's mercy (which is related to the fact that they built him a special place in their midst) reflects the lengthier list of sins in Ps. 106 (about 40 verses) followed by wyzkr lhm brytw, though there the emphasis on the Tabernacle / Temple is lacking. The same pattern is also reflected in D 1:26-30.

1:2	Heb.		N
	'ḥd ᶜśr ywm	a.	'rḥ mhlk ḥd ᶜśr ywmyn
	mḥrb	b.	hwh lkwn mhlkh mn ṭwr' dḥwrb
	drk hr śᶜyr	c.	'wrḥ ṭwr gblh
	ᶜd qdš brnᶜ	d.	mṭy ᶜd rqm dgyᶜh
		e.	ᶜl dḥṭytwn w'rgztwn qdmwy
		f.	'tᶜkbtwn wᶜbdtwn [DM: wᶜbrtwn] bhwn
		g.	mhlkyn 'rbᶜyn šnyn

N is composed of two units, a-d and e-g. Lines a-d are expansive and substitue Aramaic place names for the Hebrew ones, but generally in keeping with the practices of N. The word hr appears with ḥrb in Heb. only in E 33:6, but N uses its equivalent (ṭwr') here, perhaps because of hr śᶜyr, and also in 4:10 and 15, where no such influence is felt. The usage probably reflects the equation hr syny = ḥrb = hr ḥrb.

Lines e-g, in contrast to a-d, are similar to the midrash in v. 1 and add the further insult of having had to travel 40 years to accomplish an 11-day journey. In spite of this similarity, this addition anticipates v. 3 and should not be relocated to v. 1. The correction of wʿbdtwn to wʿbrtwn, though easily justified is unnecessary. Aram ʿbd is the equivalent of the Hebrew ʿśh which, among other things, means "to spend time."

1:3 bswp (+): expansive, as in N 33:38.
kl: for Heb. kkl, as in N 8:20.
lmymr (+): expansive.

1:5 spr (+): expansive; assumes that the word htwrh refers to the entire Pentateuch.

1:7 wkbysw (+): expansive.
wṭwr byt mwqdšh: for Heb. hlbnwn, as in 3:25, 11:24, etc. Cf. G. Vermes, Scripture and Tradition in Judaism (Leiden, 1961), pp. 26-39.

1:8 dyyry d'rʿ': for Heb. h'rṣ. Sometimes this change has been introduced to prevent hyper-literal misreadings of the text, but this is apparently not the case here. Perhaps the adjustment should be seen together with the use of msryt for Heb. ntty. The same notion is found in v. 21, but there dyyry has not been added.

1:10 sgyn wqyymyn (+): sgyn is based on 'sgy; for a parallel to wqyymyn, cf. D 29:9.

1:13 rbrbnyn ʿlykwn: for Heb. br'šykm, influenced by v. 15.

1:15 ḥkymyn wskltnym: for Heb. ḥkmym wydʿm In v. 13 we see

the problem of using *ḥkymyn* and *ḥkmyn* for Heb. *ḥkmym* and *ydᶜym*, but here the text seems to be in error, for *skltnyn* should refer to *nbnym*, as it does in v. 13.

1:16 *dynyn d-* (+): expansive, providing a direct object for the verb.

qšṭ: routine for Heb. *ṣdq*; cf. 16:18, etc.

1:17 *kmlwy d-*: expansion to avoid a hyper-literal error (2x).

mlk wšlyṭ: for Heb. *'yš*. An honest judge should fear neither great people nor lowly ones. As seen many times before, *mlk wšlyṭ* is an hendiadys, and *'yš* means more than "man."

mtbᶜ (+): expansive; used (with *qdm*) to avoid too close a connection with God.

1:24 The Heb. *wyᶜlw* has not been translated.

1:28 *ᶜd ṣyt šmy'*: routine for Heb. *bšmym*.

1:30 *hw' yᶜbd lkwn nṣḥny qrbykwn*: for Heb. *hw' ylḥm lkm*, as in 3:22, etc.

yyy (+): expansive, adds subject; cf. 4:34, which is the closest to this construction of many similar ones.

1:33 *lmtqnh*: for *ltwr*, applied to God.

bᶜmwdh d- (+): expansive, based on E 13:21 (2x), to which this translation is now quite similar.

1:34 *wtqp rwgzyh*: for Heb. *wyqṣp*. Note the absence of the circumlocution *hwh rgwz mn qdm yyy* that is found in v. 37.

w'mr bšbwᶜh: for Heb. *wyšbᶜ*; cf. *dqyymt* for *'šr nšbᶜty* in v. 35.

1:36 lmymr ṭb (+): expansive.

1:38 mšmš (+): expansive, used to describe Joshua in E 33:11 also.

1:39 lmpršh byn ṭb lbyš: idiomatic translation of Heb. ṭwb wrᶜ; cf. ydᶜyn lmpršh byn ṭb lbyš, G 3:5.

wlhwd: for Heb. wlhm; read wlhwn.

1:44 'wrᶜyyth (with DM) (+): expansive.

ᶜd šyṣyw: for the toponym ᶜd ḥrmh, taking the root as ḥrm (translated elsewhere as šyṣy', e.g. 2:34), but not referring to another specific toponym, as does bgblh, the routine translation of śᶜyr. Cf. N 14:45 and 21:3.

1:45 bql bkwtkwn: for Heb. bqlkm.

lmlykwn: for Heb. 'lykm.

Chapter 2

2:1 'mr mšh (+): added to prevent "... God spoke to me" from being misunderstood as the words of the translator. Similar to the commonly noted practice of translating 'ny yyy as kdn 'mr yyy or the like, this addition is routine in Deut.; examples include N 21:34, D 2:2, 9, 17, 31, 4:10. See also my discussion of D 3:2.

2:5 sdry qrbh (+): based on the full expression 'l ttgr bm mlḥmh, as in v. 9; here the Heb. says only 'l ttgrw bm. The same addition has been made in v. 19.

2:6

Heb.		N
'kl tšbrw m'tm bksp	a.	mzwn lyt 'twn ṣrykyn mzbwn mn lwwthwn bksp
w'kltm	b.	dmnh nḥyt lkwn mn šmy'
wgm mym tkrw m'tm bksp	c.	wlhwd myyn lyt 'twn ṣrykyn mzbwn mn lwwthwn [M: + bksp]
wštytm	d.	dbyrh dmy' slq' ᶜmkwn
	e.	lr'šy twwryh wlhltth [DM: wlḥlth] ᶜmyqth

According to the Hebrew, the Israelites were allowed to buy food and water from descendents of Esau, but not to take it without paying. But given the presence of the manna and the wonderous well that followed them in the desert, such purchases should have been unnecessary. N therefore changes the positive statements of the verse to negative ones. This was accomplished by reading the Heb. of a and c as questions and adding the appropriate comments: "Why should you buy food from them for money, while you eat the manna ...", etc. Since bksp occurs twice in the Heb., it should probably be added at the end of line c, as in M.

2:7 Cf. notes of DM.

bsᶜdkwn: for Heb. ᶜmk.

kl mn dᶜm: for Heb. dbr.

2:9 ly: read ᶜly? The same expression occurs in v. 31 also.

2:10 gwbryyh (+): cf. 1:28 and 2:11, where gwbryn is used for rp'ym. The use of this Waw is normal for gbr "man." The word may have replaced gybr-; cf. M: gybr' and N in v. 20, etc.

2:12 ḥwwrnyyh: for Heb. hḥrym; apparently the root ḥwr

"white" was understood as the basis of this proper name.

b'tryhwn: for Heb. tḥtm, as in v. 21, etc.

2:13 The Heb. lkm has been omitted but added in M.

ᶜl: for Heb. 't; cf. v. 14, where yt is used in this same construction, and I, here, which also suggests yt.

2:15 mḥwwn mn qdm yyy 'trgzyt bhwn: for Heb. yd yyy hyth bm.

ᶜd zmn dy spw: for Heb. ᶜd tmm, a routine translation of gerund with a finite verb, but the same expression is a literal translation of the Heb. in the following verse.

2:20 zmtnyyh: for Heb. zmzmym.

2:21 kbnwy dᶜnq gybryy': for Heb. kᶜnqym; cf. v. 9.

2:23 bkwprnyyh: for Heb. bḥṣrym. Apparently the Hebrew was understood as a common noun; cf. notes to 1:1.

2:27 l' ... wl' (+): idiomatic.

2:28 lḥwd lyt 'nn ḥsryn mn kl mn dᶜm (+): This verse stands in marked contrast to 2:6 as augmented, but the addition helps bridge the gap. The added phrase is similar to l' ḥsrt dbr in 2:7, translated l' ḥsrtwn kl mn dᶜm, and to l' tḥsr kl bh in 8:9, translated l' tḥsrwn kl mn dᶜm bh.

2:29 yrdnh hdn: for Heb. hyrdn; the phrase hyrdn hzh is used in 3:27, 31:2, etc.

2:30 wl' ṣb' ... dl' lmᶜbrh ...: a double negative; cf. E 10:27, where a similar construction lacks dl'.

The printed text should read kywm' as in the MS, not bywm', for Heb. kywm.

2:34 qwry tlylth: for Heb. ᶜyr mtm, as in 3:6, routinely used for ᶜry mbṣr also.

l' šyyrnn l' šzbw: double negative; cf. 5:29.

2:36 lḥyyt: for toponym ᶜrᶜr; also in 3:12, and elsewhere for ᶜr.

bnḥlh: a literal translation of Heb. bnḥl, but in keeping with the tendency in N to avoid such literal translations, M suggests ᶜl gyp nḥ-.

2:37 qrbnn: for Heb. qrbt, keeping with the many other m. pl. forms in these verses.

Chapter 3

3:2 'mr mšh (+): probably like the other verses listed in 2:1, but in N 21:34, which is very similar to this verse, the Heb. reads wy'mr yyy 'l mšh.

3:4 ythwn: yth would be better.

kl tḥwm ṭrkwnh byt mlkwth dᶜwg bbwtnyn (with DM): for Heb. kl ḥbl 'rgb mmlkt ᶜwg bbšn.

3:5 mqpyn (+): added to divide the long Heb. contruction kl 'lh ᶜrym bṣwrt hwmh into two. The word tlyln is normally used for bṣwrt, but the desire to divide the Heb. into two descriptions necessitated adding mqypn, which looks like a double reading but is not. Cf. Onk. kl 'lh krykn mqpn ṣwr; PJ: kl 'lh qyrwwy ḥqr' mqpn šwryn.

qwry mbdrth: for Heb. ʿry hprzy.

3:7 wqwryyth: read dqwryyth, as in 2:35.

3:8 mn: for Heb. myd; I adds yd.

ṭwr tlgh: for Heb. ḥrmwn, as in N 33:15.

3:9 ṭwr' dmsry pyry: for Heb. (claimed to be Sidonian) śryn, obviously relating sry and śryn.

3:10 sylywqyh: for Heb. toponym slkh. Homophony seems to be the major reason for this association; cf. Onk.: slkh (variants slk); PJ: slwwqy' (cf. N 33:15).

3:11 b'mtyh dmlk': for Heb. b'mt 'yš; cf. 1:17.

3:13 l'trh: expansive; stimulated by ambiguity of Heb. hhw'.

This verse is related to the midrash in N 34:15, as is v. 14.

3:14 The translation of Heb. whmʿkty has been erased from N; cf. DM, a.l. The text should probably contain a gentillic form, w'pyqyrwsyyh, or the like.

3:16 Read either wlšbṭyh dbnwy dr'wbny ... or wlšbṭh dbnwy dr'wbny wlšbṭh dhnwy dgdy, not wlšbṭh (s.) followed by two tribes.

3:17 mn ym' dgnysr: for Heb. mknrt.

špwʿ byt rmth: for Heb. 'šdt hpsgh.

3:23 wṣlyty (!) wbʿyty (!) rḥmyn: a double translation of

Heb. w'tḥnn. Cf. Onk. wṣlyty (in this form) and PJ wbʿyt rḥmyn.

3:24 Heb.		N
'dny	a.	yyy
yyy	b.	bbʿw brḥmyn mn qdmyk yyy
'th hḥlt lhr'wt 't ʿbdk	c.	't šryt lmḥwwyyh yt ʿbdk
't gdlk w't ydk hḥzqh	d.	yt tqpk wyt gbwrt ydk tqypth
'šr my 'l	e.	dy mn 'lh kwwtk
bšmym	f.	d'yqr škyntk šryy' bšmyy' mn lʿyl
wb'rṣ	g.	wšlṭnyk ʿl 'rʿ' mn lrʿ
'šr yʿśh kmʿśyk	h.	dy yʿbd kʿbdyk ṭbyyh
wkgbwrtk	i.	wknysy gbwrtk

The verse is translated expansively but closely. In line b, yyy has been read in its normal way, not as 'lhym, as in the TBT; cf. PJ mn qdmk 'lqym. In d, gbwrt has been added to avoid the impression that the people actually saw God's hand, though the literal translation is used in c. Unhappy with the notion of God's being literally in the heavens or on earth, the translator added the routine 'yqr škyntk and wšlṭnk in lines f and g.

There is a certain syntactic tension between this expansion of f-g and the word kwwtk, which seems more suited to a translation like dy mn 'lh kwwtk bšmyyh wb'rʿh .... Lines f-g are similar to Onk.: d't hw' 'lh' dškyntk bšmy' mlʿyl' wšlyṭ b'rʿ' (some texts add mlrʿ) and identical to part of 4:39.

The reading in N (with kwwtk) is similar to my kmkh b'lym yyy, E 15:11, translated mn kwwtk b'yly mrwm' yyy in N or to my 'l kmwk in Micha 7:18. The related line in D 33:29 is different in N. The expansions in lines f-g are paralleled in E 20:4 and D 5:8, but the entire passage (e-g) is very close to 1 Kings 8:23

wy'mr yyy 'lhy yśr'l 'yn kmwk 'lhym bšmym mmʿl wʿl h'rṣ mtḥt ... (closer than the briefer parallel text in 2 Chron. 6:14), translated in Jonathan lyt br mnk 't hw' 'lh' dškyntk bšmy' mlyl' wšlyṭ ʿl 'rʿ' mlrʿ.

3:25 kʿn bbʿw: a double translation of Heb. n'.

3:26 wl' šmʿ bql ṣlwty: idiomatic for Heb. wl' šmʿ 'ly.

3:27 The sequence of these points of the compass has been followed in G 28:14.

3:29

Heb.		N
wnšb bgy'	a.	wšrynn bḥlth
mwl	b.	bkyyn ʿl ḥwbynn
	c.	wmtwwdyn ʿl ḥṭ'ynn
byt pʿwr	d.	ʿl dy 'dbqnn lplḥy
	e.	ṭʿwwth pʿwr

Cf. 4:3. The gratuitous parallelism in b–c is striking. Both bkyyn / mtwwdyn and ḥwbyn / ḥṭ'yn occur together elsewhere.

Chapter 4

4:2 kʿn (+): seemingly extra and deleted by M, but probably idiomatic; cf. Introduction, chapt. 3.

4:3 The words ky kl h'yš 'šr hlk 'ḥry bʿl pʿwr have been omitted from N by mistake. DM has filled in the text from PJ, but the wording is appropriate for N. A closer approximation would be 'rwm kl gbr' dy 'zl (cf. D 17:3) [or 'tḥbr (cf. N 25:5) or 'dbq (cf. D 3:29 and 4:4)] lplḥy ṭʿwwt pʿwr.

4:4 *b'wlpn 'wryyth d-* (+): Cleaving to God was impossible; one could cleave to his Torah.

ḥyyn wqyymyn: a routine hendiadys; for Heb. *ḥyym.*

4:5 The word *ṣwny* should have been translated *pqd yty*, as noted by DM.

4:6 *ḥkmtkwn wswkltnwtkwn wbyntkwn*: Three terms for *ḥkmtkm wbyntkm* in Heb. This extra one appears to be *wbyntkwn*, for the root *skl* is routinely used to translate the root *byn* (e.g. 1:13, 32:28). This follows Onk. and PJ as well; cf. notes to 1:15.

4:7 *'wmh wmlkw*: for Heb. *gwy gdwl*. The hendiadys has been used frequently (e.g. v. 8), but the word *gdwl* has not been translated in either case; cf. v. 6, *'wmh rbth*.

bkl zmn d'nn mṣlyyn qdmwy hw' ʿny ytn: for Heb. *bkl qr'nw 'lyw*. The verb *qr'* is frequently translated *ṣly* in such contexts.

4:8 *whl'* (+): unexpected and deleted in I.

zkyyn: for Heb. *ṣdyqm*. Heb. *ṣdq* is often translated *qšṭ*. The meaning here is "righteous" or "proper," not "pure." Cf. the homophonous Greek *dikaia*, which actually means that.

sdr: for Heb. *ntn*, usually translated *yhb*; I: *msdr*.

4:10 *yylpwn ythwn*: taking Heb. *ylmdwn* as *ylmdwm* by reading the Heb. as Aramaic, influenced by 5:1.

4:11 *bšypwly ṭwrh*: routine for Heb. *tḥt hhr*.

ṣyt šmy': for Heb. *lb hšmym*.

4:12 *lhby* (+): expansive, as in v. 15, 4:33, 5:4, etc.

ql dbyry: for Heb. qwl dbrym, M: dbyryn. This is the word for individual units of the Ten Commandments; cf. E 20:1 ff. and Deut. 5:6 ff., 4:13, etc.

4:14 Heb. lᶜśtkm 'tm was untranslatable in its literal form, hence dy tᶜbdwn ythwn, which reflects the Hebrew of verses like 1:18, etc.

4:16 ᶜwbdykwn (+): providing an object for the verb, as in v. 25. It is followed by wtᶜbdwn, not wtᶜkdwn.

The space for the translation of psl tmwnt kl sml is hardly large enough to accommodate more than the ṣlm wṣwrh restored by Diez-Macho (presumably visible in the MS). The gap contained at least two words (cf. MS of v. 23, where the space for the translation of a similar passage is split between two lines), and ṣlm was probably part of the phrase, because it was erased by the censor. This same phrase is suggested for v. 23, the slightly larger space in v. 25, and 5:7 (also split between two lines) as well. Verses 23 and 25 read psl tmwnt kl; 5:8 has psl kl tmwnh E 20:4. In N, tmwnh is regularly translated dmw (cf. 4:12, etc.) and all of these verses contain a phrase wkl dmw .... Accordingly, the space contained only the translation of the word psl, restored by Diez-Macho as ṣlm wṣwrh in each case, even though the underlying Heb. phrases are not identical.

The Heb. of v. 16, however, contains psl, tmwnt kl sml, and tbnyt zkr 'w nqbh. The word sml occurs in the Torah only here. (In Ezek. 8:3, 5 it is translated ṣylm). The word psl is found in D 27:15 (2x), 7:5, 7:25, and L 26:1, and in each case it has been erased by the censor. Diez-Macho routinely restores it as ṣlm. If psl in v. 16 was rendered ṣlm, and tbnyt ... was rendered wkl dmw ..., why was the phrase tmwnt kl sml translated as ṣwrh, and why was this word used in vv. 23, 25 and 5:8 even though it was not based on any underlying Heb. text?

It is possible that psl was rendered in some cases as the hendiadys ṣlm wṣwrh, though one must then ask why this has not been done more consistently. (PJ also uses only ṣlm.) It is also curious why the censor removed the word ṣwrh. In any case, one must assume either 1) that for some unknown reason, in 4:16 the phrase tmwnt kl sml was rendered ṣwrh (and perhaps became the base of the usages in later verses); or 2) that the translation of this phrase was replaced by the word ṣwrh used elsewhere; or 3) N contains an error in addition to the censor's deletion, and the text originally resembled the form, if not the language, of PJ, which reads ṣlm dmw ṭᶜw dmw ddkr 'w dnwqb', (perhaps ṣlm dmw ṭᶜw wkl dmw ddkr 'w dnqbh) and three (not two) words were deleted because of their similar forms (note the suggested deletion of wtṭᶜwn in 4:19). The reading in M reflects this problem: dmn (DM: dmw) kl mn dᶜm dmn (DM: dmw) ddkr 'w dnqbh. But the phrase dmw kl mn dᶜm seems closer to the reading tmwnt kl in vv. 23, 25 than to the text of N, and it would not have been deleted by the censor.

4:17 dprḥ dṭyys: a double translation of knp. Cf. discussion in G 1:17 and 15:11.

4:19 zhr': for Heb. yrḥ; cf. G 1:14.

4:21 wqyym bšbwᶜh: for Heb. wyšbᶜ.

4:24 'š' 'klh 'š': for Heb. 'š 'klh; cf. notes to E 24:17.

'lh qnyy wpwrᶜn bqn': possibly a double translation of Heb. 'l qn', but note the same expression in E 20:6 and D 5:10.

4:25 mh dsny wmrḥq: for Heb. hrᶜ, as in 17:2.

4:26 qdm, wqdm (+): The Hebrew says that the Heavens and Earth were called as witnesses (cf. 32:1). This was changed by the translator so that the oath was simply made in their presence. Note also the treatment of this problem in 32:1.

4:28 tᶜwwn d- (+): added twice and not deleted by censor.

4:30 bzmnh d'ᶜyq lkwn: for Heb. bṣr lk. Cf. M: bzmn' dyᶜyqwn ytkwn; Onk. kd tᶜyq lk; etc. "When (b-) it is rough (ṣr) for you."

ᶜqyyh: for Heb. hdbrym, based on the above phrase.

bswp ᶜqb ywmy': idiomatic translation of Heb. b'ḥryt hymym.

4:32 br' yyy 'lhym: for Heb. br' 'lhym; cf. G 2:7.

'dm qdmyh: for Heb. h'dm, as in G 2:8.

4:33 hyydh: for Heb. h- (interrogative). This change has necessitated reordering the rest of the clause.

ḥyyh (+): expansive.

4:34 nysyyh: for Heb. hnsh, possibly seeing the Hebrew verb as an Aramaic noun. This change demonstrates that vv. 33 and 34 must be joined.

wᶜyynykwn ḥmyyn: for Heb. lᶜynyk. This is similar to ᶜyynykm hr'wt (4:3, 11:7), translated ᶜynykwn ḥmyyn.

4:37 wprq w'pq ytkwn pryqyn: redundant, possibly a double translation of Heb. wywṣ'k. Cf. E 6:7 w'pyq ytkwn pryqyn, with w'prwq later in the verse.

btwqpyh bḥyylh rbh: perhaps a double translation of Heb.

bkḥw hgdwl.

4:39 d'yqr škyntyh šryh bšmyh mn lᶜyl wšwlṭnh ᶜl 'rᶜ' mn lrᶜ: for Heb. bšmym mmᶜl wᶜl h'rṣ mtḥt; cf. 3:24.

lyt 'lh 'ḥrn br mnyh: in place of Heb. 'yn ᶜwd, but actually based on v. 35.

4:42 btqwp (+): the equivalent of btkwp (not btqyp with DM) in N 35:22.

4:43 dbyt (+): N routinely adds dbnwy d- in such contexts; cf. end of verse.

grm: for Heb. toponym r'mt.

dbrh: for Heb. toponym gwln.

4:44 sdr: for Heb. śm; also used for ntn in 4:8.

4:46 ltᶜwwth dpᶜwr (with the Daleth dotted for deletion): This is the intermediate stage between full use of the relative d- and its absence in other occurrences.

4:49 ym' dmlḥ': The more popular name for the Heb. ym hᶜrbh.

Chapter 5

5:1 bmšmᶜkwn: routine for Heb. b'znykm.

5:5 kᶜn (+): As in 4:2.

5:6-18 These verses contain the Ten Commandments, translated, expanded and embellished as in Ex. Chapt. 20. Innovations in Deut. are discussed below; for further analysis consult my notes to Exodus.

5:9 Though the Hebrew texts of E 20:5 and D 5:9 are identical, the translations are not.

N, E 20:5		N, D 5:9
... 'rwm 'nh yyy 'lhkwn	a.	...'rwm 'nh hw' yyy 'lhkwn
'lh qnyy wpwrᶜn	b.	'lh qnyy wpwrᶜn
dmtprᶜ bqn' mn ršyᶜy'	c.	mtprᶜ bqn'h
	d.	mdkr ḥwby 'bhn ršyᶜn
ᶜl bnyn mrdyn	e.	ᶜl bnyn mrwdyn
ᶜl dr tlyty'	f.	ᶜl dr tlytyy
wᶜl dr rbyᶜy'y lśn'y	g.	wᶜl dr rbyᶜyy
kd yhwwn bnyy' mšlmyn	h.	kd mšlmyn
bḥṭ'h btr 'bhthn	i.	bḥṭ' qdmyy
lhwn 'nh qr' śn'yy ...	j.	lśn'yy...

In addition to minor differences, there are major changes in lines d and g-j. The addition of line d in D 5:9 makes the translation much closer to the Hebrew; this version probably reflects the correct text. It points to the expansive translation of Heb. 'l qn' in b-c; (d)mtprᶜ cannot be the translation of pqd. And line d contains 'bhn, missing from E 20:5. In contrast, lines g-j in D 5:9 are shorter than their parallels in E 20:5; the latter text seems superior, though both are intelligible and convey essentially the same idea. In E 20:5, lines h-j appear to be a gloss, related to pqd ᶜwn 'bwt, omitted from d. In D 5:9 lines h-i are a gloss, intruding between g and j. Note the similarities with E 34:6-7 and N 14:18.

5:10 wlnṭry mṣwwth d'wryyty: E 20:6 has wlnṭwry pyqwdy'; the text of Deut. is less literal but seems preferable.

5:11 'nš: in E 20:7 gbr. There is no Heb. word underlying the translation; the same type of paraphrase, including the shift from second to third person, is also found in vv. 16, and 21.

šmh dyyy qdyšh: in E 20:7 šmh dyyy 'lhyh, for šm yyy 'lhyk.

5:12-15 Wherever possible the text is close to that in E 20:8-11, but where the Hebrew texts differ, so do the translations.

5:16 ywqr kl 'nš mnkwn yt ...: cf. E 20:12 hwwn zhyryn gbr byqryh d'bwy. The Heb. is in the singular (kbd 't ...), and the verse begins with ʿmy bny yśr'l, which occurs most typically in cases where singular directives are translated as plurals.

5:17 Almost identical to E 20:13.

5:17 (=18) Aside from the restorations of obvious deletions (cf. DM) the only noteworthy difference between this verse and E 20:14 is npq; the latter has 't' (cf. E 20:15) while the other passages, including E 20:13, have np(y)q, but note 'tyyh at the end of v. 21.

5:17 (=19) The text is almost identical to E 20:15.

5:17 (=20) While the contents are basically the same, D 5:17 and E 20:16 differ in many small points. The phrase mśhdyn śhdy šqr' may be an unnecessary redundancy, cf. Ex.: shdy. Where Ex. uses shdy šqr' four times (šqr once), Deut. has mśhdyn śhdy dšqr, śhdy šqr', mśhdy šqr, mshdyn shdy dšqr, and shdy šqr'.

Apparently the translator (or copyist) also could not decide on the use of *Śin* / *Samekh*; cf. 19:16.

Note also the difference between the usages of the prepositions *ʿm* and *l-* here and in v. 18 (cf. parallels in Ex.).

N usually uses the phrase *ḥyyt' d'py brh* (e.g. G 3:1). Note that here and in E 20:16 the phrase is *ḥywt br'*.

5:18 (21) The text follows the Hebrew where possible, expanding it, as in E 20:17, but the conclusions are different.

N, E 20:17		N, D 5:18
...*'rwm bḥwby ḥmwdyyh*	a.	... *'rwm bḥwby hmwdyh*
	b.	*ʿnnyn slqyn*
	c.	*wmṭr l' nḥt*
	d.	*wbṣwrth 'tyyh ʿl ʿlm'*
mlkwt' mtgryyn bbny 'nš'	e.	*wmlkwwth mtgryyn bbny 'nš'*
	f.	*wḥmdyn nksyhwn*
	g.	*wnsbyn* [with DM] *ythwn*

Punishment for coveting one's neighbor's possessions logically could consist of God's withholding rain, thus causing a famine in retribution for greed. Or it might fittingly take the form of a foreign power conquering the land and taking the people's possessions. Thus either b-d (not unlike 11:17) or e-g alone might be adequate. Lines f-g differ from the series of punishments in the previous verses, because they specify the association between punishment and the crime; but this is no more essential here than in some of the other cases and might mean that they are secondary. There is no obvious connection between b-d and e-g; one is unnecessary, but they are attested in E 20:17, in Frag., but not in PJ, F, N or M. Apparently the text of N in D 5:18 contains a double explanation.

The confusion in versification stems from the difference between the Ex. and Deut. texts in the use of conjunctions to introduce the latter commandments: *wl'* ... *wl'* or *l'* ... *l'*. The Heb. citations in Deut. (as well as the translation to the extent possible) are the same for Deut. as Ex. and further evidence that the Deut. text has been strongly influenced by that of Ex.

5:19 (=22) *'mr mšh* (+): also in D.

5:21 (=24) *whw' ḥyh*: The word *wqyym* is not present in Aram.

5:25 (=28) *h' špr wtqn 'yyṭybw*: probably a double translation of Heb. *hyṭybw*. The phrase *špr wtqn* is frequently used for Heb. *ṭwb* in G 1:10, 12, etc., but *'yyṭybw* is much closer to the Hebrew and probably a later corruption. Verbal forms are used in 5:26 (*yyṭyb*), in 8:16 (*lmyyṭbh*), 30:5 (*wyyṭb*), etc. Here D reads only *h' špr wtqyn* (though it has *lmyṭbh* in v. 26).

5:26 (=29) *lbh šlmh*: for Heb. *lbbm zh*.

5:27 (=30) *mšh mn šmy* (+): I *mš-*. This should be understood as *mšmyyh*, "from the heavens," not "from my name" (space for *-yh* definitely appears in the MS), Though not attested here in PJ, Frag. or the geniza fragments, Moses' ascension(s) to heaven were a popular theme in the midrashic literature; cf. Ginzberg, *Index*, p. 323. Note the implications of v. 28 for Moses' location, and how it differs from this addition.

5:30 (=33) *wtsgwn wtwrkwn ywmyn*: a double translation of Heb. *wh'rktm ymym*. The root *sgy* is used in similar constructions in D 5:16 and E 20:18, and 32:47, while *'rk* is used in D 22:7 (M: *sgy*), 4:40, 17:20 (N and I), 11:9, 4:26 (N, I: *twrkwn* as here, but M: sgy), 25:15 (M: sgy). Regardless of the extent of this inconsistency, 5:30 seems to be the only place where both verbs are used together, unless one assumes that the purpose of the glosses noted above in M and I is to augment, rather than replace, the verbs in N.

Chapter 6

6:2 Add 'twn after ytkwn.

6:4 The text of 6:4 is similar in part to G 49:1 and especially 49:2, but there are enough differences to warrant a full presentation.

N, D 6:4

a. kywn dmṭh qṣh d'bwnn yᶜqb
b. lmtknš bšlm mn gw ᶜlm'
c. knyš tryn ᶜśrty šbṭyyh
d. w'qym ythwn ḥzwr ḥzwr ldrgšyh ddhbh
e. ᶜny 'bwnn yᶜqb
f. w'mr lhwn
g. 'brhm 'bwy d'bh qm mynyh psylh yšmᶜ'l wkl bnyh dqṭwrh
h. wyṣḥq 'bh qm mynyh psylh ᶜśw 'ḥy
i. dlmh lṭᶜwwt dhwh 'bwy d'brhm plḥ 'twn plḥyn
j. 'w dlmh lṭᶜwwt [d]lbn 'ḥwh d'mh plḥ 'twn plḥyn
k. 'w l'lhyh dyᶜqb 'bwkwn 'twn plḥyn
l. ᶜnyyn tryn ᶜśrty šbṭwy dyᶜqb kḥdh blbh šlmh
m. w'mryn šmᶜ mnn yśr'l 'bwnn yyy 'lhn yyy ḥd hw'
n. yh' šmyh mbrk lᶜlmy ᶜlmyn.

The setting for this midrash is Gen. 48-49, even though

the verse around which it revolves is D 6:4. Lines a-b present this setting, and lines c-d are similar to G 49:1 i-j and 49:2 a-b. Lines c-m are generally very close to 49:2 f-m, but the equivalent of 49:2 j-k has been expanded in D 6:4 to include G 49:2 c-e. The material in G 49:2 c-e is better suited to the context of Genesis, but so is the more direct, second person, presentation of D 6:4. Indeed, the only reason why this entire matter is included here at all is to provide a suggested, albeit midrashic, origin for this verse, which became the most important one in the entire Bible for rabbinic Judaism.

The expansion of lines i-k refers to the idolatry of Terach, father of Abraham, and of Laban, brother of Rebecca. Neither of these accusations is based on any clear statement in Genesis, though Laban had his *terafim* (G 31:19, etc.). Numerous rabbinic texts portray the idolatrous activities of both people.

In line 1, *kḫdh* and *blbh šlmh* are redundant. G 49:2 has only *kḫd'*, but the same duplication occurs in G 22:6 for the Heb. *yḫdyw*. G 49:2 contains *ʿnh yʿqb w'mr*, followed by *brwk šmyh kbwdyh dmlkwtyh lʿlmy ʿlmyn*. D 6:4 lacks the connective, which attributes the subsequent line to Jacob, and adds *yh' šmyh mbrk lʿlmy ʿlmyn*, a doxology found elsewhere in N and discussed in G 35:9. Unless the purpose of this addition is simply to attribute *yh' šmyh* ... to Jacob, one must assume that this concluding line predates that in G 49:2. It is highly unlikely that the text in G 49:2 would have been replaced by this one, once the former had become the accepted liturgical practice. For additional discussion, cf. G 49:1-2.

6:5 *'wlpn 'wryyth* (+): This changes the requirement of loving God to one of loving the studying of his Torah.

mmwnykwn: for Heb. *m'dk*; cf. M Ber. 9:5.

6:6 tdyryn (+): expansive.

6:7 bmyytbkwn, wbhlkwtkwn, wbmdmkwn, wbqwmykwn: Though attested elsewhere, the nominal form used here is very rare in N and has probably been used here, as in Onk. as well, in imitation of the Heb. The same thing occurs in 11:19; both texts are extremely important in the liturgy.

6:8 ʿl 'drʿykwn: for Heb. ʿl ydk, as in 11:18 where the Heb. is also plural.

ltpylyn: for the Heb. hapax legomenon lṭṭpt. The choice of tpylyn for the second phrase avoids repeating symn or tpylyn in both halves of the verse, and does not necessarily mean that only ṭṭpt on the head were called tpylyn.

ʿl byt 'pykwn; for Heb. byn ʿynyk; cf. 14:1, and 11:18.

6:9 wtkbtwn ythwn bgw mzwzyyn wtqbʿwn ythwn btrʿy btykwn wbsyypy qwryykwn: for Heb. wktbtm ʿl mzzwt bytk wbšʿryk (here and in 11:20). The targum appears either to specify three places for the mezzuzah, instead of the two in the Bible, or to contain a double translation; but neither is in fact the case. The Biblical mzwzh meant "door post," but here in N it refers to the parchment on which the text of D 6:4-9 (and 11:13-21) was written. Hence the instructions are to write the text on the parchments (bgw mzwzyyn) and fasten them to the appropriate places (btʿry btykwn wbsyypy qwryykwn). The same translation is found in Onk.

6:12 'wlpn 'wryyth d- (+): cf. v.5.

byt šʿbwd ʿbdyyh: as in 5:6, etc.

6:13 Restore yt 'yqr škynth dyyy thwwn [dḥlyn wqdmwy thwwn

plḥyn wbšmyh (or wbšm mymryh) thwwn] mštbʿyn wmqyymyn, not as in DM.

... mstbʿyn wmqyymyn: an hendiadys or possibly a double translation of Heb. tšbʿ, cf. 10:20.

6:14 Add d'wmyh with DM. It is strange that this word has been deleted and not ṭʿwwn or ṭ'wwthwn in the same verse. The censor may have erased the wrong word, or perhaps he read d'rmyh (taken as "Romans") instead of d'wmyh. References to Romans appear to have been censored from E 12:42.

6:15 'l qnyy wpwrʿn: a routine hendiadys for Heb. 'l qn'. The same phrase is used in E 20:5 and D 5:9.

6:16 There is no reason for two different translations of the phrases l' tnsw 't yyy 'lhykm and k'šr nsytm as l' tnswn yt 'yqr škynth dyyy and hyk mh dnysytwn qdmwy. Use of 't may have occasioned the use of yt, but yth could have been used instead of qdmwy. Perhaps the testing of people should be expressed by yt (E 16:4) while testing of God is expressed by qdm (E 17:2) or by the addition of 'yqr' škynth. The small number of occurrences prevents any generalization, especially since N 14:22 has wnswn yth applied to God, but that might conceivably be understood as God's speaking of having been treated in a contemptible, human way. Whatever the explanation, D 6:16 is inconsistent. Since this expression occurs only four times, twice (now) with yt and twice with qdm, it is not clear what may have been preferred. None of these verses is attested a.l. in the available genizah fragments, and Onk. uses a preposition only in E 17:2 and here (qdm), while PJ has qdm in E 17:2 but yt here.

bnysywnh: for toponym bmsh, as in 9:22, and E 17:7. The translation of D 33:8 is also based on this interpretation, though less obviously.

6:19 lmydḥwp: for the homophonous Heb. lhdp.

6:21 Read: wprq w'pq ytn yyy pryqyn (or ... mymryh dyyy pryqyn with I).

6:24 lmqyymh ytn: for Heb. lḥytnw; cf. 5:21 (=24).

6:25 wzkw: for Heb. ṣdqh; cf. 4:8.

Chapter 7

7:3 ttʿrbwn: for Heb. ttḥtn.

7:6 lʿm ḥbybyn hyk sgwlh: routine for Heb. lʿm sgwlh, e.g. 14:2.

7:7 The text of this verse is obviously corrupt, but the situation seems to have been aggravated by the manner in which the verse was printed. Following the lines of the manuscript, the Aramaic reads:

1. l' mrbkm [Heb.]: l' mn swgy
2. ytkwn mn kl 'wmyyh 'trʿy yyy bkwn 'rwm
3. 'twn ʿm qlylyn mn kl 'wmyyh

Redivided and compared to the Hebrew we have:

Heb.		N
l' mrbkm	a.	l' mn swgy ytkwn
mkl hʿmym	b.	mn kl 'wmyyh

ḥšq yyy bkm	c.	'trʿy yyy bkwn
wybḥr bkm	d.	[wbḥr bkwn]
ky 'tm hmʿṭ	e.	'rwm 'twn ʿm qlylyn
mkl hʿmym	f.	mn kl 'wmyyh

The printed text reads l' mn swgy [yyy] ytkwn; but from the above presentations it should be clear that the insertion of [yyy]is unnecessary. The textual problem in line a can be solved without the proposed insertion by reading swgy ytkwn as swgy dydkwn or swgyykwn (M). The word dydkwn or ddkwn is used in N, but perhaps a variant spelling dtkwn (d / t interchanges are common) was altered to ytkwn. The form swgyykwn is also unknown in N, but is logically possible. Since the words swgy ytkwn in the manuscript are divided between two lines, it is also possible that the manuscript from which N was copied already contained this error or had spread the word swgyykwn so that it resembled two words. (Other manners of translation are found in Onk. and PJ but these do not aid in the reconstruction of the text).

A second textual problem in this verse is the lack of a translation for the Hebrew wybḥr bkm (d). The word ḥšq is translated 'trʿy in 10:15 (the closest parallel to this verse) and in 21:11 and 34:8 as well. The word bḥr is also translated 'trʿy in v. 6, 14:2, 18:5, etc., but bḥr in E 17:9, 30:19, etc. Probably the translator would have preferred to translate both verbs as 'trʿy, but it is unlikely that he did; though that would have appeared as a dittography and could have led to the omission of the second piece. It is also very inappropriate for his style to have translated both c-d with only one line of Aramaic, c. We must conclude, therefore, that the text originally read wbḥr bkwn (d) and these words were deleted through the homoioteleuton bkwn ... bkwn. (Both M and PJ read ṣb' ... w'ytrʿy for the verbs, but this reading is less likely in

N.) The words 'trᶜy and bḥr appear in 12:14, but unfortunately the latter is a printing error for bhd, the translation of the Heb. b'hd.

7:9 ṣdyqyyh (+): added because loving God is not enough to merit His mercies; one must deserve them.

7:10	Heb.		N
	wmšlm lśn'yw	a.	wmšlm lśn'wy
	'l pnyw	b.	bᶜlm' hdyn
		c.	'gr ᶜwbdhwn ṭbyyh
	lh'bydw	d.	mn bgll lmtprᶜh mnhwn
		e.	lᶜlm' d'ty
	l' y'ḥr lśn'w	f.	wl' mšhy 'gr ṭb lśn'wy
	'l pnyw	g.	ᶜd 'nwn yhybyn bᶜlm' hdyn
	yšlm lw	h.	mšlm lhwn 'gr mṣwwn qlylyn
		i.	dhwy bydyhwn

The Hebrew, which contains references to both sing. (a) and pl. (f), is repetitive, lines a-d being basically the same as f-h, but each unit is also composed of two balanced sub-units a-b, d and f, g-h. N translated the verse uniformly in the plural and, as seen elsewhere (e.g. G 39:10), has interpreted the type of literary balance found in the Heb. as referring to this world and the world to come. The division of the Aramaic is a-c, d-e; f, g-i, and the apparent duplication between the halves of the verse has been mirrored in the similar notions expressed in a-c and f-i. The thought here is that the evil are rewarded for their good deeds in this world so that they can be denied any basis for avoiding their deserved punishments in the world to come; cf. Introduction, chapter 4 for a discussion of how this idea is part of N's framework.

7:13 ᶜbydtykwn: read ᶜbwrykwn.

lhwn: for Heb. lk. Both make sense in the verse, though lhwn is possible a variant of lkwn, a frequent translation of lk.

7:14 wl': for Heb. l'.

l', l', 'wp l' (+): double negatives.

7:16 nksy (+): the Israelites would devour their enemies' possessions, not the people themselves.

7:20 mhwt 'wr yth: for Heb. hṣrᶜh.

7:25 Add ṣlmy, following DM.

dmḥpy (+): expansive.

sny wmrḥq: for Heb. twᶜbh; in v. 26 only mrḥqh is used. The idiom occurs in 4:25 also.

7:26 mrḥqyn: for Heb. ḥrm (2x). Usually ḥrm is translated šyṣy'; this usage is influenced by mrḥqh and mrḥqh trḥqwn elsewhere in the verse. Note also the use of rḥwq in L 12:3, etc.

Chapter 8

8:2 bmḥšbt (+): expansive.

8:3 The Hebrew words l' ᶜl hlḥm lbdw yḥyh h'dm ky have been omitted because of a homoioteleuton, and DM has restored them from another text. The restoration is an almost literal translation of the Hebrew, which may not be warranted. The key word here is Heb. ᶜl in the phrase ky ᶜl kl, omitted from N. Omission of this preposition changes the subject of the following clause from h'dm in Hebrew to kl mh dnpq in Aramaic; the verb yḥyy could conceivably accompany either one. If this is correct (and not an accidental error itself in need of correction), one might expect the previous, parallel line to have lḥmh as its subject, not br nšh. If so, the reconstructed text should read l' lḥmh lblḥwdwy yyḥy [or yḥyy?] br nšh 'rwm ....

8:5 wttpyswn: for Heb. wydᶜt.

8:7 byt (+): expansive, and routine in such expressions, e.g. v. 14.

8:8 'rᶜ dmn zyyth ᶜbdyn mšḥ: for Heb. 'rṣ zyt šmn.
wtwmryyh ḥlyyn kdbšh: for Heb. wdbš, emphasizing that dbš refers to dates, not the honey of bees.

8:9 šryyn wbryrn hyk (+): changing the metaphor to a simile.

8:11 'wlpn 'wryyth (+): forget not the Torah, replacing God; cf. v. 14, etc.

8:14 pryqyn is expected after ytkwn but lacking in N; it is added in M.

8:15 'rᶜ byt (+): a necessary explanation; cf. v. 7.
kyp šmyr ṭnrh: for Heb. ṣwr hḥlmyš.

8:17 qnwn ln yt nksyyh h'lyyn: for Heb. ᶜśh ly 't hḥyl hzh; for this translation of ḥyl cf. 7:16, 8:18, etc. The use of qny for ᶜśh may help explain how ᶜśw in G 12:5 became a reference to conversion. There were people Abraham "acquired" for God.

8:18 lmqny nksyn: for Heb. lᶜśwt ḥyl. The translation could not use ḥyl here, because it occurs a few words earlier.

8:20 ḥlp 'yn: double translation of Heb. ᶜqb, usually rendered ḥlp (e.g. 7:12).

Chapter 9

9:1 ᶜd ṣyt šmy': a slight improvement over the Heb. bšmym.

9:3 'š 'klh mt'klh: a double translation of Heb. 'š 'klh. Cf. notes to 4:24.

9:4 bzkwwtn: for Heb. bṣdqty: as in vv. 5, 6, etc.

9:5 bḥwbyhwn: for Heb.ブršᶜt.

9:6 ᶜm qšyn qdl lmqblh 'wlpn: for Heb. ᶜm qšh ᶜrp. Onk. uses the phrase ᶜm qšh qdl, and N usually translates this phrase as ᶜm qšyn lmqblh 'wlpn, e.g. E 32:9, 33:3, 34:9. The word qdl should thus be seen as a double translation, probably borrowed from Onk.; cf. also v. 13 and 10:16.

9:7 Read 'trh hdyn.

9:8 wbḥrb: Frequently the toponym ḥrb is rendered ṭwr' dḥwrb; cf. notes to 1:2.

9:9 mzwn: for Heb. lḥm; Moses abstained from all food, not just bread or meat. N frequently translates lḥm in this manner; it is not unique to this context.

9:10 b'ṣbᶜ dgbwrh mn qdm yyy: a double translation of the Heb. b'ṣbᶜ 'lhym.

hwh ktyb kl: for Heb. kkl.

knšwt (+): expansive, as in 10:4.

9:12 yt ᶜwbdhwn (+): providing an object for the verb, but interrupting the close association between ᶜmk and dy 'pqt. The addition is routine with the berb šḥt, translated ḥbl; cf. 4:16, 4:25, etc.

9:13 gly qdmy yt: for Heb. r'yty, originally ḥmyt, as indicated by the presence of yt.

qšywthwn d- (+): added in anticipation of the phrase ᶜm qšh ᶜrp.

ᶜm qšyyn qdl mn lmqblh 'wlpn: cf. notes to v. 6.

9:14 mnᶜ grmk mn qdmyy mn lmbᶜy ᶜlyhwn rḥmyn: replacing the Heb. hrp mmny; cf. Onk. 'nḥ bᶜwtk mqdmy. The statement in Exodus is reported as wᶜth hnyḥh ly, also translated mnᶜ grmk mn lmbᶜy rḥmyn ᶜlyhwn qdmy, but mn qdmyy here is either misplaced (from the end) or evidence of a double text.

wywklh hy' qdmy l-: This corresponds to the imperfect form of the verb ᶜśh, but the wording of E 32:10 and N 14:12 is better: w'yt yklh qdmyy.

rbh wtqyph wmsgyyh: for Heb. ᶜṣwm wrb. In E 32:10 only rbh wtqyp' is used, but cf. 2:21, where the same type of addition is found.

9:15 yhybyn (+): expansive.

9:18 bṣlw wbᶜyt rḥmym mn qdm [yyy] (+): routine, as in vv. 20, 24, 25, etc.

mzwn: for Heb. lḥm, as in v. 9, etc.

mh dsny wmrḥq: for Heb. hrᶜ, as in 4:25.

9:19 bql ṣlwty: for Heb. 'ly, following the addition in v. 18.

bql ṣlwty 'mr mšh: usually 'mr mšh is added after 'ly, but not after all of the other first person references to Moses. Its presence here may mean that the text once read wšmᶜ yyy 'ly 'mr mšh and was later modified to the present reading. If so, bql ṣlwty can be dated later than the original translation wšmᶜ yyy 'ly, definitely later than the use of 'mr mšh, which itself is not original.

9:20 Heb. m'd has been omitted, perhaps to lessen God's anger at Aaron.

wṣlyyt wbᶜyt rḥmyn: for Heb. w'tpll.

ᶜl ᶜsq: for Heb. bᶜd.

9:21 ṭᶜwwn: for Heb. hᶜgl.

ᶜbd ᶜprh: for Heb. dq lᶜpr.

9:22 wbbyt yqydth wbnysywnh wbqbry š'lth: routine renditions of tbᶜrh, msh and qbrt ht'wh.

9:23 bšm mymrh dyyy qdyšh: a conflate translation of Heb. lw; cf. 10:8.

9:25 The first yt ('t) has been deleted, but not the second.

The primacy of ṣly as the translation of w'tnpl is seen from the use of ṣlyyt for htnplty. Perhaps the use of bᶜy rḥmyn should be seen as a double translation, but cf. v. 20, where it appears to be an hendiadys.

9:26 wṣlyyt wbᶜyt: for Heb. w'tpll; M adds rḥmyn; cf. vv. 20, 25.

9:27 brḥmyk ṭbyyh (+): idiomatic addition.

Heb. lᶜbdyk has been omitted (but added in I), perhaps through the influence of E 32:13, a similar verse in which lᶜbdyk is positioned somewhat later.

9:28 dyyry d- (+): The earth can not speak; but cf. Sam. pn y'mrw ᶜm h'rṣ and LXX katoikountes tèn gên.

Chapter 10

10:6 bryyh dyᶜqn: for Heb. bny yᶜqn.

10:9 qrbnwy d- (+): the sacrifices might be their portion, but surely God was not.

ᶜmkwn: for Heb. lw.

10:10 wšmᶜ ql mmrh dyyy bql ṣlwty 'mr mšh: for Heb. wyšmᶜ yyy 'ly. The double layering that was described in 9:19 exists here as well. The addition of the first ql is an error. Note also that wyšmᶜ yyy is also translated wšmyᶜ qdm yyy in 26:7, etc.

10:11 lmṭln: for toponym lmsᶜ.

10:12 dtqnn qdmwy (+): expansive, as in 11:22.

'wrytt': = 'wryyth in order to accommodate the 3 m. s. pronominal suffix or 'tw.

10:16 ṭpšwt (+): expansive; in spite of the popularity of the phrase, the heart could not be circumcised.

wqdlykwn qyšyy' l' ttqpwn twb: for Heb. *wᶜrpkm l' tqšw ᶜwd*. On the use of *qdl*, cf. 9:6.

10:17 The missing phrase occurs only here and in Ps. 136:23, where it is translated *l'lhy 'lhy' ... lmry mry'*. This adds very little to our ability to check this passage (added from M), but the inconsistency of singular *'lh* and plural *rybwnyyh* may point to an imperfect text there, too; (cf. I).

bdynh (+): perhaps based on 16:19.

dmmwn (+): idiomatic, as in 16:19.

10:20 *wqdmwy thwwn mṣlyyn*: for Heb. *'tw tᶜbd*.

mštbᶜyn wmqyymyn: for Heb. *tšbᶜ*; possibly a double translation of Heb. *tšbᶜ*; M: *tymwn bqwšṭ-*, Onk. *tqyym*; PJ: *twmwn*; cf. also 6:13.

Chapter 11

11:2 *'wlpn 'wryyth*: for Heb. *mwsr*.

11:3 *nysy pryšth*: for Heb. *'ttyw*.

ᶜbdwy mšbḥth: for Heb. *mᶜśyw*.

'rᶜy': for Heb. *'rṣw*. As in 10:12 and elsewhere, the 3 m. s. pronominal suffix has been written with an *Aleph*. This is usually attributed to scribal changes of final Heh to Aleph in imitation of BTA, but it is frequent enough in N to warrent its recognition as an alternate form, not a simple error.

11:6 *q'myh*: for Heb. *hyqwm*; cf. G 7:4, where *bryytyh* is used.

ᶜm' (+): instead of *kl* in Heb.

11:11 mn mṭrh dnḥyt mn šmyy' hy' štyyh myyh: for Heb. lmṭr hšmym tšth mym.

11:12 ᶜyynwy dyyy: note the absence of a substitute for "God's eyes."

bh mstklyn bh: possibly a double translation of Heb. bh.

11:17 pyry ᶜllth: for Heb. 't ybwlh.

11:18 ptgmyyh: for Heb. dbry (debaray); perhaps read ptgmyy. The error may result from the following h'lyyn, which usually follows a word ending in -yyh. The phrase ptgmyyh h'lyyn actually occurs in 12:28 and in 6:6, the latter being part of the Shemaᶜ prayer, regularly joined to 11:13-21.

tdyryn (+): expansive, as in 6:16, etc.

11:21 Add 'rᶜh with DM.

11:24 wṭwr byt mqdš: for Heb. whlbnwn; cf. notes to 1:7.

rbh (+): routine addition with the Euphrates River; cf. notes to G 2:14.

11:28 Restore with DM, but delete ṭbth as in 9:12, 16, 11:28, 31:29. Note also the possibility that lmhlkh is wrong. A similar construction in 28:14 has lmyzl.

11:30 myšry ḥzwzh: for toponym 'lwny mrh.

Chapter 12

12:2 Add ᶜl with DM.

12:5 lbyt mwqdšh: for Heb. lšknw. It is interesting that the word škynh has not been used.

bdḥlh (+): instead of the untranslated Heb. šmh.

12:8 špr wtqn: for Heb. hyšr, as in v. 25. The phrase is also used for Heb. ṭwb; cf. G 1:12, 18, etc.

12:11 wnkst qwdšykwn: idiomatic translation of Heb. wzbḥykm.

12:12 bpylwg 'rʿ' (+): extra here, but together with ḥlq w'ḥsnh, this constitutes a stock phrase in G 44:18.

12:13 hyydyn (+): expansive

tškḥwn: for Heb. tr'h.

12:15

Heb.		N
... hṭm'	a.	... dmrḥq mn qwdšyyh
whṭhwr	b.	wddky mn qwdšyh
y'klnw	c.	khdh y'klwn ytyh
kṣby wk'yl	d.	kbśrh dṭbyyh wd'lyyh

Though the beginning of the verse is translated literally, the end (a-d) is paraphrastic. Line b is problematic, but the same expansion is included in 12:22 also. D 15:22 omits mn qwdšyh from the equivalent of line b, though it is added in M. In L 10:10 and 11:47 the terms are ms'bh and dky'. Perhaps a reading like PJ is more appropriate: (a) dms'byn mn lmqrb lqwdšy' (b) wddkyn lmqrb lqwdšy', but there is no reason to correct more than lmqrb. It is also conceivable that qwdšyh has two different meanings. In line a it means "holy things" from which unclean people normally must abstain; but in b it might mean "purification." Thus the Heb. ṭhwr would mean "pure from his purifications" and make good sense. Other places where it may have this meaning include E 19:10, 14.

12:16 Add yth as in v. 24.

12:17 lyt 'twn ršyyn: for Heb. l' twkl. Cf. the statement of Rabbi Joshua ben Qorha (Sifrei, a.l., p. 136) ykwl 'ny 'bl 'yny ršyy; Onk.: lyt lk ršw.

tynyyn (+): This tithe is normally called mᶜśr šny in MH (e.g. BT Mak. 19b).

12:20 Heb. lk has not been translated.

12:22 bśr' (+): cf. v. 15 d.

bmrḥq ...: cf. notes to v. 15.

12:23 l': for Heb. wl'.

12:31 sny wrḥyq: idiomatic for Heb. śn'.

Chapter 13

13:4 šqr' (+): as in v. 6. The term nby' šqr is common in MH, based on Is. 9:14 and many places in Jer., but the term is rabbinic, not Biblical.

h' 'yt rḥmyn: for Heb. hyškm 'hbym. Cf. Onk., PJ: h'ytykwn. This form is not used in N, but in most of the places where yš receives a pronominal suffix, it has been translated brᶜwh (e.g. G 24:42, 49, 43:4), suggesting brᶜwtkwn here. Perhaps 'yt shoudl be 'twn.

13:5 blbh šlmh (+): idiomatic.

13:6 mlyn dšqryyn: for Heb. srh.

ᶜbdy bšth: for Heb. rᶜ, as in 17:7, 12, etc., emphasizing the destruction of the evil doers rather than the evil itself. Cf. Ps. 104:35 as vocalized by the Tiberian Massorah but explained by the rabbis, BT Ber. 10a.

13:7 ḥbrk rḥmk: a double translation of Heb. rᶜk.

dḥbyb ᶜlyk knpšk: for Heb. 'šr knpšk.

13:10 ydykwn yšlṭwn byh: for Heb. ydk thyh bw.

13:17 ṣdy: for Heb. tl; note the usage of this word in G 1:2, etc.

13:18 The Hebrew word m'wmh has not been translated, but mdᶜm, mndᶜm and kl mn dᶜm are suggested in the margin. The form mn dᶜm would have created a clearer homoioteleuton mn - mn.

Chapter 14

14:1 ḥbybyn: for Heb. bnym. Cf. M Avot 3:14: ḥbybym yśr'l šnqr'w bnym lmqwm.

l' tᶜbdwn ḥbwrn hbwrn bpwlḥnh nkryyh: for Heb. l' ttgddw, following the rabbinic interpretation that explains this phrase as l' tᶜśw 'gwdwt 'gwdwt BT Yeb. 14a; cf. also Sifrei, p. 158.

ᶜl byt 'pykwn: for Heb. byn ᶜynykm: cf. 6:8, etc.

ᶜl npš dmt: for Heb. lmt.

14:4 bᶜyr: correct to bᶜyrh with M, I.

14:5 w'lyn: for Heb. w'qw.

wdyyṣyn: for the homophonous Heb. wdyšn.

wtwry br: for Heb. wt'w.

wrym'nyn: for Heb. wzmr.

14:12 brgzh: for Heb. hprs.

14:13 wbt byth: for Heb. whr'h.

'yybw: for homophonous Heb. h'yh.

14:15 ḥṭpyth: for Heb. htḥms.

ṣpr šḥph: for Heb. hšḥp.

14:17 wqqh: for Heb. whḥsydh. Is the Aramaic related to the sound of the bird's call ? Cf. šrqrqh for hrḥmh.

14:18 wdyyth ḥwwrth w'kwmth: for Heb. w't hḥsydh, as in L 11:19.

wngr ṭwr': for Heb. whdwkypt.

14:21 ltwtbyyh mn bny ᶜmmy': for Heb. lgr; cf. bny ᶜmmy', later in the verse, for Heb. nkry.

mzbnh tzbnwn ytyh: for Heb. mkr.

l' tbšlwn ...: Cf. discussion in E 23:19.

14:22 ... mh d'twn mpqyn wzrᶜyn b'py brh wmknšyn ᶜllth ...: expansion of the Heb. hyṣ' hśdh.

14:24 lmswbrh mᶜśrh tnyynh: explaining the ambiguous Heb. ś'tw.

14:25 wtprqwn mᶜśrh tnynh [with DM] bksp: for Heb. wntt bksp. This precise translation eliminates the ambiguous use of ntn in

vv. 25-26. Cf. *wtzbwn* for *wntth*, v. 26.

14:26 *wbḥmr ḥdt wbʿtyq*: for Heb. *wbyyn wbškr*.

ʿmy (+): vocative, as in 15:6, 16:14, etc.

14:27 *bpylwg 'rʿ'* (+): cf. notes to 12:12, also v. 29.

14:28 *dywmyn* (+): expansive.

Heb. *kl* has not been translated.

šnt mʿśr mskynyyh (+): cf. MH *mʿśr ʿny*. The phrase *šnt mʿśr* was borrowed from 26:12 *bšnh hšlyšt šnt hmʿśr*, translated in N as *bšth tlytyyh dhy' šnt mʿśr mskynyyh*.

14:29 *ḥwlqhwn*: read *lyt lhwn*.

Chapter 15

15:1 *dywmyn* (+): as in 14:28, 16:9, etc.

15:2 *sdr dynh wšmtth*: read *dšmṭth*.

kl gbr mry ḥwb yt ydyh: for Heb. *bʿl mšh ydw*, possibly containing a double reading; cf. MH *bʿl ḥwb*.

15:3 *'t ršyy lmdḥq*: for Heb. *tgś*. This is in contrast to the Sifrei, which unequivocally states *zw mṣwt ʿśh*. Whether the imperfect verb form should be understood as an imperative (*ḥwbh*) or an option (*ršwt*) was a routine matter of dispute between (the schools of) Rabbi Akiva and Rabbi Ishmael. The former usually saw these forms as obligatory while the latter interpreted them as optional. Cf. J. N. Epstein, *Prolegomena ad Litteras Tannaiticas* (Jerusalem, 1957) pp. 534-535 (in Hebrew).

bryyh (+): expansive.

15:4 Heb. N

Heb.		N
'ps	a.	lḥwd 'yn tṭrwn mṣwwth d'wryyty
	b.	ḥlp kn
ky l' yhyh bk 'bywn	c.	['rwm l' yhwwy bkwn mskynyn]
ky brk ybrkk yyy	d.	'rwm mbrkh ybrk ytkwn mmrh dyyy
b'rṣ 'šr yyy 'lhyk ntn lk	e.	b'rʿ' dyyy 'lhkwn yhb lkwn
nḥlh lršth	f.	'ḥsnh lmyrt yth

Line c is present in I; M also contains b-c, but has brm instead of line b. The presence of the condition 'yn tṭrwn ... in line a precludes the use of both ḥlp kn 'rwm and brm 'rwm. In fact, one might be more correct to associate ky with 'yn in a than with 'rwm in c. In any case, the addition in a does not correlate with the piece added in c. The simplest accommodation would be to delete 'rwm from line c; cf. PJ: lḥwd 'yn 'twn ʿsyqyn bmṣwwt' d'wryyt' l' yhwy bkwn mskyn' 'rwm ....

15:6 w'ynwn (+): adds subject, perhaps because the verb occurs at the end of the clause.

15:9 ptgm dḥty: for Heb. dbr.

wl' yṣwḥ: for Heb. wqr', changing the positive statement to a negative one. This is not a dittography, as suggested by DM, but a reflection of the Sifrei's statement that the oppressor will be seen as sinning even if the oppressed poor person does not cry out against him. Comparison with 24:15, wl' yqr' ʿlyk 'l yyy whyh bk ḥṭ' (where oppressing a poor person is recognized as a sin even if he does not cry out), produced the observation ykwl 'm qr' ᶜlyk yhyh bk ḥṭ' w'm l'w l' yh' bk ḥṭ' tlmwd lwmr whyh bk ḥṭ' mkl mqwm (Sifrei, p. 176). N adds the additional thought dl' yhwwy bk ḥwbh for Heb. whyh bk ḥṭ'; i.e., by not crying out to God, the poor man means to spare his oppressor the anger of God.

15:11 'yn nṭryn bny yśr'l 'wlpn 'wryth wᶜbdyn pyqwdyh (+): Note the similarity to G 3:15, 22, etc. and the fact that this verse emphasizes (but does not mention) the reward in this world only. The Heb. says l' yḥdl 'bywn mqrb h'rṣ, but N, perhaps by reading the Heb. as a question, presents just the opposite: l' hwy bynyhwn mskynyyh bgw 'rᶜ'.

15:12 'ḥtkwn (+): parallel to 'ḥwkwn.

ytyh: for Heb. tšlḥnw, prompting DM to add tšlḥ. This may be correct, as E 21:2 reads tšlḥ ytyh even though the Heb. has yṣ'. Note, however, that ytyh could be a 3 m. s. imperfect form of 'ty "he should go free."

15:16 plḥ (+): based on v. 12.

15:17 wbtrᶜ byt dynh: for Heb. wbdlt. No door is specified, but here, in PJ, and in M to E 21:6 the door of the court is noted.

ᶜwd lᶜwlm: a literal translation of the Heb.

lᶜwlm, in contrast to the suggestion in PT Qid. 1:2.

15:19 The introduction of ᶜmy bny yśr'l in the middle of the verse may attest to an original division of v. 19 into two verses. The Heb. contains two complete thoughts, and this was part of a public Torah reading, perhaps in need of further subdivision. See the similar phenomenon in 16:16.

15:22 dmrḥq mn qdšyh wddky: for Heb. hṭm' whṭhr. The note of mh qdšh in M is probably an addition to N, not a variation, as may be seen from the parallels in 12:15, cf. notes there.

Chapter 16

16:1 bzmn (+): the expansion makes the phrase the equivalent of mwʿd ḥdš h'byb in E 23:15 and 34:18, translated bzm yrḥ' d'byb'.

'rʿ' (+): expansive; cf. vv. 3, 12.

wʿbd lkwn nsyn wgbwrn b'ymmh (+): This may have been added to avoid the assumption that God's miracles were only at night. Note that v. 3 stresses the day.

16:4 blyly ywm' ṭbḥ qdmyyh dpsḥh: for Heb. bʿrb bywm hr'šwn.

16:5 lyt 'twn ršyyn: for Heb. l' twkl. It is prohibited, not impossible; hence the change from BH "can" to Aramaic "may." Cf, also v. 16.

16:6 bmṭmʿy šmš': for Heb. kb' hšmš.

16:8 knyšt ḥdwh: for Heb. ʿṣrt.

16:9	Heb.		N
		a.	ʿmy bny yśr'l
	šbʿh šbʿt tspr lk	b.	šwbʿh šbwʿyn dywmyn tmnwn lkwn
	mhḥl ḥrmš bqmh	c.	mn [zmnh] dy 't mšry mglh dḥṣdh lmḥṣd bʿwmr' d'npwth
	tḥl lspr	d.	tšrwn lmmny
	šbʿh šbʿwt	e.	šwbʿh šbwʿyn dywmyn

Routine expansions in a, b and c accompany the more significant one in c. Cf. DM for *mn* or *my* (c). Whether *my* or *mn* is preferred, *zmnh* may still be correct.

16:10 *hy' ʿṣrth* (+): The rabbinic name of the holiday is glossed to the Biblical one.

16:13 *ʿbwrh*, *wḥmr'* (+): expansive. The additions are similar to those discussed in N 18:27, 30.

16:14 The Heb. *ytwm* has not been translated in N.

16:16 In part, the Heb. of this verse resembles E 23:17 and 34:23:

	E 23:17	E 34:23	D 16:16
1)	*šlš pʿmym bšnh*	*šlš pʿmym bšnh*	*šlwš pʿmym bšnh*
2)	*yr'h kl zkwrk*	*yr'h kl zkwrk*	*yr'h kl zkwrk*
3)	*'l pny*	*'t pny*	*'t pny*
4)	*h'dn yyy*	*h'dn yyy 'lhy yśr'l*	*yyy 'lhyk*

The main difference lies in (4) translated *rbwn kl ʿlmy' yyy* and *rbwn kl ʿlmy' yyy 'lhh dyśr'l* in Exodus. N in D 16:16 has obviously been made to follow E 34:23: *rbwn kl ʿlmy' yyy 'lhkwn*.

wbḥgh dšbwʿy: added by DM for the Heb. *wbḥg hšbʿwt*, but note the gloss in v. 10.

lyt 'twn ršyyn l-: for Heb. *wl'*, as in v. 5, 17:15.

ryqnyn mn kl mṣwh: for Heb. *ryqm*, as in E 34:20, and E 23:15 M, but not N.

16:17 *kmst 'wšṭwt ydyh*: for Heb. *kmtnt ydw*; cf. 15:10, where this expression is used for the Heb. *mšlḥ ydk*.

16:19 wl' tsbwn 'pyn bdynh: for Heb. wl' tkyr pnym. The word bdynh has been added to parallel l' tsṭwn bdynh, a paraphrase of l' tṭh mšpṭ; cf. the end of the verse also.

dmmwn (+): as in 10:17, with šḥd.

nsbwy: The word is hardly equivalent to Heb. ḥkmym, but the DM's suggestion to emend nsbwy to dsbwy is unnecessary, notwithstanding the use of dnsbyn in PJ, for N here does not offer a literal translation. The Hebrew contains a synonymous parallelism:

hšḥd	yᶜwr	ᶜyny	ḥkmym
	wyslp	dbry	ṣdyqm

Bribery can blind the wise and thwart the words of the righteous; ḥkmym and ṣdyqm thus both referring to the recipient of the bribe. However, the word ṣdq, as noted in many other places, may also mean innocent, in which case the first line of the Hebrew may refer to the recipient of the bribe while the second may mention its innocent victim. While some rabbinic comments reflect the former interpretation (e.g. BT Ket. 105a), N, it seems, is based on the latter and has opted to see dbry ṣdyqm as "the words of the innocent." It has, however, accommodated the other explanation as well by using the plural nsbwy to refer to both ḥkmym and ṣdyqm who accept bribes. (M translates ḥkmym with ḥkymyyh, but this does not prove that it understood nsbwy as dsbwy, because the word is part of a larger unit.)

Chapter 17

17:1 kl mylh dpsylh: for Heb. kl mwm rᶜ, M offers ptgm byš, and this seems closer to what might be expected. Note kl mn dᶜm byš in 24:5, for Heb. kl dbr rᶜ; here, PJ and Onk. use kl mdᶜm byš. Note the common MH usage of psl in such contexts.

17:4 'tkwwn: routine for Heb. nkwn.

17:6 mymr (+): The matter is decided according to their words, not their mouths. The word is not introduced in the other phrases in the verse.

ᶜl pm tlth: The phrase ᶜl pm is based on the Heb. of 19:15 ᶜl py šlšh ....

mn dmtḥyyb lhtqṭlh: for Heb. hmt. It is impossible to kill the dead.

17:7 ydwy ... ypšṭn: the lack of agreement has been corrected by M, which suggests ydyhwn.

17:8 The Hebrew lists three pairs of cases, regarding dm, dyn and ngᶜ. This was meant to convey the idea of distinguishing "between one kind of case of each category and another"; but in keeping with the accepted rabbinic practice of leaving no doubtful phrases, N has glossed each item in the pairs, creating three lines that rhyme internally:

a. ... byn 'dm dbtwlyn l'dm dqṭwlyn
b. byn dyny mmwn ldyny npšn
c. byn mktš ṣrᶜth lmktš ntqh ...

These laws are discussed in various places in the Torah, but the technical terms are mostly rabbinic Hebrew: dm btwlym, dyny mmwn, dyny npšwt. The terms ngᶜ ṣrᶜt and ngᶜ hntq are Biblical, though the latter occurs only once.

There is a certain redundancy between ptgm bdynh and the two words dyny in b, but it is not clear that bdynh should be deleted. It seems to originate in Onk., where it is also somewhat redundant, and the terms dyny mmwn and dyny npšn are stock phrases. Note that in 22:15 Heb. btwlym is translated shdwwn. While dm btwlym (= 'dm dbtwlyn) is a stock phrase in rabbinic literature, it is possible that the difference between these verses points to a different origin for the addition to 17:8, thus explaining the redundancy as well.

17:9 khny' wlywwyy: for Heb. hkhnym hlwym.

dyyyhwwy mmny: an error for dy yyhwwy mmnyyn or the like, cf. also I and M. The Heb. hšpt may take a singular modifier, but the text has dyynyh (pl.). The word mmny does not apply to the priests and Levites. Cf. 19:17 dy yhwwn mmnyyn.

17:10 kl: for Heb. kkl.

17:15 br yśr'l (+): a clarification, possibly to eliminate any possible doubt and possibly to balance the phrase gbr br ᶜmmyn, the routine translation of 'yš nkry. The period of the second Temple witnessed a number of disputes over the title "King." One or more of them may be echoed here.

17:16 twb ᶜd lᶜlm (+): possibly a double translation of Heb. ᶜwd, often translated twice, it seems; (cf. Introduction, chapter 4).

17:19 The word htwrh has not been translated; cf. M.

17:20 ᶜm' bny (+): expansive.

Chapter 18

18:1 bny (+) expansive.

18:3 *'rʿyyh* (+): cf. the Sifrei, *zh lḥy htḥtwn* (p. 215).

18:6 *mn* (+): if *'šr* is taken as "place," only *mn* is added to clarify the Heb.

18:7 *wmšmšyn* (+): expansive.

18:8 The Hebrew *lbd mmkryw ʿl h'bwt* is difficult. N translates *br mn mwtry qwrbnwy d'ḥsynw lhwn 'bhthwn*. The associations are clear except for that between *mmkryw* and *mwtry qwrbnwy*, discussed in BT Suk. 56a and elsewhere. Perhaps the use of *'bwt* is related to the interpretations of the blessings of Isaac to Jacob (G 27:27) and Jacob to Levi (G 49:7), though this is not mentioned specifically in either place. Cf. N, a.l.

18:10 *wl' ḥdwdy ʿynyn*: DM suggests *ḥrwry* on the basis of Jastrow, s.v. *ḥrwr'* (not *ḥrwry*). Note the possible interference of the term *'ḥyzt ʿynym*, which would appear as a form of *'ḥd* in Aramaic (cf. also v. 14). The connection with the Heb. *mʿwnn* is weak, but very popular in rabbinic literature. The term is discussed more fully in L 19:26.

nṭwry nḥšyn: routine for Heb. *mnḥš* "diviner."

18:11 *byšn* (+): expansive.

wmsqy zkwrwn: for Heb. *wydʿny*. From the use of *wmsqy*, it seems that the verb *š'l* was understood to refer only to *'wb*.

wtbʿyn 'wlpn: for Heb. *wdrš*. This seems almost a mechanical translation of *drš*, for it can hardly be the precise meaning. For a more reasonable (though not necessarily correct) explanation cf. BT San. 65b: *zh hmrʿyb ʿṣmw whwlk wln bbyt hqbrwt kdy tšrh ʿlyw rwḥ ṭwm'h*.

18:13 bᶜbdh ṭbh (+): routine with šlmym.

18:15 lmlwy: for Heb. 'lyw (cf. above).

18:17 h' špr wtqn: for Heb. hyṭybw.

18:21 bmḥšbt (+): routine expansion with lb.

Chapter 19

19:2 qrwyn dšyzbw: for Heb. ᶜrym. The full term occurs in N 35:11, etc; cf. also vv. 7, 9, etc.

19:3 lkwn (+): following N 35:11.
bšlw (+): as in N 35:11.

19:6 wytḥyyb bnpšh: for Heb. whkhw npš, applying the word to the murderer not the victim; cf. v. 11.

wlh lyt sdr dyn dqṭwlyn: for Heb. wlw 'yn mšpṭ mwt, but actually closer to MH 'yn lw dyn rwṣḥ.

19:9 b'wrḥn dtqnn qdmwy: for Heb. bdrkyw.

19:10 The Heb. whyh continues the preceding clause: innocent blood should not be spilled so that the people will not be guilty. The thought can be expressed in Hebrew by the positive whyh (which is governed by wl' at the beginning of the first clause), but in Aramaic, as in English, the idea is more easily conveyed by a negative clause, which, in this case, also avoids the application of somthing bad to the listeners. Thus N offers dl' yhwwy ᶜlykwn ḥwbt špykwt 'dm zkyy. The term špykwt 'dm is similar to MH špykwt dmym.

19:11 *wyqṭwl ytyh wytḥyyb bnpšyh*: for Heb. *whkhw npš wmt*. The words *whkhw wmt* have been combined in *wyqṭwl ytyh* and applied to the murdered party, while *npš* has been applied to the murderer (cf. the MH term *ytḥyyb bnpšw*). This seems to have been done in v. 6 also, giving the impression that v. 11 contains a double translation.

19:12 *wyqṭl ytyh*: a more direct presentation of the basic idea expressed by the Heb. *wymt*.

19:13 *špwky* (+): expansive, because those who spill innocent blood must be removed, not the blood. (Whether that was the original intention of the Heb. is irrelevant).

19:15 Read *shd ḥd*, following M.

19:16 *śhd dšqr*: for Heb. *ʿd ḥms*, based on v. 18.
shdy (!) *dšqr*: for Heb. *srh*.

Chapter 20

20:1 *wrwkbyhwn*: for Heb. *wrkb*, as in E 15:1.

20:5 *šklyl*, *yšklyl*: for Heb. *ḥnkw*, *yḥnknw*.

20:6 *'pryq pyrwy*: for Heb. *ḥllw*.

20:8 The reasons for the soldier's fears are not specified in Heb. but are provided in N. Thus *hyr'* is translated *ddḥl mn ḥwbwy* and *wrk hlbb* is translated *wlbyh tbyr ʿl ʿbydtyh*. Fear of battle has been turned into fear of punishment for sins.

ymsy wytbr: a double translation of Heb. *yms*.

20:14 wkl: for Heb. kl.

20:19 'ylnh: the plural is expected, and this form may be plural; in many places Yod has been assimilated.

kl myn dprzl: for Heb. grzn. It is understandable that the translation might want to prevent limiting the prohibition to grzn (with Sifrei and Mid. Tan.), but since grzn has been generalized to przl, the phrase kl myn might be better as kl mn dprzl. M contains myn also, but PJ reads mn dprzl'. Alternatively they may represent two independent attempts to generalize the rule.

l' hyk dbr nšh 'ylnh d'py br': for Heb. h'dm ᶜṣ hśdh. N appears to have read the Heb. as a question, which was then converted into a negative statement. The use of hyk points to a perception of h'dm as hk'dm. The MS reads d'pylw, but this should be d'py; they both could be abbreviated the same way.

bšᶜt (+): expansive.

20:20 'yln ᶜbd pyryn: for Heb. ᶜṣ m'kl. The expression was borrowed from G 1:11-12. Perhaps its purpose is to make plain that only the fruit is eaten, not the trees themselves.

Chapter 21

21:1 qṭyl wmṭlq: for Heb. npl. The word qṭyl is used at the beginning of the verse, but mṭlq is sometimes the translation of Heb. npl (e.g. 22:4). The point of the translation and the Hebrew is that this person has been murdered, and did not die of natural causes, but N may contain a double translation. The MH mwšlk (=mṭlq) is used in discussing this verse in PT Sot. 9:2.

21:3 l' slq ᶜlyh šᶜbwd dnyr: for Heb. l' mškh bᶜl, reflecting

N 19:2, translated this same way.

21:4 lnḥyl dbyyr: for Heb. 'l nḥl 'ytn.

21:7 yth (+): expansive, providing a direct object to the verb.

21:8 khnyy' yymrwn (+): Recited by the priests, according to BT Sot. 46a, Sifrei, p. 244.

21:10 mnhwn (+): expansive, to clarify the terse Heb.

21:11 špyrt ḥzwwn: for Heb. ypt t'r; cf. G 12:11, 24:16, etc., where this phrase is used to translate Heb. ypt mr'h.

21:12 wtṣmy: for Heb. wʿśth. This follows the opinion of Rabbi Eliezer, who interpreted wʿśth as cutting (tqwṣ), not Rabbi Akiva, who said it meant the opposite (tgdl); cf. Sifrei, p. 245. Onk. translates trby, following Rabbi Akiva, but PJ has wtyṣmy.

21:13 wtysb yth lk l'th: for Heb. whyth lk l'šh, but actually based on v. 11.

21:14 bršwt npšh: for Heb. lnpšh, similar to the MH bršwt ʿṣmh; cf. 19:11 for a different manipulation of npš.

yhbt ršwtk ʿlh: for Heb. ʿnyth, a weakened statement compared to the Heb., but parallel to the beginning of the verse.

21:17 yqrb: for Heb. ykyr.

Add lh after lmytn, with I.

ṣʿryh: for Heb. 'nw; cf. G 49:3.

21:19 *byt dynh*: for Heb. *mqmw*.

21:20 *'kl bbśrh wšty bḥmr*: for Heb. *zwll wsb'*. The crime seems worse in the Biblical wording, but N is similar to, though less explicit than, the explanation in the Mishnah (San. 8:2).

21:21 *ᶜm'*: for Heb. *'nšy*.

21:22 Diez-Macho's suggestion to reorder N to follow M is an improvement, but the phrase *ḥwbt sdr dyn dqṭwlyn* is clumsy nonetheless. It results from joining the routine translation of *ḥṭ'* as *ḥwbh* and *mšpṭ* as *sdr dyn*. Note that the same Heb. phrase is translated without *ḥwbt* in 22:26.

21:23 *lyṭ qdm yyy kl dṣlyb*: for Heb. *qllt 'lhym tlwy*.

Chapter 22

22:1 *wtksy ᶜyynk*: for Heb. *whtᶜlmt*; cf. vv. 3, 4.

22:3 Read *lyt 't ršyy*; perhaps *lyt 't* was contracted to *lyt*.

22:4

Heb.		N
l' tr'h 't ḥmwr 'ḥyk 'w šwrw	a.	*l' tḥmy yt ḥmryh 'w twrh d'ḥwk*
nplyn bdrk	b.	*mṭlqyn b'wrḥ'*
whtᶜlmt mhm	c.	*wtksy ᶜyynk mnhwn*
	d.	*mšbwq tšbwq mh dblbk ᶜlwy*
	e.	*wmprwq tprwq*
hqym tqym ᶜmw	f.	*wmṭᶜwn tṭᶜwn ᶜmyh*

Lines d-f are almost identical to part of E 23:5:

(d) mšbq tšbq kl mh dblbk ᶜl ḥbrk

(e) wmprq tprq ᶜmh

(f) wmṭᶜn tṭᶜn ᶜmyh

Here the Hebrew reads hqym tqym ᶜmw, while in Ex. it says ᶜzb tᶜzb mw. Lines e and (e) are double translations or expansions.

22:5 mny zyynh dgbr: for Heb. kly gbr. This verse is cited in BT Naz. 59a to prove that women should not go out to war with men's weapons.

22:7 bᶜlm' hdyn, lᶜlm' d'ty (+): The addition of these two phrases corresponds to their general use elsewhere. They are added when a repetition or parallelism (or something that could be taken as redundant) can be divided and one component is made to refer to this world while the other is applied to the world to come. In this case the application coincides with statements lmᶜn yyṭb lk and wh'rkt ymym, which emphasize the reward of good in this world (cf. N 31:50, etc.). Cf. BT Hul. 142a for a slightly different interpretation.

22:8 ḥwbt špykwt 'dm zkyy: routine for Heb. dmym.

dl' ypwl mn dḥmy lh lmypl mnyh: for Heb. ky ypl hnpl mmnw.

22:10 tryhwn qṭyryn (+): expansive.

wkdn is not a mistake for wktn; it is one of many places where Daleth and Taw have been interchanged. Cf. L 19:19, D 19:5, etc.

22:12 ttᶜtpwn: for Heb. tksh. Rabbinic usage customarily applies the verb lhtᶜtp to the wearing of a garment with these fringes.

22:14 šm byšn: for Heb. šm rʿ.

22:15 ltrʿ byt dynh: for Heb. hšʿrh.

The use of shdwwth here is similar to the usage in G 38:25.

22:19 slʿyn d- (+): idiomatic, as in v. 29.

btwlth brt yśr'l: for Heb. btwlt yśr'l: The Heb. phrase btwlt bt yśr'l does not occur in the Bible. Here the text reads only btwlt yśr'l, and this phrase also occurs in Jer. 18:13, 31:3, 20, etc., but the reference is to the nation, not to an individual woman. Phrases like btwlt bt ṣywn (2 Kings 19:21), btwlt bt ṣydwn (Jer. 23:12), btwlt bt bbl (Is. 47:1), btwlt bt ʿmy (Jer. 14:17), and btwlt bt mṣrym (Jer. 46:11) are found throughout the prophetic literature and may have influenced the usage here. Cf. Onk.: btwlt bt yśr'l; PJ: btwlt' kšr' dyśr'l.

kl ywmwy ḥywy: for Heb. kl ymyw. The word ḥywy looks like a gloss, because the phrase should be kl ywmwy. The phrase kl ymy ḥyyw is common and occurs, most recently, in 17:19.

22:21 wyqṭlwn yth: for Heb. wmth.

hdh (+): The phrase mrḥqth hd' is the literal translation of htwʿbh hz't in 13:15.

22:24 ʿl ʿsq: ʿl dbr (2x), as in 23:5, etc.

ṣʿr: for Heb. ʿnh, as in v. 29.

22:26 kl mn dʿm: for Heb. dbr.

wmtḥyyb bnpšyh: for Heb. npš; cf. 13:7, 19:6, etc.

22:28 *tryhwn* (+): perhaps influenced by v. 22 or v. 24.

22:29 *kl ymmy ḥywy*: cf. notes to v. 20. Here the phrase may be an expansive translation rather than a gloss, but it is grammatically acceptable. Note also 23:7.

Chapter 23

23:1 *ybzy*: for Heb. *yglh*; cf. L 18:7 ff.

23:2 *dpsyq wdmsrs*: for Heb. *pṣwʿ dkh wkrwt špkh*.

23:3 *ytḥšb*: for Heb. *yb'*, unlike the use of *yyʿwl* earlier in the verse and in verse and in v. 2, probably because of the Heb. *lw*, as in v. 4.

23:5 *ḥlmy'*: add *ptwr* as in M; cf. my comments to N 22:5. This phrase, *ptwr ḥlmy'*, is the equivalent to a translation for *mptwr*.

23:6 *llwwṭwy*: for Heb. *'l*; expansive. Note the inconsistency between this word and the use of *qllh* later in the verse.

23:7 *wl' lṭbwthwn*: for Heb. *wṭbtm*. The reading in M is clearly superior (*wṭbthwn*), but N is interesting nonetheless. The double negative is common in N, but requires *l'* before *šlmyhwn*, also. The *l-* prefixed to *lṭbwthwn* is conceivably for the accusative particle, but it should be prefixed to *šlmyhwn*, as well. Apparently the missing *l'* was felt to be unnecessary because of its proximity to the initial *l'*.

23:9 The *mh* is unnecessary.

23:13 *w'tr mzmn*: for Heb. *wyd*; cf. Onk. *w'tr mtqn*, PJ: *w'tr mzmn*.

23:14 *bm'zny zyynykwn*: for Heb. *ᶜl 'znk*.

23:15 *wl' yḥzr ...*: for Heb. *wšb*.

23:18 *'yth npqt br*: for Heb. *qdšh*; cf. notes to G 38:25.

gbr npq br: for Heb. *qdš*. A *qdšh* or *qdš* was not a simple prostitute, but the explanation in N is closer to the literal meaning than Onk.'s suggestion, which plays on the alternative association of the root *qdš* with the concept of marriage: *l' thy 'tt' mbnt yśr'l lgbr ᶜbd wl' ysb gbr' mbny yśr'l 'yt' 'm'*.

23:19 *'gr dznw wprwq klb*: for Heb. *'tnn zwnh wmḥyr klb*.

23:20 The Aram. *mmwn ... ksp ... kl mylh* does not correspond to the Heb. *ksp ... 'kl... kl dbr*. Both *zpw mmwn* and *zpw ksp* are translations of *nšk ksp*; apparently a double translation has been introduced, while the rendering of *nšk 'kl* has been lost. Perhaps *mmwn* should be *mzwn*, but the order would still be inaccurate.

23:21 Cf. discussion of 15:3.

23:22 *tpršwn prwš dndr*: for Heb. *ky tdr ndr*.

23:24 *pyrwš spwwtkwn*: for Heb. *mwṣ' śptyk*.

23:25 *k'rys* (+): This addition makes the law analagous to those in 23:26 and 25:4, where animals are given the right to eat the produce on which they work; cf. Mid. Tan., p 153.

lyt 'pšr lk lmtn: for Heb. *l' ttn*; usually this construction is translated *lyt 't ršyy l-* ...; cf. 23:21, etc. Here the notion "may not" has been translated "can not." According to most rabbinic sources (e.g. Sifrei, Mid. Tan.). this verse refers to a worker, presumably one who should be putting the harvested crop into his master's container. Perhaps N extended this notion to a situation where the container held no more produce and the worker wanted to use his own. Fearing a possible accusation of theft, N prohibited the worker from using his own container. This hypothetical situation could have been expressed in Aramaic *'rwm tyᶜwl* ... *wtśbᶜ wlgw mny*[*h dbᶜl byth*] *lyt 'pšr lk lmtn* [*lgw mnyk lyt 't ršyy lmtn*]. Presumably the similar phrases confused the scribe, who copied about half of the text. This type of error is common in N and this reconstruction accomodates all of the text and N's style of translation as well. But I have yet to find a rabbinic parallel to support the restoration. The use of *lyt 'pšr* for a prohibited act in 33:17, line b, may be additional evidence that *'pšr* and *ršyy* are interchangeable, but 33:17 c contains an impossible act, and it may have determined the usage there.

Chapter 24

24:1 *wypryn* (+): providing the bride with her dowry was very important.

ḥn wḥsd: routine for Heb. *ḥn*, but not exactly the nuance expected.

'grt šybwqyn: cf. the form *'gr' dšybwqyn* in v. 3, changed to *-rt šybwq-* in I. the latter also seems to be attested in the magic bowl published by J.A. Montgomery, *Aramaic Incantation Texts from Nippur* (Philadelphia, 1913) no. 26.

Heb. *'w* has not been translated.

24:4 lyt hw' ršyy b^c^lh: for Heb. l' ywkl b^c^lh. On ršyy, cf. 15:3. The word hw' is redundant for b^c^lh and should probably be deleted. Reading hwh for hw' is hardly an improvement.

šbwq: read šbq with I.

24:5 ksyrwy: for Heb. ḥdšh; perhaps read bšyrwy.

kl mn d^c^m byš: for Heb. kl dbr. Obviously there was no concern about good things.

zkyy mzmn: possibly a double translation of Heb. nqy, usually translated zky. Cf. Onk., PJ: pny, Frag.: zqyq. M has only zkyy.

24:6 N

a. ^c^my bny yśr'l
b. l' thwwn 'swry ḥtnyn wklyn
c. wl' tmšknwn ryḥyyh [wrkbh]
d. 'rwm kl d^c^bd kdn
e. bḥwby npšn hw' ḥbyl

Heb.

1. l' yḥbl rḥym wrkb
2. ky npš kw' ḥbl

Lines b and c are parallel and offer figurative and literal interpretations of line 1. Since it is inappropriate to see b as the interpretation of rkb and c as corresponding to rḥym, I have added wrkbh following M1, M2, Frag., Onk. and PJ. All of these (except Onk., which lacks the equivalent of b) reverse the order of lines b and c, allowing the literal translation to precede the non-literal one, but that seems unnecessary. Lines c-e, therefore, contain the translation of the Hebrew, while a-b are added. The phrase kl d^c^bd kdn (d) is based on *kl ʿśh 'lh* in 18:12, 22:5 and 25:16.

Line b's figurative interpretation takes the verse, because of its occurence after v. 5, to include a reference to the treatment of brides and grooms. Apparently the *rḥym*, the bottom stone, was understood to refer to the bride (cf. Heb. *rḥm*) while the *rkb*, the "rider" or top stone, was the groom.

The expansion of *npš* to *bḥwby npšn* is routine. Note that both the Heb. citation (*l' tḥbwl*) and the Aramaic (*thwwn*, *tmšknwn*) are second person, while the MT is third person; cf. LXX and Peshitta for additional support for N.

24:7 *wytqṭl*: routinely for Heb. *wmt*, when it refers to a punishment.

24:8 *hyk dpqd ytkwn*: for Heb. *k'šr ṣwytm*. N should probably read *dpqdyt*. Cf. Onk., PJ: *dpqydtynwn*, but M: *[dpq]dw*.

24:13 *wyṣly ʿlk*: for Heb. *wbrkk*. Note the reverse situation in 15:9 and the translation of *ybrk* (not *yṣly*) in v. 19.

24:14 *d'gyrh*: This word seems to be a gloss, but it may be a double translation of *dmskynh wṣrykh*, because the phrase *'gryh d'gyrh* is the equivalent of the Heb. *śkr śkyr*, found in 15:18 and used there in N. As such it is an alternative to *'gryh dmskynh*....

24:15 *wl'gr pʿlyh hw' msr qdmk yt npšyh*: for Heb. *w'lyw hw' nś' 't npšw*. Apparently *'lyw* has been taken as the equivalent of *ʿlyw* and expanded.

'zdhr lk d- (+): added in imitation of the frequently used expression, E 10:28, 34:12, D 4:9, 12:13, etc.

24:16 bḥwby: for Heb. bḥṭ'w, patterned on the end of the verse.

24:19 wlgywryh: for Heb. lgr. The casual addition of Waw is common.

24:20 tyklwn ᶜwllth: for Heb. tp'r.

24:21 tbᶜrwn ᶜwllh: for Heb. tᶜwll.

Chapter 25

25:1 qdm dyynyh (+): possibly a double translation of 'l hmšpṭ, translated ldynh.

mn dḥmy lyh lmḥyybh: for Heb. hršᶜ. This is an interesting expression of the care taken in discussing a convicted criminal, particularly since it is lacking in the description of the innocent party.

25:2 mrdw 'tḥyyb lmlqh: for Heb. bn hkwt; cf. MH mkt mrdwt.

25:6 Heb. yqwm has not been translated.

25:7 ltrᶜ byt dynh (+): routine for Heb. hšᶜrh; cf. D 15:17, 21:19, 22:15, where the term is also used.

25:9 qdmwy: for Heb. bpnyw, as if it were lpnyw; cf. Sifrei, p. 310. According to BT Sot. 32a this recitation was in Hebrew, but N has translated it. Compare, by contrast, the treatment of the verse in M, where kkh yᶜśh l'yš 'šr l' ybnh 't byt 'ḥyw is not translated.

25:10 wmbṭlh mṣwwt ybwmh (+): lacking in M, Onk. and PJ, but found in PJ: wmbṭly mṣwwt' dybmh.

25:11 dḥd mnhwn: for Heb. h'ḥd, as in G 2:11, 10:25, E 18:3, etc.

bbyt bhttyh: for Heb. bmbšyw.

25:13

Heb.		N
l' yhyh lk bkysk	a.	l' yhwwy lkwn bkysykwn
'bn w'bn gdwlh wqṭnh	b.	mtql rb wmtql zᶜyr
	c.	mtql rb lmhwwy nsb bh
	d.	wmtql zᶜyr lmhwwy yhb bh.

The last four Hebrew words have been reordered in b, and c-d is a gloss to explain the reason for the prohibition; cf. v. 14.

25:14 This verse has been treated the same as v. 13. The Heb. 'yph has been conceptualized to include other sizes of measurement also: mklh rbh wmklh zᶜyrh.

25:15 yhwwy: for Heb. yhyh, though the plural is expected; M: yhwwn (2x).

25:18

Heb.		N
'šr qrk bdrk	a.	dy 'rᶜw ytkwn b'wrḥ'
wyznb bk	b.	whwwn mqṭlyn bkwn
kl hnḥšlym 'ḥryk	c.	kl dhwh lbyh mhrhr mn btr mmry
	d.	hwwh ᶜnn' plṭ ytyh
	e.	wdbyt ᶜmlq qṭlyn ytyh
w'th	f.	w'twn ᶜmy bny yśr'l

ᶜyp wygᶜ	g.	hwwytwn lᶜyyn wmšlhyyn
wl' yr'	h.	wl' dḥylw dbyt ᶜmlq
'lhym	i.	mn qdm yyy

The text of N may be divided into three units. Lines a-b translate the beginning of the Hebrew and are one complete statement. They appear almost like the quotation from the text that precedes the interpretations recorded in the expositional midrashim. Lines c-e may play on nḥšlym, and may even contain a hint of the Heb. of h-i, but they are an independent midrash. The break between b and c as well as the syntactic connection between a-b and the previous verse probably mean that the targum perceived the conclusion of the idea in v. 17 -- if not the end of v. 17 itself -- as coming after wyznb bk, but the verse division in the manuscript corresponds to that in the MT. Similarly, the inclusion of ᶜmy bny yśr'l (which is probably an expansion of bny yśr'l as in Frag.) in f separates the end of v. 18 from the beginning. Indeed, we may postulate a time when vv. 17-18 were divided differently and when, in all likelihood, the first unit ended with a literal (or quasi-literal) translation of kl hnḥšlym 'ḥryk. The midrash in c-e was then added to explain how the Amaleqites could possibly conquer the Israelites, who were protected by God's cloud of glory; as noticed in other passages, it replaced part of the original text. This cloud, so we are told, expelled all those who doubted or rebelled against God. The Heb. of h-i could apply equally well to the Israelites or the Amaleqites, but in N it has been translated as a reference to the latter.

25:19 hwwn dkyryn (+): added from v. 17.

Chapter 26

26:3 *'wdynn wšbḥynn*: for Heb. *hgdty*. The verse calls for a declaration, not a prayer, and the translation is unexpected. Apparently the emphasis should be on the connection between the recitation *whgdty* and the obligatory thanksgiving that derives from it.

Delete *wšbḥyn ywm' hdyn*; cf. DM.

26:4 *sl' dbykwryh*: for Heb. *hṭn'*, as in 28:5.

wyṣnᶜ: for Heb. *whnyḥw*; cf. Onk. *wyḥtynyh* with variants *wyṣnᶜynyh*; cf. v. 10 in N and Onk. also.

26:5 Heb.		N
wᶜnyt w'mrt lpny yyy 'lhyk	a.	*wtᶜnwn wtymrwn qdm yyy 'lhkwn*
'rmy 'bd 'by	b.	*lbn 'rmyyh sbr lmwbdh l'bwnn yᶜqb*
	c.	*mn šyrwyh*
	d.	*wšyzbt ytyh mn ydyh*
wyrd mṣrymh	e.	*wnḥt lmṣrym*
wygr šm bmty mᶜṭ	f.	*w'twtb tmn bᶜm zᶜyr*
	g.	*w'ytbrk*
wyhy šm lgwy gdwl ᶜṣwm wrb	h.	*whwh tmn l'wmh rbh wtqyph wmsgyyh*

Lines a, e, f, and h are literal translations, while c is a routine addition. Lines d and g are simple embellishments, while b contains the well known rabbinic explanation of this verse. The statement *'rmy 'bd 'by* probably means "my father was a wandering Aramean," but reading *'bd* as an intensive verb allows it to convey the meaning "an Aramean 'destroyed' my father," more appropriately understood as "... wanted to destroy ..." because he failed. Some writers have taken 'bd as a transitive verb, also meaning "to destroy." The Aramean is identified as Laban and the "father" as Jacob.

The similarities to Onk. are striking:... 'rm'h bʿ' l'wbd' yt 'b' wnḥt lmṣrym wdr tmn bʿm zʿyr whwh tmn lʿm rb tqyp wsgy. Both deviate from literalness in many of the same ways, particularly in the last phrase. For parallels in N cf. 9:14.

26:7 dwḥqn: for Heb. lḥṣnw; cf. The Passover Haggadah, pp. 43-44, where lḥṣnw is explained as dwḥq.

26:8 wprq w'pq ytn: for Heb. wywṣ'nw. This may be an hendiadys or, less likely, a double translation.

wbḥzwyn: for Heb. wbmr'.

26:9 hdyn, hd': The inconsistent usage of hdyn (m. s.) and hd' (f. s.) to modify 'rʿ' (f. s.) results from the fact that the underlying Heb. varies. When translating hmqwm hzh, N used the m. s. form, but for h'rṣ hz't the regular f. s. one.

26:10 šrwy bwkrt: a double translation of Heb. r'šyt.

mn mh (+): expansive.

Add ytyh after wtṣnʿwn.

26:12 According to rabbinic law, based on the interpretation of D 26:12 ff., etc., the cycle of tithes varied on a three-year rotation; first tithe and second tithe, first tithe and second tithe, first tithe and tithing for the poor. This is reflected here in the translation of mʿśr as mʿśr mskynyyh and in the addition of mʿśrh qdmyyh, as well as in 14:25, etc. where the term mʿśrh tnynh is used. Note the parallel in v. 13.

26:13 ḥdh mnhwn (+): "even one of them."

26:14 b'bylwtn: for Heb. b'ny; cf. L 10:19.

wl' yhbnn mynyh 'rwn wtkrykyn ᶜl npš dmyt: for Heb. wl' ntty mmnw lmt. This is hardly the original meaning of the verse, which probably referred to food offerings to the dead, but it parallels the rabbinic interpretation in PT M.S. 5:12.

26:15 mn mdwr 'yqr škyntk: for Heb. mmᶜwn qdšk.

26:17 'mlktwn ᶜlykwn: for Heb. h'mrt; cf. v. 18.

lmhlkh: for Heb. wllkt, without the conjunction.

26:18 lᶜm ḥbybyn hyk sgwlh: routine for Heb. lᶜm sglh.

26:19 rmyn wmnṭlyn: for Heb. ᶜlywn, as in 28:1.

Chapter 27

27:5 Heb. šm has not been translated. Read wtbnwn tmn.

mn dbrzl: for Heb. brzl, but normally przl. Note the use of similar phrases in D 20:19, N 35:16, etc.

27:6 ṭbyn (+): perhaps a double translation, with šlmn mn mwm, of Heb. šlmwt, but 'bn ṭbh is a gem. The translation of šlmwt as šlmn mn mwm follows the routine practice in the description of the sacrifice.

27:8 N

a. ...ktyb ḥqyq

b. wmprš y'wt

c. wmtqr'

d. *wmtrgm bšbʿym lšn*

These lines contain two to four explanations of the Heb. *b'r hyṭb*. Frag. and PJ are similar, but for line c both have *mtqry bḥd lyšn*, a clearer statement.

According to the Hebrew, Moses was to write the words on the limed rocks. Presumably *ktyb* describes this process better than *ḥqyq*. Elsewhere *b'r* is translated with the root *prš* (1:5, the only other occurrence) and *hyṭb* is given as *y'wt* in 13:15, 17:4, 19:18, etc. (but as *ṭb'wt* in 9:21). Undoubtedly line b represents the translation of *b'r hyṭb*. Lines c-d reflect the common rabbinic notion that the Torah was given in the 70 languages of the world, associated with this verse in BT Sot. 32a.

In its present form, N resembles somewhat Neh. 8:8 *wyqr'w bspr btwrt h'lhym mprš wśwm śkl wybynw bmqr'*. The interpretation of this verse, attributed to Rav in BT Ned. 37a, explains *mprš* as *trgwm*, *wśwm śkl* as *hpswqym* and *wybynw bmqr'* as *mswrwt*. This does not parallel our translation completely, but *mprš y'wt* does seem to fit the Heb. *mprš*. The term *śwm śkl*, if taken as *pswqym*, i.e. versification or division into syntactic units, could be the same as N's *mtqr'*. The Palestinian texts (e.g. BR 36:8, p. 342, PT Meg. 4:1) vary slightly but present no closer versions.

27:9 *'tmnytwn*: for Heb. *nhyyt*; cf. *'mlktwn* in 26:17-18 and the frequent use of *mny* with the priest and Levites.

27:14 *ʿmh bny yśr'l*: a variation on a stock phrase that has been introduced for the Heb. *'yš yśr'l*, as in 29:9.

ql tly: for Heb. *ql rm*; cf. 28:52.

27:15 N

a. šth šbṭyn slyqw lṭwrh dgryzym

b. wšth šbṭyn slyqw lṭwrh dᶜybl

c. wkhnyyh w'rwnh bmṣᶜh

d. wkl yśr'l mn hkh wmn hkh

e. mbrkyn hwwn hpkyn 'pyhwn klpy twrh dgryzym w'mryn

f. bryk yhwwy gbr' dl' yᶜbd [ṣlm wṣwrh with DM] wkl dmw

g. mh dsny wmrḥq qdm yyy

h. ᶜbd ydy 'wmn

i. wl' yšwwy ytyh bṭmrh

j. wmlwwṭyyh hwwn hpkyn 'pyhwn klpy ṭwrh dᶜybl w'mryn

k. lyṭ yhwwy gbr' dy yᶜbd [ṣlm wṣwrh with DM] wkl dmw

l. mh dsny wmrḥq qdm yyy

m. ᶜwbd ydy 'wmn

n. wyšwy ytyh bṭmrh

o. wᶜnyyn kl ᶜm' kḥdh w'mryn 'mn

Heb.

1. 'rwr h'yš 'šr yᶜśh psl wmskh

2. twᶜbt yyy

3. mᶜśh ydy ḥrš

4. wśm bstr

5. wᶜnw kl hᶜm w'mrw 'mn

The material is divided into four units. Lines a-d describe the setting, basically a summary of v.v. 12-14. The expansion over vv. 12-14 includes mention of the ark and the note that all Israel stood around, but everyone (except converts) has already been included in the 12 tribes in a-b. Perhaps the phrase kl yśr'l has been influenced by the conclusions of vv. 15 and 26. The phrase mn hkh wmn hkh is rare in N at best; ḥzwr ḥzwr would be expected if this were part of the original text.

Line e begins the description of the blessing (f-i) and line j, the curse (k-n - Heb. lines 1-4). While no blessing is recorded in this chapter, which contains only curses, v. 12 clearly designates half of the tribes as blessers, so the reconstruction of a blessing is a logical step. The blessing is the opposite of the curse, itself a modification of the Hebrew curse. The passage concludes with the translation of the end of v. 15 Heb. line 5, augmented by kḥdh.

The text of the curse itself (and the blessing) is close to the Hebrew except in lines n and i, where ytyh is added, and in k and f. In the latter case, the Hebrew psl wmskh twʿbt yyy should have been rendered ṣlm wṣwrh mh dsny wmrḥq qdm yyy, but the words wkl dmw have been added, completing the frequently used expression ṣlm wṣwrh wkl dmw (E 20:4, etc.).

27:16 The use of gbr' in N to vv. 17 ff. is based on v. 16 where the Heb. actually reads 'rwr h'yš.

dzl' yqryh: for Heb. mqlh; note the same expression in Sarah's description of Hagar's attitude towards her in G 16:4.

27:20 bzy ʿryth: for Heb. glh knp, based on L 18:8.

27:24 The verse is lacking and found in the margin.

27:25 Note the difference between the translation of lhkwt npš as lmqṭwl npš here and elsewhere like 19:3, 11, etc.

Chapter 28

28:1-14 Because they contain a blessing and are written in somewhat lofty prose, verses 1-14 are replete with expansions, but for the most part these expansive translations are close to the Heb.

28:3 bmh d'yt lkwn bqwryykwn: for Heb. bᶜyr.

The reconstruction should contain b'py brh, not bḥqlk, as in v. 16.

28:5 wbtnwry 'ṣwwtkwn: for Heb. wmš'rtk; cf. E 7:29 wbtnwrk wb'ṣwtk.

28:6 bmᶜlkwn lgw byt mdrškwn (based on M), bmypqkwn mn byt knštkwn: for Heb. bb'k, bṣ'tk. For other uses of byt mdrš and byt knšth together, cf. 34:31, N 24:5, etc. Note, however, the difference in the parallel text in v. 19.

28:7 lm'bšh [DM: lmb'šh] bkwn: (+): expansive.

tbyry qdl: for Heb. ngpym.

lsdry qrbh (+): expansive.

28:8 wyytwn ᶜlykwn (+): expansive, based on vv. 2 and 15.

28:12 ᶜmy (+): cf. ᶜmy bny yśr'l.

28:13 lmlkyn, lhdywṭyn: for Heb. lr'š, lznb, as in v. 44.

28:16-19 are augmented as were vv. 3-6.

28:19 byt knštykwn (2x): M has bty mdršykwn in both cases; cf. v. 6, where the text may vary.

28:20 šbqtwn 'wlpn 'wryyty: for Heb. ᶜzbtny.

28:21 mwtnh: for Heb. hdbr, as in E 9:15, etc.

28:22 ᶜd zmn dy yswpwn ytkwn: for Heb. ᶜd 'bdk; cf. v. 24 for a similar variation.

28:23 šmy' ... ḥsymyn hyk nḥšh: for Heb. šmyk... nḥšt, changing a metaphor to a simile.

mn mḥth lkwn ṭl' wmṭrh (+): based, perhaps, on 11:17; a similar addition has been made in L 20:19.

bryrh hyk przlh: for Heb. brzl.

mn lmrbyh lkwn dtyn wṣmḥyn (+): similar to the addition in L 26:19.

28:25 mtngpyn: for Heb. ngp. In v. 7 ngpym, referring to Israel's enemies, was translated tbyry qdl, as it is here in M. Note how this complements the translation of qšh ᶜrp in Onk., qšy qdl.

28:27 wbṭḥwryh: for Heb. wbᶜplym; Qere: wbṭḥwrym.

28:29 mgššyn, dmmšš: for forms of Heb. mšš. One may be an error, for it is to be expected that the same word be used for both; but both make sense as preserved.

wl' yṣlḥn 'wrḥtkwn: for Heb. wl' tṣlyḥ 't drkyk.

28:30 ysb yth: not really the equivalent of yšglnh or the Qere: yškbnh. The verse is similar to (though opposite in intention from) 20:7, which uses yqḥnh; perhaps this has influenced the translation here. It is also possible that the translator wanted to use a milder term than either of the two available in the Hebrew; cf. the statement in BT Meg. 25b kl hmqr'wt hktwbyn btwrh lgn'y qwryn 'wtn lšbḥ ....

tprqwn pyryhwn: for Heb. tḥllnw, as in 20:6; the verb prq may be used in this context without the word pyryhwn , as it is at the end of 20:6 and in M here, where yt- is used instead.

28:31 ʿbdyn ṭbyn qdm yyy 'lhkwn dy yšyzyb (!) ytkwn mn yd bʿly dbbykwn: for Heb. mwšyʿ. This eliminates the personal quality of the savior by substituting the notion that good works bring salvation. The addition is based on routine expressions in Deut.

28:32 wl' 'lhh ʿl ydykwn: for Heb. w'yn l'l ydk. The phrase yš / 'yn l'l ydy occurs (in the Torah) only here and in G 31:29, but there the phrase has been interpreted in context of Laban's threat to Jacob: 'yt ʿmy ḥyl w'wklsyn sgyn, possibly playing on 'l and ḥyl.

lmprwq ytkwn (+): perhaps in imitation of 20:4.

28:33 yth (+): adds direct object.

28:35 qdqdy r'šykwn: for Heb. qdqdk; elsewhere the word qdqd may stand alone, e.g. 33:16.

28:36 Probably add qdm after tmn.

28:38 wtzrʿwn (+): possibly a double translation or hendiadys tpqwn wtzrʿwn for Heb. twṣy'.

28:42 ythwn (+): (2x) cf. v. 33.

yšyṣwn ythwn msyqyyh, yšyṣy ythwn ḥlzwnh: double translation for Heb. yyrš hṣlṣl. Cf. Onk.: sq'h, PJ: ḥlnwn': M: ḥylnwnh (both suggested to be corruptions of ḥlzwnh: The word occurs only here in the Torah, and other uses of the word ṣlṣl do not reflect the same meaning.

28:47 wblb ṭb: for Heb. wbṭwb lb; cf. M: wbṭwb lb.

28:48 wtᶜbdwn: for Heb. wᶜbdt; usually plḫ is used; cf. M: wtplḫwn.

28:52 ᶜd zmn dykbšwn: for Heb. ᶜd rdt.

28:54 dmḫṭy: for Heb. hrk, as in v. 56; cf. the translation of rk in 20:8, but the difference from G 41:43.

wb'tt ḫwbh ṭlywtyh: a double translation of the Hebrew wb'št ḫyqw. The phrase 'tt ḫwbk is used in 13:7, and ḫwbh is used in v. 56 as well. The phrase 'tt ṭlywtyh reflects the term 'št nᶜwry found in Mal. 2:14-15 and Prov. 5:18 and also used in MH.

28:57 wbšylyyth hywṣt mbyn rglyh: these words are identical in form (but not in spelling) to the Heb. wbšlyth hywṣt mbyn rglyh. The word hywṣt (as spelled in Hebrew) points to the fact that the Hebrew has not been translated. Perhaps the reference to "coming out from between her legs" seemed too immodest; cf. the discussion in BT Pes. 3a. Onk. is also not literal: wbzᶜyr bnh' dypqwn mynh. The PT objected to the inaccuracy of the term byn rglyh, but N has retained it in contrast to PJ, which reads mbyt twrph; cf. PT Yeb. 12:1.

28:58 'wryth (the second) (+): based on v. 61.

28:62 ᶜm bmnyyn: routine for Heb. bmty mᶜṭ.

28:64 ṭᶜwn dqys wṭᶜwwn d'bn: for Heb. ᶜṣ w'bn; as in 29:16.

28:67 wyyty, dyyty (+): expansive.

28:68 blbrnyyh wb'lpyyh: a double translation of b'nywt. The first word has been restored in N 24:24.

ytkwn (+): direct object.

Chapter 29

29:7 dbyt (3x): usually N uses dbnwy d- (as in M), but there are a few cases of byt also. They both may be abbreviated b-.

29:13 kᶜn (+): deleted in M; cf. Introduction, chapt. 3.

29:14

Heb.		N
ky 't 'šr yšnw	a.	'rwm kl dryyh dqmw qdmynn
	b.	mn ᶜlm' wᶜd kdwn
ph ᶜmnw ᶜmd	c.	ᶜmn 'nwn qyymyn hkh
hywm lpny yyy 'lhynw	d.	ywm' hdyn qdm yyy 'lhn
w't 'šr 'ynnw	e.	wyt kl dryyh dᶜtydyn lmqwm mn btrn
ph ᶜmnw hywm	f.	ᶜmn qyymyn hkh ywm' hdhn

The translation has followed the structure of the Heb., but most of the verse has not been translated literally. The phrases 'šr yšnw (a) and 'šr 'ynnw (e) have been interpreted as references to the past and future generations. Usually in N the notion expressed by mn ᶜlm' may point to a different history of transmission or origin.

29:15 Read 'rwm 'twn.

29:16 yhybn gbhwn bgw btyyh: for Heb. 'šr ᶜmhm.

dḫlyn mnhwn dl' ytgnbwn (+).

The idolators feared that the idols would be stolen

because they were covered with silver and gold (yhybn gbhwn), not because they were completely constructed of the precious metals. Accordingly, N must have understood the Hebrew to mean "... their idols of wood and stone and the silver and gold on them ('šr ʿmhm)." If so, the reconstruction based on other texts is wrong, and N should read ... wyt ṭʿwwthwn wyt ṭʿwwth dqysh wd'bnyyh [wyt ksph wdhbh dy] yhybn gbhwn .... Support for this interpretation may be found in 7:25, which prohibits coveting the silver and gold on the idols (ksp' wdhbh dmḥpy ʿlyhwn). The verse uses yhybn instead of dmḥpy, but gbhwn may originate in the ʿlyhm of 7:25. Such a reconstruction allows for a certain redundancy in that mrḥqthwn and ṭʿwwthwn appear to be a double translation; but 28:36 and 64 may be the source of the association of ṭʿwwthwn with the following terms.

29:17	Heb.		N
	... pn yš bkm	a.	... dl' yhwwy bkwn gbr
		b.	dlbyh mhrhr bḥṭ'
	šrš	c.	dhw' mdmy lšryš qbyʿ b'rʿ'
	prh r'š	d.	'rwm r'šyh dḥṭh ḥly kdbšh
	wlʿnh	e.	brm swpyh mryr klʿnyth dmwth

The translation of this part of the verse is less literal than that of the beginning. Lines a-b are actually based on the beginning of the verse, translated dl' yhwy bkwn gbr ... dlbyh sṭy ʿlwy. The comparison with the root (šryš) changes the Heb. metaphor to a simile and introduces the conclusion in d-e. The idea in d-e is that the beginning of a sin is pleasant, "as sweet as honey," but the end, presumably the punishment (in the next world?), is bitter. That is hardly what the Heb. means, but some of the words have been used.

Interestingly, the word for sin is ḥṭh, incorrectly

spelled, for ḥt' or ḥṭ'h. The word wheat is spelled ḥṭh in Heb., but is translated in the six places in the Torah where it appears in the plural form ḥṭyn, ḥṭyy', etc. (though in four of the verses the Heb. form is also plural). Wheat has a sweet head and relatively bitter roots, and perhaps a pun was intended.

29:18 lwwṭyh hdyn: The word hdyn represents Heb. hz't, but either it should be plural or lwwṭyh should be singular; cf. M lwwṭh hdyn. There may have been some hesitancy to do this with "curse," but no such concern is evidenced, for example, in 11:26.

ḥwby šlwth ᶜl ḥwby zdnth: for Heb. hrwh 't hṣm'h. Heb. rwh was understood as "drunk," a state leading to unintentional sins, while ṣm'h was taken as someone who sinned "from thirst," i.e. willfully and knowingly (cf. Rashi, a.l.). The idea is also found in Onk. ... bdyl l'wsp' lyh ḥṭ'y šlwt' ᶜl zydnwt'.

29:19 'wryyth (+): as in vv. 20, 26, etc.

Add šmyh mn tḥwt (not šmy') to create the homoioteleuton.

29:22 mn: This may be a variant spelling of myn. There is no reason why N should read kl mn dᶜm dᶜśb, though it is possible that the scribe wrote kl mn instead of kl or kl myn because of the frequency of this idiom; cf. PJ: kl ᶜyśb', Onk.: kl ᶜsyb. Note, also the interchange of mn and myn in 20:19.

hyk mh d'thpkt [not d'tḥpkt as printed]: for Heb. kmhpkt.

29:28 glyyn 'ynwn (+): expansive and explanatory.

Chapter 30

30:1 wḥylwpyhwn: for Heb. whqllh. There can be no doubt that this euphemism is used to avoid the word *lwwṭyh*, but it is not clear why this is necessary here and in v. 15. In the preceding chapters, more attention has actually been given to the curses than to the blessings.

dy *sdr*: The expression *dy* *bdr* is expected, but *sdr* is attested in M and I. Note v. 17 and also *mbdrykwn* for *ndḥk* in v. 4, reflecting the use of *bdr* for *hpyṣk* in v. 3. Perhaps *sdr* comes from confusion with *sdr* and *sdrt* elsewhere in the verse.

30:8 *'lhkwn* (+): expansive, in imitation of vv. 6, 7, etc.

30:12

Heb.		N
l' bšmym hy' l'mr	a.	*l' bšmy' hy' 'wryth lmymr*
my	b.	*lwwy hwh ln ḥd kmšh nbyy'*
yʿlh lnw hšmymh	c.	*dy yswq lšmy'*
wyqḥh lnw	d.	*wysb yth ln*
myšmʿnw 'th	e.	*wyšmʿ ytn pqwdyyh*
wnʿśnh	f.	*wnʿbd ythwn*

The translation follows the Hebrew but is expansive in a and b. In a, the subject *hy'* is identified as *'wryth*, while b has been altered radically. Other examples of *lwwy* are routinely found with *my*, and a similar usage is found in v. 13. Note that here it replaces *my* in Heb. The title *mšh nbyy'* is common in N to Deut. (elsewhere in N, he is called *sprhn dyśr'l*), but the term is applied to him in the Heb. of 34:10 and parallels the usage *kywnh nby'* in v. 13.

30:13 Verse 13 resembles v. 12. The phrase *ymh rbh* is routine for *hym*; *'wryth* and *lwwy* are added as in v. 12. The expansion *lwwy hwh ln ḥd kywnh nby' dy yḥwt lʿmqy dymh rbh* parallels v. 12. For the printed *yḥh*, read *yth*.

While a number of ancient texts speak of Moses' ascension to heaven to get the Torah, and others interpret Jonah's descent in the fish as a trip through hell, I have found none that interprets the latter as a revelation or recovery of the Torah.

30:14 bmymr pmykwn: for Heb. bpyk.

30:15 ḫylwpyhn: for Heb. hrᶜ; cf. v. 1. This change is reminiscent of the adaption of wbwr' rᶜ, Is. 45:7, to wbwr' 't hkl in the daily liturgy.

30:19 yt 'wrḫh dḫyy wyt 'wrḫh dmtwth: for Heb. hḫyym whmwt.

lkwn: for Heb. lpnyk.

'wrḫh (+): added three times, twice with dḫyy and once with dmtwth.

30:20 The Heb. word lšbt has not been translated.

Chapter 31

31:7 tyᶜl: for Heb. tb', possibly reading it as tabi' rather than tabo', as in the MT; note the Heb. and Aram. of v. 23, which support the translation here.

31:9 wyt: read wlkl following M.

31:11 lmḫmyyh: perhaps originally active, in contrast to the passive vocalization of the MT, but now passive with qdm.

31:14 lmymr (+): added in imitation of dozens of places where l'mr occurs in Heb.

lmtknsh bšlm mn gw ᶜlm': a euphemism for Heb. lmwt: cf.

v. 16.

31:16 mtknš bšlm ᶜm 'bhtk: for Heb. škb ᶜm 'btyk. This euphemism is found in a fuller form in v. 14, but only the verb is used in G 47:30, w'tknš lwwt 'bhty for wškbty ᶜm 'bty. The usage here is composite, because mtknš does not go with ᶜm.

ṭᶜwwn nkryn d'yt b'rᶜ': for Heb. 'lhy nkr h'rṣ.

31:17 'py rᶜwty: possibly a double translation of pny, but note also v. 18.

31:19 šbḥ (2x) (+): idiomatic, as in v. 21, 22, etc.

31:20 'rᶜ (+): added to complete the stock expression.

31:21 byšh (+): cf. the MH term yṣr hrᶜ.

31:24 ᶜd zmn dy 'šlm ythwn: for Heb. ᶜd tmm, as in v. 30.

31:27 h' (+): The first occurrence is unnecessary; perhaps it is a double of kᶜn.

31:28 dyynykwn (+): cf. 16:18 and 29:9, from which the word may have been borrowed, but it is at least as likely that šbṭykm was read twice, once as špṭykm, rendered dyynykwn.

31:29 mh dl' špr wtqn: a circumlocution for the Heb. hrᶜ; cf. BT Pes. 3a and 28:57.

Chapter 32

32:1 N

1. kywwn dmṭh qṣh dmšh nbyy'
2. lmtknšh bšlm mn gw ᶜlm'
3. ḥšb mšh blybyh w'mr
4. wwy kᶜn ᶜly d'nh mtknš mn gw ᶜlm'
5. wl' 'shdyt bbnwy dqyrys
6. 'yn mshd 'nh bhwn qdm bny nš
7. dmyytyn wṭᶜmyn ks' dmwth
8. myytyn ᶜmh wgzyrthwn bṭln
9. brm 'nh mshd bhwn qdm šmyy' wqdm 'rᶜ'
10. dl' myytyn lᶜwlm wl' ṭᶜmyn ks' dmwth
11. brm swpyhwn blyyn lᶜlm' d'ty
12. wkn yšᶜyh nbyy' pyrš w'mr
13. ṭwlw lšmy' ᶜyynykwn w'stklw b'rᶜ' mlrᶜ
14. 'rwm šmyy' ktnnh ymswn
15. w'rᶜ' klbwš ttkly [read: ttbly]
16. brm ᶜtyd hw' yyy lmbrh šmy' ḥttyn [=ḥdtyn] w'rᶜ' ḥdth
17. 'rwm tryyn nbyyn qmw lmshdh byśr'l
18. mšh nbyyh wyšᶜyyh nbyy'
19. mšh bgyn dhwh qryb lšmy' wrḥyq mn 'rᶜ'
20. 'mr lšmy' 'ṣytw wl'rᶜ' šmᶜw
21. brm yšᶜyh nbyyh dqm mn btrh
22. bgyn dhwh qrb l'rᶜ' wrḥyq mn šmy'
23. 'mr l'rᶜ' 'ṣytw wlšmyy' šmᶜw
24. wtryhwn ᶜl dhww dḥylyn mn lšmh qdyšh
25. qmw lmshdh byśr'l
26. bgyn kdyn qm lyh mšh nbyy' dyyy w'zrz w'mr
27. 'ṣytw šmyh w'mll
28. wtšmᶜ 'rᶜ' bmymr pwmy

Heb.

1. h'zynw hšmym w'dbrh

2. wtšmʿ h'rṣ 'mry py

The lengthy midrash with which the text begins is composed of several different parts, each attempting to deal with a specific exegetical problem. The first question is why Moses called upon the heavens and earth as witnesses; and this is introduced and answered in lines 1-10, where the permanence of these witnesses is noted. Lines 11-16 question this permanence. Lines 17-25 present an alternate explanation of Moses' choice based on the relationship between 32:1 and Is. 1:2 and try to explain the word order here and in Isaiah. Line 26 introduces the actual translation of the Hebrew verse in lines 27-28.

The midrash begins (lines 1-2) by introducing the approach of Moses' death; the text reflects 31:14. Line 3 leaves no doubt about the fact that the following are Moses' thoughts (ḥšb ... blybyh); elsewhere the use of 'mr has caused some confusion, e.g. G 40:12, 18. Line 4 contains Moses' declaration of his approaching death. No such announcement is found at the end of Deut. (note, however, 4:22), but the pattern is known from the similar announcements of the deaths of Jacob and Joseph, who also addressed their families before dying (G 48:21, 50:24). The Genesis passages are translated by h' 'nh myyt (cf. h' 'nh 'zl lmmt, G 25:31 and h' 'nh m'yt, G 50:5). The use of mtknš is based on the use of Heb. 'sp (e.g. G 25:8, 49:33, N 12:15, 20:26, etc.), and, especially, the references to Moses in N 31:2 and D 32:50. Here the announcement is actually a part of Moses' greater concern about his failure to call the people to testimony (4-5). In order to do so, Moses needed witnesses, but he preferred permanent witnesses to human ones, who must, of necessity, also die.

The word *qyrys* (line 5) is, I believe, used only here in N; but it occurs in PJ to N 11:26 (though not in the parallel text in N) as well as in the Targum of Ps. 53:1 and 97:10. Though these passages confirm the usage of the term, it is no more expected in N than the entire phrase *bnwy dqyrys*, itself perhaps a reflection of the idea expressed by Dan. 3:25, Ps. 2:7, D 1:31, 14:1, etc., though a range of terms is used.

The term *ṭʿmyn ks' dmwth* (7) is quite poetic, but synonymous with *dmyytyn*. Cf. G 40:12 and D 32:34, where the *ks' dpwrʿnt'* is mentioned, and *kws htrʿlh*, e.g. Is. 51:17. Line 7 is similar to line 8, which is more closely connected to line 6 than is line 7. Nevertheless both 7 and 8 may belong in the text as seen from the parallel structure to lines 6-7 in lines 9-10.

Lines 11-15 point to the weakness in Moses' assumption about the permanence of the heavens and earth. Is. 51:6 is cited in lines 13-15.

Is. 51:6		N
ś'w lšmym ʿynykm	l. 13	*ṭwlw lšmy' ʿyynykwn*
whbyṭw 'l h'rṣ mtḥt		*w'stklw b'rʿ' mlrʿ*
ky šmym kʿšn nmlḥw	l. 14	*'rwm šmyy' ktnn' ymswn*
wh'rṣ kbgd tblh		*w'rʿ' klbwš ttkly*
wyšbyh kmw kn ymwtwn...		

The translation is literal; note, by comparison, the text of Jonathan: *zqwpw lšmy' ʿynykwn w'stklw b'rʿ' mlrʿ 'ry šmy' kttnn' dʿdy kn yʿdwn w'rʿ' kkswt' dbly' kyn tbly* .... Differences between N and Jonathan are self-explanatory; but the translation in N uses some equivalents found elsewhere in the Torah, e.g. *ṭwlw ʿyynykwn* (G 37:25). Also of note is the word *ttkly*. The manuscript definitely reads *ttkly*, probably corrupted at some point from *ttbly*. The Heb. on which it is based is *tblh*.

Line 16 continues this discussion, noting that God will

create new heavens and earth. Presumably this helps Moses very little in overcoming the impermanence of his witnesses; the availability of these new witnesses, who use the same names as the old ones, only emphasizes their ephemeral nature, noted in 11-15. This plus the fact that brm "however" begins both 11 and 16 point to the redundancy of 11-15 and 16; either argument would have sufficed. The imbalance in size between 11-15 and 16 is explained quite easily. Lines 11 and 16 are, in fact, parallel. Lines 12-15 contain the proof text from Is. 51:6 for line 11, while Is. 65:17, the proof text for 16, is lacking, probably because the language of 16 is very close to the verse itself.

Is. 65:17	N, line 16
ky hnny bwr'	ᶜtyd hw' yyy lmbrh
šmym ḥdšym w'rṣ ḥdšh	šmy' ḥttyn w'rᶜ' ḥdth
wl' tzkrnh hr'šnwt	
wl' tᶜlynh ᶜl lb	

That the verse reinforces the differences between the old and new heavens and earth is clear from the two Heb. lines omitted from N.

If my analysis is correct, and both 11-15 and 16 express the same idea, it is illogical for Moses to call upon heaven and earth as permanent witnesses. This may suggest that 16 should indeed be seen as the opposite of 11-15 -- insofar as the renewal of heaven and earth implies a measure of permanence--but the text itself is less than convincing. It is significant, though, that both arguments are based on the words of Isaiah, as is the rest of the midrash. One might argue that Moses was prepared to call upon these witnesses to the same extent that Isaiah was, since the parallel between D 32:1 and Is. 1:2 may mean that they were thinking along the same lines (17-18). But comparison of these two verses points to one important difference:

Is. 1:2	D 32:1
šmʿw šmym	*h'zynw hšmym* ...
wh'zyny 'rṣ	*wtšmʿ h'rṣ* ...

The word pairs *šmym* - *'rṣ* and *šmʿ 'zn* are both used by both prophets, but the order of *'zn* - *šmʿ* is reversed in Is. 1:2. The targum did not use the term word pairs, nor did it discuss the fact that the order of D 32:1 is found in Is. 28:23 and 42:23, but the author of this midrash may have realized that the more frequent Biblical order is *šmʿ* - *'zn*, making D 32:1 the exception, not Is. 1:2. (For additional data cf. S. Gevirtz, *Patterns in the Early Poetry of Israel*, Chicago, 1963, p. 27 and M. Dahood in L. R. Fisher, ed., *Ras Shamra Parallels I*, Rome, 1972, pp. 360-361). In any case, this difference between Moses and Isaiah is explained in 19-23. Moses, who was closer to heaven, said "give ear" (*'zn*) to the heavens, while Isaiah (and presumably the majority of Biblical writers) were closer to the earth and used this verb accordingly. Note the emphasis on *dqm mn btrh* in 21, emphasizing Isaiah's later and lowe3r station.

The words *'ṣytw* and *šmʿw* are noteworthy. As seen above, Is. 1:2 has *šmʿw* (m. pl.) and *h'zyny* (f. s.), while D 32:1 reads *h'zynw* (m. pl.) and *wtšmʿ* (f. s.). Lines 20 and 23 contain the quotations, but in both cases N uses *'ṣytw* (m. pl.), equivalent to the Deut. form and to *šmʿw* (m. pl.), used in Isaiah. In other words, both references cite the terminology as used in reference to the heavens, even though both heaven and earth are being discussed. This may be attributed to imprecision in composition or in transmission, but part of the problem results from the wish to change the imperfect *tšmʿ* to an imperative form. Any Hebrew midrash on which this passage may have been based undoubtedly would have cited the verses as in the Bible. The cónfusion is a later stage of development. (Note by comparison how Frag. and PJ avoid the problem by using the nouns šmyᶜ' and ṣyyt' in discussing the difference between these two statements.)

Lines 24-25 conclude the midrash by pointing out a simlarity between the two men, namely that both wished lmshdh byśr'l. This statement is interesting for two reasons. In terms of content, it explicitly applies to Isaiah what is merely assumed there, but actually stated only in D 31:28. Structurally, it follows the pattern observed elsewhere of contrasting like things and then noting a similarity between them (e.g. N 11:26). Note also the double reading of mn and l- with dhlyn, line 24.

Line 26 offers the transition from the midrash to the verse, the translation of which is found in lines 27-28. The people mentioned in 25 are yśr'l, the name by which they are called in the same phrase in 17, also. This highlights even further the use of bnwy dqyrys in line 5, but it is impossible to know if this implies a different origin for the two passages. Clearly lines 1-16 and 17-25 are two separate entities and routinely appear alone in the various midrashim, though the texts are joined in Frag. and PJ also. The midrashim (e.g. the Sifrei) often contain a series of analyses of this verse, and the targumim have apparently chosen to connect these two (by the word 'rwm in 17), probably because of the role Isaiah plays in both.

If my analysis is correct, the two texts (1-15 and 16-25) are independent, but the unit 1-15 seems incomplete. One possible continuation is found in Mid. Tan. (p. 181), based on Is. 62:2 wqr' lw šm ḥdš and including a series of verses related to God's name. Though the connection is not tight, it is possible that this idea has been borrowed and used as the concluding link between the two midrashic units in 24-25. Note also the connection with v. 3.

32:2 Heb.		N
yʿrp kmṭr	a.	yb́sm kmṭrh
lqḥy	b.	'wlpny
	c.	ʿl bny yśr'l
tzl kṭl	d.	wytqbl kṭl' ʿlyhwn
'mrty	e.	yt mymr pwmy
kśʿyrm	f.	krwḥyyh
ʿly dš'	g.	dmnšbyn ʿl dty ʿśbyh
wkrbybym	h.	wkrsysy mlqwš
ʿly ʿśb	i.	dslqyn wmrwwyn ṣmḥh d'rʿ'
	j.	byrḥh dnysn

The translation is expansive but follows the Hebrew. The word yb́sm, "may it be sweet," takes yʿrp as yʿrb, motivated, perhaps, by Ps. 104:34 yʿrb n' śyḥy. For other associations of ʿrp and the notion of study, cf. the many places where ʿm qšh ʿrp has been translated qšyn lmqblh 'wlpn, but note that here the association is based on lqḥy, while there, on ʿrp. Line c parallels ʿlyhwn in d. Line e contains the phrase mymr pwmy for Heb. 'mrty, routinely avoided in N. Similarly, Hebrew ʿl py yyy is translated ʿl pm gzyrt mymryh dyyy in E 17:1, N 3:16, 3:39, 33:2, D 34:5, etc., though another circumlocution is used in L 24:12. Line e here may lack the customary expression, because it was either not integral to the translation or not revised to conform to this paraphrase. It is conceivable, however, that the difference between 'mrty and ʿl py yyy allowed the translator to introduce this apparent inconsistency.

In line f, rwḥyyh "winds" has been used to translate śʿyrm, usually understood as "light rain"; cf. Heb. śʿr "storm." The choice of this aspect of the rain is noteworthy, because it is paralleled by rsysy mlqwš in h, which clearly refers to the rain itself. The translator was more concerned with completeness (and lack of repetition) than with following the Biblical parallelism. This preference is also apparent from the use of dty ᶜśbyh in g. The Hebrew uses dšh and ᶜśb in parallelism. N, however, following the usage in G 1:11-12 (translated dtyn dᶜśb), has joined these two words in g, and reworded the parallel line in i without either one. The translation of ᶜly ᶜśb as dslqyn wmrwwyn ṣmḥh d'rᶜ' generalizes the word ᶜśb, already used in g, and may read ᶜly as a verb, though this is not the case in the parallel line in g. It also plays on the Heb. rbybym with mrwwyn. Line j is an extra flourish with which the verse ends.

32:3 N

a. 'mr mšh nbyyh lršyᶜyh
b. wwy lhwn rl[šyᶜy]
c. dmdkryn šmh qdyšh bgydwpyn
d. brm lyt 'ypšr lḥd mml'ky šyrwth
e. lmdkrh yt šmh qdyšh
f. ᶜd zmn d'ynwn dyśr'l 'mryn
g. q- q- q- tlth zymnyn
h. mnhwn ylp mšh dl' lmdkrh yt šmh qdyš-
i. ᶜd zm dhwh mḥnk pmyh bᶜśryn wḥdh mylyn
j. d'nwn tmnyyn wḥmšh 'tyn
k. wkn hw' mprš w'mr
l. h'zynw hšmym w'dbrh
m. wtš- h'rṣ 'mry py
n. yᶜrp kmṭr lqḥy
o. tzl kṭl 'mrty
p. kśᶜyrym ᶜly dš'
q. wkrbybym ᶜly ᶜśb
r. ky šm
s. lkn 'mr mšh nbyy'
t. 'rwm bšmh qdyš' 'nh mṣly

u. w'twn ᶜmy bny yśr'l

v. hbw 'yqr wtwšbḥh wrwmmw l'lhkwn

Heb.

1. ky šm yyy 'qr'

2. hbw gdl l'lhynw

This passage is most easily analyzed by starting at the end, where the translation of the Hebrew appears (t, v). Note that Heb. l'lhynw has been changed to l'lhkwn to apply to the listeners. The phrase yqr wtwšbḥh wrwmmw is an expansion of Heb. gdl.

The verse itself seems to instruct the people to respond when Moses mentions God's name. Lines s and u are thus simply the respective stage cues. But the verse's Biblical context is somewhat odd, for it interrupts the introduction of Moses' exhortation. This location has prompted N's observation (i-j) that Moses' mention of God follows 21 words, or 85 letters, of introductory text, which are actually listed, in Hebrew, in lines l-r. The text in N contains 84 letters, but the final Shin, Ayyin in wtšmᶜ (m) have been omitted (intentionally) and an extra Yod has been added in kśᶜyrym (probably accidentally).

The reason for Moses' using this strange introduction is not clear from the Biblical text, but line h explains that he learned it from the angels, presumably while he was in heaven. The angels, we are told, also do not mention God's holy name until it is properly introduced; they wait for the Israelites to recite the line qdwš qdwš qdwš from Is. 6:3, which serves as their signal (d-g). (Note the possible double d'ynwn - dyśr'l in f.) This points to the power of Israelite prayer and emphasizes the importance of proper preparation and sanctity in reciting God's holy name. It thus contrasts with the preceding passage, where Moses commented "Woe to the evil ones who blaspheme with God's name" (a-c). (Note that N usually translated rš' with the root ḥyb, e.g. G 18:23, E 23:1, D 25:1.)

Seen in correct order, the passage comments on evil blasphemers, who, in contrast to the ministering angels, use God's name inappropriately. The Israelites, like the angels, should mention God's name only after a proper introduction, following the model of Moses, provided in this verse. The pieces all fit together, but it is obvious that they were not originally connected. The comparison between the blasphemers (a-c) and the angels is forced at best, mostly because the context of the piece about angels is liturgical. Lines d-g appear as an important part of this passage, because the balance between the recitations of the angels and the Israelites corresponds to that between the recitation of the Israelites and Moses, and also because they contain one of the few correlations with the Hebrew verse. Indeed, if taken to its logical conclusion, Moses emerges as the master of this entire earthly and heavenly choir, perhaps because of his having commanded the heavens and earth (and, by association, their inhabitants) to praise God (cf. v. 1).

The calculation of 21 words and 85 letters is interesting. Elsewhere we find discussions of the number of letters and words (Sifrei, p. 341, Mid. Tan. p. 186) and there are close correlations between these numbers and the traditional Jewish liturgical practices that include this verse from Isaiah. (See Finkelstein's notes to the Sifrei.) This liturgical focus points to the irrelevance of lines a-c, unless they refer to a faulty liturgical practice; but even if that were shown to be the case, the connection to what follows would still be weak. Even the relationship between d-g and h-v is tenuous. Moses' practice of preparing for his mention of God's name might be analagous to some sort of preliminary step practiced by the angels, but that is where the analogy ends. It is difficult to see how Moses' actions, as described in h-v, could be based on the angels' actions in d-g, particularly since the angels did not recite 21 words before God's name. The two must have been separate texts originally (as they are in the Sifrei) and were joined together later.

This union is not unique to N, as similar passages are found in Frag., PJ and Mid. Tan. N's version is the longest, but the formulation in Mid. Tan is the clearest and avoids the problems noted above. For purposes of comparison I cite the relevant part:

1. ... mlmd šl' rṣh mšh lhzkyr šmw šlhq- b- h-
2. 'l' l'ḥr ʿśrym w'ḥd dbr
3. šhn šmwnym wḥmš 'wtywt
4. wmy [read wmmy] lmd mšh
5. mml'ky hšrt
6. mlmd š'yn ml'ky šrt mzkyrym šmw šlhq- b- h-
7. ʿd šhn 'wm- q- q- q h- ṣb-
8. 'm- mšh dyy lhywt pḥwt 'ḥd mšbʿh mml'ky šrt
9. whry hdbrym ql wḥwmr
10. mh 'm mšh rbn šlnby'ym
11. šl' hyh bʿwlm gdwl mmnw
12. l' rṣh lhzkyr šmw šlhq- b- h-
13. 'l' l'ḥr 'ḥd wʿśrym dbr
14. šhn šmwnym wḥmš 'wtywt
15. ʿl 'ḥt kmh wkmh šl' yzkyr 'dm šmw šlhq- b- h- l ḥnm.

This presentation contains all of the elements in N. Lines a-c are found in 15; d-g, in 6-7; h-j are similar to 4-5. The discussion of 21 words and 85 letters is found in i-j and 2-3 (= 13-14), though these are in different contexts. Lines k-r simply list the 21 Hebrew words in v. 3 and are not paralleled in Mid. Tan. Lines s-v contain the expanded translation of the verse and are also lacking in the Hebrew midrash. The midrash begins with the verse and notes that Moses' precedure followed that of the angels. It concludes with the comment about other people who may misuse God's name (9-15), but the comparison is between them and Moses (not the angels, as in N) and does not declare them to be either evildoers or blasphemers, as does N. Nor is there any indication of a faulty liturgy that was in use.

The midrash provides certain logical inferences (in 5, 8, 9-15) that hold the pieces together. This text also appears composite (a seam is evident between lines 9 and 10), but the presentation is preferable to that in N. Given the emphasis in lines 9-15 (½ of the text) it is possible to understand how even this presentation might have motivated a translator to begin his text with the statement about inappropriate use of the divine name. If so, it left him with no real connection with the rest of the material; hence the weak link between a-c and d ff.

The most basic problem remains, though, namely the relation (if any) that may exist between the practice described by D 32:3, a responsive prayer of Moses and the people, and N lines d-g, a description of the angelic practice of waiting for the Israelite prayers before responding with Is. 6:3. There is little doubt that the practice of responsive prayers is Biblical. It is found in Ps. 88 and 136 and has been documented elsewhere in both the Israelite and non-Israelite rituals. Ps. 145 as preserved in 11QPs also attests to this practice. Mekh. to E 15:2 applies this procedure to E 15:1 ff, as does N in E 15:2. Apparently this antiphonal form was quite common in ancient liturgical practice (pagan and Christian as well as Jewish), and there is little reason to doubt the legitimacy of understanding D 32:3 in this manner. The idea underlying d-g is the heavenly qedusha, understood to be described in Is. 6:3 and Ezek. 3:12. Neither of these texts actually describes antiphonal practice, but Is. 6:3 reads wqr' zh 'l zh w'mr, and it was not difficult to understand the verse in this way. Accordingly, on one level, the only relationship between the practices in D 32:3 and N d-g is antiphonal practice. The angelic practice was conceived in this manner in keeping with a known liturgical procedure, not necessarily limited to D 32:3. It seems, therefore, that lines d-g, (or at least their general contents) were originally independent of D 32:3, presumably as part of the mystical and/or liturgical materials to which they related.

The arithmetic aspects of our texts are quite another matter. The three words qdwš that precede God's name in Is. 6:3 contain 12 letters. Moses' introduction to God's name in D 32:3 contains 21 words and 85 letters. This ratio of 3 to 21 or 1 to 7 is picked up in Mid. Tan. as the difference between Moses and the angels, the latter being 7 times holier than Moses and able to recite God's name with 1/7 of the preparation. These observations could derive only from a comparison of D 32:3 and Is. 6:3, and would be appropriate only after the latter had been interpreted as a heavenly antiphonal prayer. The comparison of the numbers of words reveals a meaningful difference between Moses and the angels, but the image of Moses with 1/7 of an angel's holiness does not compare well with the obvious attempt by N to make Moses the choir master who ultimately led the Israelites and, through them, the angels in glorifying God through the recitation of this prayer. In this respect N and Mid. Tan. are quite different, but both texts insist that Moses patterned his 21 words on the 3 of the angels. N, it would seem, is more interested in the practical liturgical concern than is Mid. Tan., which focuses more on the question of proper and improper use of God's name.

The comparison of 12 and 85 letters is less useful, because no arithmetically pleasing associations are forthcoming (indeed, the texts mention the 85 but not the 12). The factor of 7 (21/3) noted above is very close -- 7 x 12 = 84 -- but no tampering with the text was allowed in order to support the comparison. (Given the state of knowledge of the history of and defective spelling, it is not at all unlikely that a text of 84 letters existed or could have been found. Most of the words contain defective spelling, as is the case with most ancient poems in the Bible, and texts with *kśᶜrm*, for *kśᶜyrm*, or *krbbym* or *krbybm* are entirely possible; but this was out of the question. Also comparable is the kind of *gematriah* that adds the number of words to the numerical value of its letters, e.g. *kl* = 51, not 50, or the fact that 85 in Heb. letters is *ph* "mouth," suggesting that only after 85 letters may one open his mouth, but none of these possibilities has been exploited.)

The relationship between these midrashim that mention 21 words and 85 letters and the various liturgical practices that introduce God's name in Is. 6:3 ith 21 words or 85 letters are outlined in Finkelstein's note to Sifrei, p. 341, line 12. A summary of the scholarly datings of the *qedusha* is found in Werner, pp. 283-287. Whether the description of the heavenly *qedusha* originated before or after the presentation of these calculations is difficult to say, but the impact on the final form of the liturgy is unquestioned.

32:4 N

a. *'mr mšh nbyy'*

b. *'nh ḥmyt lrbwn kl ᶜlmyyh yyy*

c. *mplg ywm' wᶜbd yth l'rbᶜ ḥlqyn*

d. *tlt šᶜyn lᶜy b'wryth*

e. *wtlt šᶜyn ytb bdynh*

f. wtlt šʿyn mzwwg zwgyn byn gbr l'tth

g. wmrym wmmk

h. wtlt šʿyn mprns kl ʿlm' ṣdyqh

i. dlyt qdmwy šqr

j. 'rwm kl 'rḥtyh dynyn wqšwṭ

k. 'lhh hyymnh dlyt qdmwy ʿwwlh

l. zkyy wqšwṭ bdynh hw'

Heb.

1. hṣwr tmym pʿlw
2. ky kl drkyw mšpṭ
3. 'l 'mwnh w'yn ʿwl
4. ṣdyq wyšr hw'

Line a is the same introductory phrase as in v. 3; a similar one is found near the beginning of v. 1. Lines b-h describe Moses' report on how God spends the 12 hours of his day. Presumably this information, like that in v. 3, was obtained during Moses' visit in heaven (according to PJ on Sinai). According to N, the daytime is divided equally between studying the Torah, sitting in judgment, matchmaking, and providing for the world. Other reports of these activities substitute "playing" or "jousting" (mṣḥq) with the Leviathan for the matchmaking during the last quarter of the day (BT A.Z. 3b). This midrashic introduction has been included as an elaboration on the statements in the verse. Line e is easily correlated to line 2, and line 3 has been taken as a prooftext for God's rewarding and punishing (BT Taʿan. 11a), possibly the idea behind line g (a line which otherwise might be deleted as an addition to f). Line h contains a reference to ʿlm' ṣdyqh, parallel to 4. The word tmym in line 1 may be taken to refer to 1) the Torah (d) through the phrase twrt yyy tmymh, Ps. 19:8, or 2) the entire description of God as provided by d-h.

If d-h are to be correlated to the four lines of the Hebrew verse, the unit must be seen as part of a double translation, because lines i-l also provide a closer translation of these same Hebrew words. The phrase lyt qdmwy šqr (i) is preferred to the positive tmym pᶜlw. Line 2 is translated literally except for mšpṭ, which has been expanded to dynyn wqšwṭ. Parallels could also be drawn between the corresponding parts of d-h and i-l, but this is not necessary for PJ, which presents the translation as a prooftext for the midrash, thereby creating one unified passage from the two pieces in N (an independent midrash and a close translation of the Hebrew, not unlike that presented in Onkelos).

32:5 N

a. ḥblw qwdmwy bnyh ḥbybyh
b. l' qdmwy ḥblw
c. 'lh lhwn mwmh
d. d'štkḥ bhwn dr' ᶜqmnh wptltnh
e. drh dšny ᶜbdwy
f. 'wp sdr dynwy dᶜlm' 'štny ᶜlwy

Heb.

1. šḥt lw
2. l' bnyw mwmm
3. dwr ᶜqš wptltl

The Hebrew is difficult. The words šḥt lw can mean (a) "he/it harmed him/it" and are easily modified to (b) "they harmed him/it," because of the presence of the plural bnyw. This latter notion may underlie line a of the translation, but perhaps it is easiest to punctuate the Heb. šḥt lw? l'! bnyw mwmm, which could produce the three lines a-c. If the blemish is His sons' (c) then obviously it is not God's (b). Line d is clearer, though the first two words may belong in c. It modifies the Hebrew to refer to some members of a corrupt generation, but does not designate all of the people as evil, as might be assumed from the Hebrew. Lines e-f are a double reiteration of the latter part of d. While d is literal, using cognates for two of the three Hebrew words, e is less figurative than the Hebrew and uses concrete terms for ᶜqš and ptltl. Lines e-f are similar to Onk., and could be an expansion of dr' d'šny ᶜwbdwhy w'štnyw.

32:6	Heb.		N
	h lyyy tgmlw z't	a.	hl' mn qdm yyy 'twn tbᶜwn d'
	ᶜm nbl wl' ḥkm	b.	'wmh ṭpšh wl' ḥkymyyh
	hl' hw' 'byk	c.	hl' hw' 'bwk
	qnk	d.	dy qnh ytkwn
	hw' ᶜśk	e.	wdy brh ytkwn
	wyknnk	f.	wškll ytkwn

The translation is close except for minor deviations in a, d, e and f. Cf. G 1:1 and D 32:18 for parallel uses of brh and wškll.

32:7	Heb.		N
	zkr ymwt ᶜwlm	a.	'dkrw ywmyn mn ywmt ᶜlm'
	bynw šnwt dr wdr	b.	'tbwnnw bšnwy dkl dr wdr
	š'l 'byk	c.	š'lw l'bhtkwn drbrbyn mnkwn b'wryt'
	wygdk	d.	wytnwn lkwn
	zqnyk	e.	ḥkymykwn
	wy'mrw lk	f.	wyymrwn lkwn

Line a appears to contain a conflate translation for Heb. ymwt ᶜwlm. Onk. translates ywmyn dmn ᶜlm', while PJ has mn ywmt ᶜlm'. Apparently N has combined these two readings. Line c adds three words that change the focus from the wisdom of maturity to the knowledge of the Torah (also found in Frag. and PJ). The rest of the verse is translated normally for N.

32:8 bpryšwtyh lynšy: for Heb. bhprydw, taking the phrase as a reference to the dispersion described in G 11:7-8.

šbṭyyh (+): idiomatic.

32:9 'nwm ᶜmh bny yśr'l (+): The use of 'nwn is routine. Apparently bny yśr'l was added as part of the idiom with ᶜmh.

32:10

Heb.		N
ymṣ'hw b'rṣ mdbr	a.	'rᶜ ythwn šryn b'rᶜ dmdbrh
wbthw yll yšmn	b.	wbṣllth ylyl yšymwn
	c.	dbr ythwn 'rbᶜyn šnyn bmdbrh
	d.	'ḥt lhwn mnh mn šmy'
	e.	'sq lhwn b'r mn thwmh
	f.	w'gyz lhwn slwy mn ymh
ysbbnhw	g.	'šry ythwn ḥzwr ḥzwr l'yqr škyntyh
ybwnnhw	h.	'lp ythwn ᶜśrty (!) dbyryh
	i.	ᶜyyny ythwn
yṣrnhw	j.	wnṭr ythwn
k'yšwn ᶜynw	k.	hyk mh dnṭr šyknh bbh dᶜyyn

Lines a, b and j are translated literally, while g, h and k are expansive. Lines c-f are additional examples of God's favor to the Israelites in the desert; i seems to be an alternative to j.

Line a uses a phrase from E 19:2, (wšrwn bmdbr'), but this may be coincidental. Line c is close to D 8:2 ... dbr ytkwn yyy 'lhkwn dnh 'rbᶜyn šnyn bmdbrh. Line d seems to combine wymṭr ᶜlyhm mn l'kl (Ps. 78:24) and mmṭyr lkm lḥm mn hšmym (E 16:4), but the translation in N a.l. is almost identical: h' 'nh mḥyt lkwn lḥm mn šmy'. Line e is similar to Ps. 78:15, including a possible word play on wyšq and 'sq: wyšq kthmwt rbh. Line f is based on N 11:31, translated w'gyz slwyyn mn ym'.

The expansion in g presumably refers to the Israelites who camped around the tabernacle, as noted in N 2:2, though some of the phrases are closer to N 1:50-53, which describe only the Levites. It also may refer to the food, specifically the quails (in f). Note the similarity to Ps. 78:27-28 wymṭr ᶜlyhm kᶜpr š'r wkḥwl ymym ᶜwp knp wypl bqrb mḥnhw sbyb lmškntyw. Line h is an expansive translation that derives the Heb. from the word bynh, "understanding"; the telling (not teaching) of the Ten Commandments is mentioned in D 4:13.

The brief phrase ᶜyyny ythwn (i) has no basis in the verse, as there is no Hebrew word between ybwnnhw and yṣrnhw. Line i is, possibly, another insertion like c-f, though it is much shorter. PJ has 'gyn ᶜlyhwn šbᶜty ᶜnny 'yqryh in this position, while Frag. has 'qyp ythwn ᶜm yqr škyntyh. PJ's use of ᶜnny might relate to N's ᶜyyny, but it is not clear why. The verb mᶜnn has been related to the noun ᶜnn in N, but there is no connection with this verse. It might be a variation of ᶜny "to afflict" (there are possible parallels in Ps. 78, Num. and Deut.), but that would be out of tune with the eight positive statements in the verse. It might also be a play on Heb. ᶜynw (k), but, if so, the Aramaic of k is preferable. Though the parallels with Ps. 78 have been noted, it is not clear if the lines of N reflect the wording of the psalm. There can be little doubt, however, that the general style and tone of N reflect the influence of this text.

32:12	Heb.		N
	yyy	a.	yyy bmmrh 'mr
	bdd ynḥnw	b.	lblḥwdhwn yšrwn
		c.	ᶜm' bny yśr'l
	w'yn ᶜmw	d.	wl' hwwy bynyhwn
	'l nkr	e.	plḥy plḥn nwkryy

Aside from the addition of c there are two changes from the Hebrew. The verb ynḥnw (b) is causative in meaning, and has God as its subject; but N changes God's action to speaking and translates ynḥnw as an intransitive verb. As presented, b-c resemble N 23:9, translated h' ᶜm' h'lyyn šryyn lblḥwdyhwn. The presence of ᶜm' in N 23:9 may explain the insertion of ᶜm' bny yśr'l in c; if so, it points to another case of the expansion of ᶜmh to this fuller phrase. In any event, however, the phrase also provides a much needed subject for yšrwn.

The second change occurs in e, where "idolators" has been substituted for "idols," as in PJ. Perhaps the equation of bynyhwn = ᶜmw, supported by reading ᶜmw as "his people," not "with him," necessitated that 'l nkr refer to people rather than idols.

32:13 bmsyh: for the homophonous Heb. bmty.

w'yykl ythwn: for the peᶜal wy'kl, perhaps revocalizing it as a causative form.

ᶜllt tpnwqy mlkyn: for Heb. tnwbt śdy. Perhaps ᶜllt and tpnwqy reflect a conflate translation. The use of mlkyn parallels Frag. and PJ and is similar to Onk's translation, which reads the entire verse as a promise of military victories.

The order wmšḥ mšḥ ythwn has been questioned by DM, who prefers to reverse the last two words. This is an improvement, but perhaps mšḥ is extra. In either case, the words mšḥ and wmšḥ stand out by themselves, because for Heb. mšḥ N usually has rby (E 28:41, 29:7, N 35:25, etc.) Perhaps rby has a special cultic meaning that would explain its use in G 31:13 also.

kyp šmyr tynrh: for Heb. mḥlmyš ṣwr, as in 8:15.

32:14	Heb.		N
	ḥm't bqr	a.	šmyny twryn
	wḥlb ṣ'n	b.	wrkyky ᶜn
	ᶜm ḥlb krym	c.	ᶜm ṭwb dpṭymyn
	w'ylym bny bšn	d.	wdkryn bny btnyy
	wᶜtwdym	e.	wgdyyn
	ᶜm ḥlb klywt ḥṭh	f.	ᶜm ṭwb šwmnyhwn dḥṭyy'
		g.	'mr mšh nbyyh
		h.	'yn hywwn yśr'l lᶜyyn b'wryth
		i.	wnṭryn pqwdyyh
	wdm ᶜnb	j.	mn ᶜnbh ḥdh
	tšth ḥmr	k.	yhwwn štyyn kwr dḥmr

Lines a-c and f contain some changes in the positive terms "good," "fat," etc., but otherwise a-f are literal. The insertion of g is similar to that encountered in vv. 3 and 4 and does not reflect the translator's practice of preventing the misapplication of first person references to himself. Lines h-i are familiar from G 3:15, D 32:30, etc., but the threat of punishment (i.e. 'yn l' yhww lᶜyyn ...) is lacking. It resembles the division of Bilaam's prophecies into two parts; cf. N 23:10, 23, etc. The inclusion of these lines has broken the flow of the Hebrew, and j-k are translated more loosely than are a-f. The collective noun ᶜnb is taken as one grape, thus emphasizing the divine blessing. (Cf. 1 Kings 17:7-16, Matthew 14:31-21, 15:32-39.)

32:15 Heb.		N
wyšmn yšrwn	a.	*w'klw dbyt yśr'l*
wybᶜṭ	b.	*wbᶜṭw*
šmnt	c.	*wᶜtrw*
ᶜbyt	d.	*wpḥzw*
	e.	*pgšw*
	f.	*whṣlḥw*
kśyt	g.	*wqnwn lhwn nksyn sgyn*
wytš 'lwh	h.	*w'nšwn yt mymr 'lhh*
ᶜśhw	i.	*dy brh ythwn*
wynbl ṣwr	j.	*wkprw bdḥltyh dtqyph*
yšᶜtw	k.	*dhwh prq ythwn bšᶜt ᶜqthwn*

The translation follows the verse but expands it in many places. In a, *yšrwn* is translated by the clearer *dbyt yśr'l*. The list of 7 words or phrases in a-g is correlated only roughly with the 5 in Hebrew, though comparison with Onk. and PJ puts the list in perspective. Onk. reads *ᶜtr yśr'l wbᶜṭ*, *'ṣlḥ*, *tqwp*, *qn' nksyn*, citing, like the Heb., only five actions. Since there can be little doubt about the correlation of *wyšmn* (a) and *w'klw*, *ᶜtr* in Onk. confirms the correspondence of Heb. and N in c. Line b is also not a problem; the Heb. and Aram. are clear cognates. Since Onk. and N both use *qn' nksyn* for the last item, and Onk. lists only 5, this phrase must correspond to *kśyt*, in a play on *nksym* and *kśh*. This leaves three words -- *pḥzw*, *pgšw* and *hṣlḥw* -- one of which must correspond to Heb. *ᶜbyt*. Onk. has *'ṣlḥ* and *tqwp* in the positions of *šmnt* and *ᶜbyt*, but no clear correlation to N is possible because *šmnt* is clearly the equivalent of *'ṣlḥ*

(Onk.) and ᶜtrw (N). PJ reads wᶜtrw byt yśr'l wpḥzw, 'ṣlḥw, tqwp, qnwn nksyn. This suggests that pḥzw, following in order after the first three verbs, corresponds to wybᶜṭ. Line f, hṣlḥw, should be understood as a double translation of šmnt; and pgšw (e), meaning "to fight," is probably an alternate translation for wybᶜṭ. Presumably it gravitated to its present location because of its similarity to pḥzw. Note also the analysis in Aruch s. v. pgšw, where one opinion suggests that pḥzw and pgšw are variants of the translation of wybᶜṭ, while the other suggests that pgšw corresponds to ᶜbyt while pḥzw translates wybᶜt.

Line i is similar to part of v. 6, line e. The phrase dḥltyh dtqyph may reflect G 31:42, where pḥd yṣḥq (a reference to God) is translated tqyp' dysḥq (cf. G 31:53, also); the words are used in the same context in E 15:16 as well. It seems to build on an equation of "powerful" and "fearful." The expansion in k is routine in N.

32:16 wbṭᶜwwthwn: for Heb. btwᶜbt. Usually ṭᶜwthwn is used for 'lylyhm or the like, while tᶜbh is translated mrḥqh. DM has suggested that bmrḥqthwn and wbṭᶜwwthwn should be reordered, thus accommodating the translation of tᶜbh, but zrym is usually translated ḥylnyy (E 29:33, 30:33, L 22:10, 12, 13, etc.). Apparently the usage differed here because zrym refers to foreign gods, not men, and the switch was occasioned by the similarity in sound between bṭᶜwwthwn and btwᶜbt. Note also the use of bmrḥqthwn in v. 21.

32:17 Heb.		N
yzbḥw lšdym	a.	dbḥw qdm ṭᶜwwt šdyh
l' 'lh	b.	dlyt bhwn mmš
'lhym l' ydᶜwm	c.	ṭᶜwwn dy l' ḥkmw ythwn

Heb.		N
ḥdšym mqrb b'w	d.	*ḥdtn 'ynwn dmn kdwn 'tbryyn*
l' śʿrwm 'btykm	e.	*dl' 'tʿsqw bhwn 'bhtkwn*

The ambiguous *yzbḥw* is understood as a past tense -- *dbḥw*, and *lšdym* (a) is expanded to *qdm ṭʿwwt šdyh*, comparable to c, where it seems more appropriate. The word *ṭʿwwt* is lacking in Onk., but part of a full phrase in PJ, Onk: *dbḥw lšdym*; PJ: *ydbḥwn lṭʿwwn dmtylyn lšdyn*.

Line b is a paraphrase of the Hebrew, probably to preclude considering these gods as anything serious. To the same effect is the change in line d of *b'w* to *'tbryyn*, which stresses that these gods were only recently created.

32:18 *tqyph*: for Heb. *ṣwr*; cf. vv. 3, 13, 15, etc.

mmr (+): idiomatic.

dy škll ytkwn wʿbd ytkwn mḥylyn mḥylyn: a double translation of Heb. *mḥllk*, both parts of which play on the similarity of sounds. PJ omits *škll ytkwn*.

32:19

Heb.		N
wyr' yyy wyn'ṣ	a.	*wgly qdm yyy 'rwm hwh rgwz*
mkʿs	b.	*mn kʿsh*
	c.	*dy 'kʿsw ytyh*
	d.	*ʿmh bny yśr'l*
	e.	*dhwwn ḥbybyn ʿlwy*
bnyw wbntyw	f.	*hyk bnyn whyk bnn*

The two circumlocutions (in a) are routine in N, so much so that they are combined here despite the resulting clumsiness. Line c is an expansion of b, and d has been added as in many of the other verses in the chapter. Line e was generated by f, though it may have been influenced by 23:6, etc.

32:21 b'lh dl' 'lh: for Heb. bl' 'l; b'mh dl' 'mh: for Heb. bl' ᶜm. While a literal translation would be no less meaningful in Aramaic than in Hebrew (cf. Onk.), this expansion is easier to understand. It is not clear why this differs from the translation of l' 'lh in v. 17.

32:23 'mrt bmymry (+): Usually the targum avoids first person references to God. Here one has been added; presumably this was less troublesome than the literal translation of the Hebrew.

gyry mḥwwt pwrᶜnwty 'grh bhwn: for Heb. ḥṣy 'klh bm; mḥwwt = mḥbt may be a double of pwrᶜnwty.

32:24 Heb.		N
mzy rᶜb	a.	mn pḥy kpn
wlḥmy ršp	b.	w'kyly gwb
wqṭb mryry	c.	wmrwwḥy rwwḥn byšn
wšn	d.	wšn 'rbᶜty mlkwwth
bhmt	e.	dmtyln kḥywwth brh
'šlḥ bm	f.	'grh bhwn
ᶜm ḥmt	g.	ᶜm ḥmthwn dtnyny'
zḥly ᶜpr	h.	wzḥly dᶜprh

Each item in the left column has been taken as a full phrase in the translation, even when the Heb. phrases have been divided, as in g-h.

Heb. mzy rᶜb (a) is understood as "wasting" (JPS), "sucked out" (BDB), etc.; rᶜb is clearly famine. But the force of mn pḥy uncertain. Meanings of pḥ (a) include "snare," "coal," and "blowing"; each could be related to a famine without much trouble. DM, suggesting the reading mnpḥy, prefers to see the root as npḥ "swollen"; cf. N 5:21, wyt mʿyk mnpḥyn.

Heb. lḥwmy ršp (b) means "devoured by ršp, ršp being anything from a Canaanite god to a pestilence. This is reflected in the use of 'kyly in Aramaic, but gwb is a problem. Based on an understanding of bny ršp in Job 5:7 as birds, the ancient translation (including LXX and Vulg.) take ršp as birds. (Cf. ršp ṣprm in the Azitawad inscription from Karatepe.) Use of gwb in N is somewhat unexpected -- Onk., PJ and Frag. have ʿwp -- and may reflect a different exegetical tradition, though phonetic shifts and scribal changes can not be ruled out. Usually gwb refers to locusts (cf. E 10: 4, etc.). Since ršp was taken as a plague of some sort, occurs together with famine (line q), and is accompanied by a word meaning devoured, locusts remain a logical possibility. There seems to be no connection with the word ygbyhw (Targ. bgwbh') in this same verse, Job 5:7.

Heb. qṭb (c) means "pestilence," mryry means "strong" or "bitter." Aram. mrwwḥy rwwḥn byšh is not a translation but a personification, perhaps in keeping with the most ancient usages of the word. Other rabbinic texts use qṭb mryry as a demon; cf. Lam. Rab. to Lam 1:3, BT Pes. 111b, etc.

Heb. šn bhmt (d-e) has been taken as symbolic of the four kingdoms, which are comparable to animals. No further identification is presented, but this is an allusion to Dan. 7:3-7, where four animals were seen in Belshazzar's dream: a lion, a bear, a leopard, and an unidentified fourth. All four were feared, in part, for their sharp teeth, actually mentioned in the description of two of them -- the bear (v. 5) and the fourth (v. 7). Note also N's interpretation of G 15:12.

Line f is translated literally. Heb. ḥmt (g) has been separated from h to allow inclusion of an additional form of suffering. Aram. ḥmthwn dtnyny' refers to the venom of snakes (tnyn); cf. v. 33 ḥmt tnynn and N.

The phrase zḥly ᶜpr (h) is the same in Heb. and Aram. and means "things that crawl in the dust."

32:25 ythwn (+): expansive.

wbqyṭwny mdmkyhwn: for Heb. wbḥdrym; cf. G 2:24.

dmwth (+): expansive.

ynqyn wmtrkyn: for Heb. ymnq. This may be an hendiadys or a double translation (Onk. and Frag. use only ynq). Or it may result from the wish to create a phrase that can balance gbryn sbyn. Note that Onk. has created this balance by omitting any equivalent for Heb. 'yš: ynqyhwn ᶜm sbyhwn.

32:27

Heb.		N
lwly kᶜs 'wyb 'gwr	a.	'ylwly kᶜsn dśn'h dy tqp
	b.	w'ylwly d'dkr lhwn qyymh
	c.	dqyymt l'bhthwn
	d.	'brhm yṣḥq wyᶜqb
pn ynkrw ṣrymw	e.	dl' ytgbrwn ᶜlyhwn bᶜly dbbyhwn
pn y'mrw	f.	wdy l' yy'mrwn
	g.	śn'yhwn bᶜly dbbyhwn
ydnw rmh	h.	ydynn 'tprᶜn ln
	i.	mn bᶜly dbbynn
wl' yyy	j.	wl' mn qdm yyy
pᶜl kl z't	k.	'dᶜbdt (= 'tᶜbdt) d'

Line a is translated closely; 'gwr is taken as "fearful," hence "powerful" (tqp). Line b is structurally parallel to a (cf. 'ylwly d-), though the addition of c-d seems to make it even more important. Lines b-d assume an underlying Hebrew text of (b) hbryt or hšbwᶜh (c) 'šr nšbᶜty l- (or krty ᶜm) 'bwtm (d) 'brhm yṣḥq wyᶜqb. Equivalents of c are found in N 14:28, D

10:11, 31:7 and Jer. 11:10, while close parallels to the unit are found in Ps. 105: 5-10, parallel to 1 Chron. 16:15-17. No closer identification for this stock phrase is possible.

śn'yhwn bᶜly dbbyhwn (g): a double text, possibly a combination of the terms used in a and e. Line g is lacking in PJ; this seems preferable.

The phrase byd rmh occurs in E 14:8, N 15:30 and N 33:3. In each case it is translated bryš gly (cf. notes to E 14:8), but in each case the reference is to Israel. That idiom would thus be inappropriate here, and a different non-literal translation is offered in line h instead.

The sequence of words whose referents are unclear (ynkrw, y'mrw, ydnw) prevents certain identification of the pronominal element of ydynn (h), but the presence of śn'yhwn and bᶜly dbbyhwn in g seems to show that bᶜly dbynn in i refers to the enemies' enemies, i.e. the Israelites.

Heb. kl has not been translated in k.

32:28 byšn (+): idiomatic with ᶜṣh when it carries a negative meaning.

32:29 yśr'l (+): addition of the subject.

wylpwn 'wryt-: for Heb. yśkylw z't. All forms of study, learning, wisdom, etc. are interpreted to refer to the Torah; the unspecified z't has been interpreted to follow.

32:30 Heb.		N
('ykh)	a.	kd yhwwn yśr'l lᶜyyn b'wryth
	b.	wnṭryn pyqwdyh
yrdp 'ḥd 'lp	c.	hwh ḥd mnhwn rdp 'lp
wšnym ynysw rbbh	d.	wtryn mnhwn rbbh rbwth mᶜrqyn
('m l' ky)	e.	ᶜl dḥṭwn w'rgyzw qdmwy
ṣwrm mkrm	f.	tqyph šbq ythwn

wyyy hsgyrm — g. wmymrh dyyy msr ythwn

h. byd bᶜly dbbyhwn

Several parts of the verse are translated literally while other parts are not translated at all. For Heb. 'ykh, preceding a potential reward, N has inserted in a-b standard lines about studying the Torah (cf. G 3:15, D 32:14, etc.). Lines c and d are quite close to the Hebrew. The addition of mnhwn (2x) probably arose through the influence of L 26:8: wrdpw mkm ḥmš m'h wm'h mkm rbbh yrdpw; rbbh and rbwth (d) are a double translation of Heb. rbbh, that alters Heb. 10,000 to 100,000,000.

The negative 'm l' ky (e) has been made positive and the cause for God's rejection of Israel has been added. Elsewhere (e.g. v. 18) ṣwr is translated tqyp, and therefore tqyph is the equivalent of ṣwrm, and the subject of šbq. The phrase šbq ythwn is the equivalent of ᶜzbm, cf. w'šbwq ythwn in 31:17; the word mkr "sell" probably seemed inappropriate. Similarly hsgyrm was paraphrased as msr ythwn ... (g-h). Lines g-h are the opposite of Josh. 23:1 and similar to Jer. 34:20. Note that the Hebrew underlying f and h resembles Neh. 9:28 wtᶜzbm byd 'ybyhm.

32:31	Heb.		N
	ky l' kṣwrnw ṣwrm	a.	'rwm l' krwḥṣynn rwḥṣnyhwn d'wmyyh
		b.	ᶜl dḥṭynn w'rgznn qdmwy
	w'ybynw plylym	c.	'tᶜbdwn bᶜly dbbykwn dyynynn

Line a plays on the similar letters and sounds of Heb. kṣwrm and krwḥṣynn; as noted above, ṣwr is usually translated tqyp. Line b is similar to the insertion in v. 30 (e).

32:32 N

a. 'rwm ᶜm' h'ylyyn

b. ᶜbdyhwn mdmyyn

c. lᶜbdyhwn dᶜm' dsdm

d. wmḥšbthwn mdmyyn

e. lmḥšbthwn dᶜm' dᶜmwrh

f. ᶜbdyhwn ᶜbdyn byšyn

g. wkᶜwbdhwn byšyh

h. mtprᶜ mynhwn

Heb.

1. ky mgpn sdm gpnm

2. wmšdmt ᶜmrh

3. ᶜnbmw ᶜnby rwš

4. 'šklt mrrt lmw

The verse is not translated, but paraphrased and expanded. Lines a-c correspond to 1, d-e to 2, f to 3 and g-h to 4. Comparisons of Sodom and Gemorrah are too frequent to enable the identification of any one verse that may be the basis of this passage, but a comparison of God's deeds and actions to Israel's, including use of the word mḥšbt, is found in Is. 55:8-9, which may be one source of the expansion. The figurative language of 3 and 4 has been modified, as usual, in f and g-h.

32:33	Heb.		N
		a.	'rwm ᶜm' h'ylyyn
	ḥmt tnynm yynm	b.	ḥmthwn mdmyy' lḥmthwn dtnynyh
		c.	bzmnh d'nwn štyyn
		d.	wrwgzyhwn mdmy
	wr'š ptnym 'kzr	e.	lr'šy ḥwwyyh ptmnyyh kzwr'y

Line a is similar to N in v. 32 and introduces the verse. The phrase ḥmthwn dtnyny' was used in v. 24, on the basis of this verse, and the phrase here begins ḥmt ... in Heb. But the word yynm has not been translated, and ḥmthwn (the first word in b) should perhaps be corrected to ḥmrhwn, particularly in the light of line c. Note, however, that Frag. adds bzmn dhynwn štyn ḥmr for line c, and d is balanced with b; both support the text of b as preserved, though Frag.'s c is clearer. Use of r'šy for Heb. r'š is interesting because Heb. r'š is not "head" but "venom," spelled rwš in v. 32. N took r'š as "head"; cf. Onk: kryš, PJ: ryšy. The word ḥwwyyh in e is really unnecessary; it may be a gloss to explain the rare ptmnyyh or, with it, a double translation of Heb. ptnym. DM has corrected ptmnyyh to ptnwnyyh; no change is needed for kzwr'y.

32:34	Heb.		N
	hl' hw'	a.	hl' hw'
	(kms)	b.	dn ks' dpwrʿnwth
	kms ʿmdy	c.	mmzg wmtqn wmʿtd lršyʿyh
	ḥtwm b'wṣrty	d.	ḥtwm b'wṣry
		e.	lywm dynh rbh

The phrase dn ks' dpwrʿnwth (b) is a gloss to explain the amgiguous hw' in a and plays on kms in c. PJ introduces a ks dlwwṭ in v. 33 but omits the reference here; cf. also N to 32:1 and G 40:12. Frag. to v. 34 contains b-e, but not a. The word kms means neither mmzg nor mtqn, but given the context, either or both may be used. Usually mʿtd corresponds to Heb. ʿmd; apparently ʿmdy has been modified for this purpose. The addition of lršyʿyh (c) limits this punishment to those who deserve it. Line e corresponds to the similar references and additions in G 4:7, 38:25, etc.

32:35 Heb.		N
ly nqm	a.	dydy hy' nqmth
wšlm	b.	w'nh hw' dmšlm
lᶜt tmwt rglm	c.	lᶜdn dy tymwt rglyhwn dṣdyqyh
ky qrwb ywm 'ydm	d.	'rwm qryb hw' ywm tbrhwn dršyᶜyh
wḥš ᶜtdt lmw	e.	w'št dghynm mᶜtdh lhwn
	f.	wmzrz wmyyty pwrᶜnwth ᶜlyhwn
	g.	lᶜlmh d'ty

Line a has been translated literally, and b has been expanded to balance it, though it does not follow the same structure. The addition of dṣdyqyh in c balances the phrase tbrhwn dršyᶜyh in d. The latter is not a translation of 'ydm (on which cf. BT A.Z. 2a ff), but reflects the known idiom "breaking x of the wicked," cf. Is. 14:5, Ps. 3:8, 37:17.

The future of the wicked is punishment -- according to the rabbis, punishment in Gehinnom -- hence the propriety of the translation in e. Nevertheless the choice of words reflects two word plays. Relying on the weakened sound of Heth, ḥš is taken as 'št. Also, ᶜtdt "future" appears in the translation as mᶜtdh "stands (waiting)"; note Frag. ᶜtyd'. Aram. and MH ᶜtyd, ᶜtydh, etc. is routinely used to construct a compound tense, but the translator has avoided using it here. Lines f-g complete the verse. Line f repeats the basic idea in e, but g seems to be hanging on. Indeed, there is no equivalent of g in Frag. or of either f or g in PJ. Perhaps it reflects the ᶜtdt in the Heb. of e.

32:36 Heb.		N
ky ydyn yyy	a.	*'rwm d'yn hw' yyy brḥmwy ṭbyyh*
ʿmw	b.	*yt dynyhwn dʿmyh bny yśr'l*
wʿl ʿbdyw ytnḥm	c.	*wʿl ʿlbwn ʿbdwy dṣdyqyh hw' mtnḥm*
ky yr'h	d.	*'rwm gly qdmwy*
ky 'zlt yd	e.	*'rwm mṭt ydyhwn dṣdyqyh*
w'ps	f.	*w'nwn šbyqyn*
ʿṣwr	g.	*wrṭyšyn*
wʿzwb	h.	*wlyt lhwn dsʿd wsmk*

The imperfect *ydyn* has been translated with the participle (*d'yn hw'*) and *brḥmwy ṭbyyh* has been added. The idiom *ldwn* (*'t*) *dyn* x (a-b) is known from Jer. 22:16, 30:16, etc. God has regrets (*mtnḥm*) over the sufferings of his people, not over the people themselves (c). (In G 6:9 this problem has been dealt with differently). Lines e-h are paraphrased, but they remain close to the Hebrew.

32:37 Heb.		N
w'mr	a.	*w'mr*
	b.	*ʿtydyn 'ynwn 'wmyh lmymr*
'y 'lhymw	c.	*'n 'lh' dyśr'l*
ṣwr ḥsyw bw	d.	*tqyph d'trḥṣw byh*

The manuscript says *w'mr ʿtydyn* ..., but line b seems to be an alternate version of line a, not unlike the situation in lines a and b of v. 34. The second *w'mr* may be a dittography but the assumption of a double translation is more probable. Onk. and PJ have *wyymr* (as in a) while Frag. has the text of b. N simply contains both.

32:38 Heb.		N
'šr	a.	dy hwwn mqrbyn qdmwy
ḥlb zbḥymw y'klw	b.	trby nksy qwrbnyhwn
yštw yyn nsykm	c.	wḥmr nyswkyhwn
	d.	dhwwn mnskyn qdmwy
yqwmw	e.	yqwm kᶜn
wyᶜzrkm	f.	wyprwq ythwn
yhy ᶜlykm strh	g.	wyhwwy ᶜlyhwn kmglh [DM: kmgnh]

Lines a and d supplement b and c, creating a chiastic balance in the four lines. The Hebrew verbs *yqwmw*, *wyᶜzrkm* and *yhy* are grammatically inconsistent, as the first must be plural and the last must be singular; the middle one may be either. The TBT vocalizes the first two as plurals while N preferred to read the last two as singulars and to force *yqwmw* to conform. (The Samaritan text of Sadaqa, by comparison, has *yqwmw*, *wyᶜzrwkm*, *yhyw*, all unequivocally plural. The Greek versions seem to attest to *yhyw* also).

DM's change of *mglh* to *mgnh* seems well advised, for it is much closer to the Heb. than *mglh* and is attested in Onk. and PJ as well.

32:39 Heb.		N
r'w ᶜth	a.	ḥmwn kᶜn
ky 'ny 'ny hw'	b.	'rwm 'nh 'nh bmmry hw'
w'yn 'lhym ᶜmdy	c.	wlyt 'lh' 'ḥrn br myny
'ny 'myt	d.	'nh hw' dmmyt ḥyyn
	e.	bᶜlm' hdyn
w'ḥyh	f.	wmḥyy myty
	g.	bᶜlm' d'ty
mḥṣty	h.	'nh hw' dmḥy

w'ny 'rp'	i.	w'nh hw' dmsy
w'yn mydy mṣyl	j.	wlyt dmyšyzyb mn ydyy

Lines a-d and f of the Hebrew have been translated literally, but additional references to this world and the world to come have been added in e and g; objects for the verbs have also been provided in d and f and 'ḥrn has been added in c. The word dmḥy (h) is perhaps anomalous because it may be taken as a variant of mḥyy (in f), but it is used in Onk. and PJ, and goes nicely with msy (i); cf. mḥy wmsy mmyt wmḥyh, a selichah by Amram Gaon (Rosenfeld, p. 21). D 33:12 N uses tbr for Heb. mḥṣ; qṭl appears in N 24:17. The double yṭlwn wyplgwn is found in N 24:8 (DM: yqṭlwn), based on the association of mḥṣ and ḥṣy "half," translated by plg. It would seem that the choice of verb in N depends on the object, or, as here, the absence of one.

32:41 Heb.		N
'm šnwty brq ḥrby	a.	'yn 'šnnh kbrqh ḥrby
wt'ḥz bmšpṭ ydy	b.	wttwqp bdynh bqwšṭh (!) yd ymyny
'šyb nqm lṣry	c.	'ḥzr nqmth lśn'wy
wlmśn'y	d.	wlbᶜly dbbyhwn dᶜmy
'šlm	e.	'šlm lhwn gmlyn byšyn

The word bmšpṭ (b) has been translated twice as bdynh and bqwšṭh. The latter should not be changed to dqwšṭh, as suggested by DM. The Heb. yd has been translated yd ymyn in b. The change of lmśn'y to "to the enemies of my people" is paralleled in the daily Amidah, Where the same prayer is preserved with readings of wkl 'wybyk and wkl 'wyby ᶜmk mhrh ykrtw. The word lhwn (e) is unnecessary and lacking in PJ, but may have seemed idiomatic with 'šlm.

32:42	Heb.		N
	'škyr ḥṣy mdm	a.	'rwwy gyryyn [DM: gyryy] mn 'dmhwn
	wḥrby t'kl bśr	b.	wḥrby ttkl bbśrhwn
	mdm ḥll	c.	mn 'dm qṭylyhwn dᶜmy
	wšbyh	d.	wšbyyhwn
	mr'š prᶜwt 'wyb	e.	mn r'šy gybryhwn pwlymrkyhwn bᶜly dbbyhwn dᶜmy

The addition of dᶜmy in c and e is comparable to the many such cases seen in the preceding verses. Line e contains the only significant deviation from the Hebrew, and, coming as it does at the end of the verse, its length is not unusual. This length, however, is not a function of the line's position but of the double reading gybryhwn pwlymrkyhwn, both of which translate prᶜwt. Given that one word is Aram. and theother is Greek, the latter may be original, and gybryhwn is probably a gloss on the Greek word, a phenomenon noted in N 31:22 also.

32:43	Heb.		N
	hrnynw gwym	a.	qlsw qdmwy 'wmyyh
	ᶜmw	b.	šbḥw ytyh ᶜmyh byt yśr'l
	ky dm ᶜbdyw yqwm	c.	'rwm ᶜwlbn wdm ᶜbdwy ṣdyqyyh hw' tbᶜ
	wnqm yšyb lṣryw	d.	wnqmth yḥzr lbᶜly dbbykwn
		e.	wbḥwby ᶜm' 'rᶜ' lqyy'
		f.	wbrḥmwy ṭbyh
	wkpr 'dmtw ᶜmw	g.	hw' mkpr ᶜl 'rᶜ' wᶜl ᶜm'

Line b has been expanded in imitation of a, as if the Heb. read wᶜmw. In c, dm has been translated ᶜwlbn wdm, probably to stress that even the act of humiliating innocent Israelites will be punished, not just injuring them. It is unlikely that this is a double translation of dm, but cf. v. 36, line c. The introduction of line e is interesting, for it applies wkpr 'dmtw (g) to the contemporary situation. The statement probably refers to some time after 70 CE, but a closer date would only be a guess. The line is based on the Heb. of g, where both ʿm' and 'rʿ' occur, though neither e nor g translates these words exactly as they are used in Heb.

32:44 šbḥ šyrth: a routine idiom, for Heb. kl dbry hšyrh, but note the absence of kl.

32:46 wlmʿbd: for Heb. lʿśwt. Both lšmwr lʿśwt and lšmwr wlʿśwt are found a number of times in the Bible. Perhaps the use of Waw here reflects the liturgical usage found in the daily morning prayer Ahavah Rabbah.

šbḥ 'wryth: for Heb. htwrh hz't. The word šbḥ usually accompanies šyrth, not 'wryth, but there is little chance that the Heb. here originally read hšyrh. It is easier to justify a misreading of 'wryth as šyrth, but this, too, may be unnecessary. D 31:30 has šyrh in Heb., translated šyrth, taken by some sources to refer to the Torah, thus equating šyrh and spr htwrh in 31:26. Perhaps a similar equation is intended here.

32:48 bzmn: for Heb. bʿṣm as in G 7:13, 17:23, etc.

32:50 wttknš bšlm: for Heb. imperative wmt. The second use of wttknš bšlm is the more proper use of the idiom for Heb. wh'sp ..., but note the use of same phrase for k'šr mt 'hrn, etc. Use of this idiom for both mt and 'sp is noteworthy, especially when the phrase appears 4 times in such close proximity, because of the rather awkward passage that results.

32:51 *srbtwn bšm mmry*: for Heb. *m^{c}ltm by*. The translation of this phrase has been influenced by N 27:17 which reads *k'šr mrytm py* ... *bmrybt h^{c}dh lh qdyšny bmym l^{c}ynyhm*, translated *hyk mh dy srbtwn ^{c}l pm gzrt mymry* ... *lmqdšh šmy*. The verb *m^{c}l* is translated *šqr* when applied to God in L 5:15, 26:40 and N 5:6. The verb *srb* is used in N 20:24 and in N 27:14, which is part of a passage (27:12-15) that is in many ways very similar to D 32:48-52. Note also the similarity with parts of N 20:12 and the use in D 1:1.

bmy mṣwth drqm: for Heb. *bmy mrybt qdš*. As noted frequently, *rqm* is the routine rabbinic equivalent of *qdš*, but the use of *mṣwth* is unexpected. In N 27:14 the phrase is translated *my dyyny rqm* and elsewhere *my dyynyh*, when *qdš* is omitted from the Heb. (e.g. N 20:13, 24). M contains a note *bmwy dm-*, perhaps a reflection of a usage that is closer to the Hebrew, but more likely suggestive of the possible origin of the usage in N, since M in N 20:13, 20 has *my mṣwth* for *my mrybh*.

Chapter 33

33:1 *nby' dyyy*: for Heb. *'yš h'lhym*. The phrase *nby' dyyy* has been used frequently (e.g. 32:1, 3). On interchanges of *yyy* and *'lhym*, see Introduction, chapter 3. Presumably a literal translation was to be avoided, especially if it could lead to claims that Moses was a "man-God."

33:2 N

a. *w'mr*

b. *yyy mn syny 'tgly*

c. *lmtn 'wryth l^{c}my bny yśr'l*

d. wnḥ (!) byqry ʿl ṭwrh dgblh

e. lmtn 'wryt lbnwy dʿśw

f. wkywwn dy 'škḥw ktyb bgwwh

g. l' thwwn qṭwlyn

h. l' qbylw yth

i. whwpyʿ byqrh

j. lmtn 'wryth ʿl ṭwr' dpr'n lbnwy dyšmʿ'l

k. wkywwn d'škḥw bnwy dyšmʿ'l dktyb bgwwh

l l' thwwn gnbyn

m. l' qbylw yth

n. ḥzr w'tgly ʿl ṭwrh dsyny

o. wʿymyh rybwwn dml'kyn qdyšyn

p. 'mryn bny yśr'l

q. yt kl mh dy mll mymrh dyyy nʿbd wnšmʿ

r. wpšṭ ymynyh mn gw lhby 'šth

s. w'wryth yhb lʿmyh

Heb.

1. wy'mr
2. yyy msyny b'
3. wzrḥ mśʿyr lmw
4. hwpyʿ mhr p'rn
5. w'th mrbbt qdš
6. mymynw 'šdt (Qere: 'š dt) lmw

Lines 2-5 report of God's activities in four places and were easily taken to refer to four revelations because of the references to Sinai and the use of zrḥ and hwpyʿ. The tale of God's offering the Torah to the nations of the world is well known in rabbinic texts and is associated with a series of verses, especially E 24:7 nʿśh wnšmʿ (cited in g) and D 33:2. It has been worked into this verse by expanding lines 3 and 4 of the

Hebrew into full paragraphs (3 = d-h, 4 = i-m). Only two of the revelations are discussed; the Torah was declined by the descendents of Esau and Ishmael but accepted by the Israelites (n-q).

The organization of the text is quite clear, but the text is rough and betrays its composite nature. Lines a-b translate 1-2 of the Hebrew; c is complementary. According to the story, God offered the Torah to other nations before Israel, but Sinai appears first in the verse, and therefore the midrash had to take the form of a flashback. This is accomplished through the use of wnḥ (DM's correction to dnḥ is unnecessary), which is the beginning of the story of the offer to the children of Esau (=śʿyr = gblh in N). These relatives of the Jews rejected the Torah because of the provision cited in line g -- l' thwwn qṭwlyn. Similarly God offered the Torah to the Ishmaelites in i (=4); but they, too, rejected it, because they found l' thwwn gnbyn (l). The stories are similar; line g is identical to part of E 20:13 and D 5:17, while l is identical to the translation of E 20:15 and D 5:19. (Note, however, the expansions there that are not found here.)

God then returned and offered the Torah to Israel. In essence, n is identical to b; but it has been added here to put the story back in order. Line d should have related how God appeared on Sinai to give the Israelites the Torah, but left and went (wnḥ) on Mt. Gebal ..., probably to undermine the claims that the other groups might make against the favoritism shown to the other children of Abraham. The beginning of the midrash was dropped, however, when the midrash was grafted to the beginning of the verse.

Line o (= 5) describes God's revelation on Sinai, including the associated myriads of angels. Heb. w'th "came" has been read as 'itto "with him" and translated ʿymyh; mrbbt has been taken as rbbt, as well. Line p introduces q, the translation of E 24:7, which may actually be the preferred reading of N there: kl mh dy mll yyy nᶜbd wnšmᶜ; M: mymry- dyyy.

Lines r-s expand and embellish the three (or four) words in line 6. They should be aligned as follows:

Heb.		N
mymynw	r.	wpšṭ ymynyh
'š		mn gw lhby 'šth
dt	s.	w'wryth
lmw		yhb lᶜmyh

This exemplifies the frequent addition of lhby and provides a noteworthy correlation of 'wryth "Torah" and dt "law."

33:3 N

a. hl' gly wydwᶜ qdmwy
b. dl' bnwy dᶜśw
c. wl' bnwy dyšmᶜ'l
d. mqblyn 'wryth
e. 'l' kl kdn lmḥbbh
f. ᶜm' bny yśr'l
g. nḥyt rybwwn dml'kyn qdyšyn
h. d'pᶜlgb dhw' myyty ᶜlyhwn yswryn sgyn
i. l' nyyḥyn wl' šdkyn mn 'wlpn 'wryyth
j. wh' 'ynwn mdbryn w'tyyn lrgl ᶜnnwy
k. wnṭlyn wšryyn ᶜl pm dbyrwy

Heb.

1. 'p ḥbb ᶜmym
2. kl qdšyw bydk
3. whm tkw lrglk

4. yś' mdbrtyk

Though lines 1 and 2 are, respectively, the bases of e-f and g, a-g in general duplicate much of v. 2. Thus lines b-d summarize lines d-m in v. 2, while g reflects v. 2, line o. This pattern of duplication appears a number of times in Gen. 49 and, in each case, some of the material seems unnecessary. That is the case here as well, but the inclusion, in the summary of the previous verse, of translations of parts of this Heb. verse, makes separation difficult.

The reference to studying the Torah in spite of suffering brought upon the people sounds like stories associated with the Hadrianic persecution, though one cannot be certain. (Note also the addition in 32:43). Line j corresponds to 3 and refers to the clouds that led the Israelites in the desert, the connection being the use of rgl. Line k is based on 4 and refers to the travels described in Num. 33. The phrase ᶜl pm dbyrwy is not routine in N. N 33:2 has ᶜl pm gzyrt mmryh, and the change here probably reflects the desire to approximate the Heb. mdbrtyk.

33:4	Heb.		N
		a.	'mryn bny yśr'l
	twrh ṣwh lnw mšh	b.	'wryyth pqd ytn mšh
	mwršh	c.	yhb yth yrtw w'ḥsnh
	qhlt yᶜqb	d.	lqhl šbṭyyh dbyt yᶜqb

Line a is an introduction, comparable to those in 32:1, 3, 4. The addition of yhb yth (c) parallels pqd in b, but the translation yrtw w'ḥsnh is of note. The word mwršh occurs in the Torah only here and in E 6:8, where it is translated wltn [DM: yrtw] w'ḥsnh and yrty [DM: yrtw] in M. The usage here confirms the suggested reading in Ex., but it is also similar to the translation of ḥlq wnḥlh (e.g. D 10:9, 12:12). Heb. mwršh is properly "heritage," not "inheritance," and the two elements of this phrase -- yrtw and 'ḥsnh -- were used to convey this meaning.

The addition of šbṭyyh (d) seems to anticipate v. 5.

33:5	Heb.		N
	wyhy byšrwn mlk	a.	wyqwm mlk mn dbyt yʿqb
	bht'sp r'šy ʿm	b.	kknš yt [DM: bknšwt]
	yḥd	c.	kḥd' yštmʿwn lh
	šbṭy yśr'l	d.	kl šbṭyyh dbny yśr'l

The change of yšrwn to dbyt yʿqb is paralleled in 32:15 by dbyt yśr'l. The use of dyśr'l in 33:26 is similar but not identical. While the choice of yʿqb here seems to reflect a desire to balance yśr'l (d), it also leaves N very similar to N 24:17, where drk kwkb myʿqb is translated ʿtyd mlk lmqwm mn dbyt yʿqb. Ideally it should be balanced by dbyt yśr'l in d as it is in Num.

The prepositions b- and k- (b) are often interchangeable and the emendation may be unnecessary. The use of yḥd as a noun in the Dead Sea Scrolls has prompted many writers to see Heb. yḥd (c) as a noun, but N, Onk. and PJ translate it kḥd'. The rest of the line is expansive.

Note the addition of kl in d. An interesting comparison is with Esth. 10:3, wrṣwy lrwb 'ḥyw. The rabbinic interpretation there stresses rwb as majority (BT Meg. 16b). i.e. most of the Jews accepted Mordecai, while here the addition of kl means that all of them will follow this ruler. Cf. also 34:9, where a similar description -- minus kl -- is applied to Joshua and 1 Chron. 29:23, where the phrase -- minus bny -- is applied to Solomon. Note, also, the change in tense in a and the related verb in c, both of which give the verse an eschatological focus. This is accomplished by a very slight change in the vocalization of Heb. wyhy.

33:6	Heb.		N
	yḥy r'wbn	a.	yḥy r'wbn
		b.	bᶜlm' hdyn
	w'l ymt	c.	wl' ymwt
		d.	bmwtnh [cf. DM] tnyynh
		e.	dbyh myytyn ršyᶜyh
		f.	lᶜlm' d'ty
	wyhy	g.	wyhwwn ᶜwlymwy
	mtyw mspr	h.	ᶜm gybryn bmnyyn

Given the pattern established throughout N, the addition of lines b and f could be anticipated. Lines d-e are extra, perhaps referring to a second death (after punishment?) of the evil doers. Note Onk.: ... wmwt' tnyn' l' ymwt, and PJ: wl' yymwt bmytwt' dmyytyn bh ršyᶜyy' lᶜlm' d'ty. The phrase mty mspr occurs in G 34:30, where it is translated ᶜm lmnyn, and D 4:27, where it is given as ᶜm dmnyyn. Elsewhere (D 28:62) ᶜm bmnyyn is used for mty mᶜṭ (but not in 26:5, where ᶜm zᶜyr is used). Here, ᶜm is the preposition "with" (as in PJ), so mtyw is not translated in N's normal way but paraphrased, perhaps to project a more positive notion. Cf. the use of bnwhy in Onk. and wyhy ᶜwlymwy mtmnyyn ᶜm ᶜwlymhwn in PJ.

33:7	Heb.		N
a.	wz't	a.	wd' brkth dy brk mšh nbyy' dyyy
b.	lyhwdh wy'mr	b.	lšbṭh dyhwdh w'mr

c.	šmᶜ yyy qwl yhwdh	c.	šmᶜ mymryh dyyy bql ṣlwth dyhwdh
d.	w'l ᶜmw tby'nw	d.	wlwwt ᶜmyh tšlm ytyh mn sdry qrbh bšlm
e.	ydyw rb lw	e.	ydwy ytprᶜn lh mn bᶜly dbbyhwn
f.	wᶜzr mṣryw thyh	f.	wsᶜd wsmk mn śn'wy tyhwy lyh

Line a is identical to the beginning of v. 1. The difference between *yt* there and *l-* in b reflects a difference between the two Heb. texts.

Line d contains an extra piece. Onk., however, adds *bmpqyh lqrb'* to its translation of c, which would offer a good balance to the extra piece in d. PJ contains both additions, but it is not certain that N should as well. Line e continues the battlefield context, and probably contains the basis of the entire reference.

33:8 Heb.		N
wllwy	a.	wlšbṭh dlwy
	b.	brk mšh nby' dyyy
'mr	c.	w'mr
tmyk w'wryk	d.	twmyy' w'wryy'
l'yš ḥsydk	e.	'lbyšt l'hrn gbr' ḥsydh
'šr nsytw	f.	dy npyt ytyh
bmsh	g.	wqm bnsywnh
trybhw	h.	wbdqt ytyh
ᶜl my mrybh	i.	bmy dyynyyh
	j.	w'štkḥ mhymn

The changes in a-c parallel those in vv. 12, 18, etc. The

minor changes in d and e identify the 'yš. In f. npyt is changed by I to nsyt. The possible parallel in Luke 22:31 notwithstanding, the change seems advisable, particularly when f and g are taken together. As they stand, f and g contain an improper mix of metaphoric and literal usages. Usually N translates the verb nsh with nsy (G 22:1, N 14:22, D 6:16, etc.), and this seems appropriate here, as well.

wqm bnsywnh: for Heb. bmsh. Parallel with bmy mrybh (i), this should be taken as a toponym. In E 17:7 msh wmrybh is translated nsyywnyh wdyynwwtyh, a pattern repeated (for the first word) in D 6:16; D 9:22 has nysywnh. The phrase wnmṣ' n'mn, underlying the translation in j, is similar to the phrase in Neh. 9:8; mhymn is applied to Moses in N 12:7.

33:9	Heb.		N	glosses
	h'mr	a.	d'myr	
		b.	ʿl šbṭh dlwy	
	l'byw wl'mw	c.	l'bwy wl'ymyh	
	l' r'ytyw	d.	l' nsb 'pyn	bdynh
	w't 'ḥyw	e.	wyt 'ḥwy	
	l' hkyr	f.	l' ḥkm	bʿwbdh dʿglh
	w't bnw [Qere:bnyw]	g.	wʿl bnwy	
	l' ydʿ	h.	l' qnh rḥmyn	bʿwbdh dzmry
	ky šmrw	i.	'rwm nṭrw	
	'mrtk	j.	mymr pwmk	
		k.	wgzrtk	
	wbrytk	l.	w'wryytk	
	ynṣrw	m.	'ynwn zhryn	

The insertion in b applies the context of v. 8 to this verse. The three items listed as glosses in d, f and h are structurally similar to those in G 15:12, etc. Because the

Hebrew verbs in these lines are not translated iterally, one cannot be sure that these phrases are true glosses, but it appears that they are. In d, the verb r'h is translated nsb 'pyn bdynh. The phrase wl' tsbwn 'pyn bdynh is used in 16:19 for Heb. l' tkyr pnym, and 1:17 for the plural l' tkyrw pnym bmšpṭ. Clearly the idiom has been borrowed from these contexts and applied here. Perhaps these are more appropriate translations for hkyr (f), but nsb 'pyn is used for nś' pnym in 10:17 and 28:50, in the latter verse without bdynh. The addition of bᶜwbdh dᶜglh (f) is unrelated to the use of ḥkm, as is bᶜwbdh dzmry to qnh rḥmyn in h. Given that the phrase nsb 'pyn sometimes occurs without bdynh (e.g. 28:50) and that the three additions to d, f and h are not required by N, it is possible that all are glosses.

The reference in f is almost self explanatory. It refers to E 32:27-28, which describes how the Levites killed those who worshipped the golden calf and uses language similar to phrases in this verse. Line g refers to the execution of Zimri in N 25:1-15, but according to N 25:4 all the leaders of the people, not necessarily the Levites, were instructed to kill the transgressors (cf. v. 5). But Phineas, an Aaronide of the tribe of Levi, killed Zimri himself (vv. 7-8), and N has credited his act to the entire tribe.

It is not clear why k has been added, but the phrase gzyrt 'wryth is a routine translation of twrh, and the influence of line l may be responsible. Apparently brytk (similar in sound to b'wryth) was taken as twrtk. The word nṣr is usually translated nṭr (e.g. E 34:7), which would have been the most logical choice for line m. It is not clear why zhyryn was chosen, though in rabbinic texts the word often refers to those who are careful in the performance of their religious obligations, and BH nzr has been translated zhr in 33:16 and G 49:26. Several difficulties can be removed by reading wbgzrt 'wryytk 'ynwn zhryn, but not other texts seem to support this.

33:10 Heb.		N
ywrw mšpṭyk	a.	kšryn lmlph sdry dynyn
lyᶜqb	b.	bgw dbyt yᶜqb
wtwrtk	c.	wgzyrt 'wrytk
lyśr'l	d.	lqhl šbṭyh dbny yśr'l
yśymw qṭwrh	e.	mšwyn qṭrt
	f.	bwsmnyn ṭbyn
b'pk	g.	wklyyn rwgzk
wklyl	h.	wqrbn gmyr (brᶜwwh
ᶜl mzbḥk	i.	ᶜl gby mdbḥk) [cf. DM]

Each word has been expanded into a phrase that is closely paralleled elsewhere in N. The Heb. 'p, when applied to God, is usually taken as anger and translated rgz, but here 'p literally means "nose." By understanding b- (b'pk) as "against" rather than "in," N is able to use the figurative sense "anger" here as well.

33:11 Heb.		N
brk yyy ḥylw	a.	[brk yyy ḥyylwwt
	b.	šbṭh dbnwy dlwy
wpᶜl ydyw trṣh	c.	wqrbn ydwy tqbl brᶜw-]
mḥṣ mtnym qmyw	d.	tbr ḥrṣh dśn'wy
wmśn'yw	e.	wbᶜly dbbwy
mn	f.	mn qdmwy
yqwmwn	g.	l' yklyn lmyqwm

As in v. 10, the piece in parentheses has been added from the margin (cf. DM). It seems appropriate, but dbnwy (in b) is not in keeping with the phrase used in vv. 8, 9 (šbṭh dlwy) or in

vv. 12, 13, 18, etc. This piece thus cannot be assumed to be authentic here, even though the word bnwy is used in tribal constructions in Numbers. Onk. and PJ offer bryk yyy nkswy ....

On mḥṣ = tbr, cf. 32:39. The most interesting expansion is f-g. As seen above, the Heb. phrase has been divided and expanded into separate lines, in this case, perhaps because mn has been explained twice, once as "from" in mn qdmwy (f) and once as a negative construction "... so that they can not rise" in g. Note also the possible influence of Josh. 10:8 l' yʿmd 'yš mhm bpnyk, directed at Joshua by God (cf. also Josh. 1:5, D 7:24).

33:12	Heb.		N
	lbnymn	a.	wlšbṭh dbnymn
		b.	brk mšh nbyy' dyyy
	'mr	c.	w'mr
	ydyd yyy	d.	rḥymh dyyy
	yškn lbṭḥ ʿlyw	e.	yšry lrḥṣn ʿlwy
	ḥpp ʿlyw kl hywm	f.	yhwwy mgn ʿlwy kl ywmy'
		g.	wbtḥwmyh
		h.	ytbny byt mwqdšh
	wbyn ktpyw	i.	wb'ḥsntyh
	škn	j.	tšry 'yqr škyntyh dyyy

On a-c, cf. vv. 8, 13, 18, etc. Lines d-f are translated closely, but g-h and i-j are a double translation of the same Heb. words. Note that the same double translation has been introduced (without an underlying Heb. text) in the blessing of Benjamin in G 49:27; cf. notes a.l. Given the close connection between Heb. škn and škyntyh, as well as the use of equivalents to i-j in Onk. and PJ, g-h should probably be seen as secondary.

33:13 Heb.		N
wlywsp	a.	wlšbṭh dywsp
	b.	brk mšh nbyy' dyyy
'mr	c.	w'mr
mbrkt	d.	mh brykh hy'
yyy	e.	mn qdm yyy
'rṣw	f.	'rʿ' dywsp
mmgd šmym	g.	mn ṭwb 'wṣry šmy'
	h.	mn lʿyl
mṭl	i.	dmḥtyn ṭlyn wmṭryn
wmthwn	j.	mn brkt mbwʿy
tḥt	k.	mn lrʿ
rbṣt	l.	dslqyn wmrwwyn
(note word order)	m.	ṣmhyh d'rʿ'

On a-c, cf. v. 12. Lines d-f are expansive translations. The lack of balance between the parallel Heb. words mṭl (i) and tḥt (k, but really following rbṣt in l) and the similarity to G 49:25 brkt šmym mʿl brkt thwm rbṣt tḥt (Jacob's blessing of Joseph) have led some to emend mṭl to mʿl. N, however, has treated the problem by simply restoring the "missing" element of the parallelism, and line h has been added to parallel k. Both Onk. and PJ also introduce mlʿyl' or mn lʿyl, but these are to balance the rhythm. None of these versions attests to a Hebrew text of the verse that contained mʿl for mṭl. Note the similarity between N in G 49:25 and here:

N, G 49:25			N, D 33:13
mn ṭwb ṭlh wmṭr'	g.	(1)	mn ṭwb 'wṣry šmy'
dnḥtyn mn šmyy'		(2)	
mn lʿyl	h.	(3)	mn lʿyl
	i.	(4)	dmḥtyn ṭlyn wmṭryn

wmn brkt'	j.	(5)	mn brkt
mbwᶜy thwm'		(6)	mbwᶜy
dslqyn mn 'rᶜ'		(7)	
mn lrᶜ	k.	(8)	mn lrᶜ
	l-m.	(9)	dslqyn wmrwwyn ṣmḥyh d'rᶜ'

Line 2 of Gen. is similar to 4 here, and 7 of Gen. is similar to 9 here. The passages are not identical, yet when compared with each other and with the similar blessings of Isaac to his sons (Gen. 27), a clear pattern of translation emerges. G 27:28 reads mṭl hšmym wmšmny h'rṣ, translated by N mṭwb ṭl' dnḥt mn šmy' špr wmn ṭwb' d'rᶜ' ... G 27:39 has mšmny h'rṣ yhyh mwšbk wmṭl hšmym mᶜl, translated by N ... mn ṭwb' d'rᶜ' thwy mšrwyk wmn ṭwb ṭl' dnḥt mn šmy' mn lᶜyl. Comparison of these verses shows that N here has been translated in a similar way and influenced by them.

33:14	Heb.		N
	wmmgd	a.	ᶜbdh [with DM] pryn
	tbw't šmš	b.	mn ṭwb ᶜllt šmš'
	wmmgd	c.	wmbrkh [with DM] pyry mgdnyn
	grš yrḥym	d.	bkl yrḥ wyrḥ

Line a should begin ᶜbdh as do vv. 15 and 16. The word mgd seems to be the source of the word ṭwb (b), but pryn ṭbyn occurs in vv. 15-16 also, and this association is not necessarily correct. It seems that tbw't (b) has generated twb ᶜllt, creating an interesting word play. Actually mmgd has been read as a participle "makes mgd" i.e. ᶜbdh pryn; cf. vv. 15, 16. Note also, the addition of kl in d.

33:15 N

a. ᶜbdh pryn ṭbyn

b. bzkwth d'bhtn

c. dmtylyn bṭwwryy'

d. 'brhm yṣḥq wyᶜqb

e. wbzkwt 'ymhth

f. dmtylyn bglmth

g. śrh rbqh rḥl wl'h

Heb.

1. wmr'š hrry qdm

2. wmmgd gbᶜwt ᶜwlm

Line a resembles the beginning of v. 16 and, to a lesser extent, v. 14. The only Heb. words that are actually translated are hrry (in c) and gbᶜwt (in f), though qdm and ᶜwlm may have contributed to the association with the patriarchs and matriarchs of old. For a similar analysis of these Heb. words, cf. N 23:9.

33:16

Heb.		N
wmmgd	a.	ᶜbdh pyryn ṭbyn
'rṣ wml'h	b.	bzkwt 'rᶜ' wml'y'
wrṣwn	c.	wdᶜbd rᶜwth
škny snh	d.	mn d'šry 'yqr škyntyh bsnyyh
tbw'th	e.	yytyyn kl 'lyyn brkyyth
	f.	wytᶜbdn klyl drbw
lr'š ywsp	g.	ᶜl ryš' dywsp
wlqdqd	h.	wlgw qwdqdh
	i.	dgbr' dhw' [with DM] mlk wšlyṭ b'rᶜ' dmṣrym
nzyr 'ḥyw	j.	wzhyr b'yqrhwn d'ḥwy

Most of this passage is translated expansively. The word *bzkwt* in b sounds out of place and may come from v. 15, which begins this way. Lines e-j are close to the last half of G 49:26; cf. comments a.l. A significant difference is in the words *byqyr' d'bwy* added in Gen. in the middle of the equivalent of j. Note also the changes in line i, an echo of G 45:26.

33:17 Heb.		N
bkwr šwrw hdr lw	a.	*bkwrwt' wmlkwt' wyqr' whdr' lyh hwwyyn*
	b.	*kmh dlyt 'pšr lmplḥ bbkwry twryyh*
	c.	*wl' lmštʿbdh bqrny rymnh*
wqrny r'm qrnyw	d.	*kdyn lyt 'pšr lbnwy dywsp lmštʿbdh*
bhm ʿmym ynggḥ	e.	*wyhwwn rmyn wmnṭlyn wʿlyyn ʿl kl 'wmyyh d'rʿ'*
	f.	*npqyn lqrbh*
	g.	*lqbl bʿly dbbyhwn*
	h.	*wlqbl śn'yhwn*
yḥdw 'psy 'rṣ	i.	*wmqṭlyn mlkyn ʿm šwlṭnyn*
whm rbbwt	j.	*'ynwn rybbth*
	k.	*dqṭl yhwšʿ br nwn mn 'ymwr'y*
'prym	l.	*dhw' mn šbṭh dbnwy d'prym*
whm 'lpy	m.	*w'ynwn 'lpyh*
	n.	*dqṭl gdʿwn br yw'š mn mdyynyy*
mnšh	o.	*dhw' mn šbṭh dbnwy dmnšh*

Very little of this verse is actually translated, though parts are paraphrased, and all of it has had an impact on N. Line a is similar to G 49:3, but Joseph had no claim on the priesthood, which is omitted here, though *mlkwt'* has been retained even though he had no claim to royalty either. The Hebrew contains 3 words *bkwr*, *šwrw* and *hdr*. The first and last correspond to *bkwrwt'* and *hdr'*. The remaining *mklwt'* and *yqr'* may be a doublet for *šwrw*. Generally the ox (*šwr*) is a symbol of power, but *mklwt'* cannot properly refer to Joseph, and we must prefer the reading *yqr'*. (Note, however that Frag. includes *mlkwt'* and omits *yqr'* and that Akk. *šarru* -- etymologically unrelated but possibly available midrashically -- means "king." PJ actually compares Joseph to Reuben, noting that *bkwrt'* was rightly the latter's but was given to Joseph. This same notion occurs in N to G 49:3. There Joseph received *bkwrt'*, but Judah received the kingship and Levi the priesthood.

The Heb. d, *wqrny r'm qrnyw*, is not really translated in d. According to the Heb. text, Joseph had the horns of a *re'em*, but N systematically voids such metaphoric language. Accordingly, b-c contain the explanation of this "impossible" statement, while d contains the inference. Note the rhetorical form *kmh d-* ... *dkyn* .... The prohibition of working with the firstborn ox (b) is based on E 13:12. The difficulty of working (*lmštʿbdh* is correct) with the horns of the buffalo may reflect the legendary size and power attributed to this beast in rabbinic lore.

Line e is one of the few Hebrew clauses in this verse easily seen in the Aramaic. The absence of an equivalent of *bhm* seems striking; perhaps *bhwn* should be added after *wʿlyyn*, but this may be unnecessary literalism in a verse of this sort. Lines f-h are parallel to e and repeat it in language that has been used many times throughout N. Note the use of *bʿly dbbyhwn* and *śn'yhwn* together, something I have identified as double translations elsewhere.

Heb. *'psy* (i) probably means "extremes," but it also may mean "cut off"; hence its use as "nothing" (later as "zero"). Apparently N is mocking the rulers of the world by calling them 'ps. The phrase mlkyn ᶜm šwlṭnyn is routine in N.

The phrases rbbwt 'prym and 'lpy mnšh appear to mean numbers of members of these tribes, but N has treated them as objective genitives, i.e. numbers killed by the tribes. Thus, j-l and m-o have translated and expanded the text in this way. The references to Joshua's killing the Amorites are scattered in Deut. and Josh.; Gideon's killing the Midianites is described in Jud. 7:19-25. Note that similar victories of Gideon and Samson are noted in N to G 49:17-18.

33:18	Heb.		N
	wlzbwln	a.	wlšbṭh dzbwln
		b.	brk mšh nbyy' dyyy
	'mr	c.	w'mr
	śmḥ zbwln	d.	ḥdwn dbyt zbwln
	bṣ'tk	e.	bmypqkwn lprgmtykwn
	wyśśkr	f.	wḥdwn dbyt yśśkr
	b'hlyk	g.	bmyytbkwn bbty mdršykwn

Note the use of dbyt in d and f while a has only wlšbṭh, not dbnwy or dbyt. Popular rabbinic interpretation had zbwln (cf. zbn?) earning the support for two tribes, while yśśkr reaped the rewards (śkr) of the study of the Torah; hence the expansions in e and g. The addition of wḥdwn in f has balanced that line with d. Onk. has a completely different association of bṣ'tk with war and b'hlyk with the Temple; cf. v. 19 in N for a parallel.

33:19	Heb.		N
	ᶜmym	a.	h' ᶜm' dbyt zbwln
	hr yqr'w	b.	lṭwr byt mwqdš' yzdmnwn
	šm yzbḥw zbḥy ṣdq	c.	wtmn yqrbwn qrbnyn dqšwṭ

ky špᶜ ymym yynqw	d.	'rwm twgrt ymyy' yyklwn
wśpny ṭmwny ḫwl	e.	wsymn dṭmyrn ytglyyn lhwn

Line a joins this verse to the preceding one by connecting ᶜmym with zbwln. Only one identification of hr (b) is possible because of the sacrifices, and c identifies it as the Temple Mount. Lines d-e are paraphrases of the Hebrew that follow the blessing to Zebulun in G 49:13.

33:20 Heb.		N
wlgd	a.	wlšbṭh dgd
	b.	brk mšh nby' dyyy
'mr	c.	w'mr
brwk mrḫyb gd	d.	bryk mn d'pty tḫwmh dgd
klby' škn	e.	nyyḫ wšry bgw qrbh hyk 'ryh
	f.	whyk 'rywwth
	g.	lyt 'wmh wmlkw dtqwm lqwblyh
	h.	qṭylwy ḫkymyn bny qṭylyh (!)
wṭrp zrwᶜ 'p qdqd	i.	prq r'š' ᶜm 'drᶜ'

Line d is translated expansively, because only the territory, not the person, could be broadened. Lines e-g are very similar to the translation of G 49:9, the blessing of Judah. That they were borrowed from Gen. (rather than the converse) seems clear because the wording fits that Hebrew text better than this one, but in some ways the Aramaic in Deut. is superior; cf. notes to G 49:9. Line h is an addition that makes sense with bny or byny, substituted for bny, in I. This meaning (but not wording) is confirmed by PJ: wqṭwlwy ḫkymyn mn kl qṭwlyy'.

Presumably this results from the tendency to cut off an enemy's head with his arm. This may mean that the head, shoulder and arm were removed in one piece, and may account for the reversal of word order in i, also found in Frag. (but not in PJ).

33:21	Heb.		N
	wyr' r'šyt	a.	wḥm' mn šyrwyh
		b.	'rwm 'tr mzwmn hw'
	lw	c.	lbyt qbwrh lyh
		d.	tmn mqbn 'bnyn ṭbn wmrglyyn
	ky šm ḥlqt mḥqq spwn	e.	'rwm tmn mšh nbyy' swpryhwn dyśr'l qbwr
		f.	wyhwwy hyk mh dhwh ᶜlyl wnpq br'šy ᶜm' bᶜlm' hdyn
	wyt' r'šy ᶜm	g.	kdyn yhwwy ᶜlyl wnpq br'šy ᶜm' bᶜlm' d'ty
	ṣdqt yyy ᶜśh	h.	zkwth dyyy ᶜbd
	wmšpṭyw ᶜm yśr'l	i.	wsdry dynwy 'lp lbny yśr'l

Having taken lw as "for himself," the translator was forced to provide an object for the verb wyr'. It appears in b-c, having been derived through the interpretation of e as a reference to Moses' burial place (cf. 34:1 ff). The antecedent of the verb wyt' (Heb. g) can be the tribe or the ruler (mḥqq, e). Preferring the latter option, N has taken g to mean that Moses will lead the people in the future as he led them in the past (f). This understanding allows for the introduction of the phrases bᶜlm' hdyn and bᶜlm' d'ty.

Line d does not seem integral to this passage, because it speaks of gems and pearls. But the reference may be authentic. In discussing the burial of Jacob (G 50:1), reference is also made to the availability of gems and pearls, and the presentation in PJ connects the equivalents of d-e even more closely: 'rwm tmn 'tr mqbᶜ 'bnyn ṭbyn wmrglyyn dbyh mšh sprhywn dyśr'l gnyz. There may also be a connection with interpretations of spwny in v.19.

33:22	Heb.		N
	wldn	a.	wlšbṭh ddn
		b.	brk mšh nbyy' dyyy
	'mr	c.	w'mr
	dn gwr 'ryh	d.	dn mdmy lgwr br 'rywwn
		e.	w'rᶜ' [DM: w'rᶜh] tyhwwty štyyh
	yznq mn hbšn	f.	mn mbwᶜyh dnpqyn mn bwtnyyn

Lines a-c are the standard introduction to these blessings; cf. vv. 7, 8, 13, etc. In d the metaphor has been changed to a simile. The verb yznq (f) in MH may mean "squirt," but a subject had to be supplied. Perhaps Heb. 'ryh (d) "lion" and Aram. 'rᶜh "land" were close enough to allow 'rᶜ' to serve in this capacity. (Add the second mn omitted from the printed text of f.)

33:23	Heb.		N
	wlnptly	a.	wlšbṭh dnptly
		b.	brk mšh nbyy' dyyy
	'mr	c.	w'mr
	nptly śbᶜ rṣwn	d.	nptly śbyᶜ rᶜwwh
	wml' brkt yyy	e.	wmly brkn mn qdm yyy
	ym wdrwm yrš	f.	mᶜrb wym' dgynysr wdrwm' yrt

Lines a-c are standard. The rest of the verse is translated literally except for f. As it stands, e means "he will inherit the west and the Sea of Kinnereth and the south." Since the territory of Naphtali actually extended from north of Hermon to the southern tip of the Sea of Kinnereth and westward, this description could be valid only if written somewhere north east of this territory. Even so, it is not clear that all of the sea fell in his territory, though it is likely that more than half did. Moreover, the Heb. contains two geopraphic designations, while N has three. Given that Hebrew ym often refers to the west (cf. N in N 3:23, 35:5, D 3:27, etc.), one might argue that mᶜrb and ym' dgynysr are double translations.

Comparison with other texts presents additional possibility. I suggests dym' for wym' in N, changing the meaning to "he will inherit the western side of the Sea of Kinnereth and the south." This reading is supported by Onk. mᶜrb ym gnysr, though PJ has ym' dswpny wym' dṭbry'. The border of Naptali is usually reconstructed along the Jordan River and the western and south western banks of the Sea of Kinnereth. The texts in Onk. I, and N may reflect this designation and nothing more. One may also read wdrwm' as wdrwmh and reconstruct the text as "the west of the Sea of Kinnereth and its south." A look at a map of this body of water clearly substantiates such designations, and the body of water was certainly large enough to carry a series of designations; cf. ym' dbyt yrḥ, N 34:15 for the south eastern side of the lake. Note also the interpretation of the Sifrei (p. 419): ym: zh ym šl swpny; wdrwm: zh ym šl ṭbryh; yršh: mlmd šnṭl ml' ḥbl ḥlqw bdrwm.

33:24	Heb.		N
	wl'šr	a.	wlšbṭh d'šr
		b.	brk mšh nbyy' dyyy
	'mr	c.	w'mr
	brwk mbnym 'šr	d.	bryk mn bny'

yhy rṣwy 'ḥyw	e.	yhwwy mrᶜyh bšbṭyh
	f.	byn 'ḥwy lbyn 'bwhwn dbšmyy'
	g.	w'rᶜ' tyhwwy mšy bmyy'
wṭbl bšmn rglw	h.	wmsḥy bmšḥh rglwy

On lines a-c cf. vv. 8, etc. The Hebrew of d means that Asher will be "the most blessed of the sons." The translation of this should be bryk mn bny' yhwwy 'šr. Several texts read bšmyṭ' for bšbṭyh, including I and PJ, allowing d-e to mean "more blessed than the other brothers will be his pasture in the shemitah," perhaps resulting from the similar sound of b and m. Preferabably one should see mrᶜyh as a reflection of rṣwy (e), yhy rṣwy 'ḥyw being yhwwy mrᶜyh bšbṭyh. This might mean that d has lost a word or two. Perhaps it should read bryk mn bny' yhwwy or bryk mn bny' 'šr or bryk mn bny' yhwwy 'šr, in which case the loss may have occurred through the homoioteleuton yhwwy ... yhwwy. Such an argument would leave f as an extension of e. Line g applies the description in h to the earth and expands it as well.

33:25 Heb.		N
	a.	h' ᶜm' dbyt 'šr
brzl	b.	bryryn hyk przlh
wnḥšt mnᶜlk	c.	wḥsymyn hyk nḥšh
wkymyk db'k	d.	wkywmy ᶜwlymwtyhwn ywmy sybwtyhwn

Line a provides a link with v. 24. Lines b-d have been built on the very brief Hebrew, but the connection between db'k (d) and the translation is obscure. Perhaps a pun on db' - sb' is intended.

33:26 Heb.		N
'yn k'l yšrwn	a.	lyt k'lh' dyśr'l
rkb šmym bʿzrk	b.	d'šry 'yqr škyntyh bšmy'
wbg'wtw šḥqym	c.	wgywwth bšḥqyh

On the substitution of yśr'l for yšrwn, cf. 32:15 and notes to 33:5. Lines b-c paraphrase the Heb. description of God, which is unacceptable to N.

33:27 Heb.		N
mʿnh 'lhy qdm	a.	mdwr 'yqr škynth d'lh' mlqdmyn
wmtḥt zrʿt ʿwlm	b.	dmn tḥwt 'drʿ gbwrth
	c.	mdbryn šbṭyh dbny yśr'l
wygrš mpnyk 'wyb	d.	hw' ytrwd bʿly dbbykwn mn qdmykwn
wy'mr hšmd	e.	w'mr bmymryh lmyšṣyh ythwn

Lines a, b, d, and e expand the Hebrew in the routine manner of N. Line c has been added to provide a context for the unattached Heb. in b.

33:28 Heb.		N
wyškn yśr'l btḥ	a.	wšrwn yśr'l lrwḥṣn
bdd	b.	lblḥwdyhwn
ʿyn yʿqb	c.	mʿyn brkth dbrk ythwn yʿqb 'bwhwn
'l 'rṣ dgn wtyrwš	d.	l'rʿ ʿbdh ʿybwr wḥmr
'p šmyw	e.	lḥwd šmy' dʿylwwyhwn
yʿrpw ṭl	f.	yhwwn mḥtyn ʿlyhwn ṭlyn wmṭryn

The expansions in all lines except c are similar to those noted elsewhere. In c, BH ʿyn "well, fountain" has been taken as MH mʿyn "like, according to," etc. (Cf. mʿyn hbrkwt in the Friday evening, abridged version of the Amidah prayer.) The phrase dbrk ythwn yʿqb 'bwhwn has been borrowed from G 49:28, the conclusion to Jacob's blessing: wz't 'šr dbr lhm 'byhm wybrk 'wtm ....

33:29 Heb.		N
'šryk yśr'l	a.	ṭwbykwn yśr'l
my kmwk	b.	mn kwwtkwn
ʿm nwšʿ byyy	c.	ʿm dprqnyhwn qryb mn qdm yyy
mgn ʿzrk	d.	mgyn sʿdykwn
	e.	wtrys ḥyylykwn
	f.	wsdyd zyynykwn
w'šr ḥrb g'wtk	g.	wtqyp gywwy sbrykwn
wykḥšw 'ybyk lk	h.	wtbryn bʿly dbbykwn mn qdmykwn
w'th	i.	w'twn ʿmy bny yśr'l
	j.	kd thwwn lʿyyn b'wryyth
	k.	wʿbdyn pyqwdyyh
ʿl bmwtymw	l.	ʿl prqt ṣw'ry mlkyhwn
tdrk	m.	thwwn drsyn

The translation of 'šryk in a is paralleled by that of 'šry in Ps. 1:1, etc. Lines d-g are repetitive. We have divided them so that e and f do not correspond to the Hebrew text, for d and e are a double translation, as f and g probably are as well. It may be that the Hebrew should be distributed mgn - ʿzrk - w'šr ḥrb - g'wtk over the four lines. Similar expansions of single words into full phrases are found, for example, in v. 13. The word wsdyd in f is problematic (cf. DM a.l.), but its proper reconstruction will not affect the distribution of the text.

Line h has been translated literally. The addition in i is paralleled in other places, but here it is clearly a rhetorical flourish. Lines j-k stress one last time the importance of studying and observing the Torah.

The word bmwtymw in l means "backs," not "high places," as sometimes explained. The use of ṣw'ry mlkyhwn is close to the correct meaning and reflects the association of this verse with Josh. 10:24, as presented in the Sifrei (pp. 424-5).

Chapter 34

34:2 'rᶜ' (+): The first occurrence is expansive, in imitation of other places in the verse where it is used.

34:3 qrth dᶜbdh twmryn: for Heb. ᶜyr htmrym.

34:4 ly: for Heb. 'lyw. The addition of 'mr mšh confirms this reading. LXX pròs Mousên attests to the reading of the MT, as do lyh in Onk. and PJ. Apparently the translator of N read 'ly rather than 'lyw. It seems less likely the ly "to him" was misunderstood as "to me" and glossed, but this is also possible.

ḥmy yth: a simpler form than the Heb. hr'ytyk. I adds bᶜyynk, missing from N.

34:5 wmyt: for Heb. wymt as in Onk.; cf. F: w'tknš.

34:5 The subject, mšh, has been omitted.

34:6 ṭᶜwth pᶜwr: for Heb. byt pᶜwr.

34:7 bzmnh d'tknš: for Heb. bmtw; the phrase seems to lack mn gw ᶜlmh, but it is the same in F.

wl' 'štnyyw zywwhwn d'pwy: for Heb. wl' ns lḥh

34:10 mmll kl wqbl mmll: for Heb. pnym 'l pnym. Perhaps kl wqbl should be taken as klwqbl; cf. M in G 30:41, E 17:9-10, L 8:9. PJ has klw qbl, but F has lqbl. N 12:8 has ph 'l ph in Heb., but N reads mmll lqbl mmll, while M has kl wqbl, and the same situation exists in E 33:11 and D 5:4. The phrase 'pyn kl gbyl 'pyn is found in G 32:31, but no variant is given, nor is there one here.

34:12 ḥzwwyyh: for Heb. hmwr', apparently based on a text that took hmr' as hmr'h. Note also G 18:1.

TABLE OF CROSS REFERENCES

The following cross references facilitate finding discussions of N that are not found in the expected place in the commentary. All Pentateuchal Hebrew and targumic references are included.

Deuteronomy

1:1	Intro., ch. 1.- ch. 4.; D 1:2; 2:23; 32:51
1:2	D 9:8.
1:3	D 1:2
1:4	N 34:15.
1:5	D 1:1; 27:8.
1:7	Intro., ch. 2.; G 2:14; D 11:24.
1:8	D 1:1.
1:9	Intro., ch. 3.; N 11:14.
1:13	D 1:15; 4:6.
1:15	D 1:13; 4:6.
1:17	Intro., ch. 3.; D 3:11; 33:9.
1:18	D 4:14.
1:21	D 1:8.
1:23	Intro., ch. 3.
1:26	D 1:1.
1:27	D 1:1.
1:28	N 26:9; D 1:1; 2:10.
1:29	D 1:1.
1:30	D 1:1.
1:31	D 32:1.
1:35	D 1:34.
1:37	D 1:34.
1:40	N 33:8.

1:45	Intro., ch. 3.
2:1	N 33:8; D 3:2.
2:2	Intro., ch. 3.; D 2:1.
2:5	Intro., ch. 3.; N 20:21.
2:6	Intro., ch. 3.; D 2:28.
2:7	E 39:43; D 2:28.
2:8	N 33:35.
2:9	Intro., ch. 3.; D 2:1; 2:5; 2:21.
2:11	D 2:10.
2:12	Intro., ch. 3.
2:14	D 2:13.
2:17	Intro., ch. 3.; D 2:1.
2:19	N 20:21; D 2:5.
2:20	D 2:10.
2:21	D 2:12; 9:14.
2:23	D 1:1.
2:24	E 15:16.
2:31	D 2:1; 2:9.
2:34	D 1:44.
2:35	D 3:7.
3:2	N 21:34; D 2:1.
3:4	N 34:15.
3:5	N 34:15.
3:6	N 34:15; D 2:34.
3:7-10	N 34:15.
3:11	Intro., ch. 3.; N 34:15.
3:12	N 34:15; D 2:36.
3:13	N 34:15.
3:14	N 34:15; D 3:13.
3:15	N 34:15.
3:16	N 34:15.
3:17	N 34:15

3:18	N 34:15.
3:22	Intro., ch. 3.; D 1:30.
3:23	Intro., ch. 4.
3:24	Intro., ch. 4.; D 4:39.
3:25	Intro., ch. 4.; D 1:7.
3:26	Intro., ch. 4.
3:27	D 2:29; 33:23.
3:29	Intro., ch. 4.; D 4:3.
4:2	D 5:5.
4:3	D 3:29; 4:34.
4:4	Intro., ch. 3.; D 4:3.
4:6	D 4:7.
4:7	Intro., ch. 3.; ch. 4.
4:8	D 4:7; 4:44; 6:25.
4:9	D 24:15.
4:10	Intro., ch. 3.; D 1:2; 2:1.
4:12	D 4:16.
4:13	D 4:12; 32:10.
4:15	D 1:2; 4:12.
4:16	D 9:12.
4:17	Intro., ch.3.
4:19	D 4:16.
4:22	D 32:1.
4:23	D 4:16.
4:24	E 24:17; D 9:3.
4:25	D 4:16; 7:25; 9:12; 9:18.
4:26	Intro., ch. 3.; D 5:30 (=33).
4:27	D 33:6.
4:32	Intro., ch. 3.
4:33	D 4:12; 4:34.
4:34	N 20:20; D 1:30.
4:35	D 1:30; 4:39.

4:37	Intro., ch. 4.
4:39	D 3:24.
4:40	N 18:19; D 5:30 (=33).
5:1	D 4:10.
5:4	D 4:12; 33:10.
5:5	Intro., ch. 3.
5:6	Intro., ch. 4.; G 15:11; E 20:2; 20:3; D 4:12; 6:12.
5:7	Intro., ch. 4.; G 15:11; E 20:2; D 4:16.
5:8	Intro., ch. 3.; D 3:24; 4:16.
5:9	Intro., ch. 1.; G 10:9; E 20:5; N 14:18; D 6:15.
5:10	L 22:31; D 4:24.
5:13	L 23:3.
5:16	D 5:11; 5:30 (=33).
5:17	D 5:17 (=20); 33:2.
5:18	E 23:1; L 20:10; D 5:17 (=20); 5:18 (=21).
5:19	D 33:2.
5:21	D 5:11; 5:17 (=18);
5:21	(=24) D 6:24.
5:25	E 12:31.
5:26	Intro., ch. 4.; D 5:25 (=28).
5:27	Intro., ch. 1.
5:28	D 5:27 (=30).
5:29	D 2:34.
5:30	Intro., ch. 4.; D 5:30 (=33).
6:4	Intro., ch. 4.; G 22:6; 49:2; D 6:9.
6:5	Intro., ch. 4.; G 49:2; D 6:9; 6:12.
6:6	D 6:9; 11:18.
6:7	D 6:9.
6:8	D 6:9; 14:1.
6:9	Intro., ch. 4.
6:13	D 10:20.

6:16 D 11:18; 33:8.

6:24 Intro., ch. 3.;

7:5 D 4:16.

7:6 Intro., ch.3.; D 7:7.

7:7 Intro., ch. 1.; E 9:16.

7:8 E 9:16.

7:10 Intro., ch. 3.

7:12 D 8:20.

7:13 G 27:28; 30:2.

7:16 D 8:17.

7:24 Intro., ch. 3.; D 33:11.

7:25 D 4:16; 29:16.

7:26 D 7:25.

8:2 D 32:10.

8:3 Intro., ch. 1.; N 11:6.

8:7 D 8:15.

8:9 Intro., ch. 3.; D 2:28.

8:11 Intro., ch. 4.

8:14 D 8:7; 8:11.

8:15 D 32:13.

8:16 N 11:6; D 5:25 (=28).

8:18 N 24:18; D 8:17.

9:1 Intro., ch. 1.; ch. 3.

9:3 E 24:17.

9:5 D 9:4.

9:6 Intro., ch. 4.; D 9:4; 9:13; 10:16.

9:9 D 9:18.

9:12 D 11:28.

9:13 D 9:6.

9:14 Intro., ch. 4.; N 14:12; D 26:5.

9:16 D 11:28.

9:18 D 9:19.

9:19 Intro., ch. 4; D 10:10.

9:20 L 9:7; D 9:18; 9:25; 9:26.

9:21 D 27:8.

9:22 N 11:34; D 6:16; 33:8.

9:24 D 9:18.

9:25 Intro., ch. 4.; D 9:18; 9:26.

9:26 Intro., ch. 4.

9:27 Intro., ch. 4.

10:4 D 9:10.

10:8 D 9:23.

10:9 Intro., ch. 3.; D 33:4.

10:10 Intro., ch. 4.

10:11 D 32:27.

10:12 D 11:3.

10:15 D 7:7.

10:16 D 9:6.

10:17 E 18:11; D 16:19; 33:9.

10:20 D 6:13.

11:7 D 4:34.

11:9 D 5:30 (=33).

11:12 Intro., ch. 3.

11:13 G 2:15; D 6:9; 11:18.

11:14 Intro., ch. 2.; G 27:28; L 26:4; D 6:9; 11:18.

11:15 L 26:5; D 6:9; 11:18.

11:16 D 6:9; 11:18.

11:17 L 26:19; D 5:18 (=21); 6:9; 11:18; 28:23.

11:18 D 6:8; 6:9; 11:18.

11:19 D 6:7; 6:9; 11:18.

11:20 D 6:9; 11:18.

11:21 D 6:9; 11:18.

11:22 D 10:12.

11:24 D 1:7.

11:25 Intro., ch. 3.

11:26 Intro., ch. 3.; D 29:18.

11:30 G 18:1.

12:12 D 14:27; 33:4.

12:13 D 24:15.

12:14 D 7:7.

12:15 Intro., ch. 3.; D 12:22; 15:22.

12:16 L 19:26.

12:17 G 27:28.

12:22 D 12:15.

12:23 L 19:26.

12:24 D 12:16.

12:25 N 18:19; D 12:8.

12:28 D 11:18.

13:6 D 13:4.

13:7 Intro., ch. 3.; ch. 4.; D 22:26; 28:54.

13:15 D 22:21; 27:8.

14:1 D 6:8; 32:1.

14:2 D 7:6; 7:7.

14:21 Intro., ch.; E 22:30; 23:19.

14:25 L 19:23; D 26:12.

14:26 D 14:25.

14:28 D 15:1.

14:29 D 14:27.

15:1 Intro., ch. 3.

15:3 D 23:21; 24:4.

15:6 D 14:26.

15:9 Intro., ch. 1.; E 18:16; D 24:13.

15:10 D 16:17.

15:12 E 21:2; D 15:16.

15:13 E 21:2.

15:17 D 25:7.

15:18 D 24:14.

15:22 Intro., ch. 3.; D 12:15.

16:3 D 16:1.

16:5 D 16:16.

16:8 N 29:35.

16:9 D 15:1.

16:10 D 16:16.

16:12 D 16:1.

16:14 D 14:26.

16:15 E 39:43.

16:16 Intro., ch. 4.; G 34:1; D 15:19; 16:5.

16:18 D 1:16; 31:28.

16:19 D 10:17; 33:9.

16:20 L 19:15.

17:2 G 49:2; D 4:25.

17:3 D 4:3.

17:4 D 27:8.

17:7 D 13:6.

17:8 Intro., ch. 3.; E 18:16.

17:12 D 13:16.

17:14 E 1:10.

17:15 D 16:16.

17:19 D 22:19.

17:20 D 5:30 (=33).

18:3 N 18:11.

18:5 D 7:7.

18:10 L 19:26; 20:2.

18:11 L 19:31

18:12	D 24:6.
18:13	Intro., ch. 3.
18:14	L 19:26; D 18:10.
19:3	D 27:25.
19:5	D 22:10.
19:6	Intro., ch. 3.; D 19:11; 22:26.
19:7	D 19:2.
19:9	D 19:2.
19:10	N 35:27.
19:11	D 19:6; 21:14; 27:25.
19:15	D 17:6.
19:16	D 5:17 (=20).
19:17	D 17:9.
19:18	D 19:16; 27:8.
20:3	Intro., ch. 3.
20:4	D 28:32.
20:6	D 28:30.
20:7	D 28:30.
20:8	E 13:17; D 28:54.
20:16	D 5:17 (=20)
20:19	Intro., ch. 3.; D 27:5; 29:22.
21:8	N 35:27.
21:9	N 35:27.
21:10	N 31:50.
21:11	N 31:50; D 7:7; 21:13.
21:12	N 31:50.
21:13	N 31:50
21:14	E 21:8; N 31:50.
21:18	Intro., ch. 3.
21:19	Intro., ch. 3; D 25:7.
21:20	Intro., ch. 3.

21:22	Intro., ch. 3.
21:23	G 40:18-19; N 25:4.
22:3	D 22:1.
22:4	Intro., ch. 4.; E 23:5; D 21:1; 22:1.
22:5	G 27:3; D 24:6.
22:7	D 5:30 (=33).
22:8	Intro., ch. 3.
22:11	Intro., ch. 2.; L 19:19.
22:12	N 15:39.
22:15	D 17:8; 25:7.
22:17	G 16:5; L 21:13.
22:20	D 22:29.
22:22	D 22:28.
22:24	D 22:28.
22:26	D 21:22.
22:28	Intro., ch. 2.; E 22:15.
22:29	D 22:19; 22:24.
23:2	D 23:3.
23:4	D 23:3.
23:5	D 22:24.
23:6	D 32:19.
23:7	D 22:29.
23:13	N 24:25.
23:14	N 24:25.
23:15	Intro., ch. 3.
23:21	D 23:25.
23:26	D 23:25.
24:3	D 24:1.
24:5	D 17:1; 24:6.
24:6	Intro., ch. 4.; N 11:8.
24:13	Intro., ch. 4.

24:19	E 39:43; 24:13.
25:1	D 32:3.
25:2	Intro., ch. 3.
25:4	D 23:25.
25:6	G 27:41.
25:13	D 25:14.
25:14	D 25:13.
25:15	D 5:30 (=33).
25:16	D 24:6.
25:17	E 17:16; D 25:18; 25:19.
25:18	Intro., ch. 4.; E 17:16.
25:19	E 17:16.
26:3	Intro., ch. 4.
26:5	Intro., ch. 2.; G 27:41; D 33:6.
26:7	Intro., ch. 4.; D 10:10.
26:10	D 26:4.
26:12	D 14:28.
26:13	D 26:12.
26:15	E 3:8.
26:17	D 27:9.
26:18	D 26:17; 27:9.
27:3	E 3:8.
27:12-26	D 27:15.
27:15	L 19:4; D 4:16.
27:17	D 27:16.
27:20	G 16:5.
28:1	D 26:19.
28:2	G 49:26; D 28:8.
28:3	D 28:16-19.
28:4	G 30:2; D 28:16-19.
28:5	D 26:4; 28:16-19.

28:6	D 28: 16-19; 28:19.
28:7	D 28:25.
28:10	E 23:21.
28:11	G 30:2.
28:12	Intro., ch. 4.; G 30:22; E 39:43.
28:14	D 11:28.
28:15	D 28:8.
28:16	D 28:3.
28:19	D 28:6.
28:24	D 28:22.
28:26	Intro., ch. 3.
28:27	Intro., ch. 2.; L 21:20.
28:33	D 28:42.
28:36	D 29:16.
28:44	D 28:13.
28:48	L 26:13.
28:50	D 33:9.
28:51	G 27:28.
28:52	D 27:14.
28:53	L 26:29.
28:56	D 28:54.
28:57	D 31:29.
28:61	D 28:58.
28:62	D 33:6.
28:64	D 29:16.
29:9	D 1:10; 27:14; 31:28.
29:13	Intro., ch. 3.
29:16	Intro., ch. 1.; D 28:64.
29:17	Intro., ch. 3.
29:20	D 29:19.
29:26	D 29:19.

30:1 D 30:15.

30:2 Intro., ch. 3.

30:3-4 D 30:1.

30:5 D 5:25 (=28).

30:6-7 D 30:8.

30:9 G 30:2.

30:12 D 30:13.

30:13 D 30:12.

30:15 Intro., ch. 4.; D 30:1.

30:16 Intro., ch. 3.

30:17 D 30:1.

30:18 D 5:30 (=33).

31:2 Intro., ch. 3.; D 2:29.

31:7 Intro., ch. 2.; D 32:27.

31:11 G 34:1.

31:14 D 31:16; 32:1.

31:16 D 31:14.

31:17 E 23:19; D 32:30.

31:18 D 31:17.

31:21 D 31:19.

31:22 D 31:19.

31:23 D 31:7.

31:26 D 32:46.

31:27 Intro., ch. 3.

31:28 D 32:1.

31:29 D 11:28.

31:30 D 31:24; 32:46.

32:1 Intro., ch. 1.; ch. 4.; D 4:26; 32:3, 4, 14, 34; 33:1; 33:4.

32:2 D 32:14.

32:3 Intro., ch. 4.; D 32:1, 4, 14, 18;

32:4 Intro., ch. 4.; D 33:4.

32:5 Intro., ch. 3.

32:6 D 32:15.

32:10 Intro., ch. 4.

32:13 D 32:18.

32:14 Intro., ch. 4.; D 32:30.

32:15 Intro., ch. 4.; D 32:18; 33:5; 33:26.

32:17 D 32:21.

32:18 D 33:6; 32:30.

32:19 Intro., ch. 3.

32:21 D 32:16.

32:24 Intro., ch. 2.; D 32:33.

32:25 L 19:32.

32:27 G 40: 18-19.

32:28 D 4:6.

32:29 Intro., ch.4.

32:30 Intro., ch. 4.; D 32:14; 32:31.

32:32 Intro., ch. 3.; D 32:33.

32:33 D 32:24, 32:34.

32:34 D 32:1; 32:37.

32:36 D 32:43.

32:39 D 33:11.

32:41-2 Intro., ch. 4.

32:43 D 33:3.

32:46 Intro., ch. 4.

32:47 D 5:30 (=33).

32:48 D 32:51.

32:49 N 33:44; D 32:51.

32:50 D 32:1; 32:51.

32:52 D 32:51.

33:1 Intro., ch.3.; G 49:28; D 33:7.

33:2	Intro., ch. 3.; E 20:2; 20:13-17; D 33:3.
33:3	Intro., ch. 4.
33:4	E 6:8.
33:5	D 33:4; 33:9; 33:26.
33:7	Intro., ch. 3.; D 33:9; 33:22.
33:8	Intro., ch. 3.; D 6:16; 33:9, 11, 12, 22, 24.
33:9	D 33:11.
33:10	G 18:23; 27:27; D 33:11.
33:11	Intro., ch. 1.
33:12	Intro., ch. 3.; ch. 4.; G 49:27; D 32:39; 33:8, 11, 13.
33:13	Intro., ch. 3.; G 49:25, 27; D 33:11, 12, 22, 29.
33:14	Intro., ch. 2.; D 33:15.
33:15	Intro., ch. 2.; G 49:26; D 33:14; 33:16.
33:16	Intro., ch. 2.; G 49:26; D 28:35; 33:9; 33:14; 33:15.
33:17	G 49:18; 49:22; D 23:25.
33:18	Intro., ch. 3.; D 33:8; 33:11; 33:12.
33:19	D 33:18; 33:21.
33:22	Intro., ch.3.
33:24	D 33:25.
33:26	D 33:5.
33:28	Intro., ch. 3.; G 27:28.
33:29	Intro., ch. 4.; G 15:1, D 3:24.
34:1	G 14:14; D 33:21.
34:3	G 19:20.
34:5	G 5:5; D 32:2.
34:7	G 4:5-6; 5:5.
34:8	D 7:7.
34:9	D 33:5.
34:10	D 30:12.
34:11	E 4:28.

INDEX OF CITATIONS

BIBLE

(All citations from the Torah and related translations are listed in the tables of cross references that appear after each book.)

Joshua

1:4	G 2:14
1:5	D 33:11
10:8	D 33:11
10:24	D 33:29
Chapt. 13	G 49:19, N 34:15
14:13-14	N 13:22
23:1	D 32:30

Judges

7:19-25	D 33:17
12:5-6	E 15:16

1 Samuel

3:14	G 4:15
15:4	N 24:7
Chapt. 16	E 17:17

1 Kings

8:23	D 3:24
8:44	G 49:17
17:7-16	D 32:14
21:19	G 27:41

19:9	L 26:29
22:16	D 32:36
23:12	D 22:19
30:16	D 32:36
31:3	D 22:19
31:15	N 21:6
37:21	N 24:25
34:20	D 32:30
46:11	D 22:19

Ezekiel

3:12	D 32:2
4:16, 5:16	L 26:26
8:3	D 4:16
28:13	G 2:12
30:13	L 19:4
37:12	G 30:22
39:9-19	N 11:26
chapt. 47	N 34:15

Joel

2:24, 4:18	G 49:12

Micah

7:18	E 34:7, D 3:24

Zechariah

11:9	L 26:29
14:8	N 34:6

Malachi

2:14-15	D 28:54

Job

5:7	D 32:24
28:16	G 2:12
38:15	G 40:18

Proverbs

3:18	G 3:24
16:10	N 5:6

Ruth

1:2	G 46:1
1:6	G 42:1, 46:1
2:6	G 46:1
3:9	G 16:5

Song of Songs

2:8	N 23:9

Lamentations

2:20 ff	L 26:29

Esther

3:1	E 17:16
6:1	E 12:42
7:6	E 15:9
10:3	D 33:5

Daniel

3:12	G 38:25
3:25	D 32:1
10:4	G 2:14

The Jewish War

vi, 201-213 L 26:29

NEW TESTAMENT

Matthew

14:13-21 D 32:14

15:32-39 D 32:14

MISHNAH

Berachot

4:1 G 49:27

Kilaim

8:1 G 44:18-19

Pesahim

10:4 E 12:9

Ta^{c}anit

2:4 G 38:25

Megilla

3:4-6 Intro. chapt. 2, N 28:2

4:2 Intro. chapt. 2

4:4 Intro. chapt. 2 (2x), N 7:17

4:10 Intro. chapt. 1, 3; G 49:4, E 32:1, N 6:24-26

Sotah

1:7 G 38:25

BABYLONIAN TALMUD

Berachot

6a	E 12:42
18b	D 1:1
26a-b	G 24:65, 49:27
26b	N 17:13
34a	N 12:13
55b	G 40:18
57b	N 23:19

Shabbat

68a	E 32:25

Pesaḥim

3a	G 48:17, D 28:57, 31:29
18a	G 3:19
111b	D 32:24
116a	E 13:8

Yoma

21b	N 9:16
80a	L 23:29

Sukkah

11b	L 23:43
56a	D 18:8

Rosh HaShannah

11a	N 23:9

Sotah

10b	G 38:25
11b-12a	E 1:21
18a-b	N 5:22
32a	D 25:9

Qiddushin

30a	Intro. chapt. 2
32b	L 19:32

Baba Batra

15a	L 22:27

Sanhedrin

7a	E 32:5
17a	N 11:26
38a	G 1:1 (2x)
63a	L 19:26
64b	L 18:21
65a	L 19:31
65b	L 19:26, D 18:11
67a	E 22:17
106a	N 24:24
108a	G 6:8

Makkot

20b	L 19:28

Avodah Zara

2a	D 32:35
3b	D 32:4

Menahot

110a Intro. chapt. 3

Hullin

102b E 22:30

115b E 23:19

142a D 22:7

Bekhorot

13a E 13:12

38b, 45a L 21:20

Keritot

11a L 19:20

MINOR TRACTATES

Soferim

5:13 Intro. chapt. 2

PALESTINIAN TALMUD

Berachot

4:1 G 49:27

4:4 G 24:63

Shevi^c^it

6:11 N 34:15

Ma^c^aser Sheni

5:12 D 26:14

Shabbat

7:2 L 19:26

Ta^{c}anit

1:2-4	G 38:25
4:5	E 32:18

Megilla

1:9	Intro. chapt. 2
4:1	D 27:8
4:10	Intro. chapt. 3

Yebamot

12:1	D 28:57

Sotah

2:2	L 2:2
9:2	D 21:1

Sanhedrin

7:5	L 19:26
10:1	N 23:9

MIDRASHIM

Genesis Rabbah (listed by <u>parshiot</u>)

20	G 3:19, 3:21
21	G 21:33
36	D 27:8
39	Intro. chapt. 2 (n. 15)
40	G 13:7
44	G 15:17
44	G 15:12
83	G 36:39
98	G 49:4
99	G 49:3

Sifrei Deuteronomy

D 1:1	a.l.
D 33:2	Intro. chapt. 3
D 22:17	G 16:5
chapt. 1, end	G 41:43

D 14:1, D 20:19, D 21:12, D 23:25, D 32:2, D 33:23, 29 a.l.

Pirqe de Rabbi Eliezer

28	G 15:17
42	E 15:12

Avot deRabbi Nathan I

30	G 35:9

Pesiqta deRav Kahana

3	G 35:9
9:9	L 22:27

Midrash HaGadol

G 40:23, D 1:1 a.l.

Midrash VaYosha

53	E 15:12

Midrash Leqah Tov

G 42:12, E 23:5, 24:11, D 1:1 a.l.

Midrash Psalms

114, 7	E 14:22

Sefer Eliyahu

lines 76-77	N 11:26

Pereq Eliyahu

lines 98-99 N 11:26

Midrash Tannaim

D 1:1, D 23:25, D 32:1, 2 a.l.

Passover Haggadah

p. 122 Intro. chapt. 3

Yalqut Shimoni

Torah #855 Intro. chapt. 2

Midrash Tanhuma

Beshalah 16 Intro. chapt. 2 (n. 15)

Balaq 15 N 24:25

PATRISTIC LITERATURE

Onomasticon of Eusebius

at N 21:18, N 22:39, D 1:1